ILL WINDS

ALSO BY LARRY DIAMOND

In Search of Democracy

*The Spirit of Democracy: The Struggle to Build
Free Societies Throughout the World*

*Squandered Victory: The American Occupation and
the Bungled Effort to Bring Democracy to Iraq*

Developing Democracy: Toward Consolidation

Promoting Democracy in the 1990s

Class, Ethnicity, and Democracy in Nigeria

EDITED BY LARRY DIAMOND

Authoritarianism Goes Global: The Challenge to Democracy
(with Marc F. Plattner and Christopher Walker)

Democracy in Decline?
(with Marc F. Plattner)

Democratization and Authoritarianism in the Arab World
(with Marc F. Plattner)

Will China Democratize?
(with Marc F. Plattner)

Liberation Technology: Social Media and the Struggle for Democracy
(with Marc F. Plattner)

Politics and Culture in Contemporary Iran
(with Abbas Milani)

Democracy in Developing Countries (series)
(with Juan J. Linz and Seymour Martin Lipset)

ILL WINDS

SAVING DEMOCRACY FROM

RUSSIAN RAGE, CHINESE AMBITION,

AND AMERICAN COMPLACENCY

LARRY DIAMOND

PENGUIN PRESS

NEW YORK

2019

PENGUIN PRESS
An imprint of Penguin Random House LLC
penguinrandomhouse.com

Excerpt from "To the Tyrants of the World" by Abul-Qasim Al-Shabbi,
translated by Adel Iskandar. Reprinted by permission of the translator.

LIBRARY OF CONGRESS CATALOGING-IN-PUBLICATION DATA
Names: Diamond, Larry Jay, author.
Title: Ill Winds : Saving Democracy From Russian Rage, Chinese
Ambition, And American Complacency / Larry Diamond.
Description: New York : Penguin Press, 2019. |
Includes bibliographical references and index.
Identifiers: LCCN 2018058826 (print) | LCCN 2018058923 (ebook) |
ISBN 9780525560630 (ebook) | ISBN 9780525560623 (hardback)
Subjects: LCSH: Democracy. | United States—Politics and government—2017– |
United States—Foreign relations. | BISAC: HISTORY / United States /
21st Century. | POLITICAL SCIENCE / Political Ideologies / Democracy. |
HISTORY / Modern / 21st Century.
Classification: LCC JC423 (ebook) | LCC JC423 .D556 2019 (print) |
DDC 321.8—dc23
LC record available at https://lccn.loc.gov/2018058826

Printed in the United States of America
1   3   5   7   9   10   8   6   4   2

DESIGNED BY MEIGHAN CAVANAUGH

To Zin Mar Aung

Vladimir Kara-Murza

Maina Kiai

Rafael Marques de Morais

Cara McCormick

Nicholas Opiyo

Joshua Wong

*And the many other unsung heroes
of the struggle for democracy*

. . . of those men who have overturned the liberties of republics, the greatest number have begun their career by paying an obsequious court to the people; commencing demagogues, and ending tyrants.

—ALEXANDER HAMILTON, 1787

In the long history of the world, only a few generations have been granted the role of defending freedom in its hour of maximum danger. I do not shrink from this responsibility—I welcome it.

—JOHN F. KENNEDY, 1961

The desire for liberty may be ingrained in every human breast, but so is the potential for complacency, confusion, and cowardice.

—MADELEINE ALBRIGHT, 2018

CONTENTS

ILL WINDS

ONE

INTRODUCTION: THE CRISIS

No cause is left but the most ancient of all, the one, in fact, that from the beginning of our history has determined the very existence of politics, the cause of freedom versus tyranny.

—HANNAH ARENDT, *On Revolution*, 1963[1]

On a gray Sunday afternoon two days before the November 2016 U.S. election, I entered the Berkeley Repertory Theatre with twenty Stanford students to see the final performance of a production of *It Can't Happen Here*. Adapted from the classic 1935 novel by Sinclair Lewis, the play traces the rise of an ultranationalist demagogue who, in the midst of the Great Depression, snatches the 1936 Democratic presidential nomination away from Franklin Roosevelt, wins the presidency, and establishes a dictatorship in the United States.

In the novel, Lewis memorably describes his authoritarian ruler, Buzz Windrip:

Certainly there was nothing exhilarating in the actual words of his speeches, nor anything convincing in his philosophy. His political platforms were only wings of a windmill. . . . There were two things . . . that distinguished this prairie Demosthenes. He was an actor of genius. . . . He would whirl arms, bang tables, glare from mad eyes . . . [and] in between tricks would coldly and almost contemptuously jab his crowds with figures and facts—figures and facts that were inescapable even when, as often happened, they were entirely incorrect.[2]

The parallels to Donald Trump, the 2016 Republican candidate for president of the United States, were too stark to ignore. I watched the play with a level of anxiety I hadn't expected even a few weeks before—and didn't want to fully share with the students. They were also shaken by the drama, but we reassured ourselves with the obvious facts. The play was a time-bound work of fiction. Roosevelt had been reelected in 1936. The United States wasn't sunk into anything close to a depression. Trump wasn't an actual fascist. And in any case, he wasn't going to win on Tuesday, right?

When the Berkeley Rep began writing its new stage adaptation of the novel in January 2016, no primary election votes had yet been cast. There was no reason to expect that a modern-day demagogue could win the nomination of a major American political party.

Indeed, since Trump had declared his candidacy in 2015, I had spent more than a year reassuring people around the world that it couldn't happen here in the United States. First I assured them that Trump had no serious chance of winning the Republican nomination. Then I told them that he had scant chance of winning the general election. To democratic activists gathered in Seoul for the World Movement for Democracy Assembly in November 2015, to Vietnamese dissidents who had come to Taiwan to watch the January 2016 presidential election there, to college students and civic activists in Hong Kong who had organized the 2014 Umbrella Movement protests against Chinese repression, to students, professors, journalists, and legislators in Burma and Argentina, I repeated it over and over: It won't happen in the United States.

Our institutions were too strong, I insisted, to permit a reality-TV star with no prior government experience to win a major-party nomination for president, much less the Oval Office. Our democratic norms were too resilient to produce a president who crudely demeaned the press, the judiciary, and immigrants; who encouraged his supporters to physically attack protesters and to scream for his opponent to be locked up; who refused to release his tax returns; and who appealed in thinly veiled code to base racist sentiments.

I wasn't naïve. I knew that lying, race-baiting, and dirty tricks had long played their roles in presidential politics. I knew that unscrupulous men had won the office. But Trump would be a wholly new and almost unimaginable low. Polarized and unsettled though America's voters were, I didn't believe they could elect a man who, in the words of *The Guardian*'s Jonathan Freedland, "mocked opponents for their looks, belittled women, disparaged war heroes, damned ethnic and other minorities in crude, bigoted language, jeered at disabled people, beat his chest with bellicose promises of state-sponsored violence that would trample on the US constitution and trigger a third world war, and told dozens and dozens of lies every day."[3]

I was wrong. And so were most of my fellow political scientists and scholars of democracy.

It was not simply the shock of Donald Trump's election that moved me to write this book. It was the anguished knowledge of what his presidency would mean for democracy around the world.

Over forty years of travel to more than seventy countries, I had gained a deep appreciation for the unique importance of the United States to the global struggle for freedom. Even people who resented America for its wealth, its global power, its arrogance, and its use of military force nevertheless expressed a grudging admiration for the vitality of its democracy. Even those who were keenly aware of our tragic history of slavery, racism, inequality, and corporate monopolies marveled at the ability of American democracy to reform and renew itself.

And the fiercest critics I encountered were, I found, often disarmed by an American speaker's readiness to criticize his government while praising its constitutional system.

Wherever I met people struggling to achieve or build democracy, I heard the same hope: that the United States would somehow support their cause. Wherever I met dissidents risking everything to challenge corruption and oppression, I felt the heavy weight of moral expectation: that the United States would stand behind them and, perhaps as a last resort, give them refuge. And now, we had elected a president whose worldview was "America first," whose policies were rooted in contempt for immigrants and refugees, and whose rhetoric was suffused with praise for dictators.[4]

The timing of Trump's rise was particularly worrisome. For the past decade, I had been warning of a gathering tide of political corruption, polarization, and decay that was disillusioning ordinary citizens in many democracies and diminishing and destabilizing previously durable democratic systems. For most of that decade—and most of my career—I had been worried about the emerging or embattled democracies of Asia, Africa, and Latin America, as well as the formerly Communist states in Eastern Europe. Of course, I was also deeply concerned about the worsening state of my own democracy, and I had increasingly come to feel an urgent need to repair and reform democracy in the United States. But I never imagined that democracy *here* could be in danger.

Now everything was in flux. China was relentlessly rising in global power, wealth, and ambition. Another, far weaker autocratic power, Vladimir Putin's Russia, was increasingly reasserting itself as an aggressive geopolitical bully—and had just intervened with a brazen digital hacking and propaganda campaign to try to tip the American presidential election to an open admirer of Putin with autocratic leanings of his own.

Much as the post–World War II liberal order is rooted in U.S. leadership, so too is democracy worldwide anchored in democracy in America. But the global standing of the world's leading democracy had been badly hurt by both the fiasco of President George W. Bush's war of choice in Iraq and then the financial collapse of 2008. His successor, Barack Obama, had partially restored America's global image with his inspirational barrier-breaking story, his pursuit of international cooperation, and his rescue of the financial system. But with the United States chastened by Iraq and the financial crisis, Obama had drawn back from vigorous global leadership, and China and Russia were filling the void.

Other worrisome forces were on the march too. In the wake of wars in Syria and elsewhere, an immigration crisis had converged with social and economic stresses to feed a growing wave of illiberal populism across Europe. Far-right, xenophobic leaders were attacking democratic norms and institutions in Hungary and Poland. Britain had recently voted to leave the European Union. A menacing populist who had boasted of personally killing lawbreakers had won the presidency in the Philippines. The ultranationalist bigot Marine Le Pen appeared to have a real chance of winning the French presidency. Things seemed to be unraveling. Karl Marx's famous phrase from *The Communist Manifesto* kept ringing in my head: "All that is solid melts into air." A decade-long democratic recession in the world was giving way to something much worse: a crisis.

Why Democracy?

Why do we care? Why is democracy so important that people continually risk their lives for it? And why have I spent my life studying and trying to advance it? Lord knows it's not a perfect system. When the people can choose and replace their rulers, they may well embrace bad leaders and shortsighted policies. They may be swayed by money or demagoguery. They may become bitterly divided against one another and undermine their country's stability. Democracy may fail to function well—or at all. Every generation has its share of skeptics who insist that "the people" cannot govern themselves as well as an enlightened elite could. And today, we are hearing a new generation of intellectuals proclaim the superiority of "the China model" of autocratic rule combined with capitalist growth.[5]

But here's the problem: you cannot have freedom without democracy. That may seem obvious, but it's a point often lost. Philosophers may sing the praises of "benevolent" dictatorships, but there is nothing benevolent about suppressing an individual's right to speak, publish, think, pray, rally, satirize, criticize, read, and search the internet. Apologists for authoritarianism insist that people have a right to order—but without the rule of law, only the ruled are constrained, not the rulers. This kind of "order" too readily descends into tyranny and brings all of its worst consequences: torture, terror, mass imprisonment, and genocide.

Without constitutional constraints on power, there is only a republic of fear. What saves citizens from the knock on the door in the dead of night, from the risk of being silenced or removed, is a constitution, a robust body of laws, an independent judiciary to enforce them, and a culture that insists on free elections, human rights, and human dignity. Not all democracies do a good job of defending liberty, but all the political systems that protect liberty are democracies. Not all democracies do a good job of controlling corruption and abuse of power, but no dictatorship does a good job of it.

Human nature being what it is, power that is not checked will sooner or later be misused. Virtually all of the world's least corrupt governments are democracies. And they are less corrupt because their citizens are free to expose abuse and their courts are free to prosecute crimes.

For reasons I cannot fully explain, these things became generally clear to me at an early age. Mine was not a very political family, but from my earliest days in elementary school, I was drawn to politics and moved by the appeal of freedom. As a grandchild of Jewish immigrants to the United States who had fled the pogroms of tsarist Russia, I knew that bigotry begets persecution. I saw that persecution on the tattooed arm of a family friend who had survived one of Hitler's concentration camps. I hated fascism. And I hated communism too, not simply because my country was locked in an existential struggle against it but because I hated any form of overbearing state control.

I grew up inspired by visions of freedom and self-determination: the birth of new African countries, the American civil rights movement, and President John F. Kennedy's call to wage "a long twilight struggle . . . against the common enemies of man: tyranny, poverty, disease, and war itself." Mesmerized and horrified, I read about World War II, the Holocaust, and the mass crimes committed in the name of "the people" in the Soviet Union and China. Frightened and alarmed, I read about the excesses committed in the name of anticommunism by Senator Joe McCarthy, his fanatical followers, and his cowering apologists. I read about the vicious racists of the Ku Klux Klan and the extreme-right anti-Communists of the John Birch Society, which had a strong foothold in my native Southern California. I read the early 1960s political thriller *Seven Days in May*, about an attempted military coup in the United States, and I worried about the prospect of losing our freedom. In quick succession, I read George Orwell's *Nineteen Eighty-Four* and *Animal Farm*, and I was seized with dread at the prospect of a world in which liberty could disappear altogether. I didn't realize it at that time, but for me, defending and extending freedom had become an overarching moral cause.

My enthusiasm for democracy has always been quite personal. I started running for office in elementary school; I lost a race for student-body president in junior high school and won one in high school. But in one respect, my political awareness lagged behind that of my peers: my hatred of communism had blinded me to the folly and escalating immorality of America's war in Vietnam. Not until I arrived at Stanford to start college in the fall of 1969 did I fully turn against the war and join the peace movement.

In my freshman year, I majored in political activism, working late into many nights mobilizing protests and writing articles against the war. But the opposition I encountered on campus didn't come from defenders of "the system." It came from a small, intense clique of Marxist revolutionaries who thought America was beyond redemption and that violence was the only answer. I was and remain committed to nonviolence in the pursuit of democracy and social justice; the revolutionaries despised me for that and denounced liberal activists like me as naïve fools. Before they faded into well-earned oblivion, they did serious damage. On a warm spring evening in 1970, they provoked a police riot that resulted in numerous arrests and shrouded the core of Stanford's pastoral campus in tear gas. As the protests peaked, university buildings were damaged and research was destroyed. During the late 1960s and early '70s, much more serious violence plagued other American campuses and especially the country's inner cities, even as European democracies faced more intense denunciations and even terrorist violence from the revolutionary left.

While my generation grappled with the roiling public order, an older generation of policy experts feared that something profound had gone wrong. A 1975 report for the Trilateral Commission (which brought together influential elites from the United States, Europe, and Japan) warned that the advanced democracies were losing their capacity to govern. Although the authors worried about common policy challenges such as inflation, economic stagnation, and oil prices, their principal concern was that an excess of democracy was generating "an overload of demands on government." Rising pressure from protest movements, radical intellectuals, and hypercritical news media had, the report warned, resulted in an "adversary culture" that was relentlessly challenging the authority and eroding the legitimacy of democratic governments.

For the first time since the end of World War II, scholars and commentators were speaking of a broad crisis of democracy due to trouble at its core—the West.[6] Indeed, the resignation of President Richard Nixon over his attempts to subvert the 1972 election and obstruct justice suggested that the rot had been dangerously advanced. Living through the Vietnam and Watergate era taught me two lifelong lessons: that political polarization and intolerance could prove poisonous to democracy, and that the instruments of democracy—elections, the media, the Congress, the courts—could restore its health.

Because of my political and antiwar activism, I couldn't find the time to study overseas during college. But I remained intensely interested in political and economic development worldwide and resolved to experience it firsthand after I graduated. With a press credential from *The Nation* magazine, I set out to spend a month each in Portugal, Nigeria, Egypt, Israel, Thailand, and Taiwan, beginning in November 1974. Each country had a story to tell about political or economic transition, and I was eager to learn.

Over six months of travel and intense interviewing, I began to glean real-world insights into the two questions that had most fascinated me in college: Why do some countries develop while others remain poor? And why do some countries become democratic while others don't?

Landing in Portugal seven months after the revolution that overthrew a forty-eight-year-old dictatorship, I was captivated. In the smoke-filled offices and cobbled streets of 1970s Lisbon, I found a live political struggle—not just among political parties but between two different visions of political order, democratic and authoritarian. With Soviet support, a powerful Communist Party was bidding for political control. Familiar revolutionary slogans hung in the air, but with the fate of a nation in the balance, not a college campus. Half a century of dictatorship had left Portugal's political landscape fragmented and underprepared for democracy. But young and middle-aged politicians of extraordinary energy and courage were fighting for a democratic future. And ultimately, with Western support, they prevailed.

In Nigeria, I found a different story. In December 1974, the country was just a few years past a devastating civil war that had claimed roughly a million lives. Although the military regime had worked to heal the

wounds of that conflict, the country remained deeply divided along ethnic lines, particularly among the Hausa in the north, the Yoruba in the
west, and the Igbo in the east (who had attempted to secede and establish an independent state of Biafra). These divisions, along with endemic
corruption, had doomed Nigeria's first attempt at democracy after its
independence in 1960. Now the Nigerian people were tired of the military's venality, which was reaching scandalous proportions as oil wealth
began gushing into government coffers.

In Nigeria, I encountered pervasive greed, incompetence, and waste
as the get-rich-quick mentality filtered down to the lowest levels of
government. But I also met journalists who were defying the country's
generals to press for a return to civilian rule and academics who were
reimagining the country's future. I met women in the markets who
were natural entrepreneurs and saw students who demanded a political
voice. For the first time in my life, I witnessed on a daily basis unimaginable poverty and squalor alongside uplifting resilience and hope.

Each country taught me something new about why countries develop
or stagnate, about why democracies flourish or fail. I was hooked.

Democracy Under Siege

I am still learning today. After writing my doctoral dissertation on Nigeria's failed first attempt at democracy in the 1960s, I spent a year as a
Fulbright fellow in Nigeria, witnessing the failure of its Second Republic. Soon thereafter, I wound up back at Stanford and the Hoover Institution. Over the past three decades there, I have explored the ways
democracies can survive and succeed—and how they can falter and fall.

I have worked with democratic dissidents from Cuba, Vietnam, and
Egypt. I have supported human rights activists from North Korea,
China, Russia, and Zimbabwe. I have advised political transitions in Iraq
and Yemen. I have lectured in the midst of transitions in South Africa,

Kenya, Tunisia, and Ukraine. I have tried to help democrats from Nigeria, Burma, and Venezuela devise strategies to shake off authoritarian rule. I have worked with politicians and civic leaders trying to improve democracy in Mongolia, Ghana, and Taiwan. These brave people have become not simply my teachers but my friends.

Late in a lifetime spent studying and promoting democracy, I would like to be able to say that things are heading in the right direction. They are not.

And that is why I have felt the need for this book. Trump's election made me start thinking about a book that offers a comprehensive—and urgent—assessment of the rising danger to democracy in the United States and around the world. After three decades in which democracy was spreading and another in which it was stagnating and slowly eroding, we are now witnessing a global retreat from freedom.

In every region of the world, autocrats are seizing the initiative, democrats are on the defensive, and the space for competitive politics and free expression is shrinking. Established democracies are becoming more polarized, intolerant, and dysfunctional. Emerging democracies are facing relentless scandals, sweeping citizen disaffection, and existential threats to their survival. From Turkey and Hungary to the Philippines, wily autocrats are destroying constitutional checks and balances. And with the global winds blowing their way, authoritarian leaders are becoming more nakedly dictatorial.

These unfavorable gusts are not simply the exhaust fumes of decaying democracies. They are blowing hard from the two leading centers of global authoritarianism, Russia and China. And if the United States does not reclaim its traditional place as the keystone of democracy, Vladimir Putin, Xi Jinping, and their admirers may turn autocracy into the driving force of the new century.

Many other analyses are missing this crucial point. The extraordinary progress of democracy from the mid-1970s to the early 2000s was a global phenomenon, heavily facilitated by the strength, idealism, and energetic support of the United States and Western Europe. The gathering retreat of freedom is also a global phenomenon, driven this time from Moscow and Beijing. A reviving autocracy and an emerging Communist superpower are investing heavily—and often effectively—in efforts to promote disinformation and covertly subvert democratic norms and institutions. Their increasingly brazen challenge demands a vigorous global response: a reassertion of global democratic leadership, rooted in Washington's renewed understanding of its far-reaching responsibilities, and a new worldwide campaign to promote democratic values, media, and civic institutions.

Part of that, I argue, must involve a serious attack on the soft underbelly of these autocracies: kleptocracy. The money being looted from public coffers in corrupt autocracies is not only sustaining abusive rulers; it is also being laundered into the banking and property systems of the world's democracies, corroding our own rule of law and undermining our will to confront the spread of despotism. We can be the kleptocrats' foes or their bankers, but not both. By fighting kleptocracy and money laundering, we can help reverse authoritarian trends both at home and abroad.

But as the old saying goes, you can't beat something with nothing. We cannot defend and renew free government around the world unless we do so at home. Stopping the desecration of democratic norms and institutions by Donald Trump (and budding autocrats elsewhere) is vital but insufficient. The decline of American democracy did not begin with Trump, and it will not end with his departure from the White House. Our republic's sickness has its roots in decades of rising political polarization that has turned our two parties into something akin to warring tribes, willing to skirt bedrock principles of fairness and inclusion for pure partisan advantage. America's constitutional order has long been scarred by racism, deep injustices in our criminal justice system, and the soft corruption of our systems of lobbying and campaign finance. Now these deep-rooted problems are quickening in a society that has forgotten the purpose of civic education and is increasingly in thrall to social media, which privileges the profits of sensationalism and groupthink above the prophets of facts and evidence-based debate.

None of this is a cry of despair; all of it is a call to arms. As I explain in this book's final chapters, it doesn't have to go on like this. Promising and viable reforms are available. We can improve, empower, and heal our democracy—and much can be done even while Trump is in power. We can change this. *We*—democratic societies—must change this. But this effort starts with each of us as an individual.

The Power of the Powerless

In 1978, the Czech playwright Václav Havel—who would go on to become the first president of post-Communist Czechoslovakia—wrote one of the most important dissident treatises ever published. In "The Power of the Powerless," Havel insisted that the oppressed have the power to overcome their powerlessness by "living within truth" and refusing to bend to the will and lies of dictatorship. His key theme is individual responsibility and the ability of citizens, through daily acts of defiance, to make a difference even under tyrannical rule.

In four decades of studying democracy, there is no maxim of which I have become more convinced than this: individuals can determine the fate of democracy. "It is from numberless diverse acts of courage and belief that human history is shaped," said Senator Robert F. Kennedy in a moving 1966 address to South African students at the University of Cape Town, in the heyday of that country's apartheid tyranny. At the time, those words became my conviction. After many decades of research and experience, they have become my conclusion. And sometimes, I have found, people in new democracies like today's South Africa

may remember RFK's lesson better than the often comfortable, complacent, or even self-pitying citizens of older republics, who have forgotten
how quickly liberty can die.

Eager to think of itself as a science, the academic study of politics
these days is often dismissive of the role that leaders play in shaping
political outcomes. But it is not abstract economic or social forces that
bring about democracy or make it work. It is individuals—ordinary and
extraordinary citizens—who stake claims, shape programs, form organizations, forge strategies, and move people.

Making a difference involves risk and sacrifice. And when liberty is
on the line, the risks may be daunting and the sacrifice may be mortal.
But across the continents and the decades, what has most inspired me
has been the willingness of people—in the end, just people, like you and
me—to risk everything they have in the fight for freedom.

Today, in the United States, it is our turn. And the fate of global democracy rests on all our shoulders.

TWO

WHY DEMOCRACIES SUCCEED AND FAIL

Nothing is more fertile in prodigies than the art of being free; but there is nothing more arduous than the apprenticeship of liberty.

—ALEXIS DE TOCQUEVILLE, *Democracy in America*[1]

For the past three decades, I have taught a college course that asks a simple question: What makes for a stable democracy? That is not merely the logical starting question for this book; since Aristotle, it is a subject that has seized political philosophers and social scientists. Democracy does not always work; from the French Revolution of 1789 to the Arab Spring uprisings of 2011, history is littered with the corpses of revolutions for freedom that turned sour, fell apart, or descended into tyranny.

My students have often teased me about the complexity of a diagram that I introduce early in the course and keep coming back to. It looks like a really badly designed urban-transit system, with connections from many directions to the ultimate destination, which is labeled "Stable Liberal Democracy." A lot of factors shape the odds that democracy will survive. How prosperous is the country? Is it saddled with massive inequality in wealth or income? Does it have strong independent media and robust civic organizations embedded between the family and the state? Do its party system and political norms promote compromise and toleration? Is its rule of law strong enough to protect citizens' rights and check a leader who might be tempted to abuse power?

In this chapter, I'll try to distill forty years of learning and that Rube Goldberg contraption of a causal diagram. But it all boils down to this. At the far right side of the diagram, just before "Stable Democracy," is a box that says "Legitimacy." Almost every other factor in the chart passes through this station before it affects democracy, for good or ill. Ultimately, what sustains democracy is a deep and unconditional belief in its legitimacy. Unless a country's people and politicians are unconditionally committed to democracy as the best form of government—one worth obeying and defending even when their preferred parties, candidates, and policies lose out—democracy will rest on tenuous footing.[2] Then, any crisis could topple it.

For people to believe in democracy, they must believe that it can work in the long run to solve their problems: to raise living standards, manage conflict, and create a better society. They have to see that their system really is democratic, providing free and fair elections with a rule of law that maintains order and protects citizens' rights. So just before "Legitimacy" comes another box, "Performance," which covers both economic and political performance. To be stable over time, a democracy must give all groups a stake in the system by producing, maintaining, and broadly distributing prosperity. And to do that, a democracy needs a capable, professional state that can implement decisions, deliver development, and maintain order. To bring progress fairly and effectively, a democracy must restrain the most toxic and alienating element of rotten performance: corruption. We call the capacity to do all this *good governance*.

If a democracy can earn people's faith through good governance, it will survive. If it cannot, it's in trouble. A broader culture of democracy—

emphasizing tolerance, flexibility, and moderation—helps manage conflict and promote good governance. These so-called democratic norms thrive amid economic development, limited inequality, high levels of education, and a vibrant civil society. Institutional designs—ways to choose and constrain leaders, elect legislatures, and monitor government performance—can also affect how well and honestly government works. But in the end, it all comes back to legitimacy.

Beliefs about the legitimacy of democracy are not shaped just by what happens inside a country. In every era, they are shaped by the outside world, by international influences, foreign actors, and trends in global power. When a democracy dies, it is rarely a simple case of suicide; such deaths often carry a strong whiff of homicide, in which those who want to kill off democracy from the inside are aided and abetted by foes of democracy on the outside.

That's a lifetime of study in a nutshell. In what follows, I'll try to open up that shell a bit.

What Is Democracy?

First things first: What exactly is democracy? And how can we distinguish it from its pale and cynical imitations?

In its most minimal form, democracy is a system of government in which the people can choose and replace their leaders in regular, free, and fair elections. That may not sound like a lot to citizens of long established democracies, but it requires many complicated elements. To be free, elections must be open to competition from different parties and candidates, as well as to the participation—at least through voting—of all citizens.

In America, this took centuries. Every year, I ask my first-year class, "When did the United States become a democracy?" Was it in 1776, when we threw off the tyranny of King George III? Or 1789, when we finally adopted the workable federal constitution that remains in place (with surprisingly few amendments) to this day? Or 1865, with the ratification of the Thirteenth Amendment, which abolished slavery? Or 1920, when the Nineteenth Amendment gave American women the right to vote?

At some point, someone always volunteers the right answer: 1965. That was the year the United States passed the Voting Rights Act, prohibiting racial discrimination in voting and ending the sordid practices that southern states had used for a century to keep African Americans from exercising their democratic rights. Only in 1968 could an American presidential election plausibly be, for the first time, called free and fair.

Democracy also requires the freedom to vote and run for office, including running vigorous, energetic campaigns. But these liberties can be partial or illusory. Egyptians used to tell a joke about life under their longtime dictator, Hosni Mubarak: "There's freedom of speech. There's just no freedom *after* speech."

Russia's strongman, Vladimir Putin, always allows some opposition presidential candidates to surface in Russian elections, as did Mubarak toward the end of his twenty-nine-year reign. But the outcome is never in doubt: in Putin's type of "electoral autocracy," the serious alternatives to the entrenched ruler are disqualified, arrested, denounced by the state-controlled media, or otherwise confronted with such massive handicaps that any "election" becomes a farce.

If you look today at countries such as Hungary, Turkey, and Tanzania, you can find systems that look a little more like democracy. In their elections, opposition parties can campaign widely and may even win a lot of seats in parliament; challengers can criticize the ruling party without being locked up (though even that freedom has been dwindling in Turkey and Tanzania). But it's not a fair contest. The ruling party controls most of the media that matter. It has browbeaten business owners into supporting it if they want to stay in business. It has rigged the electoral rules and districts to ensure that it retains power even if it fails to win a majority of the vote. And it uses its control over other levers of power—like the judiciary and the security apparatus—to ensure that no accidents happen on the road to reelection.[3]

No wonder the playwright Tom Stoppard has one of his characters remark, "It's not the voting that's democracy, it's the counting." Democracy requires elections that are genuinely free and fair, and those are possible only in a country with a significant degree of freedom to speak, organize, monitor, and move about.

But democracy is more than just the ability to choose one's leaders. What we usually think of as full-fledged democracy is what political scientists call *liberal democracy*, which entails much more than just voting. It means strong protections for basic liberties, such as freedom of the press, association, assembly, belief, and religion; the fair treatment of racial and cultural minorities; a robust rule of law, in which all citizens are equal under the law and no one is above it; an independent judiciary to uphold that principle; trustworthy law-enforcement institutions to pursue it; other institutions to check the potential for high government officials to behave corruptly; and a lively civil society, made up of independent associations, social movements, universities, and publications, which together enable citizens to lobby for their interests and limit government power.

These elements constitute something closer to the full political package of a *good* democracy. And that is the kind of democracy that people want to keep.

The Imperative of Good Governance

Early in my career, when I began to look closely at the instability that plagued many emerging democracies, I noticed something striking. Failing democracies were invariably illiberal, "low-grade" democracies, with bad governance. If they had once been fully realized, rights-protecting liberal democracies, they had stopped being liberal before they started to fail. These crumbling democracies were either shallow and shaky from the start, like Russia in the 1990s or Nigeria in the early 1980s, or they had steadily declined in quality before they descended into authoritarianism, like Venezuela in the 1990s or Hungary today.

No liberal democracy has ever just suddenly had a heart attack and died. Its arteries of freedom, the rule of law, and the balance of power had started clogging noticeably well before the end. And it didn't take the political scientist's version of a cholesterol test or an EKG to spot the emerging symptoms.

Some of the most frequent warning signs of a democracy's decline are easy enough to spot: endemic corruption, recurrent high-profile scandals over graft, power-abusing presidents, and governments that cannot deliver jobs, rising incomes, lower crime rates, or such basic services as electricity, water, roads, and decent schools. In such waning democracies, when things went bad, government seemed to grind to a halt. Politicians were so busy scrambling after the remaining spoils of power or demonizing their opponents that little in the public interest was accomplished.

That is what I saw in Nigeria in 1983 as the Second Republic—which began amid so much hope and goodwill in 1979 after years of autocratic misrule—gasped its way toward its bruising first electoral test. Nothing was getting done. A country in the midst of an oil boom could not build more than the hollow shells of hospitals, schools, or other public infrastructure; politically connected contractors were absconding with the funds after making a mere gesture of effort. Highways were left pitted with craters, fields without irrigation, towns without pipe-borne water—all while the cranes and bulldozers, the water pumps and pipes, stood abandoned by the side of the road. Students found themselves without promised scholarship money; soldiers and civil servants waited months for salaries that were being pilfered by higher-ups.

Meanwhile, as public money leached out to pay government "ghost" workers and fake contracts, the guilty were brazenly burning down government buildings to cover up their corruption. Rice—a food staple—became scarce as top politicians hoarded it for profit. Graft-driven shortages left the gas pumps dry, stranding taxis and trucks, and forcing middle-class drivers to inch forward for hours in long lines amid merciless heat.

Nigerians told me that they were looking to the August 1983 elections as a kind of last chance to rescue their system from the paralyzing plunder. But the ruling party stole that chance, through flagrant electoral fraud. The system was no longer really democratic, and I could sense calamity coming. I knew what my university students in Kano (northern Nigeria's largest city) were thinking, and a preelection survey I had done in the state showed massive citizen disenchantment.

After the election, students marched in the streets with signs calling for the military to return. Perhaps because Nigeria's Second Republic had begun amid such wealth and optimism, the public disillusionment was particularly bitter. But this is what democratic failure often looks like: governance is bad, the economy sags, order implodes, people lose faith, and the system limps along until it is pushed over by the military, extremist militants, or the ruler himself.

Tragically, bad governance often goes hand in hand with the manipulation of ethnic and religious differences. If parties and politicians are going to grab the gold that comes with power and then not deliver much in return, how can they recruit support from their unhappy citizens? The answer—with stunning consistency across regions and cultures—is that they rely on extended family ties. These are not immediate blood relations but a kinship of shared ethnic identity, based on language, race, religion, or some notion of common ancestry.[4] Instead of boosting the entire society, corrupt politicians deliver patronage to their cronies and their ethnic kin. That can mean government contracts at inflated prices; government jobs for unqualified supporters; and all manner of other payments, kickbacks, and preferences.

This is the game of patronage politics on steroids. Such systems are not only a huge drag on economic development but also a formula for political instability—breeding ethnic conflict, political polarization, and pervasive citizen disgust. Once ordinary people see that the political class is grabbing public wealth and advantage at every turn, they ask, *Why not me?* And if they can't get it through politics, they will get it through crime.

Moreover, unless you are a small, oil-rich kingdom, there is never enough public wealth to go around. So illicit activity of all kinds circles around politics in chronically corrupt states: drug trafficking, sex trafficking, kidnapping, smuggling, organized crime, money laundering. Just look at Mexico or Russia: the criminals in government and those outside it can become not only similar but inseparable.

When this kind of predatory system reaches its kleptocratic nadir, democracy is long gone, replaced by a dictatorship fueled by greed. But even if things do not get quite this dire, democracies can be left quite corrupt and riddled with patronage politics. And it is these low-grade democracies—whose logic is loot first and worry about the public later—that are most vulnerable and prone to fail.

With pervasive corruption comes a host of other ills. In such graft-ridden countries as Pakistan, Kenya, Guatemala, and Ukraine, the rule of law becomes anemic as the judiciary becomes corrupted. Without a justice system worthy of the name, citizens are left at the mercy of predatory police officers, landlords, mafias, and soldiers. Minorities, women, and the poor are prone to being targeted for abuse. The consequences for democracy are grim: a hollowed-out state that can't deliver much; chronic ethnic conflict and violence; and a poverty trap in which the country can't take off economically because few will invest in such a void of accountability, transparency, and the rule of law.

Over the years, I have found that the greatest damage to democracy is done where it is least visible: in the culture. When democracy withers, it often has a lot to do with what citizens think, believe, and value.

Pervasive greed, opportunism, and corruption shatter trust not only in government but in our fellow citizens as well. Society then fragments as the poor cling to their local power brokers and try to capture the crumbs that fall from their political tables. No one expects that anyone else will behave honestly, so nearly everyone demands or pays bribes, buys or sells votes, and watches their backs.

In the 1990s, the Harvard political scientist Robert Putnam brilliantly captured this phenomenon in a classic work that explained why the southern part of Italy was so much poorer and less well governed than the country's north.[5] The root cause of the disparity, he found, was a dearth of social capital—the "trust, norms, and networks" that enable people to cooperate as equals to improve their community and their individual circumstances. When a democracy is on the right track, becoming what Putnam calls a "civic community," people trust one another and form all manner of associations to combine in pursuit of larger ends. The culture of civic engagement and the practice of responsible governance then reinforce each other in a virtuous circle. Development proceeds, and democracy thrives.

This is the kind of society that Alexis de Tocqueville famously found and celebrated in his monumental nineteenth-century study *Democracy in America*. In such a civic community, people may disagree about politics and diverge over faith and culture, but they show mutual respect and tolerate their differences. Disputes are eased by citizens' common attachment to their country, constitution, and laws. Entrepreneurs invest, workers produce, and parties compromise. Citizens pay their taxes, obey the laws, and respect the political system because it works, by and large, for the common good.

On the other hand, in a predatory system—one like Nigeria's Second Republic, Haiti under the Duvaliers, or Cambodia under Hun Sen today—institutions exist but do not function. Legislators do not deliberate, judges do not adjudicate, and citizens do not participate. The police do not protect innocents, and the state does not deliver services. Every transaction is twisted to immediate advantage. No one has confidence in the future or their fellow citizens.

To lose in an election in such an unhappy country is to risk permanent disempowerment and destitution. Add in the deliberate mobilization of ethnic or religious grievance, and elections become "do or die" affairs in places such as Kenya, Nigeria, and Bangladesh. Defeat can mean not just an electoral setback but indefinite subordination to the ruling group.

While the extreme form of predatory society has taken shape in some severely repressive and failed states—countries like Congo, Somalia, Sudan, Zimbabwe, Iraq, Afghanistan, Burma, Haiti, and Turkmenistan—a lesser form is common in struggling democracies. Look at any measure of corruption, such as Transparency International's Corruption Perceptions Index, and you will find a pattern. The least corrupt countries, with the exception of Singapore, are the prosperous liberal democracies of the West, which have been highly stable (at least until now). The Scandinavian countries top the list, followed by the rest of northern Europe, New Zealand, Australia, and Canada, with the United States trailing behind, just ahead of Ireland and Japan.[6] Then comes a mix of more recently established democracies from southern Europe, Eastern Europe, Asia, and Latin America, along with some authoritarian regimes.

Down below the midpoint among the 176 countries surveyed, the lights start blinking. This is where we find many autocracies, as well as countries that have endured repeated democratic failure and instability, such as Argentina and Sri Lanka (tied for the rank of 95), the Philippines and Thailand (tied at 101), Pakistan and Tanzania (116), Ukraine and Nepal (131), and Venezuela (166).

High levels of corruption are not only a cause of democratic failure but an effect of decadent institutions. Thus the path to controlling corruption—through robust accountability, the rule of law, and a vigorous civil society—is also the path to sustainable democracy.

The Formula for Success

That gives us a picture of what makes democracies fail. So what makes them succeed? Over the long haul, we have learned, democracies need a strategy for restraining the most destructive flaw in human nature: our greed for power and wealth. Without such a formula, a society's most cunning and ambitious people will find ways to parlay small advantages into ever larger ones, build monopolies, and exploit the less fortunate. Then inequality will become entrenched, corruption will become a way of life, and society will sink into a vicious cycle of cynicism, distrust, and domination of the weak by the strong.

Those worried about the health of democracy today will naturally want to know what the formula is. The design of a constitution can make a big difference. So can effective state and political institutions, including the judicial system, independent agencies that control abuses of power, and civilian control over the military and police. It also helps a lot if a society is prosperous and limits economic inequality. The more liberal democracies are, the stronger and more resilient they are too.

But sustaining democracy begins and ends with culture. If people believe in democracy and are willing to defend it as a way of life, the level of economic development and the precise design of institutions matter a lot less. But if democracy lacks this kind of broad support, it will always be a fragile reed.

So what is the culture of democracy? How do we build it and keep it strong?

The paramount component is democratic legitimacy—the resilient and broadly shared belief that democracy is better than any other imaginable form of government. People must commit to democracy come hell or high water, and stick with it even when the economy tanks, incomes plunge, or politicians misbehave.

As the great social scientists Seymour Martin Lipset and Dankwart

Rustow noted decades ago, that democratic commitment usually begins pragmatically: politicians choose democracy as a way to manage their differences, and citizens accept it because it gradually gives them better lives (and not just freer ones).[7] But eventually, this belief has to sink deeply into people's hearts and minds, so that it no longer depends on an answer to the question "So what have you done for me lately?" Usually, this sort of profound belief in democratic legitimacy results from long experience, from years in which a democratic system manifestly succeeds in maintaining order and improving living standards. Think of the United States, Britain, and Canada over many decades before the Great Depression, or of Germany and Japan in the decades after World War II.

My fellow democracy scholars call this widely shared and unconditional commitment to a constitution and its norms *democratic consolidation*. The problem is that it's hard to know whether democratic commitments are solid or fair-weather until the political climate gets bad—a challenge we are witnessing today as the winds of authoritarianism and nativism whip again through Europe and the United States.

Moreover, advanced democracies face a newer challenge. For a long time, most of us assumed that consolidation was a one-way street; unless an asteroid hit the United States, we could be confident that democracy would endure. But what happens when the performance of the system suffers more than a temporary shock—when incomes for a large swath of the working and middle class stagnate for years or even decades, and when people no longer believe that their children's lives will be better than theirs? That is the situation now in the United States, where by 2016 the median household income had recovered, after the financial collapse of 2008, only to its 1999 level.[8] As wages for lower- and middle-income families decline or stagnate, significantly "fewer Americans are growing up to be better off than their parents," with rural areas in the steepest decline, as a Brookings Institution study has noted.[9] People who see their incomes and status slipping can be particularly susceptible to demagogic appeals that threaten democracy.

A deep and wide belief in democratic legitimacy can immunize the public against the siren songs of authoritarian populists in difficult times. It smooths the way to political compromise and prevents democracy from veering toward polarization and deadlock. It can inspire politicians to put the defense of democracy ahead of immediate partisan or personal advantage if an elected strongman starts to mess with the rules of the democratic game. And finally, it tends to draw ordinary citizens into more measured positions and more civil behavior.

Democratic legitimacy is a master norm that implies many others. A culture of democracy is also a culture of intellectual and political flexibility. Politicians and civic advocates may have strong ideologies and quarreling agendas, but the bulk of them must be open to evidence and reason and willing to bargain and compromise. Democracy requires trust in the decency and benevolence of other citizens, tolerance for different points of view, and thus a bit of modesty and doubt about one's own political stances. Intellectual openness promotes tolerance, as the late China scholar Lucian Pye once put it, by embracing "the idea that no one has a monopoly on absolute truth and that there can be no single, correct answer to public policy issues."[10] In turn, political tolerance requires social tolerance, because democratic governance must reconcile not only divergent policy preferences but also the claims and sensitivities of different classes and identity groups.

A culture of democracy is also a culture of moderation. Democracy can't function when politics is dominated by opposing camps of "true believers" who view compromise as betrayal and dismiss discordant evidence as fake. Democracy also requires a tone of civility and mutual respect. When contending politicians and activists vilify one another as evil and immoral, the rules of the democratic game can get stretched surprisingly quickly—often even to the point of violence, which is toxic to democratic stability. After all, how could you compromise with evil, accept its legislative victories, or—God forbid—let it assume power?

So all these norms are crucial to democracy: legitimacy, tolerance, and trust; moderation, flexibility, and compromise; civility, mutual respect, and restraint. Alongside them goes one more: a disposition toward authority that is, as my late Stanford colleague Alex Inkeles put it, neither "blindly submissive" nor "hostilely rejecting" but rather "responsible . . . even though always watchful."[11] If people are cynical about authority, government cannot win their cooperation and respect, resulting in political polarization and government deadlock—thereby further alienating citizens and driving them to defect from the democratic rules. But the opposite syndrome is also bad for democracy: a slavish deference to authority and a willingness to surrender one's freedoms to some movement that promises to magically deliver society from all its woes.

The great social-democratic philosopher Sidney Hook, writing in the era of Hitler, Stalin, and Mussolini, eloquently captured this insight in a way that anticipated the rise of modern autocrats like Putin, Hugo Chávez in Venezuela, and Recep Tayyip Erdogan in Turkey. Working democracy, he wrote, requires "an intelligent distrust of its leadership," including a hardy skepticism "of all demands for the enlargement of power, and an emphasis upon critical method in every phase of education and social life." He added, "Where skepticism is replaced by uncritical enthusiasm and the many-faceted deifications which our complex society makes possible, a fertile soil for dictatorship has been prepared."[12]

In a healthy democracy, intelligent skepticism on the part of the public is accompanied by prudent self-restraint on the part of political leaders. The Harvard political scientists Steven Levitsky and Daniel Ziblatt call this *forbearance*—the avoidance of "actions that, while respecting the letter of the law, obviously violate its spirit."[13] If the spirit of democracy is tolerance, trust, and compromise, then forbearance is the regulator valve that insulates these norms from political pressure. Forbearance keeps politicians from using every measure of their legal authority (and some that skirt it) to crush the other side in a quest for permanent political victory.

The most influential academic study of the transition to democracy, by the late Argentine political scientist Guillermo O'Donnell and my former Stanford colleague Philippe Schmitter, makes a similar point. Most often, replacing a dictatorship with a democracy requires a negotiated compromise in which bitter political rivals guarantee each other's vital interests and agree not to push their own agendas to the hilt. The democrats say to the autocrats, in essence, *Just leave power and we won't prosecute you.* The left says to the right, *Allow a free and fair election and if we win, we'll respect your property rights.* And South Africa's apartheid rulers said to the country's black majority, *Give us some constitutional protections for our wealth and rights, promise to abjure revenge, and we'll grant you democracy.*[14]

The problem for new democracies is that this mutual restraint may be merely tactical, honored only until such time as one side can win enough power to obliterate the other. Old democracies face the inverse problem: as the memory of tyranny fades, people tend to take democracy for granted. They lose sight of democracy's fragility, become complacent about its norms, and carelessly cross the line into incivility, intolerance, and power grabbing.

When an old democracy loses track of what made it great, ruling parties refuse to listen to their opposition or compromise with it. Opposition parties retaliate with obstruction and government shutdowns. Hyperpartisanship intensifies, and the fabric of trust and mutual respect wears thin. This is the path to democratic dysfunction and crisis. And it is the path that the United States is now on.

The Social Conditions for Democracy

Many scholars once thought that much of the non-Western world was doomed to despotism, arguing that, say, Asian or Muslim countries lacked the liberal Enlightenment values often linked to a culture of democratic compromise and toleration. But even setting aside those hidebound assumptions about societies in the Middle East and Asia, time and more recent scholarship have shown that cultures do change, as a result of social and economic conditions that can enable a democratic culture to emerge and take root. Democracy is hardly just for the West. (Remember, the world's largest democracy is India, with some 1.3 billion people, followed by the United States and then Indonesia, a Muslim-majority country of over 260 million.)

Political scientists know quite a bit about the conditions that make democracy more likely to thrive. One key condition is wealth, but not just any form of it. When countries rely on oil or other mineral wealth, the riches are usually controlled, skimmed, and squandered by a narrow elite running a corrupt state. In Saudi Arabia, Iran, Russia, and other oil-rich autocracies, this generates severe economic inequality, stunts free enterprise, and swells the state's repressive apparatus. This is hardly a formula for tolerance, trust, and peaceful competition for power.

On the other hand, when countries become wealthy through the gradual expansion of private enterprise, small businesses, and the rule of law, a far healthier dynamic takes hold. Income and wealth are more fairly distributed. Levels of education and knowledge steadily rise. Social capital grows alongside financial capital. The landscape becomes thick with professional associations, interest groups, unions, cultural organizations, anticorruption watchdogs, mass media, and universities. Under such conditions, these different groups may clash, even intensely, over policies, but they will respect one another's right to exist.

When most of society belongs to the middle class or a reasonably secure and improving working class, politics takes on a different hue. Then, as Lipset noted decades ago, even the lower classes can afford to approach politics with greater flexibility and a longer time horizon, seeking gradual reform instead of revolutionary change.[15]

Education is particularly key here. When people are educated at least through high school, it broadens their outlook on life. They become more tolerant of differences and nuances. This inclines them to become more active, informed, and rational citizens, and thus restrains them from being seduced by extremists. (Increasingly, though, in wealthy countries like the United States, college seems to be the educational threshold that brings these benefits.)

After all, it is a lot harder to be politically tolerant and patient when you don't have a job, don't know where your next meal is coming from, or live in dread of losing your grip on your rung of the economic ladder. Sinking status breeds bitter resentment. Desperate poverty breeds desperate politics.

All this explains why countries become more primed for democratic change—and more likely to make it stick—as they become richer and better educated. In his classic 1991 work *The Third Wave*, Samuel P. Huntington identified a per capita income "zone of transition"—roughly about $3,500 to $14,000 in today's nominal dollars—in which democratic transformations tend to occur.[16] The higher countries are in that zone (or even above it), the more likely they are to sustain democracy. Most of the durable democratic transitions of the past few decades— such as Greece and Spain, Brazil and Chile, South Korea and Taiwan, Poland and South Africa—occurred in this zone.

Yet poverty does not preclude democratic progress. A sizable minority of poor countries (including nations in the world's poorest region, Africa) are democracies, although they tend to be of lower quality. Citizens in poor countries—especially those in Africa—often express strong

commitments not just to democracy but to the liberal values of pluralism. And the prosperous and well educated are not always democracy's
most dedicated defenders.

Several developing countries, including Botswana, have also managed to launch and sustain democracy at a fairly low level of per capita
income—but they overcame the odds because their wealth was better
distributed and the values of tolerance and pluralism were well entrenched. In Botswana, which had been a colonial backwater, traditional
norms constrained the ability of chiefs to amass oppressive wealth and
power, and after the country won its independence, its government pursued a pragmatic policy of state-led capitalist development that distributed benefits all around.[17]

Still, as democracy has spread to all corners of the globe, its success
has remained strongly related to economic prosperity. Consider the
United Nations' broader measure of development, the Human Development Index, which measures not only per capita income but also life
expectancy and educational levels. By this U.N. yardstick, twenty-four
of the world's twenty-five richest countries are democracies (with tiny,
wealthy Singapore the lone autocratic exception). With virtually every
step down the ladder of development, the percentage of democracies
declines. Among the world's poorer countries, only 40 percent are
democracies—and mostly low-grade ones. Among the eleven poorest of
all countries, only two are democracies.

Ethnic divisions can also make it harder for democracy to take root.
When a society is deeply divided along largely binary identity lines—
secular vs. religious, Christian vs. Muslim, Sunni vs. Shia, white vs. black,
Kikuyu vs. Luo, Sinhalese vs. Tamil—democracy is sorely strained. Deep
ethnic divisions need not doom a country to authoritarianism or civil
war, but democracies in such societies as India, Nigeria, and Iraq require
well-designed constitutional systems to give each group a stake in power
and a feeling of worth and security.

Getting the Institutions Right

For all the importance of these underlying conditions, countries are not captives of their histories and social inheritances. Their ability to become democratic depends on what political and societal leaders do with the power they gain—in particular, with how they design and operate the political institutions of democracy. Will they choose presidential or parliamentary government? Will they empower or constrain executives? How will members of parliament be elected? How will the government be monitored, the constitution defended, and the rule of law upheld?

My fellow political scientists have argued for decades about which setups work best, with many of our quarrels centering around the merits of presidential vs. parliamentary systems of government. Understanding the gist of these debates helps explain the strengths of democracies worldwide—and their vulnerabilities too.

The bulk of democracy experts tend to favor parliamentary rule, along the lines of Britain or Germany, for several reasons.[18] A parliamentary system—in which control of government goes to the party or coalition with the most seats in the elected legislature—avoids the problems of American-style divided government, which can face paralyzing deadlock if one party controls the presidency but not the Congress. In a parliamentary system, a prime minister generally needs majority support in parliament to form a government; if she cannot get it solely from her own party, she needs to form a coalition; and if the coalition cracks, her government falls, requiring either a new coalition or new elections.

Democracy experts like the efficiency and elegance here. Such a system may strike many Americans as less stable than our familiar fixed terms for our presidents, but the parliamentary model actually offers greater flexibility in overcoming crises, better prospects for passing legislation, and an easier path to succession if the head of government should die or disgrace the constitution.

Many developing countries—first in Latin America, then in Africa and Asia—have tried to imitate the American presidential system. But the U.S. model has another major drawback: the presidency offers a more direct path to autocracy. The chief executive gets a guaranteed period in office and wide discretion to make appointments, issue orders, and oversee the security forces. No wonder many budding autocrats—most recently, Recep Tayyip Erdogan in Turkey—have finished their demolition of democracy by transforming their constitutions from parliamentary systems to presidential ones.

Still, abuse of power is not limited to presidents. Plenty of prime ministers have gored their own parliamentary democracies, including Indira Gandhi of India, who declared emergency rule in 1975, and, more recently, Sheikh Hasina of Bangladesh, who had trampled on constitutional norms so thoroughly by 2014 that the opposition party boycotted that year's election, giving her even freer rein to oppress her critics.

Well-designed institutions can make a difference in several other realms. One is ensuring that the electoral system is well run and widely seen as fair. This has been a key factor in the mounting dysfunction of democracy in the United States, where our system has handed the presidency to two clear losers of the popular vote since just 2000, and where partisan elected secretaries of state administer elections in most states.

A second major problem area has to do with electing members of a legislature. In the United States, most members of Congress are elected through a system that scholars call *first past the post*. Only one person is elected per district, and whoever gets the most votes wins, whether he claimed a majority or not. This system, inherited from the British, seems natural to Americans. But it is no longer the way that most democracies elect their parliaments, and fortunately, as we will see, it is beginning to be challenged and replaced in some American cities and states.

Many democracies have found an appealing alternative: using some version of proportional representation, a system that elects legislatures not from single-member districts but from multimember districts of varying size. (In a few countries, like Israel and the Netherlands, the entire country is a single district.) Each party then receives a share of seats proportional to its share of the overall popular vote. (Citizens in such systems typically vote for a party list rather than just one candidate, and if, say, the Republican Party gets 53 percent of the national vote, it gets about 53 percent of the seats in the legislature.) Such systems do a significantly better job of representing their citizens' preferences, making every vote count, including those of women and minorities, and encouraging people to cast their ballots.

But proportional representation's strength is also its weakness: by enabling lots of parties to win at least a few seats in parliament (usually if they clear a minimum threshold of between 2 and 5 percent of the vote), this system can fragment the legislature and enable more extreme forces to enter. If the local Communist Party gets 4 percent of the popular vote, it shows up in the legislature. That was the curse of democracy in Weimar Germany in the late 1920s. Because of an extreme form of proportional representation, the German Reichstag was divided among many parties, crossing the whole political spectrum. As Germany's economic and social crisis deepened in the next decade, the parties that gained the most were the Communists on the far left and the Nazis on the far right, making it harder and harder to form a government without one of them—with unspeakably tragic consequences.

After World War II, when grieving German democrats redesigned their system, they required parties to win at least 5 percent of the vote to enter parliament. For seventy years, that kept extremists out of the postwar parliament, the Bundestag. But in 2017, amid an anti-immigration backlash, the far-right Alternative for Germany unexpectedly won nearly 13 percent of the vote and became the third-largest party in parliament. That would not have happened in a first-past-the-post system.

Since both proportional representation and first-past-the-post systems have serious flaws, experts have looked for another way. The most promising alternative is known as *ranked-choice voting*, and it has been used for a century to elect Australia's lower house of parliament. Under this system, a candidate in a single-member district must get a majority of the vote (or nearly so) to win. But instead of voting for just one candidate, people rank their choices—giving candidates a one, two, three, and so on. If no one wins a majority of the first-preference votes, the candidate with the lowest number of votes is eliminated, and those ballots are then recast for those voters' second choices. This process continues in an "instant runoff" until someone wins a majority (or the largest vote in the last round).

I like this system a lot—and so does a growing array of democracy scholars and reformers. Ranked-choice voting, we are finding, encourages moderation, coalition building, and civility in political life. Where districts are competitive, candidates can no longer just appeal to a narrow base to win: they have to craft broader messages to attract the second- and even third-choice votes of people who did not rank them first. This dynamic makes it much more difficult for an extremist or single-issue grievance candidate to win. And it could help remedy much of what ails American democracy.

Restraints on Power

Even if your democracy has figured out a voting system that works for it, it will face another challenge: How can your political institutions constrain politicians from amassing wealth and abusing power? A strong liberal democracy needs robust checks and balances. The American Constitution was designed, in James Madison's famous words, to make "ambition counteract ambition" by giving each of the three branches of the U.S. government "a will of its own."[19]

But experience has shown that having an independent judiciary and legislature is not enough to ensure good government. Liberal democracy requires a network of other institutions to disperse and check political power. During the twentieth century, new independent agencies arose to monitor the government and perform sensitive functions of regulation and oversight: central banks, electoral commissions, audit agencies to examine government accounts, and specialized bodies to regulate finance, telecommunications, and public health.

The United States created many federal regulatory agencies to prevent monopoly practices and protect the public interest. Oddly, though, it never established something that other liberal democracies now routinely have: strong agencies with national authority to administer elections and investigate corruption in the executive branch and the legislature. As both the oldest democracy and a federal system, the United States is saddled with some antiquated arrangements: each of the fifty states administers its own elections, with varying rules on voting standards, and Congress investigates its own ethical lapses. Moreover, criminal investigation of a president falls to a Justice Department that is housed within the executive branch and to a federal law-enforcement agency, the Federal Bureau of Investigation, that presidents have tried to influence and use for their own ends—and that the current president, Donald Trump, has repeatedly tried to bend to his will.

Any extra mechanism to investigate malfeasance, such as an accountability commission or a more independent prosecutor's office, must be fair, fearless, and politically independent, not beholden to the politicians it is supposed to monitor. Such watchdogs should be fired only for good and provable cause—not just because they threaten to bring down dishonest officeholders. And they need the power to prosecute or impose penalties, with guarantees of due process.

This is why, in the wake of Watergate, President Richard Nixon's 1970s assault on the U.S. system of justice and free elections, Congress established the Office of the Independent Counsel to investigate charges of wrongdoing by high-level officials. But both parties came to see the institution, especially during Kenneth Starr's sprawling investigation of

President Bill Clinton, as a runaway train. It was replaced in 1999 with new regulations allowing the attorney general to appoint a special counsel when the Justice Department had a conflict of interest or saw a compelling "public interest."[20] The new rules gave special counsels operational autonomy but still enabled the president to order their dismissal.[21] That vulnerability has been central to the crisis of American democracy under Trump.

Why would political leaders agree to have their power monitored and limited by bodies they cannot control? Even in well-established democracies, few leaders welcome the prospect of searching, independent scrutiny. So real independence comes only when civil society organizes to demand it.[22] Without strong, well-focused public pressure, countries usually wind up with muzzled watchdogs. And public vigilance and devotion to these institutions must be sustained over time.

In an enduring democracy, power must be not only chosen but checked. To see why, look at the recent history of Thailand. After 1997, it adopted an innovative constitution with strong institutions of accountability. Then in 2001, a billionaire tycoon named Thaksin Shinawatra won a stunning electoral victory by mobilizing a resentful and neglected countryside against Thailand's long dominant urban elite.

Like the election of the billionaire populist who would pull off a similar feat in the United States fifteen years later, Thaksin's was bitterly controversial. Thailand's National Anti-Corruption Commission ruled that, as a cabinet minister, Thaksin had falsified a mandatory declaration of his assets and thus was legally barred from becoming prime minister. Thaksin fought back, mobilizing "the people" against the elite and suing in the Constitutional Court. By a single vote (often rumored in Bangkok to have been purchased), the court allowed him to assume office.

As prime minister, Thaksin delivered on many of his populist promises, but he also subverted Thailand's constitutional norms. He attacked his opponents as unpatriotic and "stupid." He turned the country's accountability institutions around to investigate journalists and critics.

"Bad people deserve to die," he declared as he launched murderous assaults on drug dealers and on violent resistance by minority Muslims in the south. He hounded the media, demanding "positive" news and threatening critics with libel suits and even criminal investigation.[23] He won reelection in a landslide and accelerated his erosion of checks and balances. Then, in 2006, the military overthrew him. Thai democracy has not yet recovered.

The parallels are, I think, pretty clear. Thailand's tragedy shows that even the most beautifully designed constitution can be abused. The ultimate defense of liberal democracy lies not in the constitution but in the culture—in free, informed, and principled citizens who will not tolerate the abuse of their democracy or their rights. And that is as true in the United States as it is in Thailand.

THREE

THE MARCH AND RETREAT OF DEMOCRACY

For a century and a half after Tocqueville observed the emergence of modern democracy in America, successive waves of democratization washed up on the shore of dictatorship. Buoyed by a rising tide of economic progress, each wave advanced further and ebbed less than its predecessor. History, to shift the metaphor, does not move forward in a straight line, but when skilled and determined leaders push, it does move forward.

—SAMUEL P. HUNTINGTON, *The Third Wave*[1]

The Tides of Freedom

History shows us that democratic change does not happen in isolation. Rather, democracy surges forward and retreats in waves, across regions and the whole globe. And in recent decades, the support of the United States—as an exemplar, an inspiration, and a source of aid and expertise—has had a great deal to do with whether the tide is coming in or going out.

As the late Harvard political scientist Samuel Huntington explained, what defines a historical wave is its balance of gains and losses. In a democratic wave, the number of countries making the transition to democracy greatly exceeds the number moving away from it, and overall levels of liberty rise. In a reverse wave, the opposite is true: democracy shrinks, and so does human freedom. This concept isn't perfect, but it reminds us that democratic progress can be rolled back. It also underscores why the current global assault on democracy—with scant protest from the United States—is simultaneously so historic and so troubling. To understand today's crisis, we need to understand yesterday's waves.

Huntington argued that the first wave of global democratization began with the democratization of the United States, which he dates (disputably) to 1828, when more than half of all white American males became eligible to vote. Gradually, the first wave engulfed most of Western Europe as well as a few countries in Eastern Europe (such as Poland), Canada, Australia, New Zealand, and four South American countries. A century later, more than thirty countries had "established at least minimal national democratic institutions," Huntington wrote, although we would regard some of them today as only semidemocratic.[2]

While democracy expanded in the world, it also met setbacks: failed revolutions, aborted transitions, breakdowns of constitutional rule. As this first wave was cresting, a reverse wave began gathering in 1922, when the Italian Fascist Benito Mussolini marched on Rome, prompting Italy's king to appoint him prime minister. Mussolini quickly disposed of what Huntington called Italy's "fragile and rather corrupt democracy." Democratic reversals soon followed in Portugal, Poland, and the Baltics.

The crucial turning point came in 1933, when the Nazis took power in Germany. Hitler and Mussolini spread fascism across Europe, while civilian and military upheavals finished off democracy in Japan and most of Latin America. As liberal societies struggled with the prolonged economic depression of the 1930s, doubts about democracy grew, even in Britain and the United States. With Nazi Germany and imperial Japan on the march, many concluded that dictatorship was the solution to national frailty, uncertainty, and decay—and even the expression of a new global zeitgeist. It took the defeat of the Axis powers in World War II to halt this momentum and launch the second wave of democratization.

The second wave restored democracy to most of Western Europe, introduced the first real democracies in Japan and Turkey, and spread democracy further into Latin America. But this wave was short-lived, ending in 1962. With the exception of Costa Rica, Venezuela, and Colombia, most of the new and restored Latin American democracies—including Argentina, Brazil, and Peru—fell in a wave of military coups.

The second wave also saw the birth of many new democracies (and quasi democracies) through decolonization, as the European empires in Africa, Asia, and the Middle East collapsed after World War II. These burgeoning democracies were mainly former British colonies that had some experience with elections and the rule of law—India, Sri Lanka, Jamaica, Botswana, Gambia, Ghana, Nigeria, Burma, and Malaysia. The first four of these democracies have survived (save for a brief period of emergency rule in India under Indira Gandhi in 1975–1977 and a more recent democratic interruption in Sri Lanka). But most multiparty constitutional systems in the Third World—including in Turkey, South Korea, Indonesia, the Philippines, and across Africa—ultimately gave way to military, one-party, or one-man rule. By Huntington's count, the number of democracies during the second wave peaked at fifty-one before slipping back down to just twenty-nine.[3]

Democracy on the Upswing

On April 25, 1974, a youthful cabal of left-wing military officers overthrew one of the longest-surviving dictatorships in Europe, Portugal's Estado Novo (New State). Thousands of citizens poured into the streets of Lisbon to cheer on the military rebels and place carnations in the barrels of their rifles, which gave the coup its name: the Carnation Revolution. The Portuguese were exhilarated at their liberation from nearly half a century of political oppression and economic stagnation. And the country's NATO allies were relieved to be rid of an embarrassing anachronism—a religiously conservative autocracy, rooted in Europe's fascist past and mired in pointless wars to try to hold on to its African colonies.

When Portugal's dictatorship fell, no one imagined that it would launch a third global wave of democratization. Portugal had scant democratic experience, and its immediate neighbor, Spain, remained under Francisco Franco's dictatorship. In the next year and a half, rival military factions plotted, workers went on strike, peasants seized farms, the Soviets backed the Communists, and the turmoil threatened to unleash civil war. But prodemocracy officers won control of the country's fractured military, and courageous and pragmatic politicians like Socialist Party leader Mario Soares bested Portugal's Communists in electoral politics. In 1976, Portugal became the second new democracy in the third wave.

In 1974, Greece had become the first, returning to democracy when its seven-year-old military dictatorship collapsed after a defeat by Turkey in Cyprus. In 1978, Spain became the third: after Franco's death in 1975, a young conservative prime minister named Adolfo Suárez skillfully added his country to the democratic tide.

Most Westerners were too preoccupied to imagine a new democratic trend. On April 25, 1974, as soldiers were rebelling in Lisbon, Special Prosecutor Leon Jaworski was battling in Washington to obtain the sixty-four White House audiotapes that would help bring down Richard Nixon's presidency. The United States was mired in the Watergate scandal and struggling to extricate itself from the war in Vietnam, even as Secretary of State Henry Kissinger was overseeing a dictator-friendly foreign policy amid a still raging Cold War. Outside of the West, few countries were democratic.

But aspirations for freedom were stirring in Asia and Latin America, and changes in U.S. politics and foreign policy would soon encourage them. In 1973, Congress began to push for human rights and punish offenders with cuts in American aid. Then in 1977, a new president of deeply Christian faith, Jimmy Carter, began to change U.S. foreign policy from the top down.

Carter elevated human rights in American foreign policy—and as the historian Arthur Schlesinger Jr. put it, "on the world's conscience"— through strong public statements, foreign aid cuts for selected abusers, and the creation of a new bureau for human rights at the State Department.[4] U.S. pressure not only spared the lives of political prisoners and activists but also gave hope to democratic movements worldwide. The new American policy undermined the legitimacy of military autocrats, pressured them to liberalize, and strengthened moderates. In 1978, for instance, Carter sent stern warnings and U.S. warships to the Dominican Republic after the military stopped the vote count to prevent the opposition from winning the presidency. The country's strongman, Joaquin Balaguer, was defeated, and a new (if tentative) democracy emerged.[5] In the late 1970s and early '80s, a wave of transitions followed, moving Ecuador, Bolivia, Peru, Argentina, Brazil, and Uruguay back from military rule to democracy.

The Democratic Revolution

When Ronald Regan defeated Carter in the 1980 presidential elections, there still seemed little reason to expect a new worldwide eruption of freedom. Reagan had vowed to take a tougher line against Soviet repression, but he and his new U.N. ambassador, Jeane Kirkpatrick, had condemned Carter for naïvely ignoring Communist tyrannies while pressuring authoritarian U.S. allies like the shah of Iran and Nicaraguan president Anastasio Somoza to liberalize. This double standard, they ar-

gued, simply ushered in even nastier regimes that were hostile to the
United States to boot.[6] In his 1981 inaugural address, Reagan vowed to
"match loyalty with loyalty."[7] This meant renewing support to faithful
autocratic friends of the United States, including Augusto Pinochet's
Chile, the Philippines under Ferdinand Marcos, a coup-prone South
Korea, and apartheid South Africa.

By the time Reagan left office in January 1989, all four regimes would
be gone or fading. So would the Soviet Union itself.

The transformation of Reagan's foreign policy was the product of
both circumstance and his own passionate belief in freedom. On June 25,
1982, Reagan delivered a historic speech at the British Parliament that
turned Marxism on its head, predicting that the deepening contradictions of the Soviet system would leave it on "the ash heap of history."
Many American liberals still saw Reagan as an unreconstructed Cold
Warrior, but at Westminster, he was among the first to recognize that a
"democratic revolution" was sweeping the world—and that it deserved
American support. Reagan proposed a new American initiative "to foster the infrastructure of democracy." The next year, with unusually bipartisan support, Congress established the National Endowment for
Democracy.

By 1982, the proportion of democracies in the world had increased
only modestly, to 34 percent from the 30 percent figure of 1974. Even
as some new democracies were arising, others were failing, including
Turkey, Bangladesh, Ghana, and Nigeria. And the new growth in democracies was coming disproportionately in tiny island states with populations of less than one million people.

Then in February 1986, a political miracle happened. The people of
the Philippines rose up in the first of a series of nonviolent popular
movements to bring down dictatorships. After two decades in power, the
venal Marcos had faced intensified condemnation ever since his main
opponent, the charismatic Benigno Aquino, had been assassinated in
August 1983. Human-rights abuses mounted; the ruling family's plun-

der deepened. A seeming reincarnation of Marie Antoinette, First Lady Imelda Marcos embodied the regime's sickening greed and excess, with her multimillion-dollar shopping sprees and her three thousand pairs of shoes.[8] In November 1985, shortly after a visit from a Reagan emissary urging reform, the besieged Marcos suddenly announced what he termed a "snap election" to restore domestic and international confidence in his rule.

Marcos assumed that the opposition was too fractured to mount a serious challenge. But he failed to anticipate four factors that heralded a new era—for the Philippines and the world.

First was a dramatic reorientation of the Roman Catholic Church, whose gradual evolution toward activism against oppression had accelerated in 1978, when John Paul II became pope. In the mainly Catholic Philippines, Cardinal Jaime Sin—lovingly dubbed by Filipinos "the greatest Sin of all"—broke with the regime a year later, demanding an end to martial law and democratic elections. In 1986, Sin helped unite the opposition around the candidacy of Aquino's widow, Corazon. When Marcos brazenly stole the election, Sin blessed and encouraged mass public protests. That was the second factor Marcos never anticipated: hundreds of thousands of Filipinos—"a living, breathing river of humanity," as Secretary of State George Shultz put it[9]—mobilizing to defend the vote.

The third factor was proof that Marcos had stolen the election. More than half a million volunteers (along with numerous international observers) had watched the balloting and vote counting at most of the ninety thousand polling stations, documenting massive vote fraud and conducting a parallel "quick count" that suggested Aquino had won decisively.[10] The military split in the face of the demonstrations, and Marcos prepared to use force to crush both the military rebels and the civilian protesters.

It took the fourth factor—American engagement—to produce the dictator's peaceful exit. The Reagan administration dissuaded Marcos from suppressing the vote monitors, who had received financial support from the recently established U.S. National Endowment for Democracy.[11] Reagan also sent an American delegation, led by Richard Lugar, a widely respected Republican senator, to monitor the election. When the crisis broke, Lugar endorsed the independent vote count, as did the local Catholic Church.

Even as evidence of massive fraud mounted, Reagan was reluctant to abandon Marcos, a steadfast American ally. But as the so-called People Power Revolution surged, Reagan turned. He threatened to cut off military aid if Marcos used force and agreed to recognize Aquino as president.[12] On February 25, a U.S. Air Force plane flew the Marcoses to exile in Hawaii, with twelve bags full of gold, jewelry, clothing, and cash valued at $15 million.[13]

The democratic wave that had started in southern Europe and spread to Latin America now broke over Asia. In October 1986, under pressure from the U.S. Congress and increasingly bold internal opposition, Taiwan's authoritarian ruler, Chiang Ching-kuo, lifted martial law and allowed opposition parties to organize. Over the next decade, the island—transformed by three decades of booming economic development—dismantled its antiquated authoritarian structures. In 1996, Lee Teng-hui became the first democratically elected president of Taiwan.

In April 1987, it was South Korea's turn. Like Taiwan, South Korea had been a poor, rural country in the 1950s but had morphed into an urban, highly educated, middle-class society. Increasingly, the South Korean people wanted not just prosperity but freedom. But the country's military dictator, Chun Doo Hwan, balked, which launched the burgeoning middle class into massive street protests. Chun wanted to use force to suppress the turmoil, but the Reagan administration warned him off.[14] With internal and international pressure rising, Chun's designated successor, Roh Tae Woo, agreed to hold a direct presidential election and release political prisoners. Six months later, Roh bested the divided opposition in a free election, inaugurating a democracy that, like Taiwan's, has deepened over three decades.

Several more Asian transitions soon followed. For the first time since a military coup in 1976, Thailand's parliament chose an elected member of parliament as prime minister in 1988.

In Pakistan, democratic change came after an increasingly Islamist military dictator, General Zia ul-Haq, was killed in a plane crash in August 1988. Three months later, the charismatic Benazir Bhutto, daughter of a martyred former prime minister, won democratic elections and became prime minister.

In the former East Pakistan, Bangladesh, opposition was mounting against the rule of another military strongman. The country elected a civilian government in 1991. That same year, a widespread People's Movement emerged to challenge the absolute monarchy in Nepal. Despite bloody government repression, the protesters forced the king to legalize political parties and then surrender power.

But not every freedom movement succeeded. In April 1989, a small group of Chinese students and intellectuals gathered to mourn the death of Hu Yaobang, a reformist former general secretary of the country's Communist Party. This soon swelled into a broader appeal for a free press, a pluralistic society, and the rule of law. In May, university students in Beijing launched a hunger strike, swelling the numbers of protesters in Tiananmen Square into the hundreds of thousands. Protests spread from Beijing to more than a hundred Chinese cities. As students, workers, and other social groups joined, their ranks expanded into the millions.

On June 4, the Communist Party launched a deadly military assault on Tiananmen Square. At the time, the Chinese government acknowledged some two hundred civilian deaths, but a recent British report has put that number at more than ten thousand.[15] With them died the hope for democratic change in China for more than a generation.

Democracy's Big Bang

By 1989, the proportion of democracies in the world had increased to 40 percent. This was impressive though not yet transformative. But much more explosive democratic change was gathering.

Most of the remaining authoritarian holdouts in Latin America were giving way. In 1988, Chile's fractious political parties—with support from the Catholic Church and a staunchly prodemocracy U.S. ambassador named Harry Barnes—united to beat a plebiscite that would have given junta leader General Augusto Pinochet another eight years in power. Pressure from the Reagan administration and funding from the National Endowment for Democracy helped tip the balance. The next year, a broad democratic coalition defeated Pinochet's favored candidate and completed one of Latin America's most iconic transitions from military rule to democracy.

In 1989, a thirty-five-year-old dictatorship fell in Paraguay, and the drug-running Panamanian dictator Manuel Noriega was ousted in a U.S. military invasion after fraudulent, violent elections and escalating harassment of Americans. Nicaragua's far-left Sandinista dictator, Daniel Ortega, was soon defeated at the polls after U.S. economic and diplomatic pressure got him to agree to international election monitoring.

The most historic changes, however, were occurring in Europe. Mikhail Gorbachev's liberalizing reforms of the Soviet Union diminished the prospect that Moscow would use force to crush Eastern European protests, as it had in Hungary in 1956 and Czechoslovakia in 1968. Anti-Communist demonstrations proliferated across the Soviet empire, inspired by the stirring moral leadership of dissidents like the Czech playwright Václav Havel, the dogged resistance of the Polish trade-union movement Solidarity, and the defiance of other writers, journalists, students, and activists.

On October 18, 1989, East Germany's aging hard-line ruler, Erich

Honecker, was ousted amid massive demonstrations. Tens of thousands of citizens fled west across East Germany's borders. Having vowed that the Berlin Wall would stand for "a hundred more years," Honecker was left to watch helplessly as it collapsed—soon followed by the East German state. A year later, Germany was reunited as a democracy.

Throughout 1989, democratization swept through the region. The change was largely peaceful, except in Romania, where a week-old revolutionary movement executed the country's hated dictator, Nicolae Ceausescu, and his wife, Elena, following a hasty trial.

By 1991, Poland had elected its first democratic leader in more than sixty years; Hungary and Czechoslovakia had become nascent democracies; Bulgaria was moving toward full democracy; and Yugoslavia was breaking up into its component republics. (Rapid multiparty elections were not an unalloyed good, however: the voting would bring to power ultranationalists in Serbia and Croatia who would drag the Balkans into war and give the world the hideous phrase "ethnic cleansing.")

In 1991 came the biggest change of all: the Soviet Union collapsed. Gorbachev had failed to grasp what Ronald Reagan had long clearly seen—the irreparable contradictions of the Communist system. Gorbachev's reforms, too little and too late, only paved the way for the Soviet empire's disintegration.

In one of history's great ironies, the godless Soviet state died on Christmas Day. Post-Soviet Russia struggled to establish democracy. The nearby Baltic states did far better, hoping to integrate themselves quickly into Europe. But in Uzbekistan and other republics in central Asia and the Caucasus, the old party bosses and secret police leaders simply reconstituted their long-standing dictatorships without the Communist label.

The Soviet collapse produced global shock waves. In Africa, it ignited a "second liberation," heralded by two events in February 1990. In bankrupt Benin, a coalition of civil-society forces peacefully seized power from a quasi-Marxist military dictator and launched a transition to democracy that survives to this day. And in South Africa, the white supremacist rulers of the apartheid state—reeling from years of international sanctions but now less worried about the specter of a Communist takeover—released Nelson Mandela from twenty-seven years of imprisonment, legalized his African National Congress, and entered into negotiations over a transition to democracy. This produced another miracle in 1994: a peaceful end to apartheid and the country's first multiracial and genuinely democratic elections. Black South Africans endured hourslong lines to cast their first votes, which gave the presidency to the beaming, stunningly magnanimous Mandela.

Across Africa, opposition parties were legalized, personal and press freedoms were widened, new constitutions were adopted, and multiparty elections were held. Often, as in central Asia, authoritarian rulers simply reinvented themselves as Potemkin democrats. But in Zambia and Malawi, dictators were defeated at the polls. By 1997, most African states had held multiparty elections. More than a dozen of them were democracies—a record for the continent.

Percentage of Democracies in Countries of
More Than One Million People, 1974–2017

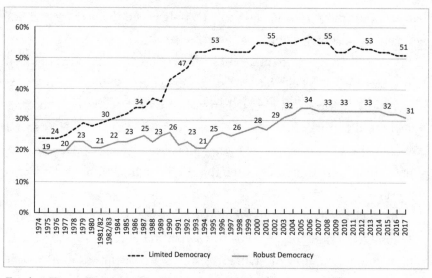

Freedom House, "Freedom in the World 2018," and the author's own assessments.

For the first time in history, most of the countries on Earth were democracies (at least in the limited form of choosing their leaders in free and fair elections), and a third of all states were fairly liberal, or what I call "robust," democracies (see chart on page 52).[16] And for the first time, democracy had become a truly global phenomenon, with a critical mass of freely elected governments in every region except the Middle East.

In the early years of the twenty-first century, three more "people power" revolutions unfolded. First in Serbia in October 2000, then in Georgia in November 2003, and finally in Ukraine in the fall of 2004, massive popular mobilizations defeated autocrats in elections. When the rulers nevertheless declared victory, these movements turned out hundreds of thousands of citizens to protest peacefully, at great personal risk. In Georgia, demonstrators marched with roses as they peacefully took control of parliament. In Ukraine, marchers wore the color orange as they claimed the central square in Kiev.

Each of these *color revolutions*, as they came to be known, took advantage of slivers of media independence to expose the old regimes' vote frauds and publicize protests. And each prevailed, in part, because the security forces split in the face of widespread nonviolent civil resistance.[17]

A Third Reverse Wave?

It was virtually inevitable that democracy's rapid march during the 1980s and '90s would at least slow. By 2000, most of the countries with favorable economic, social, and geographic conditions for democracy had already adopted it. And at least some countries that became democratic under unfavorable conditions—of poverty, ethnic conflict, and totalitarian legacies—seemed likely to slip back. But with the world's sole superpower, the United States, joining with Europe in promoting democracy, and with democracy riding high as the only legitimate form of government in the aftermath of the Cold War, there seemed no reason to presume that a third reverse wave was inevitable. Even in the five years after the shock of the September 11, 2001, terrorist attacks on the United States, the world added seven more democracies.

However, after 2006, three decades of progress ground to a halt. The proportion of democracies peaked that year at 62 percent of all countries (and 58 percent of those with populations over one million). Since then, democracy has eroded, falling in 2017 to just 51 percent of countries with more than a million people.

By then, the Arab Spring had come and gone. In 2011, when Arab populations rose up to challenge their dictators, it seemed like democratic change was finally coming to the last major regional holdout from the third wave. By February 2012, popular protests had toppled autocrats in Tunisia, Egypt, Libya, and Yemen, challenged them in Syria and Bahrain, and cried out for reform in Morocco, Algeria, Jordan, Iraq, Kuwait, and Oman. But most of these openings were soon shut by internal divisions, external subversion, and the obstinacy of established power centers like the military in Egypt. As of 2019, only Tunisia's democratic experiment has survived. Syria and Yemen are mired in civil war, Libya has collapsed, and most Arab regimes are as authoritarian as—or more so than—they were on the eve of the Arab Spring.

The backlash of the Arab autocrats was part of a steady global slump in human rights. The independent group Freedom House found that 2017 was the twelfth consecutive year in which the number of countries declining in liberty significantly outstripped the number of those gaining. Most worrisome, big declines in freedom are now being seen in some Western countries, including Poland, Hungary—and the United States.

The world has plunged into a democratic recession. For some time, many of my colleagues disagreed, arguing that the big picture seemed to stand: the majority of states are democracies; most people in the world live in democracies; and there is a critical mass of democracies in every region (except the Middle East).[18] But as the numbers continue to creep downward and as liberal democracy's rivals gain momentum, the case for democracy's global health gets harder and harder to make.

The numbers mask a deeper decay. The next chapters will detail the key elements of this alarming deterioration: the rise of illiberal, anti-immigrant populist movements in Europe and the United States; the steady decline in the quality of American democracy; and the surge in global power of Russia and China, which are avidly undermining democracies and liberal values around the world. Without U.S. leadership, the democratic recession could spiral down into a grim new age of authoritarianism.

In earlier reverse waves, military coups were the main method of the democratic recession. Not today. The death of democracy is now typically administered in a thousand cuts. In one country after another, elected leaders have gradually attacked the deep tissues of democracy—the political independence of the courts, the business community, the media, civil society, universities, and sensitive state institutions like the civil service, the intelligence agencies, the military, and the police.

Whether the agent of destruction was a right-wing nationalist like Vladimir Putin in Russia or a left-wing "Bolivarian" socialist like Hugo Chávez in Venezuela, the effect was the same. The structures and norms of democracy were gradually eviscerated, one by one, until all that was left was a hollow shell. Elections were still held, and opposition parties even won seats, but the ruler and his party had an iron grip on power that only grew tighter over time.

When democracy is slowly suffocated, it can be hard to locate the precise moment of asphyxiation. In the once vibrant democracy that used to be Venezuela, the moment of death came no later than 2004, when a referendum to recall President Chávez was defeated by extensive institutional fraud.[19] By then, Chávez had already rewritten the constitution to inflate his powers, and he moved ruthlessly to neuter any institutions that could check his power. Under Chávez's brutal and inept successor, Nicolás Maduro, Venezuela has increasingly become a failed state.

In Russia, where democracy was thinner and younger, it was killed off more quickly, at the hands of Vladimir Putin.[20] After inheriting the presidency from the ailing Boris Yeltsin, Putin—a politically insecure former KGB agent—ravaged Russia's weak and nascent democratic structures. Lacking a real party, he staffed the Kremlin with KGB and military loyalists. He ruthlessly subdued Russian oligarchs who had become billionaires when state assets were up for grabs in the go-go 1990s. Russia's wealthiest men either fell in line with the new tsar or were stripped of their media empires, their business fortunes, and even their lives. Gradually, many of Russia's most intrepid journalists, critics, and opposition leaders were assassinated.

In Turkey, Recep Tayyip Erdogan watched Putin's power grab with keen interest. After he became prime minister in 2003, at the helm of a moderately Islamist party, liberal and secular Turks feared that he would bring creeping Islamization to a country founded by Mustafa Kemal Atatürk as a resolutely secular republic. But in his early years in office, as Erdogan and his Justice and Development Party (known by the Turkish acronym AKP) pursued integration into the European Union, Turkish democracy grew stronger. When the EU authorized the start of formal negotiations on Turkish membership in 2005, more liberalization followed, including wider freedom of expression and greater scope for the Kurdish minority to use its language and culture.

But as the prospect of EU membership faded, so did the restraints on Erdogan's strongman instincts. Following the authoritarian playbook of Putin and Chávez, Erdogan and his party solidified control over the judiciary and the civil service, arrested journalists, intimidated dissenters in the press and academia, threatened businesses that might dare to fund opposition parties, and extended control over the media and the internet. After eleven years as prime minister, Erdogan won the presidency in

2014 with the explicit goal of converting Turkey from a parliamentary democracy to a presidential regime.

Amid growing fears that Erdogan was becoming a dictator, middle-ranking military officers staged an ill-advised and poorly executed coup attempt in July 2016. Erdogan beat back the putsch by rallying his followers. This gave him a pretext to launch what Freedom House has called "a sprawling witch hunt, resulting in the arrest of some 60,000 people, the closure of over 160 media outlets," and the dismissal of nearly one hundred elected mayors.[21] Turkey is now a fractured country, one where despotic rule has alienated even some of Erdogan's earlier, more moderate allies.

The global trend is sour. Freedom, tolerance, and the rule of law are being challenged in even the most advanced liberal democracies. Across the poorer countries of Asia, Africa, Latin America, and the Middle East, the descent of democracy continues. The whole spectrum of regimes is shifting downward.

In the Philippines, a ruthless populist president, Rodrigo Duterte, has engineered the removal of the chief justice, jailed a leading senatorial critic, hounded human rights activists, dismissed the mass media as "bullshit" and "garbage," and waged a "drug war" that has claimed more than twelve thousand lives in extrajudicial killings.[22] Democracy is under serious pressure from autocratic leaders or parties in Bolivia and Peru; from religious extremism in Indonesia; and from corruption and criminality in Brazil, Mexico, and South Africa. With Brazil mired in the most sweeping corruption scandal in its history and a wave of violent urban crime that is claiming 175 lives per day, a right-wing populist with open authoritarian sympathies, Jair Bolsonaro, was decisively elected president in an October 2018 runoff election.[23] The lone surviving democratic experiment from the Arab Spring, Tunisia, is withering under pressure from corruption, poor economic performance, regional insecurity, and the resurgence of old authoritarian forces. In Asia, Burma's

once promising democratic opening has reverted to military domination while a feckless civilian leadership fails to restrain the large-scale
ethnic cleansing of the country's Muslim Rohingya minority—now an
ongoing crime against humanity.

The problem is not just that democracies are declining; it is that autocracies are becoming steadily more repressive and aggressive. When
the Cold War ended, authoritarians like Hun Sen in Cambodia and
Yoweri Museveni in Uganda felt compelled—even as they rigged elections and arrested critics—to tolerate opposition parties, presidential
challengers, a nettlesome press, and a vigilant civil society. But as the
global climate has changed, those restraints have evaporated. Inspired
by the new swagger of Xi Jinping's China and Vladimir Putin's Russia, and emboldened by the new silence from Donald Trump's America,
today's autocrats tyrannize their opponents openly and without apology.

In October 2017, Museveni—then in his thirty-second year in power—
sent soldiers onto the floor of parliament to beat up opposition legislators for opposing his effort to lift presidential term limits. Several of the
legislators were hospitalized, and some had grenades tossed into their
homes. That month, a leading Ugandan human rights activist, Nicholas
Opiyo, wrote me: "The whole region is in a steep democratic recession
partly because of the loud silence from their western allies. In the past,
the state was a little reluctant to be this brute and violent and had some
measure of shame. It is all gone."

FOUR

THE AUTHORITARIAN TEMPTATION

> I get a growing feeling that liberal democracy is something we
> have taken for granted for too long.
>
> —PER OHLSSON, COLUMNIST FOR THE SWEDISH
> NEWSPAPER *Sydvenskan*[1]

n April 2010, a former prime minister named Viktor Orbán stormed
back to power in Hungary, still youthful but slightly paunchier. When
he first won the office twelve years earlier, aged just thirty-five, Orbán had displayed an authoritarian bent, purging the civil service and
centralizing political power, but he had lacked the parliamentary numbers to remake Hungary's democracy. Now, after eight years in opposition and two bitterly close electoral defeats, Orbán was determined
never to lose power again.

His quest for permanent dominance was aided by economic stress
and his foes' political blunders. In 2006, Orbán's main rival, Socialist
prime minister Ferenc Gyurcsány, told his parliamentary caucus in private, "We lied morning, noon, and night" to the electorate.[2] The speech
soon leaked; rarely had a governing party been caught admitting such
flagrant deception. Moreover, the Socialist government spent freely and
piled up debt, leaving Hungary ill prepared for the global financial crisis
that broke in 2008.

In 2010, with the winds of scandal, deceit, and economic hardship blowing hard, Hungary's Socialists lost more than half their vote and the bulk of their parliamentary seats. The big winner was Fidesz, which Orbán had reshaped from "a liberal party for upwardly mobile young professionals into a conservative-nationalist party catering to those who saw themselves as the losers of the transition."[3] It became the first party in post-Communist Hungary to win an absolute majority of the vote.

Magnifying the landslide was a Hungarian quirk. Seeking more stable government, Hungary's constitutional drafters had ensured that larger parties would get additional seats beyond their proportion of the vote. So Fidesz won more than two thirds of the seats. That supermajority gave it the ability to amend Hungary's constitution at will, and thus to destroy the institutional pillars of liberal democracy.

Orbán and his party wasted no time. "In its first year in office, the Fidesz government amended the old constitution twelve times, changing more than fifty separate provisions along the way," one study noted, removing checks on Orbán's ability "to impose upon Hungary a wholly new constitutional order using only ideas and votes from Fidesz."[4]

First, Fidesz eliminated the requirement for a near consensus in parliament to rewrite the constitution. Next it packed the Constitutional Court. There followed a burst of measures to strip and politicize other institutions meant to constrain executive power. Fidesz dismissed members of the Election Commission and replaced them with party loyalists. It established a new Media Council with "powers to levy hefty fines" on outlets whose coverage Orbán's government did not deem "balanced."[5]

Now unfettered, Fidesz rammed an entirely new constitution through parliament. That document further reduced the authority of the Constitutional Court, established a new party-controlled body to politicize the rest of the judiciary, and extended party control over other accountability institutions—including the State Audit Office, the Central Bank, even the Central Statistical Office.

Fidesz has since governed by the dictum attributed to the mid-twentieth-century Brazilian autocrat Getúlio Vargas: "For my friends, anything; for my enemies, the law." Opposition figures were arrested in front of television cameras. State-owned radio and TV stations were purged and converted into government mouthpieces.[6] Critical media outlets saw their advertising revenues plunge. Whistle-blowers were harassed. Meanwhile, Fidesz enriched its relatives and allies, creating a new class of friendly business oligarchs.[7]

Within two years, Orbán and his party had not only secured unassailable power; they had also wired the Hungarian system to explode if the opposition somehow managed to win a future election. Aided by gross gerrymandering, Fidesz retained its two thirds parliamentary majority in the 2014 elections, even though its vote share fell below 45 percent.

Orbán has become Europe's most influential right-wing populist, trumpeting what he terms a new type of "illiberal democracy," hostile to immigrants and so-called foreign influences. He has played on historical resentment over the fall of the Hapsburg Empire and bolstered sympathy for Hungary's wretched, bigoted post–World War I authoritarian regime.[8] Vowing to "defend European Christianity" against the migrant exodus from Syria, Iraq, Afghanistan, and elsewhere, Orbán has denounced refugees as "poison" and erected more than one hundred miles of razor-wire fences to keep them out.[9] After years of his escalating pressure on Budapest's Central European University, one of post–Communist Europe's most important bastions of independent thought, the university finally announced in October 2018 that it would relocate to Vienna.

Borrowing a page from Russian president Vladimir Putin, whom he openly admires, Orbán passed a law requiring Hungarian associations to disclose whether they receive foreign grants. Like Putin, Orbán keeps "weaponizing an indignant xenophobia," as the Hungarian human rights activist Miklós Haraszti has put it, to deflect discontent over his corruption and misrule.[10] As parliamentary elections approached in 2018, the prime minister resorted to unvarnished racism by telling a group of city councils, "We do not want our color . . . to be mixed in with others." Hungary has few nonwhite immigrants, but, as the top U.N. human rights official has noted, Orbán "has managed to portray Muslims and Africans as an existential menace to Hungarian culture."[11]

Orbán says he has founded an "illiberal democracy." His government is indeed illiberal, as seen in its intolerance of pluralism, its crackdown on dissent, its contempt for European values, and its warmth for Putin. But Orbán's system is no longer democratic. A decade after joining the European Union in 2004, Hungary became the first EU country to leave democracy.

The Populist Peril

Populism is as old as politics itself, but today, it has become the primary internal, self-generated threat to democracy worldwide. To understand why so many democracies are at risk today, we must understand populism.

The word implies its key feature: a cheap and cynical route to popularity. This involves mobilizing the honest, deserving "people" against a range of enemies to be confronted and quashed: corrupt elites, powerful international institutions, foreign banks and governments, refugees, migrants, and undeserving alien minorities.[12]

The enemies and aims may vary, but all forms of populism share four core features. Populist movements are antielitist, condemning the arrogance and dominance of the powerful and the privileged, who look down upon and exploit "the people." They are anti-institutional, vowing to uproot institutions that the populists deem hostile to the interests and values of the people. They are plebiscitary, mobilizing the popular majority in a direct, emotional relationship with the populist leader and movement, rather than working through the filters of representative democracy. And finally, they are ultramajoritarian, opposed to the checks and balances that might limit an elected government's power to swiftly impose radical reforms.

These four features spell danger for democracy, but they do not necessarily ensure a descent into authoritarianism. At times in the life of a democracy, some elements of populism can deliver helpful reforms that break up monopolies, lessen injustice, and expand political participation. That was the lesson of the Progressive era in the United States.

But populist politics always means dancing with the devil. All forms of populism tend to become runaway trains. If you weaken the brakes on political action, you may pass reforms faster, but you also risk smashing checks and balances, the rule of law, and even the foundation of democracy: the free and fair competition for political power. In the 1930s, President Franklin Roosevelt's attempt to pack the U.S. Supreme Court was motivated by a democratic impulse—to overcome some conservative justices' obstruction of his New Deal agenda. But if Roosevelt had succeeded in remaking the court, he would have done serious long-term damage to America's democratic institutions.[13]

Increasingly, populism is showing a snarling face—in Venezuela, Turkey, Bolivia, Hungary, Poland, and more. Three other aspects of populism give it this authoritarian menace. First is its hostility to pluralism, the core democratic principle that different political views and interests are legitimate and necessary. Second is illiberalism, which seeks to restrict the rights of opponents or ethnic minorities, narrowing their freedoms of speech, information, association, and assembly. And the third is nativism, which demonizes foreigners and immigrants and whips up fears of cultural pollution and physical threat to mobilize the "true" people.

The more populism demeans all forms of difference, the more it threatens all forms of democracy. The weaker the institutional restraints, the greater the risk that populism will become autocratic. So authoritarian populists always set out to knock away the checks and balances as quickly as possible.

As we have seen, democratic failures these days usually don't happen through the old-fashioned means of a sudden military coup. Rather, they come through creeping authoritarianism, a more subtle but equally lethal process that gradually eviscerates political pluralism and institutional checks until the irreducible minimum condition for democracy—the ability of the people to replace their leaders in free and fair elections—is eliminated.

Creeping authoritarianism moves relentlessly, with no fixed sequence or neat separation to its stages. But it does have a generic playbook, which I call "the autocrats' twelve-step program":

1. *Begin to demonize the opposition as illegitimate and unpatriotic,* part of the discredited or disloyal establishment, hopelessly out of touch with the real people.
2. *Undermine the independence of the courts*—especially the constitutional court—by purging judges and replacing them with political loyalists, or by restructuring the judiciary so it can be packed and placed under partisan control.
3. *Attack the independence of the media,* by denouncing them as partisan fabulists, mobilizing public fervor against them, starving them of advertising revenue, taxing them, regulating them—and finally taking over their ownership through politically loyal businesses and party-linked crony capitalists.
4. *Gain control of any public broadcasting,* politicize it, and make it an instrument of ruling party propaganda.
5. *Impose stricter control of the internet,* in the name of morality, security, or counterterrorism, thus further chilling free speech and the freedom to organize.
6. *Subdue other elements of civil society*—civic associations, univer-

sities, and especially anticorruption and human rights groups—by painting them as part of the arrogant, effete, selfish elite that have betrayed the people and the country. Make university professors afraid to criticize the government in their writings and classrooms. Render student groups liable to prosecution for peaceful protest. Create new, fake civic organizations that will be faithful to the populist leader and party.

7. *Intimidate the business community* into ending its support for political opposition. Threaten to unleash tax and regulatory retribution on businesses that fund opposition parties and candidates—and then bankrupt them if they do.

8. *Enrich a new class of crony capitalists* by steering state contracts, credit flows, licenses, and other lucre to the family, friends, and allies of the ruler and his clique.

9. *Assert political control over the civil service and the security apparatus.* Start referring to professional civil servants and military officers loyal to the democratic constitution as members of a "deep state." Purge them and use the state's intelligence apparatus as a weapon against the enfeebled opposition.

10. *Gerrymander districts and rig the electoral rules* to make it nearly impossible for opposition parties to win the next election. Ensure that the ruling party can retain its grip on power even if it fails to win most of the vote.

11. *Gain control over the body that runs the elections,* to further tilt the electoral playing field and institutionalize de facto authoritarian rule.

12. *Repeat steps 1 to 11,* ever more vigorously, deepening citizens' fear of opposing or criticizing the new political order and silencing all forms of resistance.

This program may sound familiar. It is, more or less, the way that populist leaders such as Hugo Chávez in Venezuela, Recep Tayyip Erdogan in Turkey, and Viktor Orbán in Hungary dismantled the democratic systems that once stood in their way. (In Russia, Vladimir Putin—though not a full-blown populist—used many of these same techniques, but he moved more quickly and ruthlessly.) It is a playbook that other autocrats in the former Soviet empire, such as Poland's Jarosław Kaczyński, have studied and sought to emulate. And it is a script that has unsettling echoes for the long established democracies in Western Europe and the United States.

Eastern Europe's Illiberal Wave

In recent years, a tide of illiberal populism has swept through Central and Eastern Europe, warped politics in Western Europe and the United States, and tested the limits of liberal democracy. In the former Soviet satellites, populist parties have had an ambitious goal: to capture the state outright. The exact formula for such a takeover has varied, but it has included attacks on the institutions that could stop ruling parties from permanently holding power, assaults on courts that could protect civil rights, and the sustained marshaling of resentment against diversity, migrants, globalization, and the European Union.[14]

No post-Communist democracy has moved more quickly to copy— and even outdo—Hungary's authoritarian turn than Poland. Once again, a conservative party that had lost parliamentary power was determined never to surrender it. In Poland, the populist right's bitterness was deepened by the death of President Lech Kaczyński in a 2010 plane crash that many of the party faithful—including the president's twin brother and successor as party leader, Jarosław Kaczyński—blamed on Russian sabotage.

After the right-wing Law and Justice Party (known by the Polish acronym PiS) returned to power in October 2015, the new government swiftly set out to pack Poland's Constitutional Tribunal; it refused to swear in three judges appointed by the previous government and added five handpicked judges of its own. Then Poland's new government effectively prevented the tribunal from annulling any of its legislation by requiring a two-thirds majority of judges to make a decision binding and by giving parliament the power to terminate a judge in midterm. The tribunal ruled this legislation unconstitutional, but the PiS government refused to recognize the ruling. In December 2015, Orbán and Kaczyński jointly committed themselves to the twin goals of "illiberal democracy": placing their understanding of the people's will over the rule of law and placing their national sovereignties over the dictates of the European Union.[15]

Poland's slide away from liberal democracy quickly accelerated. Circumventing normal parliamentary debate, the PiS passed a law taking control of all public broadcasting boards. As in Hungary, the government led a "purge of journalists and media workers suspected of lacking enthusiasm for the government's political agenda."[16] Public television became a crude, progovernment, anti-Muslim bullhorn.

Another hasty law strengthened domestic surveillance and limited freedom of assembly, in the name of fighting terrorism.[17] Tens of thousands of Poles mobilized. These protests mushroomed in July 2017, when the PiS offered new legislation to fire all judges of the Supreme Court (the country's highest appellate court) and politicize the judiciary. Under rising pressure from its citizens, Europe, and the United States, the government temporarily backed down, but in July 2018 the PiS forced the retirement of twenty-seven of the seventy-two Supreme Court justices, again sparking nationwide protests[18] and then another tactical retreat under EU pressure. In November 2017, neofascist organizations brought tens of thousands of marchers into Warsaw's streets, hoisting signs screaming "White Europe," "Sieg Heil!," and "Ku Klux Klan." The PiS interior minister declared it "a beautiful sight."[19]

One of the key forces driving the illiberal slide in the former Soviet imperium was the region's intense backlash against Europe's refugee crisis, the EU's shared asylum policies, and the EU's "compulsory quotas to redistribute refugees among EU member states."[20] Poland, Hungary, Slovakia, and the Czech Republic angrily rejected this shared humanitarian burden.[21]

The brutalities of Hitler and Stalin had left these four countries ethnically homogeneous, without the diversity of today's Western Europe.[22] These countries hosted some of the lowest proportions of foreign-born citizens in Europe (near zero in Poland, less than 5 percent in Slovakia and Hungary, and 7 percent in the Czech Republic, compared with roughly 13 percent in Germany and the United Kingdom), but they were among the most vulnerable to nativist fearmongering.[23] Orbán railed against a nonexistent "Muslim invasion" to engineer a surge in his declining popularity.

But the migration crisis, which proved alarming to many European societies with little direct exposure to Islam or racial diversity, was hardly the only driver of political change. Neither was economic recession: Polish voters had their share of grievances, but Poland's economy increased by two thirds between 2000 and 2014 and was growing at a respectable 3.5 percent rate in 2015, the year of the PiS landslide.[24] In democracies, one can never dismiss the electorate's cyclical readiness for political change. In Poland in 2015, after eight years of rule by a smart, liberal, yet slightly boring and detached ruling coalition, the populist insurgents had the fresher message, the snappier command of social media, and the more generous social welfare promises.

The surge of illiberal populism took root amid a deeper economic and sociological divide—one separating urban, younger, better-educated, and more mobile cosmopolitan citizens from rural, small-town dwellers who tended to be older, less educated, and more bound to national, religious, and cultural traditions. In Central and Eastern Europe, these were easily seen as, respectively, the "winners" and "losers" of the post-Communist era.[25] And the same type of social divide between globalization's beneficiaries and victims was starting to fuel a populist wave in the West as well.

The fear of collapsing economic security and falling social status has always provided fodder for extremists. In his 1960 classic *Political Man*, Seymour Martin Lipset warned that declining middle-class groups were a crucial base of support for far-right movements, in reaction—or revenge—against sweeping social and economic changes; big, impersonal corporations and institutions; and urban, intellectual elites.[26] Authoritarians' appeals have always tended to find greater resonance among people in more rural and isolated areas who are less exposed to diverse people and views.[27]

A related cultural factor was also at work. In much of post-Communist Europe, liberal values never became deeply entrenched the way they had in Western Europe, and civil society was generally weaker and less political. This rendered Eastern European societies "more vulnerable to attacks on abstract liberal institutions such as freedom of speech and judicial independence," as the Polish analyst Sławomir Sierakowski has put it,[28] and on liberal values such as secularism, feminism, and LGBT rights.

Left and right began to blur as cultural and economic nationalism merged. Opportunists on the left embraced the new xenophobic mood; with Orbán paving the way, opportunists on the right discarded market principles in favor of welfare programs and a stark suspicion of foreigners. Instead of the old European ideological divide between the pro-market right and the pro-welfare left, a new split emerged, one pitting illiberal nationalists against pro-European liberals.

By 2017, populist parties had won power in seven Central and East European countries (Hungary, Poland, Slovakia, the Czech Republic, Bulgaria, Bosnia, and Serbia). They had become junior coalition partners in two more, and they constituted the primary opposition in another three. Between 2000 and 2017, the average populist vote share in the region more than tripled, to 32 percent, and the number of populist parties doubled, to twenty-eight.[29]

The virus was spreading. In 2016, Slovakia's beleaguered, scandal-plagued social democratic prime minister, Robert Fico, campaigned for reelection by trying to harness anti-immigration and anti-Muslim sentiment. "I will never allow a single Muslim immigrant under a quota system," he vowed.[30] He held on to his job, but only at the helm of a fragmented coalition; his party lost 40 percent of its seats. A neo-Nazi party entered Slovakia's parliament for the first time, winning nearly 10 percent of the seats, and the total vote share of the right- and left-wing populist parties swelled to a majority.

In the Czech Republic, the left-of-center president, Miloš Zeman, embraced the anti-immigrant fever while nurturing strong ties to Moscow. It wasn't enough. In parliamentary elections in October 2017, populist parties decimated the political establishment. The populist, anti-immigrant billionaire Andrej Babis—who campaigned against corruption while being under police investigation for it—became prime minister, even while the left-wing populist Pirate Party and the far-right, extremist, anti-Muslim Freedom and Direct Democracy Party each won 10 percent of the vote. Hungary's ruling illiberal party also faces a rising challenge from the far-right Jobbik, a formerly anti-Semitic party that now describes itself as "radically patriotic Christian" and which won a fifth of the vote in 2018, making it the third-largest party in parliament.

The populist surge reminds us that European nations can quickly forget their history too. In Croatia, the agent of right-wing nationalist backlash was a culture minister who openly declared his admiration for the country's Nazi puppet state during World War II.[31]

The region's drift toward authoritarianism affirms an age-old lesson: institutional restraints are only as strong as the norms that underpin them. Courts need outside support from parties, civic associations, media outlets, universities, and religious actors unwilling to be complicit in the erosion of democracy.[32]

A final factor has made life easier for Europe's new illiberal populists: the relatively weak response from the European Union. The prospect of EU membership had been a powerful inducement for entrenching liberal institutions and norms in the 1990s, and maintaining good standing in the EU—with its full voting rights and lucrative subsidies—could well have restrained the authoritarian trend of recent years. For far too long, the EU balked at imposing sanctions on Hungary, in part because center-right parties in the European Parliament had included Orbán's Fidesz in their parliamentary bloc and feared that kicking him out could help their more liberal rivals.[33] Moreover, Orbán deftly exploited fears among European liberals who worried that the main alternative to him was the much more extreme Jobbik Party. Finally, in September 2018, Orbán's transgressions against democracy, civil rights, and the rule of law became too much even for many on the right and center right, and the European Parliament voted by more than the required two-thirds margin to pursue EU sanctions on Hungary.[34]

The EU had a freer hand against Poland's populists since the PiS sits outside the European Parliament's main party coalitions, enabling the EU to move more quickly to condemn Polish assaults on judicial and media independence. But the European response has so far failed to move much beyond rhetoric and scrutiny, though those steps are escalating.[35] The union's most powerful weapon—suspending a country's voting rights—requires unanimous agreement from the other states, and the norm-busting governments of Hungary and Poland have vowed to protect each other from this fate.[36] And so illiberalism breeds more illiberalism.

The Wave Rolls West

Throughout Western Europe, in some of the most established democracies on Earth, more and more people are also heeding the siren's call.
They have come, as the Bulgarian political scientist Ivan Krastev has put
it, to "associate migration with the rising risk of terror attacks, with the
Islamization of their societies, and with the overburdening of the welfare state." The result has been growing anxiety and a "fear that foreigners are taking over their countries and endangering their way of life."[37]

Internal migration within the European Union only exacerbated
the jitters, helping deliver a shocking British vote to leave the EU on
June 23, 2016. That so-called Brexit vote came after a decade of surging
migration from Central and Eastern Europe. By 2016, Britain hosted
some 3.5 million migrants from other EU countries, with two thirds of
them holding jobs.[38]

The more immigration in Britain rose, the more the country's divide
over diversity and national identity deepened. Once again, socially conservative, less educated, working-class white voters who felt left behind
by socioeconomic change were pitted against highly educated, cosmopolitan, young urbanites.[39] As older, white, and working-class voters
outside Britain's big cities grew alienated from the traditionally blue-
collar Labour Party and felt ignored by the Conservatives, they drifted
either out of politics or toward the far-right British National Party and
the anti-EU, anti-immigrant U.K. Independence Party. By 2015, UKIP
had become Britain's third-largest party, winning one of every eight
votes. A year later, the "left behind" constituencies combined with the
prosperous but less racially diverse Conservative suburbs to produce
huge votes for Brexit, giving the referendum its narrow, 52 percent
majority.

Brexit was a turn away from European integration, not liberal democracy. But Brexit's support base was strikingly similar to that of anti-immigrant populist parties across Europe—and behind the American nativist Donald Trump. The new populist parties fared distinctly less well in Western European parliamentary elections than they had in the East, but their average vote share still crept up to 13 percent by 2017.

In 2017 in Germany, roughly that same percentage was enough to launch the anti-immigrant Alternative for Germany (AfD)—which contains a substantial far-right faction that "shades over into ethnic and even racist nationalism"[40]—into parliament for the first time. At a stroke, the country that knew the perils of democratic collapse better than any other in Europe had an illiberal populist movement as its third-largest party.

France was also rocked by the new populism. In the 2017 elections, the anti-immigrant National Front had hoped to efface its shabby history of racism, xenophobia, and anti-Semitism and enter the political mainstream. The National Front's presidential candidate, Marine Le Pen, was soundly beaten by a young, charismatic centrist, Emmanuel Macron, a surprise political phenomenon who emerged from outside the established party system. However, as *The New York Times* reported, "nearly 34 percent of eligible voters did not cast a ballot or cast a blank or null one, suggesting that a large number of people could not bring themselves" to vote for Macron.[41] Worse, Le Pen doubled her party's best previous showing, winning a third of the vote and positioning her far-right movement as an alternative if Macron falters. By September 2018, as Macron struggled to address France's economic and social problems, polls showed the National Front drawing even in popularity with Macron's centrist party.

Populist parties have also advanced elsewhere in Western Europe. The right-wing populist Freedom Party failed in its 2017 electoral bid to lead Austria's government, but it won more than a quarter of the vote and became an influential coalition partner. In 2015, in the depths of

Greece's economic crisis, the left-wing populists of Syriza won power with 36 percent of the vote. The party's Spanish ideological cousin, Podemos, which staked out a similarly radical stance against austerity and inequality, won a quarter of the seats in Spain's 2016 elections.

Even in Europe's historically most liberal democracies, populist parties have been gaining as the proportion of immigrants has risen— to 17 percent in Sweden, roughly 12 percent in the Netherlands and Norway, and 9 percent in Denmark.[42] The far-right, anti-immigrant Sweden Democrats nearly doubled their parliamentary strength in 2014 by winning 13 percent of the vote; they did even better in September 2018, capturing 17.6 percent of the vote and coming close to the second-largest party. In 2015, the ideologically similar Danish Peoples Party nearly doubled its vote share to 21 percent, becoming proudly tolerant Denmark's second-largest party. In 2017 in the Netherlands, the far-right Freedom Party won 13 percent of the vote after promising "to reverse the 'Islamization' of the Netherlands," including closing mosques, banning the Quran, and "forbidding women from wearing headscarves."[43]

Nowhere in Western Europe have populist parties made more dramatic electoral gains than in Italy. In 2018, two such parties took power after routing a sober, establishment, center-left coalition: the far-right anti-immigrant League Party (which pledged to take Italy out of the eurozone) won 17 percent of the vote, while the fiercely euroskeptic and antiglobalist Five Star Movement won 33 percent. Five Star has progressive leanings on some economic, environmental, and social issues, but it and the League share a populist antipathy to immigration, globalization, the EU, and the Italian political establishment. Whether or not their postelection coalition government lasts, they have turned Italian politics in an unsettling new direction.

The rise of Europe's far right has exerted a gravitational pull on its center right, pulling older conservative parties to the right on immigration and other issues and toward younger leaders with more extremist leanings. From Austria and Greece to France and Britain, traditional right-wing parties are lurching toward anti-immigrant populism.

Moreover, the growing presence of populist parties in Europe's parliaments has made it harder to form coalition governments with some ideological coherence.[44] After a disappointing electoral showing in 2017, Germany's ruling Christian Democrats again had to turn to their chief rivals, the Social Democrats, to assemble a government, leaving the far-right populist AfD to lead the opposition. Established parties in Europe increasingly face a painful choice: bring the new populists into government, as in Austria and Switzerland, or unite as a ruling coalition against them, at the risk of making them the leading alternative if voters decide to punish the entire establishment.[45]

All this helps "normalize" the new populist parties. As they march deeper into the political arena, these movements are becoming more professionally organized and superficially acceptable without abandoning their core illiberal beliefs.

In Western as in Eastern Europe, right-wing populist parties generate, stoke, and mobilize the fear that immigration will erase cultural heritages and national identities. Some such parties, like the Sweden Democrats and Germany's AfD, have at least some roots in previous fascist, Nazi, and white supremacist movements. Others, like the French National Front and the Austrian Freedom Party, claim to have shed their earlier histories of neo-Nazism and anti-Semitism, evolving toward a more mainstream mélange of nativism and libertarianism blended with a loathing of immigration and globalization and a crowd-pleasing push for social welfare programs for the indigenous population (but not for minorities or newcomers). Many parties shelter factions that are even more extreme than their official face.

With a few minor and ambiguous exceptions, today's European populist parties are not overtly antidemocratic. But their demagogic appeals to the "true" people and their hostility to pluralism, minority rights, foreign influences, and the deliberative elements of representative democracy are unmistakably illiberal—and potentially authoritarian.

Nativist parties and movements do not fit well with a commitment to liberal values, as American history has shown.[46] All political projects rooted in cultural exclusion tend to slide down some alarming slippery slopes. And it is no coincidence that right-wing social conservatives have repeatedly revealed an affinity for authoritarians.[47] Indeed, in the United States in 2016, they flocked to just such a candidate: Donald Trump.

The Rise of Authoritarian Populism in America

When Trump was elected president on November 8, 2016—the twenty-seventh anniversary of the fall of the Berlin Wall—Europe's new populists celebrated. As one account put it, "Orbán was euphoric. 'I feel liberated,' he said, from the constraints of the European Union and political correctness."[48]

Long before the Brexit vote, Trump had identified the voter base for a populist assault on the liberal institutions and values of American democracy. He was the American Orbán, targeting the same constituencies that powered the right-wing populist march across Europe: older, white, working- and middle-class voters outside the major cities who feel threatened by immigration, globalization, drugs, and new cultural norms associated with multiculturalism, gay rights, feminism, and "political correctness." No wonder Trump's erstwhile chief White House strategist, Steve Bannon, embraced Europe's illiberal populists; in March 2018, he told a cheering crowd at France's National Front party convention, "History is on our side."[49]

As adroitly as Orbán and Kaczyński at their most demagogic, the

American former reality-TV star painted a stark portrait of the threat from Mexican and Muslim immigration. In his June 16, 2015, speech announcing his candidacy, Trump declared of Mexican immigrants, "They're bringing drugs. They're bringing crime. They're rapists. And some, I assume, are good people."

But the demagoguery had begun years earlier, in the spring of 2011, when Trump first considered a run for the presidency and signed on to the racist "birther" movement insinuating that Barack Obama was not a legitimate, U.S.-born president. Even after the Hawaii-born Obama wearily released his long-form birth certificate in April 2011, Trump kept tweeting deliberate falsehoods about the president's birthplace and suggested that Obama's "real" birth certificate might show he was Muslim.[50]

Trump's attacks on Islam and its adherents, sometimes presented in the guise of tough talk on counterterrorism, were similarly unsubtle— and profoundly illiberal. He called for surveilling American mosques, possibly closing some of them, and considering a database to track Muslims living in the United States. After a terrorist attack in December 2015 murdered fourteen people in San Bernardino, California, Trump demanded "a complete and total shutdown of Muslims entering the United States until our country's representatives can figure out what is going on."[51] He falsely and repeatedly insisted that he had watched "thousands and thousands" of Arab Americans in New Jersey cheering as the Twin Towers fell on 9/11. On CNN, he flatly declared, "Islam hates us."[52]

The unifying thread of Trump's campaign was the manipulation of grievances and fears: of immigrants, terrorists, Muslims, minorities, and criminals, especially nonwhite ones; of a hostile world that was cheating America in trade deals, stealing its jobs, and attacking its people; of lies and betrayal and weakness by the country's corrupt political establishment. And so he made a promise, in his speech accepting the Republican nomination, to "laid-off factory workers," to "communities crushed" by unfair trade pacts, and to "the forgotten men and women" of America: "I AM YOUR VOICE."[53] His "Make America Great Again" slogan was code for restoring the pre-1960s social order on race and gender.

No major presidential candidate since George Wallace in 1968 had played so blatantly to racial prejudice and fear, to anxieties about crime and social change, and to resentment of what Wallace termed "bureaucrats and intellectual morons trying to manage everything" for the true and deserving people.[54] The segregationist Wallace—with his contempt for elites, hippies, "welfare cheats," and the Supreme Court—appealed not just to white southerners but also to white working-class voters in America's industrial heartland. Foreshadowing Trump's isolationism, Wallace dismissed foreign aid as money "poured down a rat hole" and vowed to make America's European and Asian allies pay more for their own defense.[55] Like Trump, Wallace drew and wouldn't reject the support of ultraright elements, including the John Birch Society and white supremacists. But Wallace ran in 1968 as a third-party protest candidate with no chance of winning—though he did get more than 13 percent of the vote and carry five states with forty-five electoral votes. In 2016, decades after the civil rights movement, Trump won a major-party nomination, and then the presidency itself.

It was not just Trump's program but his contempt for democratic norms that heralded the entry of authoritarian populism into the main arena of U.S. presidential politics. As with Wallace in 1968, violence hung in the air of Trump's campaign rallies, and he encouraged it. At his final rally before the Iowa caucuses, Trump urged, "If you see somebody getting ready to throw a tomato, knock the crap out of them. . . . I will pay for the legal fees."[56] The next month, when a supporter did just that to a protester at one of his rallies, Trump promised to consider covering the legal bills.[57] Trump celebrated "the good old days" before "political correctness," when you could punch protesters "in the face" and watch them "be carried out on a stretcher." Trump suggested that if his democratically nominated rival, Hillary Clinton, won, the only way to stop her from picking liberal, pro-gun-control judges would lie with "the Second Amendment people"—a clear reference to gun violence and assassination.[58]

Exceeding even Wallace's authoritarian cynicism, Trump fanned hysteria about the integrity of the election, warning that Clinton was rigging the election, that the dead would rise, and that illegal immigrants would swarm in the millions to cast fraudulent ballots against him. He vowed to accept the election result only "if I win" or if it is "clear."[59]

All this was more than rank opportunism. Trump's incitement was a violation of the hallowed but unwritten rules of conduct that bind democratic politicians and their supporters to the U.S. constitutional system and keep our electoral struggles from descending into violence. These norms entail respect for the Constitution, the democratic process, and the rule of law; they affirm the rights of candidates to compete, of journalists to monitor, and of skeptics to criticize. But now, for the first time since 1860, as the historian Douglas Brinkley warned, a major-party candidate for president was questioning the legitimacy of the democratic process—and three quarters of his own party followers were persuaded by his slurs.[60]

Throughout the campaign, Trump heaped scorn on Clinton, threatened to jail her, and encouraged fevered, banana-republic-style rally chants of "Lock her up!" He derided the reporters covering his campaign as "absolute scum."[61] The Republican nominee dismissed their reporting of inconvenient facts as "fake news," tweeted tirades against critical journalists and news outlets, and vowed as president to "open up those libel laws" to enable public figures to sue a newspaper for writing a "hit piece."[62]

As a candidate, Trump questioned the rules of the democratic game, the legitimacy of his political opponents, freedom of speech and the press, and "politically correct" norms against violence—something no

American president had ever done.[63] Trump ran as a norm-shattering, nativist, illiberal, antidemocratic populist. He would govern as one too. And as the world's most powerful democracy began to yield to the authoritarian temptation, dictators and demagogues around the world saw an opening, and even a model, for their own escalating attacks on freedom.

FIVE

THE DECLINE OF AMERICAN DEMOCRACY

He moves restlessly back and forth as the ovation continues . . . , making jerky salutes, darting intense glances as he grins, rejoicing, exultant, feeling his power and measuring with pleasure the hecklers who are essential to his act. His very first sentence denounces *The New York Times*. The crowd roars as he flecks the intellectuals, the hecklers. . . . There is menace in the blood shout of the crowd. . . . [He] is the ablest demagogue of our time, with a bugle voice of venom and a gut knowledge of the prejudices of the low-income class.

—RICHARD STROUT, ON GEORGE WALLACE'S 1968 CAMPAIGN
RALLY AT MADISON SQUARE GARDEN[1]

After Donald Trump's 2016 victory, many shocked Americans—out of hope as much as fairness—waited nervously for his inauguration to get a sense of what kind of president he would be. After all, Trump had been a real estate deal maker and a reality-TV star. Perhaps the menacing populism of his campaign would yield to the pragmatism of a businessman who prided himself on mastering "the Art of the Deal" and who, in his earlier life in New York City, had not been particularly ideological or even partisan.

Those hoping for Trump to pivot might have recalled Richard Nixon's victory speech on November 6, 1968, after one of the closest, most polarizing campaigns in American history. Nixon had been harsh, savaging Hubert Humphrey, his opponent, and the Democrats as soft on communism, weak on crime, and vacillating on the Vietnam War. Nixon had embraced a "Southern strategy," invoking "states' rights" and law-and-order themes to attract whites upset over federal action to end segregation. He even tried to sabotage peace talks by secretly urging South Vietnam to wait for a better deal under him.[2]

On the night of his victory, however, Nixon embraced a sign seen on the campaign trail: "Bring Us Together." His presidency advanced pragmatic, bipartisan initiatives to establish the Environmental Protection Agency, launch a war on cancer, negotiate arms control with the Soviet Union, and open relations with China. If Nixon, the anti-Communist demagogue, could go to China, maybe Trump could pirouette as well.

But if Trump shares Nixon's paranoia and vindictiveness, he showed from the outset that he lacks the pragmatism and grasp of governance that let Nixon accomplish much before he self-destructed with Watergate. Trump has proven unable to rise above his divisive, defensive, and duplicitous instincts. He falsely insisted that he would have won the popular vote save for millions of (nonexistent) fraudulent votes for Hillary Clinton, tweeted that flag burners should be deported or jailed, denounced critical media outlets as "fake news," promoted absurd conspiracy theories about his political opponents, refused to divest himself of massive conflicts of interest, dismissed Russia's interference in the 2016 campaign, and became the first elected president in half a century to refuse to release his tax returns—and all *before* his inauguration.

Trump's presidency has brought more direct and chilling assaults on the norms and institutions of democracy, including:

- attacking judges and courts who ruled against his attempts to fulfill his campaign pledge to ban all Muslims from entering the United States;[3]
- pardoning a notorious Arizona sheriff, Joe Arpaio, who had been convicted of "willfully defying court orders to stop detaining illegal immigrants and racially profiling Latino drivers";[4]
- lying so routinely and egregiously that, at one point in 2018, *The Washington Post*'s fact checkers estimated that the president was making more than 6.5 false claims per day;[5]
- demonizing the media as the "enemy of the people" and threatening to exert regulatory pressure against such independent outlets as NBC, CNN, and *The Washington Post*;
- refusing to defend American security in the face of overwhelming evidence of a coordinated Russian digital assault on the 2016 U.S. election, and a resumption of Russian malevolence in the 2018 midterm election;
- pressuring U.S. intelligence officials to go beyond the known evidence to declare that his 2016 campaign had not colluded with Russia;
- demanding expressions of loyalty to himself from the director and deputy director of the FBI;
- firing FBI director James Comey—the first time an FBI chief had been fired in the absence of clear ethical violations;[6]
- bullying Attorney General Jeff Sessions, one of his earliest and most important campaign backers, to end his recusal from the Russia investigation and turn a blind eye to likely criminal wrongdoing by some Republican lawmakers, and then firing Sessions the day after the 2018 elections;
- unconstitutionally appointing as acting attorney general to replace Sessions an individual who had not been confirmed by the Senate;[7]

- dictating from Air Force One in July 2017 a false statement for Donald Trump Jr. that mischaracterized the purpose of his son's meeting during the campaign with a Russian lawyer offering dirt on Hillary Clinton;
- demeaning and obstructing Special Counsel Robert Mueller's investigation of the Russian intervention and laying the ground-work in conservative media outlets for Mueller's firing;
- attacking the Office of Government Ethics, an independent watchdog agency, and pressuring it to stop investigating Trump's conflicts of interest;
- halting the long-standing White House practice of releasing visitor logs;[8]
- appointing a tendentious Commission on Election Integrity to investigate not Russia's election hacking but baseless charges of large-scale voter fraud that supposedly hurt the GOP;
- refusing to clearly condemn the white supremacists and neo-Nazis who staged violent, racist demonstrations in Charlottes-ville, Virginia, in August 2017;
- holding rallies as president that hooted for the jailing of his vanquished 2016 Democratic rival;
- writing on Twitter that America's "biggest enemy" is not Russia, ISIS, or North Korea but our own news media;[9]
- scorning constitutional guarantees of due process by tweeting that undocumented immigrants should be "immediately" sent back from where they came, "with no Judges or Court Cases" to evaluate their claims;[10]
- and repeatedly branding his foes as traitors—from saying that *The New York Times* had "virtually" committed "treason" by run-ning a critical essay in September 2018 by an anonymous senior administration aide to calling some congressional Democrats "un-American" and "treasonous" for not applauding a passage in his 2018 State of the Union address.[11]

And this is only a partial list. It omits Trump's willful exaggeration of the size of his inaugural crowds, his misogynistic comments, his shameless promotion of his hotel and golf properties, his nepotism in giving his daughter and son-in-law senior White House jobs, his petty vindictiveness against critics (for example, revoking the security clearance of former CIA director John Brennan), his lax management of security precautions and clearances, his false depictions of crime statistics and other data, and his eliciting of obsequious televised praise from one cabinet officer after another. Nor does it address other alarming aspects of his mental and moral unfitness for office: his unrelenting fury over the Russia inquiry, his lack of impulse control, his overflowing vengefulness, his contempt for the professional work of military and intelligence officials, his impatience with and inattention to his national security briefings, and "his lack of understanding about how government functions and his inability and unwillingness to learn."[12]

All of this demeaned the office of the presidency, the ethical standards of government, and the culture of our democracy. But we must distinguish boorish and erratic statements from undemocratic ones—and bad policies from authoritarian and illegal actions.

We can survive sleaze and vulgarity in a president. We can challenge and reverse bad policies. But the threat that Trump poses to America's democratic institutions and norms is unprecedented. Only Richard Nixon at the height of the Watergate crisis so squarely shook the pillars of American democracy—and by then he was heading toward impeachment and removal from office, before he was finally driven to resign. Trump, by contrast has posed a unique threat to our constitutional system from the outset of his presidency, for he is, in the words of Madeleine Albright, "the first anti-democratic president in modern U.S. history."[13]

As this book goes to press, some of the restraining institutions in our democratic system have more or less held. Despite what *Washington Post* media analyst Margaret Sullivan has called "the most sustained attack any president has ever made on the press,"[14] the independence, investigative energy, and subscriptions of major mainstream media outlets have thrived.[15] Trump has failed to intimidate judges and investigators. Comey's successor as FBI director, Christopher Wray, has defended the battered bureau's independence and continued to probe Russian malfeasance. Mueller has pressed on with his investigations, which have led to an escalating cascade of indictments and plea agreements. Trump was forced to disband his risible "election commission" after states refused to play along, out of widespread and bipartisan concern that the body's real aim was to promote voter-ID laws that would have suppressed African American and Latino votes.[16] Numerous administration officials caught up in corruption, venality, or illegality have been forced to resign, including National Security Adviser Michael Flynn, Health and Human Services Secretary Tom Price, Interior Secretary Ryan Zinke, and Environmental Protection Agency Administrator Scott Pruitt. American public opinion has remained consistently disapproving of Trump's conduct in office. Hence, despite robust economic growth and a continuation of the longest period of sustained job growth in modern U.S. history, the American electorate dealt Trump a sharp rebuke in November 2018 by giving control of the House of Representatives back to the Democratic Party.

But Trump has still done profound damage to American democracy, and so long as he remains in office, much worse is possible. Trump has already seriously eroded the independence and morale of the panoply of American intelligence agencies, the Justice Department, and the nation's premier law-enforcement agency, the FBI. Some of these actions— such as the firing of FBI director Comey and later the hiring of the rabidly biased Acting Assistant Attorney General Matthew Whitaker— seem to be thinly veiled attempts to obstruct justice in the Mueller investigation.[17] His first Supreme Court nominee joined with four other conservative justices to uphold the third version of Trump's ill-disguised and discriminatory attempt to ban foreign Muslims from entering the United States, as he promised on the campaign trail.[18] His assaults on the media have continued so relentlessly that they prompted retired admiral William McRaven, who oversaw the 2011 Navy SEAL raid that killed Osama bin Laden, to denounce them as "the greatest threat to our democracy in my lifetime."[19] Trump has also kept hammering away at the legitimacy of political opposition, and the ability of Muslims, Latinos, transgender people, and more to be full American citizens. And he has shown an abiding scorn for the vision of political pluralism laid out by our Founders.

The current crisis is even more dangerous than the Watergate era, in several respects. During the first two years of Trump's presidency, enthusiastic or enabling Republicans controlled both houses of Congress, leaving Trump largely free from the rigorous congressional scrutiny enshrined in the Constitution to prevent executive abuses. In particular, Republicans on the House Intelligence Committee, led by Chairman Devin Nunes, persistently sought to undermine the investigation into Russia's election meddling and defend Trump at all costs.[20] Second, the country—and especially the Congress—is far more politically and ideologically polarized than during the 1970s. Even though Trump's overall public-approval ratings hovered under or around 40 percent during most of his first two years in office, they exceeded 80 percent among Republicans.[21] And third, the rise of Twitter and other forms of social media now give a president the ability to communicate constantly, directly, and emotively with millions of intensely loyal followers while fragmenting American society into bitterly opposed and increasingly extreme networks of belief and opinion. Add to this the staunch support that Trump draws from the uber-partisan Fox News channel, and the United States has seen, in the words of the *New York Times* columnist Thomas Friedman, a "president with no shame" being "backed by a party with no spine and a network with no integrity."[22]

As a result, during Trump's first two years in office, very few congressional Republicans (even obvious skeptics) were willing to openly confront Trump's serial violations of democratic norms. And the one who most forcefully did so—Senator Jeff Flake of Arizona—felt liberated to fully speak out only when he announced, from the Senate floor on October 24, 2017, that he would not seek reelection.

Flake leveled a damning charge against his fellow Republican politicians: complicity. The senator had grasped one of the most important lessons about why democracies crumble. Democracy is never vanquished by the actions of a lone autocrat. It takes a complicit and divided legislature, court system, and civil society to let an autocrat get away with it. Flake went on to censure what none of his fellow Senate Republicans have had the courage to do, the entire pattern of Trump's governance: "the personal attacks, the threats against principles, freedoms, and institution, the flagrant disregard for truth and decency." He also warned of the damage to global freedom and prosperity by the withdrawal of American leadership. And he continued:

> Without fear of the consequences and without consideration of the rules of what is politically safe or palatable, we must stop pretending that the degradation of our politics and the conduct of some in our executive branch are normal. They are not normal. . . .
>
> And when such behavior emanates from the top of our government, it is something else. It is dangerous to a democracy.[23]

Flake urged his fellow senators not to "remain silent and fail to act . . . because we might provoke a primary challenge." But it was precisely the likelihood of defeat at the hands of angry pro-Trump voters in the next Arizona Republican primary that led Flake to withdraw from a reelection fight and speak his mind instead. Flake had considerable popularity, but he had concluded that "a traditional conservative," one "who is devoted to free trade, who is pro-immigration, has a narrower and narrower path to nomination in the Republican Party."

We cannot have a healthy democracy when one of our major political parties is seriously ill. We cannot have a thriving republic when Congress shirks its constitutional duties. Trump is certainly exacerbating the woes of American democracy, but he is not their sole author. The quality of our republic has been decaying for decades—all of which makes today's crisis more grave.

The Great Estrangement

In 2012, when Jeff Flake was a six-term congressman, he won the Republican Party's Senate nomination in a primary that drew 516,000 voters—only a sixth of all registered voters in Arizona. Adding the 12 percent who voted in the Democratic primary, that was a 28 percent turnout—compared with 74 percent of registered Arizona voters in that November's general election.

When party primaries draw such a small slice of the electorate, the most ideologically motivated voters tend to turn out: more conservative Republicans, more liberal Democrats. In Arizona, it takes only about 8 percent of the total number of registered voters to choose the Republican nominee—which can mean the angriest, most right-wing, and most pro-Trump 8 percent of the overall electorate. Flake didn't think he could stand up to Trump and survive the wrath of that fanatical 8 percent—and he was almost certainly right. Moreover, had Flake tried to placate the far right, the lurch rightward could have fatally weakened his chances in the general election, which he won in 2012 by only three percentage points.

Increasingly in American politics, congressional voting behavior—and congressional cowardice—is being driven by this fear of being "primaried" into oblivion. Such worries have spurred Republicans in particular to eschew compromise and fall into line with extreme positions. GOP politicians today must fear not only the decentralized anger of militant voters but the concentrated—and immensely well-funded—opposition of special-interest groups like the National Rifle Association

(NRA), political action committees (PACs) like the Club for Growth, and deep-pocketed "independent expenditure committees," or super PACs.

Among the single-issue groups, the NRA is typically one of the most powerful electoral forces, spending more than $50 million in 2016 on campaigns. If you want to understand why so many Republican members of Congress don't want to touch serious gun-safety legislation, think about the damage that even a modest portion of that $50 million could do in a low-turnout primary election. And think about the mobilizing power of a lavishly funded organization with five million loyal, dues-paying members who are willing to cast their vote on gun issues alone and who receive regular, stark instructions from the NRA on how to do so.[24]

A tidal wave of opaque money is drowning American democracy. As a result of the 2010 Supreme Court decision in *Citizens United* (and related federal court rulings), super PACs can raise and spend unlimited amounts of money from corporations, unions, and individuals to campaign for and against candidates, so long as these efforts are not coordinated with any candidate.[25] For the 2016 electoral cycle, more than two thousand super PACs raised and spent over a billion dollars.[26]

Then there are the 501(c)(4) social welfare organizations, including the NRA. Under the law, they can spend tax-exempt donations to elect and defeat candidates—and they do not even have to disclose the identity of their individual or corporate donors, so long as they "spend less than 50 percent of their money on politics."[27] In 2016, the top five "dark-money" election spenders were all conservative Republican organizations.[28] In 2018 (for the first time since 2008), liberal groups had a slight edge in dark-money campaign spending, and total outside spending by all kinds of groups was almost evenly divided between liberal and conservative groups.[29]

Even if the partisan balance remains, however, the problems for political transparency and accountability persist. As the nonprofit Campaign Legal Center observed in 2017, since the *Citizens United* decision, the country has faced "a proliferation of super PACS that are staffed by close associates of candidates, receive blessings from the campaigns they support, and spend more than ever."[30]

The combination of rising polarization and gushing campaign-finance spigots has claimed several prominent Republican casualties in recent primary election cycles. Among the most stunning was the May 2012 primary defeat of Richard Lugar, the widely respected six-term Indiana senator who had served as chairman of the Senate Foreign Relations Committee. Lugar lost by twenty points to a little-known, hard-right challenger, Richard Mourdock, who explicitly criticized Lugar's bipartisanship. The insurgent candidate mobilized a fervent grassroots effort with support from the NRA, the national Tea Party PAC, the conservative PAC Club for Growth, and FreedomWorks (which grew out of the political network of the wealthy, conservative Koch brothers). Lugar's real crime, as the *Christian Science Monitor* noted, was being "too willing to compromise with Democrats."[31]

Lugar was one of several prominent Republican Senate candidates defeated by the Tea Party in the 2010 and 2012 primaries. All were seen by the GOP's right flank as too moderate, flexible, and pragmatic, even though they were all well to the right of center. Lugar and Utah senator Robert Bennett, defeated for renomination in 2010, both voted conservative well above 60 percent of the time on key bills.[32]

This dynamic often backfired on the GOP. In the 2012 general election, the giant killer Mourdock was defeated by Joe Donnelly, then a Democratic congressman, after suggesting that it was God's will that a pregnant rape victim should bear the child of her assailant. In Nevada, Colorado, and Delaware, other far-right Tea Party candidates also blew winnable seats for the Republican Party. And in the biggest shocker, Democrat Doug Jones won a December 2017 special election for a U.S.

Senate seat in the deeply red state of Alabama when his Tea Party Republican opponent, Roy Moore, became mired in credible charges of sexual predation on teenage girls.

But with Tea Party support, several high-profile conservative challengers have won, going on to reshape the Republican Party on Capitol Hill. Since coming to the Senate in 2010 after knocking out Robert Bennett, Utah's Mike Lee has maintained a 100 percent conservative voting record (as scored by FreedomWorks). Other Tea Party success stories from 2010 and 2012 have been almost as faithful to the movement: Kentucky senator Rand Paul has a lifetime score of 98; South Carolina's Tim Scott, 85; Texas's Ted Cruz, 88; and Florida's Marco Rubio, 80.[33]

Fewer prominent Republican moderates have fallen since 2012, but that is mainly because fewer of them remain. Most have either retired, been defeated, or moved preemptively to the right. When moderate Senator Bob Corker (with a lifetime voting score of 69) announced his retirement in 2018, a more conservative, unabashedly pro-Trump congresswoman, Marsha Blackburn (score of 86), easily won election as his replacement from Tennessee.

Apart from Trump's own stunning march to the nomination, the most shocking Tea Party upset came in 2014, when Eric Cantor of Virginia became the first House majority leader to lose a primary election. Considered a likely future Speaker of the House, Cantor had money, power, and a rising national profile. But his far-right, establishment-bashing challenger, David Brat, accused Cantor—a strong conservative who had nevertheless shown some flexibility on immigration—of favoring "amnesty" for illegal immigrants. Brat won by more than 10 points. (However, in the "blue wave" election of 2018, he was defeated for reelection by a moderate Democrat, Abigail Spanberger.)

These Tea Party victories intensified a long-term trend of increasing polarization in Congress. In the late nineteenth and early twentieth centuries, a wide political gulf separated the Democratic and Republican parties in the Senate and especially the House. Then for half a century, from the late 1920s until the 1970s, ideological polarization abated. Moderate Republicans from the Northeast and the West and conservative Democrats from the South gave each party enough diversity in its congressional ranks to enable shifting coalitions that cut major deals on budgets, taxation, civil rights, environmental protection, and other major issues.

But since the late 1980s, party moderates have become a dying species in Congress, which is also increasingly polarized along geographic lines. Save for House districts dominated by racial minorities, the South has gone virtually solidly for conservative Republicans. Meanwhile, the coasts have been drifting more solidly to the left: liberal Democrats now hold all six West Coast Senate seats and most of those in the Northeast. In the 2018 elections for the House of Representatives, Republicans were virtually wiped out in the eight Northeastern states extending down to New Jersey.[34]

As Thomas Mann and Norman Ornstein noted in their prescient 2012 book *It's Even Worse Than It Looks*, the 111th Congress (during the first two years of Barack Obama's presidency) marked the first time in modern U.S. history that Republicans and Democrats in the Senate had no ideological overlap.[35] As *National Journal* (then a weekly magazine, now a website) put it in 2014, "The ideological sorting of the House and Senate by party, which has been going on for more than three decades, is virtually complete."[36] And the same polarizing trend is now apparent in state legislatures as well.[37] In fact, the 2018 elections were the first in 108 years to give a single party control of both houses of the state legislature in every state but one. "It's a reflection of polarization," said one expert. "We have red state legislatures and blue state legislatures."[38]

Mann and Ornstein argued that congressional polarization is "asymmetrical," driven mainly by the Republican Party's leap rightward. There are some signs that this may be changing as progressive primary voters push the Democratic Party to the left in the Trump era. Most dramatically, in a mirror image of Cantor's defeat, a likely future Democratic House Speaker, Joseph Crowley, was defeated in his 2018 New York primary election by a charismatic twenty-eight-year-old democratic socialist, Alexandria Ocasio-Cortez. Another democratic socialist, Rashida Tlaib, narrowly won the Democratic nomination for a Michigan House seat. Both candidates were easily elected in November (Tlaib unopposed), but so were a number of Democratic moderates like Spanberger in swing districts.

Polarization in America still disproportionately means a tilt to the right. The political scientists Keith Poole and Howard Rosenthal have developed a sophisticated scoring system to measure the ideological character of congressional voting, in which a score of 1.0 is perfectly conservative and a score of -1.0 is perfectly liberal. From the mid-1970s on, House and Senate Democrats became somewhat more liberal, as moderate-to-conservative Southern Democrats retired or were defeated. But the big changes were among the Republicans. House Republicans grew steadily and dramatically more conservative, moving from an average score of 0.2 in the late 1970s to one of about 0.7 by 2014—a huge shift. Senate Republicans also moved sharply right, and in both the House and the Senate, moderate Republicans almost disappeared.[39] As a result, Poole and Rosenthal conclude, "polarization in the House and Senate is now at the highest level since the end of Reconstruction."[40] This trend will likely accelerate with the retirement and defeat of a number of Republican moderates in 2018.

That doesn't mean that the American public is hopelessly polarized. As my Stanford colleague Morris Fiorina has long argued, it is not primarily the public that has become deeply divided along partisan and ideological lines but rather politicians, political activists, and campaign donors.[41]

Why? One key factor has been the massive geographic realignment. The South has become overwhelmingly Republican, and New England has become overwhelmingly Democratic.[42] As the Democratic Party

pushed through sweeping civil rights initiatives in the 1960s, Republican senator Barry Goldwater carried five states from the heretofore reliably Democratic Deep South in 1964; the Democrats then lost every
southern state but President Lyndon Johnson's own Texas in 1968.
Nixon pursued his Southern strategy, and the South has remained
heavily Republican in most subsequent presidential elections. In the
1980s and early 1990s, the insurgent House Speaker Newt Gingrich
enlarged and radicalized the Republican House caucus with slash-and-
burn tactics that refused all cooperation with Democrats in committee
and on the floor. Hyperpartisanship intensified on each side while trust
in Congress plummeted.[43]

Underlying this partisan realignment have been deeper regional
shifts in economic activity, social values, and identity. As Jonathan Rodden, another Stanford political science professor, explains, manufacturing moved from the dense northeastern cities to more sparsely populated
exurban and rural areas with cheap land and labor. These rural areas
shifted heavily Republican, and religious and social conservatives flocked
to the changing GOP. Meanwhile, Democrats became more exclusively
a party of the postindustrial, socially liberal cities, with their ethnic diversity, high rates of public sector unionization, and immersion in globalization, immigration, innovation, and the knowledge economy.[44] Thus
political polarization in the United States (and other advanced democracies) now falls heavily along an urban-rural divide, with the suburbs as
the battleground.

Increasingly, culturally conservative Americans living in the country's
heartland view the urban knowledge elite—defined by Fiorina as "people who work in academia, the professions, the entertainment industry,
the media, and the higher levels of government"[45]—as arrogant and
condescending. Working-class white Americans in the Rust Belt often
feel that they are losing ground economically and that the country's cultural and political elites are biased toward every group but them. Rural
and exurban whites are increasingly trying to define themselves as an

identity group, seeking to recover a lost sense of recognition and re-spect.[46] This has helped fuel an intense politics of resentment.

Trump instinctively grasped how to exploit such cultural grievances, winning more than 70 percent of the vote among whites with no college education.[47] A quick glance at a map of the 2016 presidential vote by county would no doubt please Trump: the country is overwhelmingly red, save for the coastal areas and some scattered urban patches of blue in the Midwest.[48]

These days, Democrats and Republicans live not just in different re-gions but in separate moral worlds. Even though America has more po-litical independents than ever before (and more than either Republicans or Democrats), the two parties are more homogeneous and further apart than at any point in decades.[49]

A contributing factor to this great rift has been partisan gerrymandering—the process of drawing electoral district boundaries to give one party a partisan advantage. To ensure "one person, one vote," legislative district boundaries must be redrawn after each decennial census. In most states, this task continues to fall to the legislature. When one party controls both houses of the state's legislature as well as its governorship, that party can muscle its way to maximizing its likely share of seats for both state legislative races and the U.S. House.

Both parties have brazenly gerrymandered when they had the power to do so, but Republicans have benefited the most. The table on pages 97–98 shows the worst victims of partisan imbalance in 2016—parties whose share of the seats trails their share of the votes by more than 10 per-centage points, in states with five or more House representatives. In fifteen of these nineteen states, Democrats are the victims of extreme gerrymandering.

Take North Carolina, where Democrats got 47 percent of the con-gressional vote but only three of the thirteen House seats. The Repub-lican chairman of the state legislature's redistricting committee—which was forced by the courts to redraw the lines before the 2016 elections—

freely admitted to drawing "the maps to give a partisan advantage to 10 Republicans and three Democrats because I do not believe it's possible to draw a map with 11 Republicans and two Democrats."[50]

This sort of cynical partisanship goes a long way toward explaining why the Republicans were able to capture more than 55 percent of the House's seats in 2016 by garnering only 49 percent of the total vote (compared with 48 percent for the Democrats). And the unfairness is becoming more extreme as the revolution in "big data" and computer modeling enables legislators to slice and dice districts ever more precisely to maximize partisan advantage. Having nonpartisan commissions redraw districts clearly makes for more democratic results, as is apparent from the part of the table showing the results for four states that use this method to draw congressional districts.

Imbalance in 2016 Between House Vote and Seats in Selected States

STATE	LOSING PARTY	PERCENT OF VOTE	PERCENT OF SEATS	NUMBER OF SEATS WON
Alabama	Democratic	33	14	1 of 7
Connecticut	Republican	36	0	0 of 5
Georgia	Democratic	40	29	4 of 14
Indiana	Democratic	40	22	2 of 9
Kentucky	Democratic	29	17	1of 6
Louisiana	Democratic	31	17	1 of 6
Maryland	Republican	36	13	1 of 8
Massachusetts	Republican	15	0	0 of 9
Michigan	Democratic	47	36	5 of 14
Missouri	Democratic	38	25	2 of 8

STATE	LOSING PARTY	PERCENT OF VOTE	PERCENT OF SEATS	NUMBER OF SEATS WON
North Carolina	Democratic	47	23	3 of 13
Ohio	Democratic	41	25	4 of 16
Oklahoma	Democratic	27	0	0 of 5
Oregon	Republican	38	20	1 of 5
Pennsylvania	Democratic	46	28	5 of 18
South Carolina	Democratic	39	14	1 of 7
Tennessee	Democratic	34	22	2 of 9
Virginia	Democratic	49	36	4 of 11
Wisconsin	Democratic	50	38	3 of 8
STATES WITH NONPARTISAN COMMISSIONS				
Arizona	Democratic	43	44	4 of 9
California	Republican	35	26	14 of 53
New Jersey	Republican	45	42	5 of 12
Washington	Republican	45	40	4 of 10

Source: https://ballotpedia.org/United_States_House_of_Representatives_elections,_2016.

Gerrymandering is only part of the great estrangement. Democrats tend to be tightly clustered in urban centers, where their votes are more concentrated geographically.[51] Drawing district boundaries that simply look "natural" can thus give an advantage to the Republicans. But gerrymandering accentuates the unfairness. And it does something else. When Democratic seats in conservative southern states are limited to districts with high concentrations of African Americans, the possibility of electing more moderate Democrats from swing districts in those states is largely foreclosed. The reverse is true—a loss of possible moderate House Republicans—when liberal Democrats dominate redistricting in states like Massachusetts and Maryland. More generally, when dominant parties gerrymander, they reduce the number of competitive "swing" districts, which are somewhat more likely to produce moderates who have to appeal to independents to win. That only aggravates the polarization that is diminishing our democracy.

The Fragmented Media Landscape

Another new factor driving today's polarization has been the transformation of the media landscape, both through the proliferation of partisan outlets prone to "narrowcasting" and the rise of social media. The days of a common public sphere, in which most Americans got their news from one of the three nonpartisan network news broadcasts and their local newspaper, are long gone. Americans' news sources are far more fragmented—among cable TV news and opinion programs, radio talk shows, and social media sites, especially Twitter and Facebook.

In 1987, the Federal Communications Commission revoked its famous Fairness Doctrine, requiring equal time for contrasting views. Conservative radio talk shows ushered in a new era of hyperpoliticized broadcasting. Hosts including Rush Limbaugh, Sean Hannity, Laura Ingraham, and the conspiratorial Glenn Beck gained huge national followings and commercial success by airing hard-edged conservative viewpoints and take-no-prisoners denunciations of Democrats, the left, and any kind of compromise with them.

This became the formula for a new generation of extreme commentators and media platforms. Breitbart.com blazed a similar trail online. The eight most popular radio talk shows are all conservative, and for the past three decades, the flame-throwing Limbaugh has consistently led the list, with fourteen million listeners today.[52]

The rise of highly partisan news broadcasts, notably Fox on the right and MSNBC on the left, is further deepening the rift. These cable net-works still have many fewer viewers than the three main TV networks, but, like talk radio, they intensify and polarize the views of activists. These harder-line activists, in turn, disproportionately influence which candidates get political money, energy, and volunteers—and thus who wins party primaries. On the right, these activated media consumers advanced the Gingrich revolution in Congress during the Clinton ad-ministration and then helped drive the Tea Party surge during the Obama years. On the left, such partisans have driven political insurgen-cies of their own: Howard Dean in 2004, Obama in 2008, Bernie Sand-ers in 2016.

Social media sites are ideally suited to the politics of provocation. Online content travels instantly and can go viral in minutes. Twitter lets users post without disclosing their real identities, which may enable whistle-blowers to expose corruption and human rights activists to con-front dictatorships, but also enables racists to spew venom and lets hos-tile governments mess with election campaigns.[53] When anyone can style her- or himself as a journalist, a columnist, or a videographer, the media landscape may be democratized, but it is also stripped of profes-sional standards.

The more lasting danger to democracy from social media may simply be that it is making the electorate less capable of handling com-plexity. As sources of information have proliferated, attention spans have radically diminished. Social media companies—especially Face-book, Google, Instagram, and Twitter—are locked into what the Center for Humane Technology calls a "zero-sum race for our finite attention, which they need to make money."[54] Hence social media engineers de-sign platforms and write algorithms that prioritize what captures peo-ple's attention—sensational and emotive messages, even if they are based on outright falsehoods or conveyed by computerized "bots," automated accounts that pretend to be human (such accounts may comprise 10 per-cent or more of all Twitter accounts). As people get hooked, shocking posts go viral, the number of users keeps growing, the ad revenues pour in, and American society gets angrier, more polarized, and more readily manipulated.

Social media firms are also accumulating staggering amounts of user data, which enables companies, governments, political campaigns, and criminals to "microtarget" all kinds of constituencies. In 2016, the Trump campaign, which outspent Hillary Clinton on Facebook, reportedly targeted "13.5 million persuadable voters in sixteen battleground states, discovering the hidden Trump voters, especially in the Midwest, whom the polls had ignored."[55] And of course, Trump himself made incessant and electrifying use of Twitter, driving news coverage and drowning out his more temperate rivals.[56]

The Center for Humane Technology sees a worrisome menu of manipulation. It includes pushing lies directly to specific zip codes, races, or religions; finding people who are already prone to conspiracy theories or racism; delivering messages timed to prey on citizens when we are emotionally vulnerable (such as Facebook's finding that depressed teens buy more makeup); and creating millions of fake accounts and bots impersonating real people, fooling millions with the false impression of consensus.[57]

Recent research suggests that the average American probably encountered multiple fake propaganda stories in the final month of the 2016 campaign.[58] This is actual "fake news," and it can spread farther and faster than the real thing—often in organized campaigns accelerated by trolls (online human provocateurs who post deliberately inflammatory and disruptive propaganda) and bots. Examining all news stories distributed on Twitter from its founding in 2006 through 2017, three MIT researchers found "that falsehood diffused significantly farther, faster, deeper, and more broadly than the truth in all categories of information." In particular, fake political news spreads wider, travels faster, reaches more people, and goes more viral than any other category of information.[59]

The internet offers many gifts, from helping children with their science homework to providing support systems to cancer patients. But it is also a medium made for populist demagoguery. Donald Trump understood that better than anyone who has ever sought the presidency. Unfortunately, Vladimir Putin understood that too.

Democracy Diminished

The United States has never been a perfect democracy. Since its inception, our new republic has been scarred and limited by slavery, racism, sexism, nativism, the near extermination of the Native American population, monopoly capitalism, corruption, and repeated assaults on civil liberties.

Within a decade of the adoption of the Constitution, the Alien and Sedition Acts under President John Adams put it under strain. President Abraham Lincoln suspended habeas corpus during the Civil War. President Woodrow Wilson persecuted critics of U.S. involvement in World War I under a new Sedition Act. In the early days of World War II, more than 100,000 Japanese Americans were rounded up in a wave of nativist phobia and detained in internment camps. During the Cold War, Senator Joseph McCarthy destroyed many lives with his demagogic brand of anticommunism. During the Vietnam War, protesters were often targeted for government surveillance, much of it illegal. And after the September 11, 2001, terrorist attacks, the George W. Bush administration's counterterrorism agenda ballooned to include the secret, warrantless wiretapping of many Americans' communications and the use of torture by the CIA to interrogate terrorism suspects.

We should bear this history in mind when we ponder the danger to constitutional rights and norms in the Trump era. Even with the troublesome USA Patriot Act after 9/11, Americans' civil liberties have still been far better protected in recent years than they were in previous periods of war. But in the future, wars, terrorist attacks, or exaggerated fears of foreign subversion could provide Trump with pretexts to assail core American freedoms. (Just imagine what Trump might propose in the wake of a mass-casualty jihadist attack on U.S. soil.)

In recent years, independent assessments have documented the decline in the quality of democracy in the United States. The widely respected group Freedom House rates political rights and civil liberties on a scale from zero to 100; the United States slid from a peak of 94 in 2010 to 86 in 2017—a sharper fall than in any other major Western democracy.[60] This decline has been fed by deepening congressional dysfunction, the flood of money into our politics, and racial injustices in our criminal justice system. But Freedom House also identifies several causes unique to the Trump era: the Russian hacking of the 2016 election, the apathy of the Trump administration's response, the administration's pervasive "violations of basic ethical standards," and a worrisome "reduction in government transparency."[61]

As Washington has become more starkly polarized, norms of civility have melted, and Congress's ability to work across party lines has plummeted. The frequency of legislative gridlock on major issues has doubled in half a century, to an annual average of about 60 percent.[62]

Polarization has also prevented Congress from checking presidential abuse of power and from deliberating seriously and openly. To pass the Republicans' promised tax reform—a sweeping, immensely complicated piece of legislation—in December 2017, the House and Senate raced the bills through while "Democratic Senators complained that they only received copies of the bill and amendments within hours of voting on them, and from lobbyists rather than the legislative sponsors."[63]

Our democracy is also being eroded by the dark flows of political money mentioned earlier. Those funds have strings attached. The problem is not just campaign spending but lobbying, which remains highly skewed toward corporate and industry actors. Leading the pack in 2017 was the U.S. Chamber of Commerce, which spent $82 million in lobbying.

Of the top twenty spenders on lobbying in 2017, only one was not a corporation or industry association: the Open Society Policy Center (in eleventh place), supported by the liberal billionaire George Soros, which spent roughly $16 million advocating progressive policies on human rights, immigration, and criminal justice reform.[64] The top ten lobbyists spent almost twenty times as much plumping for the interests of pharmaceutical companies, real estate agents, hospitals, doctors, Boeing, Google's parent company Alphabet, and business in general.

Toward the end of his campaign, Trump proposed some reasonable reforms to "drain the swamp," limit the political influence of donors and special interests, and slow the revolving door between lobbyists and government. But the early years of his administration saw instead a surge in sleaze. At the end of 2017, the nonpartisan Campaign Legal Center warned that Trump's top donors were winning troubling levels of access and influence—and that "more than half of Trump's nominees have ties to the industries they are now tasked with regulating."[65]

How Resilient Is Our Democracy?

Is the picture I've painted an alarmist one? If anything, I fear it is understated.

After Trump's first year in office, many and perhaps most political analysts and observers seemed to conclude that U.S. institutions were proving to be resilient and limiting the long-term damage that he could inflict on American democracy.[66] As they saw it, Trump was talking a nasty line but not doing much to undermine civil liberties and constitutional constraints. Yes, he snarled at the media, but he did not seize journalists' files, jail them, shutter media outlets, or censor the press.[67] Yes, he pilloried federal judges who ruled against him, but a great many of them continued to do so.

I don't buy this, grateful as I am for the courage shown by reporters, jurists, and others. I am more alarmed by Trump's presidency than anything I have seen in American politics in my career—and I find the arguments for complacency thoroughly unconvincing.

Clearly, the United States is not Hungary or Turkey, where the weakness of counterbalances has given illiberal leaders the whip hand. But then, authoritarian assaults on democracy often proceed gradually, and a key factor in their success is how long they are permitted to proceed. Two years are not a very robust test, and Trump's early tenure has been profoundly disturbing.

What is most distressing is not Trump himself but the willingness of so many Republican politicians, conservative groups, and right-leaning media outlets to go along with him or exploit his ascendancy. In a striking reprise of President Franklin Roosevelt's ill-fated Depression-era effort to pack the U.S. Supreme Court, the head of the Federalist Society, a judicial advocacy organization, proposed in 2017 "to double or even triple the number of authorized judgeships on the federal Courts of Appeals"—a transparent attempt to overcome resistance by judges who have stood in Trump's way.[68] *The Wall Street Journal*'s editorial page has, after an internal purge, gone from opposing Trump on principle as a vulgarian bereft of conservative values to apologizing for his excesses and indulging his conspiratorial mind-set. Elsewhere, Republicans in Congress who have long believed in U.S. leadership abroad have shrugged at Trump's protectionism because he passed a tax cut that favored corporations. Evangelicals who have long preached family values have overlooked his vulgarity and dalliances with porn stars because he has nominated youthful conservatives to the Supreme Court. And well before Trump became president, more than twenty states, largely through Republican-controlled legislatures, were working to roll back efforts to make it easier for citizens—especially poor people and racial minorities—to register and vote. In the wake of the surge of African American and other minority voting in 2008, when Barack Obama was elected president, virtually the entire South has moved in this undemocratic direction, and in 2018 Republican-controlled states also sought to suppress the Native American vote.[69]

We also do not know how lasting the damage to the federal government will prove—not just to the FBI, the CIA, and other intelligence agencies but also to the Internal Revenue Service, the Environmental Protection Agency, the foreign service, the career prosecutors and staff of the Justice Department, key regulatory agencies like the Consumer Financial Protection Bureau, and the many other elements of the civil service that Trump has systematically belittled, demoralized, ignored, or starved of funding. So sweeping has been the Trump administration's blithe contempt for government that it even infected the Department of Agriculture, which serves Trump's most loyal constituency—rural voters.[70]

Nor can we fully judge the harm from Trump's indulgence of the far right and his open invitations to physical violence. We do know that cities that hosted Trump campaign rallies in 2016 had a 12 percent higher rate of assault on the day of the rally than on a typical day.[71]

Years before the 2017 violence in Charlottesville that left one dead, and before the 2018 murder of eleven Jewish worshipers at Pittsburgh's Tree of Life Synagogue, neo-Nazi and white supremacist groups had been growing in the United States.[72] Now hundreds of thousands of "heavily armed citizens filled with hate and anger" toward African Americans, Jews, Latinos, and other minority groups are rallying behind a new generation of charismatic leaders of the self-styled "alt-right." But they are also marching in support of Trump's agenda. As Daryl Johnson, a former senior analyst for domestic terrorism at the Department of Homeland Security, has put it: "the border wall, the travel ban, mass deportations of illegal immigrants—these ideas were touted on white supremacist message boards merely ten years ago. Now they're being put forth as official U.S. policy."[73]

As long as this is what passes for presidential leadership, American democracy will be in grave and deepening danger.

SIX

RUSSIA'S GLOBAL ASSAULT

The Russians interfered in our election during the 2016 cycle. They did it with purpose. They did it with sophistication. They did it with overwhelming technical efforts. It was an active, measured campaign driven from the top of that government. . . . They're coming after America. They think that this great experiment of ours is a threat to them. So they're going to try to run it down and dirty it up as much as possible.

—FORMER FBI DIRECTOR JAMES COMEY,
SENATE TESTIMONY, JUNE 8, 2017[1]

After World War II, as Americans were settling into what they hoped would be a long period of peace, George F. Kennan punctured many of his fellow citizens' illusions with one of the most influential cables in American diplomatic history. Writing from Moscow, where he was the number two official in the U.S. embassy, the writerly diplomat warned in his now famous Long Telegram that the Soviet Union was waging a global effort to enlarge its power and undermine Western democracies. Underpinning the "Kremlin's neurotic view of world affairs," Kennan argued, was "a traditional and instinctive Russian sense of insecurity" and a "fear of more competent, more powerful, more highly organized" Western societies. The USSR's leaders knew that their "fragile and artificial" regime was "unable to stand comparison or contact with political systems of Western countries."

Kennan saw the Soviet leadership as anxious, fearful, and hamstrung by a lack of good information. From this portrait, he predicted a relentless Soviet campaign to "disrupt national self-confidence" in the United States and Western Europe, "to increase social and industrial unrest, to stimulate all forms of disunity" within Western democracies.[2]

When the Soviet Union collapsed in 1991, many hoped that Russia's historic tendencies toward autocracy, insecurity, and insularity would give way to a more open and democratic state. For a moment, that seemed genuinely possible. Under President Boris Yeltsin, Russia saw the emergence of competitive politics, independent media, civic organizations, and a nascent market economy. This was all shallow and tentative, but it harbored prospects for genuine Russian cooperation with the West.

That hope was short-lived. With freedom and openness came massive corruption, economic dislocation, and the concentration of power in the new Russian presidency. The old Soviet state was "privatized" by a new generation of Russian oligarchs who captured fantastic wealth even as ordinary citizens were being cut loose from the old socialist safety net. Under Yeltsin, according to a 2018 U.S. Senate report, "hyperinflation, austerity, debt, and a disastrous privatization scheme combined to decrease GDP by over 40 percent between 1990 and 1998, a collapse that was twice as large and lasted three times longer than the Great Depression in the United States."[3] For most Russians, the demise of the USSR brought not modernization and integration into the West but poverty and national humiliation. And then there emerged a new leader, Vladimir Putin, who vowed, in essence, to make Russia great again.

Putin, a former KGB officer who had been posted in East Germany when the Berlin Wall fell, rose with astonishing speed through the turbulent politics of the 1990s: deputy mayor of St. Petersburg, head of the KGB's successor organization (the FSB), deputy prime minister, prime minister, and finally acting president when the faltering Yeltsin abruptly resigned at the end of 1999. Masterfully manipulating intense nationalism fanned by the brutal Russian war in Chechnya, Putin won election in his own right a few months later, in a balloting marred by irregularities and criticized by international observers. He quickly centralized power in the Kremlin, eliminated rivals and critics (some of whom died in unsolved murders), and amassed one of the largest personal fortunes of any ruler in the world.[4]

Since 2000, Putin has made Russia an ever more repressive kleptocracy. Aided by massive oil and gas revenues, he has rebuilt Russia's military strength, invaded Georgia in 2008 and Ukraine in 2014, and provoked conflicts with the West. Putin needs to keep Russian society distracted from his failures to modernize the economy, improve ordinary Russians' quality of life, and stop Russia's population size from declining during his nearly twenty years in power.

Putin's view of Russia and the world is strikingly similar to that of the Soviet leaders whom Kennan described in the Long Telegram. Putin believes that the West is seeking to encircle Russia and keep it weak. He views the "outside world as evil, hostile and menacing, but as bearing within itself germs of creeping disease," to borrow Kennan's phrasing.[5] Despite Putin's unrivaled power, he is deeply insecure about the legitimacy of his rule. Hence he panics at the sight of popular demonstrations, which he blames on Western plots to unseat him.

This is precisely what happened in December 2011, when tens of thousands of Russians took to the streets of Moscow and other cities to protest fraud in recent parliamentary elections, shouting, "Putin is a thief" and "Russia without Putin."[6] Putin blamed Secretary of State

Hillary Clinton for inciting the demonstrations, the largest since he came to power. Clinton had expressed "serious concerns about the conduct of the election" and called for full investigations into the reports of fraud and intimidation.[7] Putin was furious. He claimed that hundreds of millions of dollars in "foreign money" were being spent to foster political change in Russia.[8] And in language whose meaning would become clear only years later, he declared, "We need to safeguard ourselves from this interference in our internal affairs."[9]

Russia's despot had long resented U.S. and European efforts to support democratic "regime change" in the region and beyond, including the 2004 Orange Revolution in Ukraine and the Arab uprisings of 2011. He was particularly unnerved by the Libyan revolution that overthrew (and lynched) the longtime dictator Muammar Qaddafi—and he was infuriated by Ukraine's 2013–2014 Euromaidan Revolution, which brought down one of his key partners, the autocratic, pro-Russian president Viktor Yanukovych.[10] As the Russian-born American journalist Julia Ioffe noted, "To Putin, it was clear what had happened: America had toppled his closest ally, in a country he regarded as an extension of Russia itself. All that money America had spent on prodemocracy NGOs in Ukraine had paid off."[11]

These challenges sent Putin back to the playbook Kennan had described in 1946—now updated for the digital age. He would try, as Kennan had warned, to stimulate division, increase social and racial unrest, and undermine the self-assurance of the major Western democracies—and work to divide them from one another. But his means would be something the Soviet Union never imagined but would have eagerly employed: social media. His immediate target would be Hillary Clinton and the 2016 U.S. presidential election. But more broadly, his target would be democracy itself.

The Hacking of American Democracy

In March 2016, Hillary Clinton's presidential campaign and the Democratic Party became the target of an "all-out blitz" of highly sophisticated email "phishing" attacks, "part of a massive operation aimed at vacuuming up millions of messages from thousands of inboxes across the world."[12] Among the prizes the attackers obtained were 50,000 emails from Clinton's campaign chairman, John Podesta. The attacks, which were part of a Russian government–linked operation known as Fancy Bear, continued throughout the spring. They cracked into the files of the Democratic National Committee and targeted a wide range of Democratic elected officials, campaign workers, strategy firms, and think tanks. Ultimately, the Russian operation captured more than 150,000 emails from more than a dozen Democrats.

These intercepted messages would subsequently be leaked (mainly through WikiLeaks)—by Russia's military intelligence organization, the GRU[13]—at moments exquisitely timed to foment division within the Democratic Party, discredit Clinton, and reverse her campaign's momentum. When the first emails were leaked on the eve of the Democrats' July 2016 convention, they inflamed anti-Clinton sentiment on the party's left, forced the resignation of the party's chairwoman, and moved some Bernie Sanders supporters to sue the Democratic National Committee. On October 7, the Podesta emails began to appear, snapping attention away from the previous day's *Washington Post* blockbuster: the discovery of a 2005 videotape in which Trump bragged obscenely about his sexual assaults on women. With each week in the campaign's final stretch, a new batch of hacked emails would pour onto social media sites, triggering a fresh "media stampede" looking for scandal.[14]

Soon after the July email leaks, both technical and political experts pointed to the Russian government—and its leader—as the likely source. Throughout the campaign, Trump had heaped praise on Putin, but

Clinton had a long history of confronting the Russian leader. Within the Obama administration, she had often taken a tougher line than the president, including comparing Putin's annexation of Crimea in 2014 to "what Hitler did back in the '30s." Michael McFaul, who had been Obama's top White House official on Russia and then U.S. ambassador to Moscow, astutely speculated in July 2016 that the leaked emails were Putin's "payback" against Clinton.[15]

Only after the 2016 election did we begin to learn the full scope of Russia's operation. U.S. intelligence agencies were unanimous in concluding—as Trump's own spy chief, Director of National Intelligence Dan Coats, later confirmed—that Russia was responsible for hacking emails as well as distributing "fake news" during the campaign.[16]

In January 2017, the outgoing director of national intelligence, James Clapper, issued an assessment—representing the consensus judgment of the CIA, the FBI, and the National Security Agency—that Putin had personally ordered an "influence campaign" to damage Clinton's campaign, help elect Trump, and "undermine public faith in the U.S. democratic process." The U.S. intelligence assessment added that "the Kremlin sought to advance its longstanding desire to undermine the U.S.-led liberal democratic order, the promotion of which Putin and other senior Russian leaders view as a threat to Russia and Putin's regime."[17]

The intelligence community's report concluded that "Putin, his advisers, and the Russian Government developed a clear preference for President-elect Trump over Secretary Clinton." When Clinton seemed likely to win, the Russian campaign sought to damage her credibility and capacity to govern. But as Trump gathered momentum, Moscow tried to help put him over the top.

The U.S. intelligence assessment noted that "Moscow's influence campaign" had blended "covert intelligence operations—such as cyber activity—with overt efforts by Russian Government agencies, state-funded media, third-party intermediaries, and paid social media users or 'trolls.'" Moscow's digital operatives also probed the voter-registration databases in more than twenty American states and gained entry into several of them[18]—raising the possibility that Russia could wreak future havoc not just on election campaigns but on the fundamentals of the American electoral process itself.

In February 2018, Robert Mueller, the special counsel investigating Russia's election interference, announced a federal grand jury indictment of thirteen Russian individuals and three Russian organizations. Mueller revealed a more audacious and carefully prepared Russian campaign than had previously been understood.

Among the indicted entities was the vast Internet Research Agency, run by a Russian oligarch close to Putin. By May 2014, the indictment alleges, the agency was charged with waging "information warfare" against the American electoral process. (The Russian agency's attacks came shortly after Moscow annexed Crimea and launched a covert war in eastern Ukraine, plunging U.S.-Russian relations to new post–Cold War lows.) The Kremlin effort aimed not only to sow discord and distrust but also to defeat Trump's Republican primary opponents and help elect him president. As one news report put it, "The indictment details an extremely sophisticated conspiracy in which defendants traveled to the United States to conduct research, employed specialists to fine-tune social media posts to 'ensure they appeared authentic,' and stole real people's identities to purchase online ads."[19]

The Russian operatives' research guided them to target voters in swing states, especially Florida.[20] Their Facebook ads (some purchased with Russian rubles) exploited hot-button social and racial issues and, as *The Washington Post* noted, "showed a shrewd understanding of how best to use Facebook to find and influence voters most likely to respond to the pitches."[21] The operation was even nuanced enough to realize that one shrewd way to cut Clinton's support among minority voters was to urge them either not to vote or to cast a ballot for Jill Stein, the Green Party candidate. (As CNN political analyst Harry Enten has noted, "the number of votes cast for Stein" in the three pivotal states of Michigan, Pennsylvania, and Wisconsin "exceeded Trump's margin of victory over Clinton.")[22]

The Russian onslaught of disinformation spewed forth from organized "factories" of trolls. Plunging into online conversations posing as angry Americans, they pushed "both sides of hot-button issues like race, immigration, guns, and even the Confederate flag," as Vice News noted, and organized "real-life rallies on both sides of the same issue."[23]

In one infamous case, two online communities (each with a quarter of a million members or more) organized rival protests at an Islamic center in Houston on May 21, 2016. One group, Heart of Texas, mobilized to "Stop Islamization of Texas." The other, United Muslims of America, rallied to "Save Islamic Knowledge." Neither group was Texan or American in origin; they were both established and run from St. Petersburg, Russia, by paid trolls whose job it was to tear American society apart.[24]

After the 2016 election, Russian trolls continued using fake social media accounts to organize rallies protesting Trump's victory—and competing rallies supporting him. One now famous troll operation, masquerading as the "Unofficial Twitter of Tennessee Republicans" (going by the Twitter handle @TEN_GOP), spent two years boosting Trump, Brexit, and the European far right. The account buddied up with leading American conservatives while pummeling Clinton, progressives, Muslims, and the mainstream media. As Ben Nimmo of the Atlantic Council's Digital Forensics Research Lab has noted, the account "was a heavyweight voice on the American far right. It had over 130,000 followers; it was retweeted by some of Trump's aides. When it was suspended, in July 2017, voices across the American far right protested."[25]

Today, Russian information warfare against American democracy continues, employing what Nimmo calls "a full-spectrum state communications effort" including both social and traditional media. The work of Russian trolls and bots is amplified by tweets from RT, Russia's international television broadcaster, and even from Russia's diplomatic missions.[26] Russian trolls have created hundreds of Facebook and Instagram accounts, such as Black4Black and BlackMattersUS, which have gathered hundreds of thousands of followers. These accounts feverishly pit identity groups against one another even as they gather personal and business information that can help them refine their political messaging, buy political ads, and intervene more deftly in American politics—or simply commit criminal fraud.[27]

Special Counsel Robert Mueller is likely to have the last word on whether Trump or his campaign actively colluded with Russia's vast digital effort on his electoral behalf. But we do know that, one month after the March 2016 email hack, a Russian-linked intermediary boasted to one of Trump's foreign policy advisers, George Papadopoulos, "that the Kremlin had 'thousands of emails' worth of dirt on Clinton."[28] And that June, when one of his father's former Russian business partners offered, as "part of Russia and its government's support for Mr. Trump," to "provide the Trump campaign with some official documents and information" that "would incriminate Hillary and her dealings with Russia," Donald Trump Jr. wrote back, "I love it."[29] The president's son agreed to a follow-up Trump Tower meeting between a "Russian government attorney who is flying over from Moscow" and the younger Trump, "campaign boss" Paul Manafort, and Trump son-in-law Jared Kushner.[30]

This was not simple "meddling." It was deep and flagrant political intervention—and a serious attack on American democracy. Russia's efforts had a significant impact on the 2016 presidential campaign. The "drip, drip, drip" of the hacked emails deepened divisions in the Democratic Party and intensified negative views of Clinton. The effect was especially damaging among Bernie Sanders's supporters—12 percent of whom voted for Trump in the general election.[31]

The impact probably grew as the race narrowed in its fateful final month, when, as FiveThirtyEight notes, Americans "were clearly paying attention to" each new weekly tranche of sensational WikiLeaks releases.[32] Given the relentlessness of Russia's campaign, Facebook's own estimate that 126 million Americans received fake Russian posts on its site, Russia's strategically targeted online attempts to suppress Clinton's voter turnout in key battleground states, and the fact that Trump won the Electoral College with only very narrow margins of victory (totaling some eighty thousand votes) in Pennsylvania, Michigan, and Wisconsin,[33] I have concluded that Hillary Clinton would almost certainly have won the Electoral College if there had been no Russian intervention. The most exhaustive academic analysis to date, by the widely respected University of Pennsylvania professor of communications Kathleen Hall Jamieson, comes to the same assessment.[34] James Clapper, then the director of national intelligence, is even more emphatic. Noting the precise and savvy targeting of the Russian influence campaign, Clapper writes in his memoir, "Surprising even themselves, [the Russians] swung the election to a Trump win."[35] Putin succeeded in both of his apparent aims in hacking the 2016 election: on the one hand, to sow division and discord in American democracy, and on the other, to punish Clinton and elect Trump.

In February 2018, President Trump's own intelligence chiefs warned that Russia viewed its 2016 intervention as successful and was preparing to try it again in the 2018 midterm elections.[36] By then, the German Marshall Fund's Alliance for Securing Democracy was tracking some six hundred Twitter accounts linked to Russian influence operations.[37] These were seizing on new political controversies to inflame American sociopolitical tensions—for example, blasting out extreme pro- and anti-gun messages within hours of the tragic shooting of seventeen people in a high school in Parkland, Florida. The Russian accounts were also flaying prominent Republicans who favor policies "detrimental to Putin's interests, notably on Ukraine or in support of sanctions against Russia."[38] Laura Rosenberger, a former Obama administration staffer and Clinton campaign aide, observed, "America is under attack, has been under attack, remains under attack, and . . . the U.S. government is not doing enough about it."[39]

Russia's Malign Reach

The United States in 2016 was not the first target of Russian election interference, and it will not be the last. The German Marshall Fund has identified Russian efforts to undermine some twenty-five democracies since 2004, including the Baltic states and most other European Union countries, as well as Georgia and Ukraine. Building on Soviet-era tactics of subversion and disinformation, a Senate report also finds, these operations have spread money, lies, propaganda, and various tools of harder power to aid those sympathetic to Moscow and damage its critics—as well as the NATO alliance and democracy itself.[40] These Russian activities are opportunistic and promiscuous, willing to support parties and movements at both extremes: in Germany, for example, Moscow has tried to help both the far-right Alternative for Germany and the far-left Die Linke, which succeeded the East German Communist Party.

The unifying thread in all this is Russia's assault on truth itself—on the very notion that there can be "an objective, verifiable set of facts."[41] Nowhere was this better captured than in the title of Peter Pomerantsev's 2014 book on the deceit and decadence of Putin's Russia, *Nothing Is True and Everything Is Possible.*[42] Kremlin disinformation operations do not need to—and do not really aim to—persuade democratic publics that Russia's positions are right, only that a democracy's government and political leaders cannot be believed or trusted. As John Lansing, the CEO of the Broadcasting Board of Governors (an independent federal body now known as the U.S. Agency for Global Media), put it in public testimony in 2017, "If everything is a lie, then the biggest liar wins."[43]

Russia's media tactics heavily exploit the old Soviet-era tactic of "whataboutism." Russia's propagandists deflect all criticism onto grounds of moral relativism by asking such questions as "What about the police shootings of blacks in the United States?" We criticize Putin's annexation of Crimea; Putin asks, *What about the U.S. annexation of Texas?* We criticize Russia's military intervention in Syria; the Kremlin propaganda machine asks, *What about the U.S. invasion of Iraq?* As the *Washington Post* reporter Dan Zak observed, this time-tested deflection technique "appears to broaden context, to offer a counterpoint, when really it's diverting blame, muddying the waters and confusing the hell out of rational listeners."[44]

Wittingly or not, Trump has repeatedly played the "whataboutism" game himself as he has sought to defend or soften criticism of Russia and Putin. In February 2017, for instance, when Bill O'Reilly, then a Fox News host, asked the president how he could deal with a "killer" like Putin, Trump replied, "There are a lot of killers. You think our country's so innocent?"[45]

Before he began working to compile the famous "dossier" on Trump's Russia ties, the former British MI6 agent Christopher Steele surveyed Russian efforts to influence the politics of Britain, France, Germany, and Italy. As summarized by *The New Yorker*'s Jane Mayer, Steele's "Charlemagne" report chronicled "persistent, aggressive political interference by the Kremlin: social-media warfare aimed at inflaming fear and prejudice, and 'opaque financial support' given to favored politicians in the form of bank loans, gifts, and other kinds of support."[46] The Kremlin favored several right-wing, illiberal populist, or ultranationalist parties and politicians, including former Italian prime minister Silvio Berlusconi and the far-right French leader Marine Le Pen, whose National Front received some eleven million euros in Russian loans in 2014.

As in the 2016 U.S. election, the Kremlin's European operations had dual purposes. In the long run, Moscow sought to undermine liberal democracies by strengthening their extremist political forces. More immediately, it sought to wreck the European Union and thereby end the painful sanctions that Europe and the United States had imposed on Russia as punishment for its aggression in Ukraine.

Numerous other accounts have substantiated the key findings of Steele's "Charlemagne" report. In particular, a trenchant and comprehensive analysis by the Senate Foreign Relations Committee's minority Democratic staff, released in January 2018, documented "Putin's Asymmetric Assault on Democracy" throughout Europe. The report noted that today's "malign influence operations" have built on the logic and history of Soviet "active measures" campaigns from the Cold War. Putin has used many of the same tools to establish total political control at home and to undermine democracy abroad. Russian propaganda, disinformation, and covert funding have targeted national elections in such European countries as France, Germany, Italy, the Netherlands, and Sweden, and they also fanned support for the 2016 Brexit referendum that took Britain out of the European Union.

At the same time that Russian trolls and bots were working to tilt the 2016 American election, they were tweeting pro-Brexit messages from thousands (and possibly tens of thousands) of fake accounts, which suddenly disappeared after the June 23 vote that shook the foundations of the European Union.[47] The Brexit campaign—whose erstwhile leader, Nigel Farage, has strenuously opposed sanctions on Russia—might also have received significant illicit Russian funding.[48] In short, in a close referendum vote, Russia helped tip Britain into leaving the EU—a major achievement for a Kremlin that has the destruction of European unity as one of its major aims. The Kremlin's ambition to fracture the Atlantic alliance would later get an additional boost when President Trump took to hectoring and berating America's European allies during the July 2018 NATO summit.[49]

An emboldened Kremlin also tried to break apart Spain by stoking separatist sentiment online in advance of the October 2017 referendum on independence for the restless region of Catalonia.[50] In Italy's March 2018 parliamentary election campaign, Russian disinformation networks again used "questionable sources, biased experts, and sensationalist headlines that were shared by tens of thousands" of social media accounts. As one Spanish journalist put it, Russian networks became "very influential in radicalizing the public debate over the immigration crisis," which came to dominate all other issues in the Italian election and paved the way to victory for right-wing, populist, anti-immigrant parties.[51]

In short, Russia is waging a global assault on democracy. Moscow's goals are not limited to election campaigns, and its means are not restricted to social media. Putin's lavishly funded state media outlets—notably RT and Sputnik (a radio and internet news network operating in thirty-one languages)—reach across the globe with "high production value and sensational content." Their programs elevate pro-Russian and anti-Western voices (ideally from inside the West), advance Russian policy objectives (such as Brexit and Catalonian independence from Spain), distort facts, promote cynicism about democracy, and, as in the Soviet era, propagate wholly manufactured conspiracy theories to discredit the United States.[52]

During the Cold War, the Soviet Union peddled wild-eyed fictions about the CIA killing President John F. Kennedy and Washington creating the AIDS virus as a biological weapon. Now Putin's propaganda machine manufactures stories that the United States has been covertly testing chemical-warfare methods in Ukraine. A leading target has been Ukraine's embattled democratic government, which Kremlin-controlled propaganda outlets denounce as fascist and accuse of atrocities in a military conflict that Russia refuses to acknowledge as its own.

The Russian attack machinery also operates through a vast network of other state or state-linked actors, including the security services, public and private companies, organized crime, think tanks, and pseudo-independent organizations. As the Senate Foreign Relations Committee's minority report noted, these "infiltrate decision-making bodies . . . promote the Kremlin's narrative," and funnel money to sympathetic parties, politicians, and front groups.[53] Although the Kremlin seeks allies on both the far left and the far right, Putin has a particular affinity for ultra-right, white nationalist, anti-Semitic groups that despise Muslims, immigration, gay rights, and feminism and claim to defend "traditional values."[54] The foes of democracy abroad are aiding and abetting the foes of tolerance at home.

Sharp Power

Of course, Russian officials do not see things this way. They insist that Russia's efforts to influence politics, opinions, and policies in the West is much the same as the "soft power" that Western democracies project through their foreign broadcasts, cultural activities, educational exchanges, and grants to independent media and civil-society organizations.

But for scholars like Harvard University's Joseph Nye, who invented the concept, soft power is a country's ability to persuade, attract, and inspire others to adopt a favorable view of its policies, values, and overall system. This does not require democracy, but it does imply openness, positive engagement, and some willingness to reason with facts.[55] Russia, China, and other authoritarian states like Iran are doing something quite different when they try to work their will in other countries through means other than the old-school, hard-power techniques of military might and economic coercion. Today's autocrats increasingly use wealth, stealth, deception, and diversion to discredit democracy, corrupt influential voices, control information flows, censor unfavorable reporting, and intimidate critics. They seek to shape thinking more through negation than attraction. This is not a "charm offensive" but something much more covert, corrupting, and sinister.

In an influential 2017 report for the National Endowment for Democracy, Christopher Walker and Jessica Ludwig vividly call the autocrats' efforts not soft power but "sharp power." Like the tip of a dagger, they write, these regimes are attempting "to cut, razor-like, into the fabric of a society." For Russia, this entails "a relentless, multidimensional attack on the prestige of democracies" and on the ideas, norms, and values of democracy itself.[56]

Russia is also making strides to modernize its military power, particularly its ability to wage a high-speed, mechanized war, enhanced by the use of drones, high-tech tanks, electronic jamming, computer hacking, and long-range air defenses. Combined with its improvements in the range and accuracy of its weaponry, these aggressive investments pose a new and serious threat to NATO.[57] Nevertheless, Russia is fundamentally a declining power whose malign intentions and nationalist bravado cannot disguise its outstripped economy and shrinking importance to the twenty-first-century world.

Another autocratic power is also cutting deep into the fabric of democracies around the world: China, an enormous, proud country that is rapidly emerging as the next superpower. China's methods are more patient and incremental than Russia's, relying heavily on the geopolitical leverage that comes with Beijing's massive aid and investment, the omnipresence of its firms and immigrants, and the burgeoning flows of its money—overt and covert—to associations, parties, politicians, media, think tanks, and universities abroad. Increasingly, these forms of influence seek to compromise the independence of critical democratic institutions, stifle public criticism of China, and preempt foreign and defense policies that could hinder China's rise to global dominance.

In the long run, the greatest external threats to global democracy are the ambitions of a rising China, not the resentments of a falling Russia. China's global reach and power will increasingly and inevitably dwarf

Russia's. Through China's "hidden world of inducements, threats, and plausible deniability," as the Australian journalist and policy adviser John Garnaut has put it, a quiet invasion is unfolding.[58] And all this is happening at just the moment when Donald Trump's United States is retreating from its decades-long role of global leadership and when the American model of liberal democracy is decaying from within.

SEVEN

CHINA'S STEALTH OFFENSIVE

It is increasingly clear that China and Russia want to shape a
world consistent with their authoritarian model—gaining veto
authority over other nations' economic, diplomatic, and security decisions.

—NATIONAL DEFENSE STRATEGY
OF THE UNITED STATES, 2018[1]

n November 2017, an Australian book manuscript caused a storm of
international controversy. Unsparing and richly documented, *Silent
Invasion* by Clive Hamilton, a professor of public ethics at Charles
Sturt University in Canberra, exposed a stunning array of Chinese efforts to manipulate Australia's politics and society. The independent
publishing house Allen and Unwin was set to publish this work, as it had
for others by the author. But as the book was about to be typeset, Allen
and Unwin pulled the plug, fearful of retaliation and legal action from
the Chinese government or its agents.[2] (Reportedly, two other publishing houses also backed away from the manuscript.)[3]

Like many other Australians, Hamilton had grown uneasy over signs
of growing Chinese influence in his country. In April 2008, as the Olym-
pic torch passed by on its way to Beijing, he had joined a pro-Tibet
protest on the lawn of Parliament House in Canberra, only to find tens

of thousands of "angry and aggressive" Chinese students abusing a much smaller crowd of Tibetan protesters and Australian sympathizers.[4] The bullying encounter left him shaken, but he returned to his scholarship and advocacy on environmental issues.

Then in mid-2016, Australia was rocked by a scandal involving a rising star in the opposition Labor Party, Sam Dastyari. The youthful senator not only had received undisclosed personal payments and generous campaign donations from business interests linked to the Chinese government but had also become a leading advocate for accommodation with Beijing. Defying his party, Dastyari urged Australia to respect China's claim to virtually all of the South China Sea.

The resultant "cash for comment" scandal triggered more serious scrutiny of an expanding web of Chinese influence in Australia. Central to this web were Chinese business interests and wealthy Chinese immigrants to Australia, who had become among the largest donors to both of Australia's main political parties.

Dastyari, who denied intentionally echoing Beijing's line, was briefly demoted to Labor's parliamentary back bench but soon returned to a position of leadership. In December 2017, however, he was forced to resign from the Senate after a double bombshell. First, a video surfaced showing that, contrary to his claims, his earlier deference to China's territorial claims had been explicit, extended, and read from prepared remarks. Then reports revealed that Dastyari had warned Huang Xiangmo, a Chinese businessman who had funneled money to him, that his phone was probably being bugged by Australia's intelligence services.[5] That same month, *The Australian* newspaper reported that China's security tsar had privately threatened earlier in 2017 to pull Chinese-Australian support away from the Labor Party if it did not back an extradition treaty that Beijing wanted.[6]

By then, Clive Hamilton had finished his manuscript. After months of controversy, the book was published in 2018 by a different house,

Hardie Grant. Hamilton's work remains an alarming exposé of a campaign by the Chinese Communist Party (CCP), starting around 2004, to penetrate Australia's society, economy, and politics—"from our schools, universities and professional associations to our media; from industries like mining, agriculture and tourism to strategic assets like ports and electricity grids; from our local councils and state governments to our political parties in Canberra."[7]

Most shocking is the success China has enjoyed in co-opting major Australian civic and political figures, including former prime ministers and foreign ministers. "When they travel to China, they are feted and fawned over," Hamilton writes. In a decade and a half of facilitating business deals after leaving as prime minister in 1991, Bob Hawke built a personal fortune in the tens of millions of dollars.[8] Soon after Andrew Robb left office as trade minister in 2016, he signed a deal with a CCP-linked Chinese conglomerate that paid him nearly $700,000 annually "for unspecified services."[9]

A crucial object of Beijing's influence strategy in Australia is the Chinese diaspora, more than a million strong. They have been subjected to intense monitoring and growing intimidation by Chinese informant networks and intelligence operatives. Some have been warned that their relatives in China will face harm if they don't stop their "anti-China activities."

China is working not only to silence criticism of its government but to mobilize active Australian support for its policies. The modus operandi is to make actions choreographed from Beijing look authentically Australian. Rallies are "astroturfed," made to look like effusions of grassroots sentiment when they are really funded, promoted, and organized by the CCP through its Australian "united front" networks.

In late June 2018, the Australian parliament passed a bill—hailed as "the most significant counter-espionage reforms in Australia since the 1970s"[10]—that strengthens the state's ability to prosecute covert foreign-influence operations in politics and civil society. Another bill created an American-style registry of foreign lobbyists.[11] In November, the parliament adopted a third bill that bans foreign donations to political parties, candidates, and campaigns. But China has now become central to Australia's prosperity, accounting for a third of its export earnings while sending it a million tourists a year.[12] A growing array of Australian business leaders and policy elites offers claims like "China is our destiny" and "We are living in a Chinese world."[13] Beijing's ultimate goal is to compromise Australia's sovereignty, break its alliance with America, pull it into the Chinese orbit, and, as Hamilton puts it, secure Australia "as a reliable and stable supply base for China's economic growth."[14] And China's ambitions hardly end there.

How China Wields Sharp Power

Like Russia, China is using the openness and pluralism of democracies to subvert them, at the very time that Beijing's rule at home is becoming increasingly rigid, repressive, and personalistic. As the cautionary tale of Australia shows, China and Russia offer the world's democracies a one-way street for influence: the giant dictatorships enjoy largely unfettered access to American society while allowing foreign journalists, researchers, students, universities, foundations, think tanks, and corporations to engage their societies only on terms they tightly control.

China's goals, however, are more sweeping than Russia's—and so are its resources. Like Russia, China seeks to weaken the Western democracies' alliances, undermine the U.S.-led liberal order, and expand its own economic and geopolitical power. Like Russia, China seeks hegemony over what it sees as a rightful regional sphere of influence. But beyond this, we start to see striking differences between the two huge autocracies.

The problem with Russia is managing the anger, insecurity, and resentments of a former superpower; the problem with China is managing the ambitions, swagger, and overreach of a new one. Russia wants to renew its dominance over the areas Moscow once controlled within the Soviet Union and its Communist satellite states, and to regain some of the broader international influence the USSR once enjoyed. China seeks hegemony over all of Asia and the Pacific, and it is aggressively cultivating ties with ethnic Chinese communities to sway policy in countries like Singapore.[15] But it also increasingly aspires to challenge the United States for global leadership—economically, politically, and, some believe, eventually militarily.

Beijing's goal is nothing less than "Globalization 2.0," based on the "China model" of authoritarian, state-directed capitalism, which produces impressive growth rates while dispensing with tedious Western standards of accountability or moralistic Western lectures on freedom and rights.[16] China's leaders think their model can compete head-to-head with their increasingly battered rival, American-style democracy and capitalism. Increasingly, Beijing's influence operations extend far beyond Asia, into every region of the twenty-first-century world that China wants to lead.

China's methods of projecting "sharp power" differ in important respects from Russia's. For one thing, Beijing has a lot more money to spend. In recent years, its foreign aid flows have averaged $38 billion per year, though the bulk of that comes as export credits or loans at market or close-to-market rates.[17] If one calls that "aid," this would make China the largest bilateral source of foreign assistance, surpassing even the United States.[18]

This type of lending can plunge weaker countries into a debt trap that requires them to sell off their strategic assets to China. Such was the plight of Sri Lanka, whose corrupt, autocratic ruler had piled up an estimated $8 billion of debt to Beijing.[19] To whittle that down by about a billion dollars, Sri Lanka granted China in 2017 a ninety-nine-year lease of its deepwater port in Hambantota, which faces Indian Ocean trade routes and enables China to thrust its economic might and its naval forces "into India's sphere of influence."[20]

The technological edge of China's efforts is also raising concerns. As part of its "digital silk road," China is enlisting its giant telecom companies (such as Huawei) in modernizing the information infrastructure of countries across Asia and Africa. Their assistance can include upgrading mobile-phone spectrums and laying high-speed, fiber-optic lines.[21] But this means that China's technological leaps into the digital surveillance of its own citizens may well be baked into the systems that it builds abroad—and passed along to other authoritarian regimes.[22] Already, China has been exporting internet-control technology to other autocrats, and new possibilities for surveillance will emerge as China builds its own space-based communications network, which will utilize more than 150 satellites covering the entire globe.[23]

China is also using its riches to create new international financial institutions, the New Development Bank and the Asian Infrastructure Investment Bank, in which China is the largest shareholder and leading player. The latter bank, to which China has pledged $50 billion, has more than eighty countries as members, including all the major industrialized countries save the United States and Japan.[24] Through its Belt and Road Initiative, China is prepared to spend more than a trillion dollars to forge a bloc of economic and strategic ties stretching throughout south, central, and west Asia, all the way to Europe and Africa.[25] Eager for "subsidized Chinese loans to pay for badly needed infrastructure projects," more than seventy countries have signed up—and by 2017, Chinese lending to these countries had, as the veteran China scholar Minxin Pei noted, "reached a staggering $292 billion."[26] Many of these countries might have been lured by the vast opportunities for corruption that go along with huge infrastructure projects, especially when financed by a donor uninterested in transparency.

As David Shambaugh, a longtime China expert at George Washington University, observes, "This scale of investment is unprecedented: even during the Cold War, the United States and the Soviet Union did not spend anywhere near as much as China is spending today." China's pledges of foreign spending "add up to $1.41 trillion; in contrast, the Marshall Plan cost the equivalent of $103 billion in today's dollars."[27] Nothing like this global vision or investment is coming from the United States—or any collection of Western democracies. The huge cost of the Belt and Road Initiative is provoking rumbles of criticism within China,[28] but even if it is only partially realized, it will vastly extend China's economic clout and political sway.

While China's foreign aid goes disproportionately to the world's autocrats (often helping earn compliant U.N. voting in return), its influence activities focus on the world's democracies.[29] Through media deals, investments, partnership agreements, charitable and political donations, positions on boards of directors, and more, China is playing a longer and more patient game than Russia. Beijing is seeking wider and deeper infiltration into the vital tissues of democracies: their media, publishing houses, entertainment industries, technology companies, universities, think tanks, nongovernmental organizations (NGOs)—and even their governments and political parties.

China thus utilizes a much more far-flung and comprehensive network of organizations than Russia can muster, based on the discipline and muscle of the CCP.[30] Communist united-front activities exploit divisions inside democracies and build alliances with overseas Chinese social groups and prominent individuals while also managing information, promoting propaganda, and engaging in espionage.[31] Of course, such Leninist tactics still pervade Russian influence efforts as well. But China's initiatives now proliferate more widely and resourcefully (if less visibly) than Russia's. And China's Communist Party goes far beyond anything that Russia can mount in manipulating bonds of identity and

community within its enormous diaspora—some sixty million people[32]—
to spread propaganda, mobilize influence, and brand protests against its
infiltration as "anti-China, anti-Chinese, and Sinophobic."[33]

Media. A key prong of China's global influence operations has been
the aggressive, multibillion-dollar international expansion of its state-
controlled media agencies. These include the Xinhua News Agency,
China Daily (the party's English-language newspaper), *Global Times* (a
tabloid affiliated with the *People's Daily*, the party's official newspaper),
China Global Television Network (the international arm of China's domestic state broadcaster), and China Radio International. Xinhua's
180 overseas bureaus give it the fourth-largest global presence among
wire-service agencies (behind the independent Agence France-Presse,
Associated Press, and Reuters).[34] Simultaneously reporting news and
disseminating party propaganda, these official media outlets "constitute
the major weapons in what China considers a 'discourse war' with the
West," warns Shambaugh.[35] Unlike public and private media in Western
democracies, such as the BBC, CNN, or Germany's Deutsche Welle,
these state and party media offer a uniformly rosy view of China, its
government, and its intentions. A 2015 estimate put China's external
propaganda spending at $10 billion—some five times the 2016 U.S.
budget for public diplomacy.[36]

China's state media, like *China Daily*, also push their content to international audiences indirectly, through agreements with national and local media outlets to carry their articles. Paid newspaper inserts are
laid out to look like a local newspaper's own editorial work. Even if
the immediate impact is modest, the revenue that these inserts provide
"creates dependencies" that can "influence content in the parent publication."[37] Media-cooperation agreements provide additional Chinese
funding, as well as partnerships and exchanges that discourage media
criticism of China and advance an alternative media model very different from democratic-style "watchdog journalism" to scrutinize the
powerful.[38]

In 2014, the state-supported Australian Broadcasting Corporation (ABC) "made the extraordinary concession of largely eliminating news and current-affairs content from its Chinese-language programming," as the Australian China expert John Fitzgerald put it.[39] When Prime Minister Malcolm Turnbull visited China in April 2016, the ABC "even censored Chinese translations of its *own* commentaries" dealing with sensitive issues like human rights or the South China Sea dispute.[40] The next month, China signed six agreements with private Australian media conglomerates, which consented "to circulate CCP propaganda on network television and in prominent publications."[41] In addition, the party's Central Propaganda Department was granted outright control of content for Chinese Australian community media outlets.[42] In Australia's Chinese-language media, Chinese authorities vet guests and even callers to ensure compatibility with Beijing's views. In Australia today, the BBC's Chinese-language broadcasts are gone; "virtually all that can be heard on these stations is local chatter supplemented by the voice" of the Central Propaganda Department, carried live from Chinese state radio broadcasts.[43] A similar cloud of censorship has befallen the Chinese-language print media in Australia, as more and more of their owners toe Beijing's line in exchange for "business opportunities in real estate, education and professional services" in China.[44] And establishments large and small have been pressured to stop carrying publications critical of the Chinese government, especially those linked to Falun Gong, a spiritual movement banned by Beijing.

While Australia has been on the cutting edge of China's strategy to gain control of Chinese-language media abroad, it is far from unique. In the United States, "China has all but eliminated the plethora of independent Chinese-language media outlets that once served Chinese American communities," both by buying or co-opting existing outlets and by establishing new ones.[45]

Universities. China exerts growing influence in colleges and universities around the world through cooperative agreements and exchanges, especially involving a global network of some 525 Confucius Institutes.[46] Funded and directed by the Hanban, an organization within the Chinese Ministry of Education that has links to the party's external propaganda arm, these institutes promote the study of Chinese language and culture while often conveying the Chinese government line.

In addition to a cash grant, each Confucius Institute comes with a Chinese partner institution that provides the instructors and textbooks. On prestigious American campuses, the relationship may involve little more than funding and polite association. But where Beijing's money is more sorely needed, its leverage is also greater, and the institutes can place sensitive speakers and topics off limits, such as the 1989 Tiananmen Square massacre, Tibet, and human rights. "Most agreements establishing Confucius Institutes feature nondisclosure clauses and unacceptable concessions to the political aims and practices of the government of China," the American Association of University Professors warned in 2014. "North American universities permit Confucius Institutes to advance a state agenda in the recruitment and control of academic staff, in the choice of curriculum, and in the restriction of debate."[47] Similar concerns have been raised in Australia, Europe, and Latin America. The compromise of academic freedom and transparency has led "at least seven schools in four countries" to terminate their Confucius Institutes. More are now doing so in the United States.[48]

China also seeks to deter critical reporting and analysis by denying entry to "scholars, journalists and others who write or speak in ways that Chinese officials deem politically offensive."[49] Upon landing in Beijing in July 2014, the Indiana University historian Elliot Sperling was deported for what was presumed to be his vocal support of a leading Uighur human rights dissident, Ilham Tohti. The distinguished American sinologists Andrew Nathan and Perry Link were banned from traveling to China after they edited and published *The Tiananmen Papers*, a 2001 compilation of secret Chinese documents on the 1989 protests.

Independent foreign correspondents and news organizations, like *The New York Times* and Bloomberg, have been blacklisted or have encountered greater obstacles to operating in China.

As China grows more powerful, Chinese think tanks are being tasked with promoting the party line, and foreign academics are feeling pressure to adapt.[50] As David Shambaugh has noted, "like its propaganda apparatus, China's censorship machine is going global. And it appears to be having an impact. In a troubling trend, foreign China scholars are increasingly practicing self-censorship, worried about their continued ability to visit China."[51]

An especially troubling vehicle for Beijing's influence is the Chinese Students and Scholars Association, which connects and supports overseas Chinese students—including the roughly 350,000 who study in the United States—through a network of campus chapters that includes 150 in America and some 200 in France, Germany, and Britain. While these chapters often function as run-of-the-mill campus social clubs, they have become controversial for their frequent lack of transparency, financial ties with Chinese embassies and consulates, parroting of Chinese government positions, and periodic efforts to suppress criticism of Beijing. The associations have also been accused of monitoring campus activities, alerting Chinese authorities to campus events on issues like Tibet or human rights, and reporting back to the government on "unpatriotic" Chinese students and even research.

Some Chinese students at U.S. universities have been harassed for speaking their minds. After her May 2017 commencement address at the University of Maryland, a Chinese senior named Yang Shuping was pilloried on Chinese social media for praising America's cleaner air and political openness and then declaring, "Democracy and freedom are the fresh air worth fighting for."[52] Free-speech advocates have criticized the Chinese Students and Scholars Association (and the Chinese embassies and consulates supporting and instructing its campus chapters) for attempting to censor or control the speech and behavior of overseas Chinese students, including directing them to protest "anti-China" activities. When the University of California, San Diego, selected the Dalai Lama as its 2016 commencement speaker, the association's local chapter (which admitted coordinating with the Chinese consulate in Los Angeles) threatened the university with "tough measures."[53]

Business and Politics. China's vast overseas investments are not only extending Chinese economic leverage; they are also building politically valuable partnerships by making many influential local actors rich.

As in Australia, high former government officials in Great Britain, France, and Germany are finding lucrative work with Chinese interests after they leave office.[54] Such dubious deals are increasingly realigning politics and foreign policy even in democracies. For instance, in exchange for "a more forthcoming Czech attitude" toward China, the populist Czech president Miloš Zeman secured a prized license for Czech business in China.[55] Then a leading Chinese oil and financial services conglomerate, CEFC China Energy, led by the tycoon Ye Jianming, began making enormous acquisitions in the country as top officials "rotated back and forth between the president's office and CEFC."[56] As the money poured in, Zeman became, according to *The New York Times*, "a big backer of Beijing," endorsing its claims over Taiwan and heaping praise on the Belt and Road Initiative.[57] Claiming "to have liberated Czech foreign policy from EU domination," Zeman even appointed Ye—who has strong links to China's military—as an economic adviser.[58]

Throughout Europe, Beijing is gaining sway among politicians and intellectuals keen "to attract Chinese money or attain greater recognition on the global plane." Hence, European countries "increasingly tend to adjust their policies in fits of 'preemptive obedience' to curry favor with the Chinese side," as one important study put it.[59] With Chinese investment pouring into Greece, transforming Piraeus "into the Mediterranean's busiest port," Greece has repeatedly blocked EU resolutions condemning China's human rights record and its aggression in the South China Sea.[60]

Playing the China card also serves the interests of authoritarian populist rulers in Central and Eastern Europe. It erodes confidence in liberal democracy by suggesting the existence of a more successful authoritarian model, and it gives illiberal populists another way to warn the EU off serious sanctions.

Chinese diplomats and journalists have also been reaching out to Europe's new far-right parties, like Alternative for Germany.[61] And across Latin America, China is forging sympathetic ties with parties, politicians, officials, and other leaders with generously funded trips, exchanges, and other support, in hopes of enlisting "influential people" as "de facto ambassadors of the Chinese cause."[62]

China's vast market and economic might give it enormous leverage, enabling it to pressure American and other Western companies into toeing the CCP line on the status of Taiwan and Tibet and influencing their home governments' policies toward China. At the same time, the growing presence of Chinese corporations in Western countries permits China to achieve various strategic objectives, not least of which is the acquisition of intellectual property.[63]

Philanthropy. Recent years have seen a stunning expansion in charitable donations from wealthy Chinese individuals and foundations linked to the Chinese government and the party. These gifts provide new avenues for projecting Chinese sharp power. While they do not necessarily come with explicit political strings, the prospect of such generous funding can encourage self-censorship.

The current lead player in this sphere is the China–United States Exchange Foundation, which "promotes the positions of the Chinese government through the research grants it gives to American institutions."[64] Its founder is Hong Kong's former chief executive, Tung Chee-Hwa, a billionaire with close ties to China's Communist leaders who is currently vice chairman of the Chinese People's Political Consultative Conference (a prestigious advisory body to the government). As Bethany Allen-Ebrahimian has noted in *Foreign Policy* magazine, foundation representatives say that it is not an agent of the CCP, but "the foundation has cooperated on projects with the People's Liberation Army and uses the same Washington public relations firm that the Chinese Embassy does." It has also registered in the United States as a foreign agent.[65] In January 2018, the University of Texas, under pressure from Senator Ted Cruz and other China critics, rejected the foundation's offer to fund the university's new China center.

In New York in 2017, a charitable foundation was established by one of China's largest, most opaque, and heavily indebted business conglomerates, HNA Group.[66] With an estimated $18 billion in assets, the Hainan Cihang Charity Foundation is set to be the second-largest foundation in the United States. But because its ownership structure is so murky—its resources come from what many observers presume to be a front company for the Chinese state or the Communist Party—it cannot get and is not seeking tax-exempt status in the United States.[67] The foundation, headed by a former German vice chancellor, has pledged major gifts to Harvard and MIT and has promised to give away $200 million over the next five years.[68] This is a lot of money with which to foster charitable views toward the world's most powerful dictatorship.

Popularity Contest

For decades, American politicians have assumed that their model—liberal democracy with an open market economy—was far more appealing to people worldwide than China's model of dictatorship and state-run capitalism. These days, that is less and less true.

Among thirty-six countries it surveyed on the question in 2017, the Pew Research Center found that the gap in favorable global attitudes between China and the United States was narrowing. Positive views of the United States declined, on average, from 64 percent in surveys in 2014–2016 to 50 percent in 2017. Meanwhile, favorable views of China went down only slightly, from 52 percent to 48 percent. In Australia, the Netherlands, and Spain, favorable views of China exceed those of the United States by more than ten percentage points. In Canada, Germany, France, and Britain, levels of positive feeling toward the United States and China are within five points of each other. Only in Italy, Poland, and Hungary does the United States have a clear, large advantage in public opinion. But in four Muslim-majority, Middle Eastern countries and in several Latin American countries (including Mexico, Chile, and Peru), China is now better liked than the United States. No doubt much of this shift stems from distaste for Donald Trump's performance as president.[69] But China's patient, resourceful efforts to win friends and influence people are also paying off.

That is particularly clear in Asia. From 2014 to 2016, across the twelve countries surveyed by the Asian Barometer (a consortium of public-opinion survey projects in east and southeast Asia), on average, 50 percent of people chose China as the most influential country in the region; only 30 percent picked the United States. In Asia, 74 percent (on average) see U.S. influence positively, but China is also in positive territory, with 58 percent taking a favorable view of Chinese influence.

China's gains in Africa can be seen through the Afrobarometer, which conducts similar surveys across thirty-six African countries. In 2015, 31 percent of Africans on average thought that the United States had the best model, while a quarter chose China's. (The survey was conducted before the election of Trump, with his unsubtle appeals to racism

and his January 2018 description of African states as "shithole countries.")[70] Across Africa, two thirds of the public say that China's increasingly robust economic activities—including its infrastructure and
business investment—have "a lot" or "some" influence on their economies, and 62 percent see that influence as positive. Africans generally
strongly support democracy, but they are drawing closer to the world's
most powerful authoritarian regime.

China's New Brawn

As China's influence is growing, so are more traditional measure-
ments of its power, including its economic and military might. China's
economy will inevitably exceed that of the United States. (A country
with one quarter of China's population cannot forever maintain an
economy more than four times as large as China's.) The United States
and Europe will probably remain richer in per capita terms than China
for decades, but by 2050, China's economy may be half again as large
as America's. Inevitably, China's growing wealth will give it growing
power.

The United States retains the world's most powerful military, but
that balance is rapidly shifting. "China has increased its defense spending nearly fivefold over the last decade," notes the Center for Strategic
and International Studies, an independent Washington think tank, in a
2018 report. China's military spending is now more than twice Russia's;
it exceeds the combined defense outlays of Japan, South Korea, the Philippines, and Vietnam and is second only to the United States.[71] China is
also busily building up air, sea, and satellite capabilities designed to push
the United States farther back into the Pacific and make China the
dominant military power in Asia, including highly accurate antiship
missiles that could sink an American aircraft carrier.[72] Already, Steven
Lee Myers of *The New York Times* writes, China can "challenge Ameri-

can military supremacy in the places that matter most to it: the waters around Taiwan and in the disputed South China Sea."[73]

China's economic rise and military expansion are closely linked to its quest for technological superiority. Under its "Made in China 2025" national industrial strategy, China is aggressively seeking to gain global dominance in cutting-edge, transformative technologies, including artificial intelligence, supercomputing, cloud computing, robotics, drones, electric cars, virtual reality, blockchain, gene editing, and other biotech.[74]

China has been using any and all means to pursue these technologies— from industrial espionage and cyber theft to the dispatch of large numbers of students to U.S. graduate programs in science and technology to investments in American and European tech start-ups. It has even compelled foreign corporations to transfer their technologies as a condition for access to the vast Chinese market.[75] These relentless efforts to steal, appropriate, or force the transfer of U.S. high technology were a major factor precipitating Trump's imposition of punitive tariffs on China in mid-2018, an initiative that cheered many Asians worried about China's hegemonic ambitions.

In addition, China is rapidly developing its own scientific breakthroughs, partly by building on the foundations of stolen or acquired technology. China's spending on research and development has now risen to about 2.5 percent of GDP, up from 2.1 percent just a few years ago. While the U.S. overall effort is higher, at 3 to 4 percent, the U.S. government component of that has declined from 2 percent in the 1960s to 0.7 percent today.

Someday, China's unabating, carefully orchestrated campaign to capture the technologies of the future will end U.S. military superiority— and perhaps sooner than we care to imagine. Already, the United States and its Asian allies are finding it hard to push back. China keeps flexing its muscles and having its way. Beijing's 2013 declaration of an air-defense identification zone overlapping with South Korean and Japanese airspace now appears to be a fact of regional life. So does Beijing's

2012 naval seizure of the Scarborough Shoal, a strategic, disputed reef much closer to the Philippines than to China. And so does China's audacious dredging of reefs in the hotly disputed Spratly Islands, creating artificial islands on which China has been building military bases, including a runway that can handle strategic bombers. China is digging in to control the South China Sea. The idea, as Minxin Pei has noted, is "to show countries in East Asia that China is the strongest player in the region, while the United States is not to be relied upon."[76]

Today, China is the world's most dynamic power. Plenty of political leaders and commentators abroad dislike its heavy-handed attempts to win influence and gain control—which in many cases amount to a new form of colonialism—but many others are lured to China's side by money, power, ambition, and simple admiration for its sheer success.

Both China and Russia are taking advantage of an epochal moment in post–World War II history. The edifice of liberal institutions so carefully constructed after World War II by President Harry Truman, Secretary of State Dean Acheson, and the victorious democratic alliance is badly cracking. America and Europe cannot indefinitely dominate such bodies as the World Bank and the International Monetary Fund without hollowing them out and tempting China to establish powerful rival structures.

That is why the Trans-Pacific Partnership (TPP), the twelve-nation Pacific Rim free-trade agreement signed in 2016, was so visionary and so necessary. Not only did the TPP advance economic integration and offer impressive labor and environmental standards; it was also a strategy for constructing a new economic and political order in Asia dominated by transparent rules rather than Chinese mercantilism, all while preserving a vital leadership role for the United States. President Trump's decision to withdraw the United States from the TPP was the most grievous self-inflicted wound to America's global leadership since the creation of the liberal world order after World War II. Trump's pullout was a massive gift to authoritarian China and a body blow to democratic aspirations in southeast Asia. It was also a stunning symbol—and accelerator—of both China's rise and America's descent. As the great democracy that dominated world politics in the twentieth century retreated, the great dictatorship that aims to dominate world politics in the twenty-first could hardly believe its luck.

EIGHT

ARE PEOPLE LOSING FAITH
IN DEMOCRACY?

The claim of a universal value is that people anywhere may have
reason to see it as valuable.

—AMARTYA SEN[1]

N
ot only is autocracy on the march, but its practitioners now
purport to embody the moral and cultural spirit of our times. In
Asia, Africa, Latin America, the Middle East, and even parts of
the democratic West, a growing chorus of elites is arguing that "the
China model" of authoritarian state-led capitalism is the wave of the future. Following in the footsteps of Singapore's Lee Kuan Yew, the strongman who led his country from rags to riches in just two generations,
today's autocrats insist that rapid economic development requires order
over freedom, and that despotic rule provides a much better fit with
non-Western cultures than liberal democracy.

But is this what the autocrats' people want? And what do citizens in
the established democracies think of the authoritarian challenge? Are
people losing faith in democracy?

The short answer is: no. None of the large-scale surveys of public
opinion show any popular groundswell for dictatorship.

That does not mean we can relax, however. In the United States and its peer democracies, doubts about democracy are increasing. So are significant pockets of support for authoritarian options—growing constituencies that illiberal populists could rally to erode freedom in times of trouble.

That looming danger is more palpable in a few countries—such as Brazil, Mexico, the Philippines, and Tunisia—where democracy has done a poor job of containing crime and corruption. Yet citizens in established democracies still overwhelmingly see democracy as the best form of government. And the self-serving cultural arguments for autocracy—that it better reflects "Asian," "Islamic," or other non-Western values, or that poor people are too preoccupied with survival to care about freedom—simply do not square with the mountains of evidence. In fact, people in Africa, the world's poorest continent, exhibit strikingly high levels of support not simply for democracy but for a host of liberal values and institutional checks on their rulers. And even in the Arab world—which remains a desert for democracy—the data shows widespread aspirations for democratic and accountable government.

The main threat to democracy today is not the values or opinions of the people; it is the corruption and lust for power of the rulers (even many elected ones), as well as the weakness of oversight institutions like parliaments and courts.

It is hard to write a book on government by the people without understanding something about the opinions of the people. Yet it is hard to assemble a comprehensive snapshot of global views of democracy because different surveys are conducted at different times using different measures. Nevertheless, the data tells a powerful story. People around the world can resist the lure of autocracy and embrace democracy—if their leaders deliver economic progress and govern with respect for democratic principles and the rule of law.

What Do the American People Think?

In a provocative 2016 article in the *Journal of Democracy*, the political scientists Roberto Foa and Yascha Mounk challenged the long-held assumption among my fellow experts that the advanced industrial democracies of the West are firmly entrenched. Political scientists call democracies *consolidated* when they enjoy such broad and deep legitimacy that no significant political force would dare try to acquire power by undemocratic means—and when no leader who tried to eviscerate the norms, checks, and balances of democracy could get away with it. Under such happy conditions, democracy becomes the only game in town. But for a democracy to be truly resilient, this consensus must prevail among not only its elites but also its major parties, interest groups, and mass public. This unconditional faith in democracy as the best and most just form of government roots democracy like an oak.[2] And this faith, Foa and Mounk argued, is precisely what is now beginning to weaken.[3]

Tracking public attitudes toward democracy in the United States and Europe over two decades, Foa and Mounk warned of an emerging "crisis of democratic legitimacy" in Western public opinion. "Citizens in a number of supposedly consolidated democracies in North America and Western Europe have not only grown more critical of their political leaders," they wrote. "Rather, they have also become more cynical about the value of democracy as a political system, less hopeful that anything they do might influence public policy, and more willing to express support for authoritarian alternatives."[4]

Recent survey evidence suggests that Foa and Mounk are only partially correct—but that we still have serious cause for concern. Let's look at the United States first. In July 2017, I joined other scholars in the independent, nonpartisan Democracy Fund Voter Study Group to survey attitudes toward democracy among a representative sample of five thousand Americans.[5] The good news was that the American public still overwhelmingly backed democracy as the best form of government: some 86 percent said it's a good or very good system, 82 percent said it's very important to live in a democracy, and 78 percent said democracy is always "preferable to any other kind of government." And Americans were not as disillusioned with our democracy as one might have thought, given Washington's polarization and dysfunction. About six in ten Americans were at least somewhat satisfied with the way democracy is working in the United States,[6] which compares well with other advanced democracies.

But we found some bad news too. In addition to the above three questions about support for democracy, our 2017 survey also measured people's feelings toward two authoritarian options: "a strong leader who does not have to bother with Congress and elections," and rule by the army. Nearly a quarter of Americans (24 percent) turned out to hanker for a strongman. That was significantly less than what Foa and Mounk found in 2011, but according to a thirty-eight-nation survey conducted by the Pew Research Center in 2017, it was higher than in several other peer democracies, such as Canada (17 percent), France (12 percent), and Germany (just 6 percent, thanks to bitter memories of the Nazi past).[7]

Moreover, support for military rule has steadily risen in the United States, from 8 percent in 1995 to some 18 percent in 2017. This is not only much higher than in Canada (10 percent) and Germany (4 percent) but also higher than in democracies that depend profoundly on the army—namely, Israel (10 percent) and South Korea (8 percent). (However, in-depth interviews by the Voter Study Group suggest that American respondents think of "army rule" more in terms of the military's maintaining law and order rather than its suspending the constitution and governing directly.)

Several other disturbing trends are lurking beneath the surface. First, American support for democracy is not as robust as we would have hoped. Across all five questions we asked in our 2017 Voter Study Group poll (the three about democracy and the two about authoritarian options), only a modest majority of Americans—54 percent—consistently held a prodemocracy position. In fact, 28 percent gave a nondemocratic response on at least two of our five items.

Worse, our public's ambivalence and hostility to democracy are caught up with today's highly polarized politics. We have endured waves of illiberal sentiment in America before, of course. We don't know how much of the American public was willing to support a dictator during the 1930s or the anti-Communist hysteria of the 1950s, and those numbers might have been higher than today's. But in those previous eras, for all their challenges, we did not have a president whose own commitment to democracy was profoundly in doubt. In this respect, Donald Trump represents an unprecedented danger to American democracy, and that peril is reflected in the deeper patterns of our data.

Among Americans who supported a candidate in the 2016 presidential primaries, Trump supporters were substantially more supportive of a "strong leader" (32 percent) than supporters of any other major-party candidate, all of whom favored a "strong leader" at some 20 percent or less. Those who voted for Trump in the 2016 general election were nearly twice as likely as Hillary Clinton voters to back a strong leader (29 percent to 16). And those who switched from voting for Barack Obama in 2012 to Donald Trump in 2016 had the most authoritarian leanings of all, with an alarming 45 percent of Obama-to-Trump voters supporting a "strong leader."

Such patterns are familiar from overseas; it is quite common for citizens on the political right to be more supportive of authoritarian options than those on the left. For instance, Italian fans of Silvio Berlusconi's center-right Forza Italia and British backers of the nativist U.K. Independence Party are much more supportive of the "strong leader" option (at a rate of over 40 percent) than others in their countries. French citizens sympathetic to the country's xenophobic National Front favor military rule much more than do the backers of other parties.

In Trump's America, such autocratic attitudes are increasingly mixing with hyperpartisanship and ideological polarization. In the Trump era, Republicans are much more likely to endorse a "strong leader" than are Democrats (by 31 percent to 21). Self-identified conservatives are more than twice as likely as liberals to endorse a "strong leader" (30 percent to 13). And when we divide our sample into cultural conservatives, moderates, and liberals (according to their views on issues such as abortion, gay rights, race, and religion), the gap between cultural conservatives and cultural liberals on backing a strongman is even wider—some 20 percentage points.[8]

In the United States today, racism and religious intolerance turn out to strongly correlate with support for autocracy. An alarming one in six Americans was willing to embrace a racial, or arguably plain-old racist, view of American identity, saying that being of European heritage is important to being an American. Those Americans are four times more likely to favor a "strong leader" than those who say European heritage is "not important at all"—and are much more likely to question democracy itself.

A similarly depressing pattern holds true with Americans who favor increased surveillance of mosques or the targeting of Muslims during airport screenings. Such respondents are three times more likely to favor a "strong leader" than those who strongly oppose such religious profiling.[9] These are the subterranean constituencies that Trump continues to mobilize when he harps on culture-war issues, stokes anti-Muslim animus, declines to unequivocally condemn white supremacists, or attacks the intellects of African American critics, from Representative Maxine Waters of California to the basketball star LeBron James.[10]

Trump-era partisanship is also increasingly eroding American public support for checks and balances on presidential power. Overwhelming majorities of Americans still say that the president should be monitored and held accountable by the courts (91 percent), Congress (81 percent), and the media (75 percent). But the president's backers are dramatically less supportive of such checks on his power than are his critics. Pro-

Trump Americans are nine times more likely than their anti-Trump fellow citizens to oppose congressional oversight of the president (36 percent to 4), ten times more likely to oppose media scrutiny of him (48 percent to 5), and five times more likely to say that the president "should not be bound by laws or court decisions he thinks are wrong" (15 percent to 3).

A final worrying pattern encompasses both America and other major democracies: people with lower education levels tend to be substantially more supportive of authoritarian options.[11]

All these rumblings in American public opinion are particularly concerning because of the uniqueness of our historical moment.[12] Trump is not the only one testing and trashing democratic norms; a wave of illiberal populism is sweeping across many advanced industrial democracies, led by demagogues who target immigrants and minorities. The polling data suggests a close affinity between politicians who play the race and immigration cards and citizens who opt to "follow the leader." As more voters feel threatened by tectonic shifts beyond their control—including immigration, globalization, income inequality, and economic insecurity—illiberal populists such as Trump, Viktor Orbán, and Marine Le Pen claim that they are merely responding to these anxieties. They are actually stoking them.

Moreover, as we saw in chapter 5, America's two big political parties are more ideologically sorted and distant from each other than they have been in a century, even as they are about as closely competitive with each other as they have ever been. This dynamic is driving an increasingly hyperpartisan style of zero-sum politics. When party affiliation takes on the intensity of tribal identity, the odds get stacked against political compromise, and it becomes exceedingly hard for moderates to confront extremists and norm breakers in their ranks. It is especially difficult for Republicans in Congress to do so when the main norm trampler is their party leader and president.

And of course, the worrisome trends in U.S. public opinion are seriously exacerbated by social media's corrosive ability to swiftly spread false, hateful, and extremist messages—and by the cynical exploitation of America's political polarization and susceptibility to viral propaganda by Russia and other foreign actors who wish our democracy ill.

The danger, then, is not that alarmingly high numbers of Americans are defecting from democratic ideals; the problem is that American levels of democratic commitment appear fragile and partisan at precisely the moment when our democratic politics are under unprecedented assault.

Is Democracy a Luxury for the Rich?

These trends at home are profoundly unsettling. But I draw considerable hope from looking at public opinion in some far less fortunate parts of the planet.

For a long time, experts presumed that poor people were much less likely to care about democracy. A particularly influential theory, first propounded by the American psychologist Abraham Maslow in the mid-1940s, argued that there is a universal hierarchy of human needs, under which the basic requirements for material sustenance and physical safety take precedence over "higher-order" needs for esteem, belonging, and personal fulfillment.[13] Over the years, as the theory has been refined, its adherents have argued that people in poor, chaotic countries will favor "survival values" that focus on income and safety, while people in prosperous countries will back "self-expression values" that emphasize people's ability to choose, respect diversity, and demand not just democracy but a deeper structure of freedom and accountability.[14] From this perspective, socioeconomic development is exceptionally powerful: the more prosperous the society, the more it will propel countries in the direction of the "self-expression values" and, as a result, toward democracy.[15]

This school—known as *modernization theory*—expects that if democracy does arise in the world's poorer countries, it will rest on thinner cultural ground and be less liberal than in democracies in wealthier nations. Public support for democracy in impoverished areas, this theory argues, will be rather shallow and one-dimensional, lacking the commitments to freedom, tolerance, the rule of law, and checks and balances that distinguish truly liberal democracy.

How does this theory hold up in the face of public-opinion data? It works rather well to explain the continuing strong support for democracy in most wealthy democracies. And with its emphasis on the links between economic well-being and democratic attitudes, it can also explain some of the erosion in support for democracy in the United States and parts of Europe as a result of "declining real income linked with rising income inequality."[16] But public support for democracy in many middle-income and poor countries turns out to be higher, broader, and deeper than is often assumed.

First, consider the developing world region with the largest proportion of democracies, Latin America. Among the eighteen Latin American countries surveyed in 2017 by Latinobarometer, a major annual public-opinion survey, majorities in every country continue to agree with the proposition (inspired by Winston Churchill) that "democracy may have its problems but it's the best system of government." On average, 69 percent agreed with that sentiment, with percentages ranging from 54 percent in Mexico to 84 percent in Uruguay.

This regional average has declined ten points since 2013, when it hit a peak of 79 percent. Underlying this has been a steady decline in satisfaction with democracy's performance in Latin America. In Mexico, Colombia, Peru, and Brazil—all of which have experienced chronic problems of violence or corruption—less than 20 percent of the public are satisfied with the way democracy is working. Only 3 percent of Brazilians think that their country is governed for the benefit of all, rather than for the gain of a "few powerful groups."[17]

The picture is murkier in East Asia, where we have public-opinion data from the periodic Asian Barometer, with which I have also been involved.[18] If we compare the region's three richer democracies (Japan, South Korea, and Taiwan) with four democracies in the middle-income range (Indonesia, Mongolia, the Philippines, and Thailand), we see some of the shallowness of support for democracy that the modernization theorists would have anticipated.

All these countries, from the richest to the poorest, do overwhelmingly value democracy in the abstract; on average, in 2014–2016, 89 percent of people in these countries agreed with our proposition that "democracy may have its problems but it's still the best form of government." But when these publics are asked about authoritarian alternatives, people in East Asia's less prosperous countries are more likely to equivocate, or worse. When we asked whether "we should get rid of parliament and elections and have a strong leader decide things," support for this type of strongman rule was endorsed by a third of the public in upper-middle-income Thailand and the lower-middle-income Philippines—which actually elected a strongman ruler in 2016, Rodrigo Duterte.

The Asian Barometer also probed Asians' commitment to such liberal values as free expression, the rule of law, and legislative scrutiny of the executive branch.[19] That includes asking whether people agree or disagree with such illiberal ideas as letting the government "decide whether certain ideas should be allowed to be discussed in society," having judges accept "the view of the executive branch" in important cases, and agreeing that a government that is "constantly checked by the legislature" cannot "possibly accomplish great things."

Income levels seem to make a big difference in these responses. On average, these illiberal propositions were rejected by three quarters of the public in prosperous Japan and about two thirds of those in South Korea and Taiwan. But the people of some less well-off Asian democracies were less firm. Only about 50 percent of Indonesian respondents opposed these ideas, on average, and the numbers were a little over 40 percent in Mongolia, Thailand, and the Philippines. (That rejection level was essentially the same in four nearby autocracies, Cambodia, Malaysia, Burma, and Singapore.)

For old-school political scientists, the region with the most surprising public views is the world's poorest, Africa. We might expect support for democracy and such liberal values as free expression and the rule of law to be much weaker in low-income Africa than in middle-income Asia. Not so. Across twenty-two countries in sub-Saharan Africa and nearly thirty thousand respondents surveyed in 2016–2018, high proportions of the African public—from Benin to Zimbabwe—embraced not only democracy but its liberal components too. On average, 72 percent of the public in these mainly poor countries agreed that "democracy is always preferable" to other forms of government.[20]

African support for democracy is somewhat lower than the average response among the above seven middle- and upper-income countries that we discussed in East Asia, significantly wealthier places that have had mainly democratic experiences over the past generation. But Africans' enthusiasm for self-government is notably higher than Latin Americans'. And Africans—many with painful firsthand experience of abuse at the hands of dictatorships and juntas—dislike authoritarian options at least as much as East Asians. On average, 85 percent of Africans surveyed rejected one-man rule, compared with 69 percent of East Asians. And some 75 percent of both Africans and East Asians spurn rule by military junta.

An older generation of political science theorists would have been most astonished by Africans' robust commitment to liberal values, such as a multiparty system, parliamentary scrutiny of government performance, and media checks on the powerful. Roughly three quarters of Africans supported free elections and two-term limits on the presidency, and 70 percent backed media scrutiny of government wrongdoing.[21] Moreover, average levels of support for these core principles of liberal government—and for democracy itself—have been strikingly resilient in Africa since 2005.

If you ask ordinary Africans what the problem is with their countries, they are pretty clear: their rulers. Across the eighteen countries that have been surveyed four different times from 2005 to 2016, the pattern is always the same: a whopping gap between Africans' demand for democracy (74 percent in 2015) and their perceptions that democracy is being delivered (47 percent).

I should conclude with a word about the Arab world. If any region might be expected to devalue democracy, it would probably be the Middle East, which has the world's lowest levels of democracy. After popular uprisings for freedom broke out in 2011, the short-lived Arab Spring went down to crushing defeat everywhere except tiny Tunisia.

But the data from another regional survey, the Arab Barometer, shows the same surprising pattern of public aspirations for democracy and hostility to authoritarian rule.[22] Across ten Arab countries surveyed in 2011 and a dozen polled in 2013, 72 percent of Arabs, on average, agreed with the old Churchill thesis. For the six countries where the question was asked in 2016, average support was even higher—81 percent.[23] When Arabs were asked more specifically about a democratic system that ensures civil rights, political equality, and executive accountability, they were even more positive: in 2013, about 85 percent approved of such a system.

Arab publics do strongly prefer—by about 75 percent, on average—that political reform be gradual, not immediate. But they are not longing for dictators to deliver them from disorder. In fact, the average percentage of Arabs who reject an "authoritarian president" untroubled by a parliament and elections has increased over time, from 75 percent in 2007 to 80 percent in 2011 and 83 percent in 2013 (with a similar percentage among the six countries surveyed in 2016). That compares quite favorably with other regions, as shown below. Nor do Arabs evince much enthusiasm for Islamist dictatorship; solid majorities everywhere see it as thoroughly "unsuitable."

In Tunisia, the one Arab Spring country still trying to make democracy work, people hold withering assessments of their elected government, which they view as pervasively corrupt and ineffective. Between 2011 and 2016, the proportion of Tunisians saying that democracy is bad for the country's economy increased from one sixth to one half. Yet Tunisians' view of democracy as the best system of government grew from 70 to 86 percent during those same years.[24] Perhaps people are not as impatient and materialistic as some of the theorists assume.

Attitudes Toward Democracy and Authoritarianism, by Region

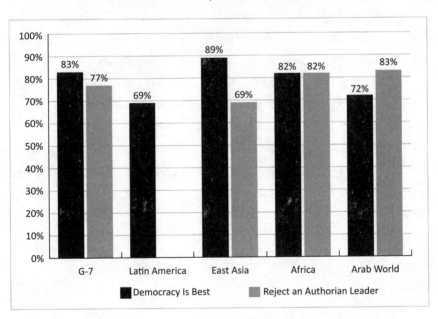

Pew Research Center, Latinobarometer, Asian Barometer, Afrobarometer, Arab Barometer.

The regional patterns can be summed up simply: democracy is a universal value. In every region of the world surveyed, large to overwhelming majorities of the public, on average, said that democracy is the best form of government *and* that an unaccountable strongman is a bad idea. Indeed, regions of the world often written off as apathetic if not auto-cratic turn out to support democracy and reject strongman rule at aver-age levels about equal to those among wealthy G-7 democracies like the United States, Great Britain, France, and Japan.[25]

The Public's Faith

All told, the global public-opinion data has a clear and perhaps surpris-ing message: the greatest enemy of democracy is not poverty. Poor peo-ple across Africa and in Asian countries like Cambodia and Burma want democracy; they just want it to work for them, not their ruling elites.[26] Citizens in the developing world still often see the lure of authoritarian-ism, but it tempts not so much the poor as the disillusioned.

Economic progress and fairness are vital to the growth of democracy. But the most important condition for sustaining public commitment to democracy turns out to be fidelity by those in power to liberal norms: transparency, accountability, tolerance, respect for the law, and an insis-tence on the essential role of political opposition. Democracies that govern decently and embrace these values will not only deliver more prosperity, they will also renew public faith in democracy as the best form of government yet devised.

NINE

MEETING THE AUTOCRATS' CHALLENGE

This is exactly what our adversaries want. . . . They know that their power and influence are inferior to ours, so they seek to subvert us, and erode our resolve to resist, and terrorize us into passivity. They know they have little to offer the world beyond selfishness and fear, so they seek to undermine our confidence in ourselves and our belief in our own values.

—Senator John McCain, remarks to the Munich
Security Conference, February 17, 2017[1]

P eople around the world may want democracy, but Russia and China do not want it for them. The most threatening feature of the current global order is the surge in power and initiative of these giant autocracies. Of course, we should not ignore the challenge to democracy posed by regional autocrats—especially those in Iran—or by nonstate terrorist groups such as Al Qaeda and ISIS. But among the world's foes of democracy, only two leaders—Vladimir Putin and Xi Jinping—have enough power and ambition to undermine the entire global liberal order. Any campaign to defend and revive democracy around the world must thus be defined by a strategy to confront and contain the authoritarian thrusts of Russia and China.

Our goal should not be a new cold war. But we will need the same sobriety, foresight, and tenacity of that earlier "long twilight struggle." More than we did in the Cold War, we must recognize the limits of American power, and thus the need for democratic alliances. And we will need to navigate between two extremes: a vigilance so extreme that it provokes paranoia, xenophobia, and imperial overreach; and a confidence so disabling that it leaves vacuums to be filled by surging authoritarianism.

Seventy years later, the famous Long Telegram that the visionary American diplomat George F. Kennan sent from Moscow remains eerily salient. But today's challenge is more complicated because it stems from two powerful global adversaries, not one, and because it comes at a time of diminished American strength and resolve, amid alliances that are eroding rather than gathering. Even so, eight strategic principles from Kennan's day still apply.

First, we must grasp the nature of the threat. Around the world, free societies face a wide range of efforts by Russia and China—from the overt to the subtle—to enhance their power by infiltrating democratic processes, eroding democratic values, and breaking democratic alliances. We must not only document efforts to project authoritarian power—soft, sharp, and hard—but see the larger pattern of malice that connects them.

Second, we must educate democratic societies about the scale, motive, and elements of the autocrats' threat. Denial and hysteria are common human instincts in the face of peril, but neither is useful in crafting a strategy. Because authoritarians can now project power in such diverse and often elusive forms, and because the postindustrial democracies are decades removed from their existential struggles to defend freedom, it is easy to deny or downplay the threats that Russia and China pose. Most people don't want to admit vulnerability—for themselves or their country. And it is understandable that democratic citizens should want their countries to pull back from heavy international burdens after their leaders misled them into wasteful debacles like the 2003 U.S.-led invasion of Iraq. The impulse to put spending at home over major investments in defense and diplomacy is a natural one, and even more powerful in Europe than in the United States. But if the democracies are to forge a serious strategic response to the autocrats' offensive, they will need to build public support for it.

Third, the democracies must strengthen their collective military resolve and capacities in the face of China's and Russia's rapidly expanding and modernizing military power. Few things are better demonstrated in history than this: appeasement will fail to deter aggression by rising (or reviving) authoritarian powers. In the face of such threats, peace and security can be preserved only through a robust combination of military strength and diplomatic initiative. We must seek to cooperate and de-escalate tensions with Beijing and Moscow whenever possible, whether that involves new arms-control agreements or finding common ground on such regional challenges as North Korea. We should also avoid gratuitous actions and rhetoric that demonize or demean our adversaries (not to mention stigmatizing their ethnic kin in the United States) while doing little to improve our own security. But where Russia and China commit limited acts of aggression—whether in Ukraine or the South China Sea—they must face resistance and costs, or more brazen acts of aggression will follow. Kennan's observation about Soviet power in 1946 remains true of Russia and China today: these autocracies may be impervious "to the logic of reason," as Kennan put it, but they are "highly sensitive to the logic of force." As such, they "can easily withdraw"—and usually do—when "strong resistance is encountered at any point. Thus, if the adversary has sufficient force and makes clear his readiness to use it, he rarely has to do so."[2]

Fourth, we should treat Russia's and China's leaders and societies with respect. Moscow and Beijing are trying to project power today, in part, as responses to profound experiences of national humiliation. For many Russians, the collapse of the Soviet Union in 1991 was shattering, carrying with it the loss of the Soviet empire, the end of Moscow's leading role in global affairs, and the shredding of the socialist safety net. Russian per capita income (in U.S. dollars) fell by 60 percent between 1990 and 1999.[3] From 1990 to 2013, average life expectancy in Russia improved at only a fraction of the rate of the rest of the world (by 1.8 years, compared with 6.2 years for the world), placing Russia "in 108th position— between Iraq and North Korea."[4] In this same period, China has been a huge economic success story, but it is still responding to the "century of humiliation" at the hands of Western and Japanese imperial powers, beginning with the Qing Dynasty's defeat by Britain in the first Opium War in 1839–1842 and continuing through the second Sino-Japanese War overlapping with World War II. Since the Communist Party seized power in 1949, it has been determined to recover the territories and glory that China lost during this painful period. Respect does not mean conceding to Russian claims on its former Soviet territories (or even on Crimea) or Chinese claims to the South China Sea, not to mention any effort to menace democratic Taiwan. But avoiding unnecessary conflict does require recognizing that China and Russia are great and proud countries with historical grievances that must be understood—and with contemporary ambitions for global influence that can sometimes be accommodated without greatly damaging our core interests and values.

Fifth, when possible, we should separate corrupt leaders from their societies and deter autocratic regimes with carefully targeted measures. Treating Russian and Chinese *societies* as enemies is dangerous. The authoritarian regimes in Moscow and Beijing are using increasingly forceful and far-reaching methods of propaganda to generate intense "patriotic" support for their own leadership and spur nationalist resentment of the West while also censoring international information that could create more complex and skeptical public views. Gratuitous confrontations that pit Western democracies against Russian or Chinese society only play into the hands of leaders who are adept at exploiting international conflicts to boost their public support and delegitimize their critics. Our goal must be to punish the regime—the ruling oligarchical elite in Russia, the Communist Party leadership in China—and not the larger societies. This requires creative and surgical methods to sanction individuals, expose gross corruption, and thwart thrusts abroad. But a general trade war with China, of the kind that President Trump launched in 2018, carries huge risks of collateral damage. We should look for more precise, effective ways to engage each society and create distance between it and its leaders.

Sixth, we must remain true to our democratic values. In the Long Telegram, Kennan urged his colleagues to find the "courage and self-confidence to cling to our own methods and conceptions of human society. After all, the greatest danger that can befall us . . . is that we shall allow ourselves to become like those with whom we are coping."[5] We cannot prevail in a global struggle to defend freedom by descending to the cynical tactics of disinformation, coercion, and corruption of our authoritarian adversaries. If we do so, Putin will achieve his purpose: to show that no virtues, ideals, or real differences separate the Russian and Chinese systems from those of the Western democracies—that every country is just an amoral rival in a global struggle for power.

Seventh, we must reinvent the postwar liberal democratic order for the current era. In the twenty-first century, as Brazil, India, Nigeria, South Africa, and other emerging-market countries play a larger role in world politics, we are witnessing what Fareed Zakaria has termed "the rise of the rest."[6] We must develop a more inclusive, multipolar world order that can secure our democratic values and interests. We must, as Kennan urged in 1946, offer "a more much more positive and constructive picture of the sort of world we would like to see."[7] With its Belt and Road Initiative and other global strategies, China is trying to shape a world order that replaces strong Western leadership with Chinese authoritarian leadership. We must draw the emerging-market countries—particularly India—into an alternative vision, one built on inclusive governance, a balance of power, and the rule of law.

Finally, we must repair and strengthen our own democracies so they can be models worth emulating. Unless we have confidence in our own system of free government and show that it can work to address the problems of our society, we cannot compete effectively with rival authoritarian models.

The rest of this book is dedicated to tackling the above challenges. As the old saying goes, "you can't beat something with nothing." Unless the democracies of the world improve their own performance, they will provide increasingly fertile ground for Russian and Chinese efforts to penetrate and subvert them. Unless the United States and other wealthy democracies wage a vigorous global campaign to counter authoritarian disinformation and advance democratic ideas, knowledge, and tools, China and Russia will win the information war. Unless the established democracies renew their resolve to support aspiring democrats around the world, their authoritarian competitors will triumph, boosted by lavish assistance from Russia and China—which will expect to have their debts repaid. Unless we launch a concerted global campaign against kleptocracy and money laundering, we will leave ourselves vulnerable to foreign manipulation even as we ignore the most glaring weaknesses of our authoritarian foes. And unless we work to make the internet a safer space for democracy, the online world will become a highway to political polarization, acrimony, and authoritarian propaganda.

All this we can—and must—do. And the obvious starting place is the many specific things we can—and must—do to counter and contain the dangers that Russia and China pose to democracy in the United States, the West, and around the world.

Standing Up to Putin

Russia under Vladimir Putin is a resurgent but still opportunistic power. Putin is like a burglar walking down a corridor of apartments, testing to see which doors are unlocked. When he gets the chance, he breaks in; when he cannot, he moves on. We must lock our doors and raise the costs of his criminal behavior, whether in the digital, financial, or physical worlds.

Any strategy to counter the Kremlin's global assault on democracy should start with listening to the people who share our liberal values and understand Putin much better than we do: Russia's democrats. One of the bravest of them is Vladimir Kara-Murza, a journalist and activist whom the Putin regime has twice tried to murder by poison. These assassination attempts were made with a highly sophisticated toxin that could probably have been administered only by one of Russia's intelligence services. Each attempt nearly killed Kara-Murza, forcing him to endure a perilous and lengthy recovery. The first attempt on his life came just three months after the assassination of his political mentor and dear friend, Boris Nemtsov, a top leader of the Russian opposition who was gunned down in February 2015 just steps from the Kremlin. Despite all this, Kara-Murza has not flinched in his campaign for reform in Russia.

Kara-Murza offers three guidelines for dealing with Putin's threat to democracy. "First," he told me, "stop saying Russia when you mean Putin." Putin wants to frame the conflict as a battle between a decadent and overbearing West and the Russian people, who are merely trying to preserve their culture and sovereignty. But our conflict is not with the

Russian people; it is with Putin's predatory ruling elite, which has hi-jacked Russia's state and its vast natural-resource wealth. We are not the only victims of Putin's crimes; more than 140 million Russians are his victims too. Western diplomatic statements must clearly distinguish be-tween Putin's kleptocracy and the Russian people who chafe beneath it. And we need to constantly work to separate the two.

Second, do not offer Putin gratuitous praise. The last thing we should do is to congratulate him on his election "victories"—a mistake both Presidents Obama and Trump have made. These were not real elections but charades meant to mimic a democratic process and lend some shroud of legitimacy to Putin's dictatorship. Russian democrats are urg-ing us: *Please don't validate this sham exercise in democracy. Don't encourage Putin. And don't discourage Russian democrats who are trying to fight for the real thing.* We need a new golden rule for autocrats like Putin: If you can't say something critical about him, don't say anything at all.

Third, we need to pressure regime elites where it hurts: their assets and their ability to enjoy them. This means targeted sanctions on those responsible for human rights abuses, predatory corruption, and other crimes. A milestone on the road to accountability came in 2012 when President Obama signed the Magnitsky Act, named for the Russian anti-corruption whistle-blower Sergei Magnitsky, who was beaten to death in a Russian prison in 2009. The Obama administration placed eighteen Russian government officials and businesspeople on the law's list, barred them "from entering the United States, froze any assets held by U.S. banks and banned their future use of U.S. banking systems."[8] In March 2014, after Russia annexed Crimea and launched military operations in eastern Ukraine, a U.S.-led coalition of Western governments began imposing sanctions on numerous other Russian government officials, military officers, oligarchs, banks, and companies—thereby preventing them from traveling to or doing business with the West.

Targeted sanctions are effective because they punish corrupt and abusive individuals, not the Russian people at large. Kara-Murza recalls

Nemtsov's saying that the Magnitsky Act was the most pro-Russian legislation ever passed in a foreign country "because it targets the people who abuse the rights of Russian citizens and who steal the money of Russian citizens." "For now," Kara-Murza says, "we can't stop the kleptocrats from stealing in Russia, but we can stop them from spending their stolen riches in the West." Putin and his ruling mafia's intense desire to be rid of these punitive measures seems to have been a major factor motivating them to try to elect a more sympathetic American president in 2016.

The Kremlin now appears to be suffering from at least some buyer's remorse. On April 6, 2018, the Trump administration announced new sanctions that cut much more deeply into the core of Putin's power network. Citing Russia's intervention in the 2016 election and its ongoing cyber attacks, Washington froze the U.S. assets of "more than three dozen Russian individuals and entities," blocked them from doing business in America, and barred their access to Western financing. Among those sanctioned were some of "Putin's closest business allies and the companies they own."[9] These included Putin's son-in-law, Kirill Shamalov; Russia's ninth-richest businessman, Viktor Vekselberg (worth an estimated $14 billion); the chief executive of the Russian state-owned energy giant Gazprom, Alexey Miller; and Oleg Deripaska (worth about $6.7 billion), a close Putin business ally who was previously linked to disgraced former Trump campaign chairman Paul Manafort.[10] When markets opened the following Monday, the Russian stock market fell 11 percent, the ruble dropped more than 4 percent, and Russia's fifty richest businessmen were estimated to have lost $12 billion in wealth.[11]

These new sanctions closely followed a wave of expulsions of Russian "diplomats" (actually known or suspected intelligence operatives) from Western embassies and consulates after the Kremlin's audacious attempt to murder one of its former intelligence agents, Sergei Skripal, in the United Kingdom with a Soviet military-grade nerve agent. In March 2018, the United States, Britain, and some twenty-five other Western democracies expelled more than one hundred Russian operatives "in a show of solidarity" that *The Guardian* called "the biggest concerted blow to Russian intelligence networks in the west since the cold war."[12]

But the West is still pulling its punches. Despite the assassination attempt on Skripal, the use of chemical weapons on British soil, and a string of more than a dozen spectacular murders and suspicious deaths of Putin's enemies living in the United Kingdom, the country remains, in the words of anticorruption activist and author Oliver Bullough, "wide open to the Kremlin's kleptocratic cash."[13] Its government and private institutions—including "banks, law firms, accountants, private schools, art galleries, and even Conservative Party fundraisers"[14]—have been deeply and in many cases knowingly complicit in laundering and profiting from these looted riches. To varying degrees, other Western democracies have also provided havens for pro-Putin oligarchs to launder their wealth, burnish their reputations, and live in arrogant splendor. As *Washington Post* columnist Anne Applebaum has noted, "the Russian government treats Britain with disdain because the Russian government thinks it has bought the British elite. Worse than that, it may be right."[15]

Trump has long claimed to have been tougher on Russia than Obama, despite Trump's refusal to condemn Putin and admit that the April 2018 sanctions were largely forced on him by Congress and his own national security team. But neither American president—and no Western government—has been tough enough on Putin. And none has implemented the kind of robust and comprehensive strategy that is needed. What would such a strategy look like?

As we shall see in the next chapter, its cornerstone would be a determined global campaign against kleptocracy. This will require legal and regulatory changes to make our democratic societies more lawful and transparent, even if they make some of our banks, real estate agents, law firms, and lobbyists less magnificently rich.

We can also extend targeted sanctions to a broader swath of Putin's allies. This should include bans on visas for not only the oligarchs but their families, as well as a radical revision of the "golden visa" programs that let wealthy foreigners, often with dubious sources of wealth, instantly obtain visas (and fairly rapidly move toward permanent residency and even citizenship) in exchange for "investing" some minimum sum.[16] In their crudest forms, in countries such as Malta and Cyprus, these schemes "offer virtually scrutiny-free EU citizenship for rich outsiders" in exchange for "quick cash." The main beneficiaries are "Russian and Chinese businesspeople who would otherwise be barred" from the European Union.[17]

We can raise the costs and ramp up the pressure on Putin's circle in many other ways. For starters, we need to make bolder, more energetic use of our intelligence means to expose the corruption of the Russian ruling elite, starting with Vladimir Vladimirovich Putin. The Russian dictator is believed to have a personal worth in the tens of billions of dollars.[18] He is deeply insecure about his legitimacy and regards any reporting about his rapacious corruption (and that of his closest cronies) as an existential threat. We do not need to resort to Putin's own tactics of Soviet-style disinformation. Financial intelligence—which we may already have—and truthful investigative reporting can do a lot to weaken and delegitimize him.

We also must do a much better job of documenting Russian subversion efforts and explaining to the public the danger they present. We must not allow the response to become a partisan issue. As Laura Rosenberger and Jamie Fly (themselves a bipartisan policy team) write, we need an integrated, well-coordinated effort across the full range of U.S. and allied government agencies to track and deter Russia's ambitious campaign. The advanced democracies will need new ways to share intelligence and "learn lessons from each other about what countermeasures work, and which don't." (French president Emmanuel Macron's campaign blunted the impact of Russian disinformation during his 2017 race by planting false information on his campaign's own servers, for instance.) Fortunately, both NATO and the EU are developing coordinated approaches to identifying and rebuffing Russian cyber attacks by disinformation and other means.[19]

This is urgent. The Russians, the Chinese, and other adversaries have been hacking, sacking, and probing our electricity grids, banks, corporations, and other critical infrastructure. In the case of Russia, this cyber aggression has included 2016 intrusions into more than twenty state voter-registration databases, as well as the 2017 NotPetya malware campaign, which Trump's own White House called "the most destructive and costly cyberattack in history."[20] In July 2018, the Department of Homeland Security revealed that hackers working for the Russian state had penetrated the most secure digital control rooms of American electric utilities, putting the Kremlin in a position to cause major power blackouts in the United States. "They are waging a covert war on the West," said Michael Carpenter, a former senior Pentagon official.[21] We must not only modernize our digital systems and harden our defenses against malware but disrupt our foes' cyber warfare capacities and deter them by developing stronger offensive capabilities.

Beyond all this, some general steps would help defend democracy from both Russian and Chinese influence operations. For one thing, democracies should boost their capacities to monitor Russian and Chinese news bureaus, journalists, and businesspeople, who often serve as intelligence agents for their authoritarian states. This means better electronic and human intelligence, as well as investing in Russian- and Chinese-language training for our own operatives and analysts. For another, the United States and its West European friends need to train scholars, journalists, watchdog organizations, and policy professionals from less prosperous democracies in Russian and Chinese methods so that they can identify, expose, and resist covert operations to which poorer countries are especially vulnerable.[22]

We also need to tackle the problem of Chinese and Russian state-run media outlets. A basic asymmetry is at work: these authoritarian propaganda instruments can freely broadcast in our democracies, even as the independent news networks of Western democracies, such as CNN and the BBC, have little to no access to the Russian and Chinese viewing publics. The same is true for journalists: ours are severely restricted in China and Russia (or even denied visas) while theirs have much freer rein in the United States. The problem, of course, is that we oppose censorship in principle, and they do not. We should not block internet access to the autocrats' programming. But it isn't obvious why they should enjoy market access to American cable television when America's free and tough-minded news media do not have a similar opportunity to reach Chinese or Russian viewers. We should be demanding symmetrical access for Western electronic media, as both a trade issue and a freedom issue. And we should take into account the extent of reciprocal access for American journalists when deciding on American visas for Chinese and Russian journalists.[23]

Standing Up to Xi

In the summer of 2018, as I was completing this book, I took an extensive trip across parts of Asia that are on the front lines of China's ambitions: India, Thailand, Hong Kong, and Taiwan. In India, I talked with foreign policy thinkers, scholars, human rights activists, and recently retired diplomats, including a few who had risen to the pinnacle of India's impressive career foreign service. In Taiwan, I met with old friends who now held senior roles in that nation's progressive government and other figures in Taiwan's vibrant democratic politics, civil society, and news media. In Thailand and Taiwan, I lectured to students and colleagues about the rising challenge posed by China. In Hong Kong, I spent moving and memorable hours with elected legislators, politicians, and student leaders from the so-called pan-democrat camp, from moderates who simply want Beijing to deliver on its promises of autonomy and democracy for Hong Kong to radicals who are fed up with the intimidation of the Chinese Communist Party and demand outright independence.

Many of my interlocutors were quite progressive and antiestablishment, including Joshua Wong, a slender, bespectacled student protest leader from Hong Kong's 2014 Umbrella Movement. After being sentenced to a second stint in prison in early 2018, he declared, "They can lock up our bodies, but they cannot lock up our minds."[24]

In the United States, these activists would have been part of the "resistance" to Donald Trump, and indeed, most of them were appalled by his vulgar rhetoric, illiberal attitudes, and authoritarian instincts. Yet they joined with many savvy strategists and conservative commentators in a surprisingly widespread—and to me, stunning—sentiment: gratitude at seeing a U.S. president finally stand up to China.

From India to Japan, from Singapore to Taiwan, I found not only mounting fear of China's ambitions but also growing hunger for a counterweight to it. And you can't counterbalance a rising autocratic superpower without the existing democratic one.

Any such counterstrategy would need civic, political, economic, and military dimensions. Democracies must start by understanding how China is exercising its influence, forging ties, and attaching conditions on its friendship.

That includes confronting Chinese sharp power in the crucial realm of education. University administrators and other education leaders are increasingly recognizing that secret agreements and foreign-government dictates are inconsistent with the mission of education in a free society. That doesn't mean banning all partnerships with China, which would be antithetical to the spirit of democracy and open inquiry. But all agreements for Confucius Institutes and similar ventures should be fully transparent. Faculty, students, and the public should know what personnel and resources China is providing—and whether strings are attached.

Many Chinese offers will need vetting and control. Some colleges and universities will have the resources to assess the language textbooks and other curricular materials that China is providing. Those that can't need help. These schools could form a consortium and recruit expert advisers to ensure that China's materials do not promote political propaganda or bar discussion of certain subjects.

Chinese students abroad deserve protection for their intellectual freedom. Colleges should provide some confidential means to ring the alarm bell when China's government uses the long arms of its influence to try to suppress discussion of subjects it considers taboo or intimidate overseas Chinese students who publicly defy the CCP line on sensitive matters. And student organizations should have to report any funding they receive from a foreign government and secure approval from university authorities. When funding is coming from an autocracy known for trying to stifle freedom of expression at home and abroad, the burden of proof should be on the student organization to demonstrate that its independence and freedom of expression are not being compromised by its receipt of funds.

This principle goes for think tanks and university research projects as well. Foreign funding of all research and program activities should be fully disclosed, along with any objectives or conditions on which the funding depends, so that outside observers can assess whether the money's source might be compromising.

An even stronger imperative is to strengthen U.S. government tracking of Chinese (and other foreign) efforts to influence American policy. When foreign grants have that purpose, U.S. recipients are legally required to register under the Foreign Agents Registration Act (FARA). This legislation, and the Justice Department's enforcement of it, could stand to be strengthened.[25]

Democracies need to raise both public awareness of and legal barriers to authoritarian intrusions into their political lives. For starters, this requires banning foreign contributions to political campaigns, as the Australian government recently passed into law. Such contributions are illegal at the federal level in the United States, but not in all states and municipalities. Anyone in the United States lobbying for a foreign government should have to register under FARA, not simply be allowed to register as a lobbyist, as is now the case. And this should apply to lobbying state and local governments as well. Beyond this, the so-called Drain the Swamp Act, from Representative Peter DeFazio, an Oregon Democrat, would ban all former political appointees to U.S. government positions from lobbying for a foreign government or political party. I would go further: we should extend such a ban to former members of Congress as well (not to mention former presidents, vice presidents, or, in other democracies, prime ministers). The door to political corruption from abroad should be firmly and irrevocably shut.

Since Chinese influence operations are increasingly global, many countries around the world urgently need help in developing tools and knowledge to expose and resist them. Foundations in the wealthy democracies could help to train other countries' journalists and academic researchers in how China's influence activities work, how to track Chinese corporate investments in their countries, and how to monitor the business ties of their own former officeholders. American state and local governments and civil society actors need help—ideally from a federal agency that they could voluntarily approach—in vetting the authenticity of approaches from Chinese individuals, associations, and companies seeking various forms of cooperation and partnership.[26] These may be as they purport to be, and worth evaluating on the merits. Or they could be embedded in the murky and complex architecture of China's official international influence operations, seeking covertly to extend CCP influence into the deep tissues of American democracy.[27] Democracies should also learn from one another about which laws, standards, and tools work best for disclosing (if not banning) foreign campaign contributions, and what digital tools China is selling autocracies to censor the internet and intercept citizens' communications. Finally, financial support from nongovernmental foundations could help independent media in less affluent democracies to better resist China's efforts to buy favorable coverage and bully criticism. We must all be far more aware of the ways that authoritarian influence can penetrate and corrupt open societies.

The High-Tech Threat

On March 22, 2018, President Trump ignited a storm of controversy by authorizing the imposition of tariffs on up to $60 billion in Chinese imports, which he called a response to Beijing's relentless efforts to capture U.S. technology through theft, hacking, and pressure on American companies. The president had a point about China's agenda, even if his riposte was ham-fisted: no development would more profoundly threaten the future of freedom than for an increasingly authoritarian China to achieve military superiority over the United States.

That prospect would have seemed far-fetched even five years ago. But China is now so rapidly advancing its capabilities—in cyberspace, hypersonic weapons, antisatellite systems, drones, robotics, artificial intelligence, advanced computing, and more—that within a decade or two, it may be able to win a war with the United States.

That does not, of course, mean that Trump can win a trade war today. In starting one with China, Trump risked harming not only American farmers and industries but also many economic actors in other parts of Asia. We need a smarter, more comprehensive response. And fortunately, as Congress wakes up to the scope of China's challenge, support for this kind of approach is growing.

The definitive report on China's strategy to acquire by any and all means cutting-edge technology—prepared for the Defense Innovation Unit Experimental (DIUx), a small Pentagon program founded late in the Obama administration and headquartered in Silicon Valley—suggests several more targeted measures to address China's drive for dominance.[28] In particular, we need to strengthen the key mechanism for reviewing foreign investments that could threaten American national security, the Committee on Foreign Investment in the United States (CFIUS). Although CFIUS has long had the power to block foreign investments, the process has been too cumbersome—involving fourteen different U.S. government agencies—to pull off within the committee's mandated ninety-day time frame. With limited resources and jurisdiction, CFIUS has been able to review only about 150 transactions per year—a fraction of the number that have serious implications for U.S. national security.

In an important step forward, in July 2018, Congress gave CFIUS significantly greater scope to review and block foreign acquisitions of U.S. companies and real estate that could harm American national security or competitiveness.[29] The committee may need even more resources and authority to respond quickly to the multiple threats (and not only from China) to American technological leadership.

China's actions also have major personal-security implications in the digital age. Consider the recent Chinese corporate acquisition of the gay dating site Grindr, which is headquartered in Los Angeles.[30] The purchaser was a little-known Chinese online gaming firm called Kunlun, which is not a state company, and Grindr has assured its users that their data will be safe. But some cybersecurity experts have rung alarm bells about the possibility that Beijing could gain broad access to user data. Grindr often serves to facilitate discreet gay hookups, making it "a tantalizing source of information" for Chinese intelligence agencies, which, as one report noted, are building "massive databases" on individual Americans "to have handy" and perhaps use "as leverage in blackmail scenarios."[31]

The DIUx report identifies several other steps to ensure that China does not become the dominant technological leader for decades to come. A crucial one is to increase federal government funding for research and development, which has fallen from 2 percent of GDP in the 1960s to

0.7 percent today (a level below that of China, Japan, South Korea, Germany, and several other countries). Of course, the U.S. private sector invests considerably more than that, but federal funding is crucial to ensuring that we make big, bold bets on complex future technologies, some of which require outlays on infrastructure.[32]

We also need a smarter approach to the question of visas for expert talent. America must do much more to incentivize our students to study science, technology, engineering, and math (the so-called STEM fields). For now, the United States has "a persistent and dramatic shortage of STEM workers."[33] Meanwhile, many Chinese students hope to do graduate work in these critical areas. Either we need to rethink our open doors to Chinese students keen to do advanced graduate study in those technological fields most critical to our national security, or we need to induce them to stay in the United States indefinitely once they get their valuable degrees. Shortening their visas to work in America after they graduate, as the Trump administration announced it would do in May 2018, seems entirely the wrong approach.[34]

At the same time, we need to recruit much more science and engineering talent from countries that do not pose a manifest threat to our national security, such as India. More broadly, the United States should greatly expand the number of foreign expert (H-1B) visas it grants each year so that our companies and universities can hire from abroad the STEM stars we will need to lead the industries of the future. U.S. corporate demand for visas to recruit such foreign workers vastly outstrips what Washington now grants. Studies show that not only does each expert foreign worker create 1.83 jobs among resident Americans, these workers also increase the number of patents awarded to U.S. firms—and thereby buttress America's edge in technological innovation.[35]

All this casts today's debates about immigration in a different light. Immigration *is* a national security issue, but not in the way that Donald Trump and his fellow nativist populists assert. Part of what distinguishes the United States from its two great autocratic rivals is its ability to attract people from all over the world brimming with technical gifts and creative energy. Keeping our gates open to this influx of talent and entrepreneurship will continue to make America great. And assimilating these immigrants into taking on democratic citizenship is a profound opportunity for American democracy. It is a field on which China and Russia—and every other autocracy in the world—simply cannot compete.

TEN

FIGHTING KLEPTOCRACY

The pathway of kleptocracy . . . is: steal, obscure, and then spend.

—Oliver Bullough[1]

I n 2006, the widow of a discount-retail magnate sold her 23,000-square-foot mansion in Washington, D.C., for $15 million in cash. The ornate residence—with seven bedrooms, eleven and a half bathrooms, an elevator, a cinema, "Italian marble floors and a chandelier that had once hung in the Paris Opera House"—is perched strategically in the capital's prestigious Embassy Row district, among the homes of the city's celebrities and power brokers, half a mile from the official residence of the vice president and a mile from the Russian embassy. One of Washington's top political lawyers, Vernon Jordan, lives across the street, and after the 2016 election, the top Trump aide Kellyanne Conway would move in next door. At the time, the home's sale was one of the most expensive in Washington's history. Yet the only thing known about the buyer was the name of the obscure company to which the mansion was officially sold.[2]

Eleven years later, a *Washington Post* report would reveal that the likely real owner was one of Russia's most powerful oligarchs, Oleg Deripaska—the same man who was added to the U.S. sanctions list in

April 2018 for his ties to the Russian government and for suspicions of money laundering, "threatening the lives of business rivals, illegally wiretapping a government official, and taking part in extortion and racketeering."[3]

Deripaska, one of the world's largest aluminum producers, with vast holdings in such other sectors as energy, insurance, and transportation, is a close ally of Russian president Vladimir Putin. The oligarch had long had difficulty getting a U.S. visa, but this did not stop him from periodically traveling to the United States on a Russian diplomatic passport. That let him visit his reported Washington mansion and two Manhattan residences he is said to have purchased through a trust in the British Virgin Islands—a $4.5 million town house in 2006 and a $42.5 million house in 2008.[4] During those years, the Russian metals magnate was not prevented from forging ties with Washington fixers like Paul Manafort, who would briefly chair Donald Trump's presidential campaign and then go on to be convicted of bank and tax fraud in 2018. Nor, according to *Harper's*, was Deripaska barred from donating money through his holding company to prestigious organizations such as the Council on Foreign Relations (which says it was unaware that the money was coming from Deripaska) and the Carnegie Endowment for International Peace (which says it wouldn't take such funds today).[5] Much more troubling is the vast array of lawyers and lobbyists who stand ready—for generous fees—to help dubious figures like Deripaska launder their reputations and break free of international sanctions. "Oleg Deripaska understands better than most Russian oligarchs how money buys influence in Washington," said Michael R. Carpenter, a former official of President Obama's National Security Council.[6] And, observe *New York Times* correspondents Andrew Higgins and Kenneth P. Vogel, "helping deep-pocketed foreign interests massage [American] sanctions and tariffs" has become "one of the fastest-growing elements of the lobbying business."[7]

Standing behind global oligarchs like Deripaska are the autocratic rulers who lead, in effect, state-sponsored crime rings. Putin may be the richest, but he is only one of many. Take Malaysia's former prime minister Najib Razak: he and his cronies are accused by the U.S. Justice Department of stealing some $4.5 billion between 2009 and 2015 through an astonishingly brazen "pump and loot scheme" that siphoned off money raised from government-backed bonds. The Malaysian conduit for the theft was a government development company, 1MDB, which laundered the funds through a complex global web of regional financial centers, secretive shell companies, and giant European and American banks. U.S. court filings allege that "the money went to buy luxury real estate in Manhattan and Beverly Hills; paintings by Monet and Van Gogh; a chunk of one of the world's biggest music-publishing companies; a $35 million Bombardier Global 5000 business jet; a $260 million superyacht called *Equanimity*; and $8 million in jewels bestowed as gifts upon Australian supermodel Miranda Kerr."[8] The stolen funds also covered $85 million in "Las Vegas gambling debts" and tens of millions more invested in a movie production company, which then made a critically hailed Hollywood epic about delirious greed, *The Wolf of Wall Street*.[9]

Like corrupt autocrats and oligarchs from dozens of other countries around the world, Oleg Deripaska and Najib Razak could penetrate American society because of gaping legal holes that not only permit but welcome the laundering of dirty money. As one keen observer has put it, the lack of effective regulation has made the United States, not notorious financial safe havens like Switzerland and the Cayman Islands, "the leading incorporator of anonymous companies."[10] The U.S. Treasury Department estimates the annual flow of laundered money into the United States at $300 billion—equal to 2 percent of the American economy.[11] The comparable estimate is even more startling in the United Kingdom: some $120 billion, equal to nearly 5 percent of the British economy.[12] By one estimate, as much as 8 percent of total global wealth, 30 percent of African wealth, and 50 percent of Russian wealth is held in largely secret offshore accounts.[13]

Global transfers of untraceable funds have enabled a stunning array of venal dictators and their family members, political allies, and business cronies to acquire property and influence in the West as well as to corrupt democracy and the rule of law within free nations. The West "has largely failed to export its democratic norms and is instead witnessing an increasingly coordinated assault on its own value system," warned the Russian anticorruption analyst Ilya Zaslavskiy in a recent paper for the Hudson Institute's trailblazing Kleptocracy Initiative. "This destructive import of corrupt practices and norms comes not only from post-Soviet kleptocratic regimes like Azerbaijan, Kazakhstan, and Russia, but also from China and other countries around the world whose ruling elites now possess far-reaching financial and political interests in the West."[14]

As Charles Davidson, the executive director of the Kleptocracy Initiative, warned in 2017 congressional testimony, kleptocracy is "a relatively new" but ominous threat to our democracies that "should have us on high alert."[15] The online Cambridge Dictionary defines kleptocracy as "a society whose leaders make themselves rich and powerful by stealing from the rest of the people." Modern-day kleptocracy, however, is something more than massive, predatory corruption: it also uses the international financial system to move, mask, and secure ill-gotten fortunes across borders.

As we have seen, nothing more readily saps democracy of its public legitimacy than the widespread perception that government officials are mainly there to enrich themselves, their cronies, and their parties rather than to serve the public. From Brazil to Mexico, from Ukraine to Tunisia, from Mongolia to Moldova, large-scale, endemic corruption poses the single most urgent internal threat to democracy—and renders it all the more vulnerable to external subversion.

The opportunity to loot the public treasury also perpetuates undemocratic behavior and gives both official and hidden ruling elites an overriding incentive to cling to power. From Russia to Venezuela, from Nigeria to Kenya, from Pakistan to Malaysia, kleptocracy has been the most important obstacle preventing democracy from emerging and taking hold. And when illicit funds pour covertly into the banking systems, property markets, and company registries of "advanced" democracies such as America and Great Britain, they too become corrupted and diminished.

In the absence of strong rules and explicit oversight, a powerful authoritarian state like China can work through its wealthy associates to penetrate the politics and policy debates of democracies. A growing number of kleptocracies are "using corrupt businessmen as proxies to advance their political goals" in the West, warns Zaslavskiy.[16] Publicly, these regimes employ lobbyists and publicists to influence Western governments; covertly, they lure current and former public officials with the prospect of money and lucrative employment.

China often deploys such tactics, but probably no Chinese business association with a Western notable can top the relationship that former German chancellor Gerhard Schröder has built with Russia's energy industry. Since he left power in 2005, Schröder—a Social Democrat who pursued an increasingly pro-Russia course during his seven years in power—has become a very wealthy man, "serving as a board member of several consortia in which Russian-government-controlled energy company Gazprom is either the majority or sole shareholder."[17] An outspoken opponent of Western sanctions against Russia, Schröder was elected in September 2017 as chairman of the board of a major target of those sanctions, Russia's largest oil company, Rosneft.

Smaller kleptocracies can play this game adroitly as well. Another post-Soviet regime awash in oil money, Azerbaijan, has managed to neutralize the Council of Europe, a body "whose function is to defend the European Convention of Human Rights" and which the late Czech

president Václav Havel once called "the most important European political forum."[18] In 2000, many liberal members of the Council of
Europe's parliamentary assembly went along with a motion to admit
Azerbaijan, hoping that membership would gradually transform its authoritarian practices. Instead, as Gerald Knaus, chairman of the European Stability Institute, has put it, "Azerbaijan set out to transform the
Council of Europe." The regime showered council deputies with "silk
carpets, gold and silver items, drinks, caviar and money," all while relentlessly attacking the dictatorship's European critics. Elections in
Azerbaijan continued being flagrantly rigged, and the country's president, Ilham Aliyev (whose family has ruled Azerbaijan for twenty-five
years), continued holding some one hundred political prisoners—while
insisting that he could not possibly have any *because* he was a member of
the Council of Europe. In 2009, a parliamentary delegation from the
council endorsed a referendum Aliyev was pushing to remove presidential term limits, calling it a vote for "greater stability." The two German
members of that delegation later became paid lobbyists for Azerbaijan.
Subsequent Council of Europe monitors praised Azerbaijan's farcical
electoral charades with terms like "free, fair and transparent."

Few examples of reciprocal corruption have been as brazen as the
recycling of kleptocratic oil revenue from francophone Africa to political campaigns back in France. Since the 1960s, French politicians have
maintained a special relationship with oil kleptocracies like the Bongo
regime in Gabon, which has bled the country's treasury for half a century. French companies got favorable terms to produce and market African oil; African autocrats got stupendous personal wealth and security
guarantees from the French military. (The Bongo family's thirty-three
French properties include three mansions in Paris and a villa on the
Riviera.) In return, as the intrepid political scientist Brett Carter has
reported, the autocrats "transferred a share of the oil revenue . . . back
to France to fund" Gaullist and other party election campaigns. The

bagman for President Jacques Chirac and his government claimed to have collected some $20 million from African kleptocrats between 1997 and 2005.[19]

When his country's oil wealth proved insufficient for the Republic of Congo's plundering dictator, Denis Sassou-Nguesso, he borrowed money on international markets and then hired lobbyists and bribed politicians to win debt relief. When he ran into debt trouble again in 2017, he hired the disgraced former head of the International Monetary Fund, Dominique Strauss-Kahn, to push for a new round of relief.[20] Like other African kleptocrats, Sassou-Nguesso has also doled out generous contracts to Washington lobbying and PR firms in an effort to launder his reputation and win favorable treatment for his government.[21]

Some francophone kleptocratic dictators seem to have been investing in international media to launder their image. The magazine *Forbes Afrique*, which routinely heaps praise on Sassou-Nguesso, is owned by a Canadian Congolese businessman who "has been implicated in Sassou-Nguesso's money-laundering apparatus."[22] The corrupt dictators of Cameroon and Equatorial Guinea, Paul Biya and Teodoro Obiang, jointly own the magazine *Africa 24*. As Carter notes, the most prominent magazine in francophone Africa, *Jeune Afrique*, "has long had a reputation for selling political coverage to Central African autocrats," which was partially confirmed by a 2005 leaked document.[23]

Kleptocracy, with its corrosive reciprocal effects on democracy, is not limited to Africa's francophone states. Since it struck oil in the 1960s, Nigeria has seen its political elite make off with tens of billions of dollars, the bulk of it recycled into Western property, investments, and banks. The most extreme kleptocrat, the former military dictator Sani Abacha, is believed to have stolen more than $4 billion, most of it sent abroad, during his five years of rule in the 1990s.[24]

In Angola, in just the year 2008, a report by the anticorruption watchdog Global Witness identified a discrepancy of up to $10 billion in the government's own reporting of its oil revenues. Isabel dos Santos, the daughter of Angola's longtime kleptocratic president, José Eduardo dos Santos, "has become one of Portugal's most powerful figures by buying large chunks of the country's banking, media and energy industries," according to *The New York Times*.[25] Even after Isabel dos Santos was fired as head of Angola's oil company in late 2017, after her father finally stepped down from the presidency, her net worth was estimated at $2.2 billion.[26] Such wealth and ambition have won her a place among the West's jet-setting glitterati, letting her swan around at international film festivals while Angola ranks at 150 out of 188 countries in the world in overall human development.

This is not because Angola is poor—in pure money terms, it is a middle-income country—but because its ruling elite have plundered its wealth. Average life expectancy at birth in Angola is only fifty-three years, one of the lowest in the world. Nigeria's is similar. Each of these two oil-rich countries also lags behind the African average in infant mortality and child mortality. As a result, 7 percent of Angola's and Nigeria's infants die before their first birthday, and 10 to 12 percent of children die before they turn five.[27]

In 2015, I ran up against the corrupting impact of this wealth in a small but unsettling way. I was speaking in El Salvador at the Ministerial Conference of the Community of Democracies, which gathers the foreign ministers of some one hundred democracies every other year to renew a commitment to their shared values. But somehow Angola—one of the world's most authoritarian governments—was participating as a full member. In all the years of contentious debates and inevitable compromises over which governments should participate (and thus enjoy a claim to democratic status), this was by far the most egregious affront to the founding purpose of the community. I denounced the decision to include Angola in my public remarks at the conference, only to have the Salvadoran foreign minister defend it with the hackneyed claim that every country had to move at its own pace toward democracy. In private conversations, I was told that Angola was there because Portugal, a member of the community's governing council and Angola's former colonizer, had insisted on it. Months later, after discreetly inquiring in Portugal, I was told that the Portuguese government had pressed the matter as a result of pressure from . . . Isabel dos Santos.

One could dismiss this as a small and symbolic matter. But in Portugal itself, efforts to investigate Angolan corruption and money laundering were short-circuited a few years ago—with an apology from the Portuguese foreign minister—when Angola threatened to pull its investments from the country. And international reports continue to fault Portugal for lax enforcement of multilateral standards on international bribery and money laundering.[28]

International flows of dirty money are not just degrading our own democracies in the West. They are also threatening national sovereignty and security worldwide. By entrenching and empowering the new kleptocrats, these transactions heighten the dangers of political violence, human rights abuses, or the outright collapse of fragile states. When the bottom falls out of political order—whether in Libya or Haiti, Liberia or Yemen—the United States and its Western allies are frequently drawn in. And when kleptocracy sets in, as in Afghanistan, it can be difficult for the United States to get out.[29]

More directly, our security is threatened by a simple fact: if corrupt foreign officials can utilize U.S. shell companies to launder their finances, so can terrorists, drug cartels, human traffickers, and other organized crime networks. Consider the following:

• For years, the notorious Russian arms dealer Viktor Bout allegedly used one of his U.S.-based shell companies to transfer arms to the Taliban.[30] Fortunately, Bout was arrested in Thailand and then extradited to the United States in 2010. He was also a significant arms supplier to African warlords and a major stoker of civil wars. Bout was convicted in 2011 of intending to sell arms to Colombia's FARC rebels to use against U.S. forces. He is now serving a twenty-five-year prison sentence in the United States.

- In four American states—Delaware, Nevada, South Dakota, and Wyoming—it is now so easy to register an anonymous shell company that, as one Kleptocracy Initiative report warned, "ISIS could be operating companies and trust funds domiciled in Delaware."[31]
- In a recent investigation, the U.S. Government Accountability Office was unable "to identify the true beneficial owners of foreign-owned buildings used for about one-third of the federal government's 1,400 'high-security' leases." This raises the absurd and dangerous possibility that the leasing agencies—including the FBI, the Secret Service, the Drug Enforcement Agency, and the Department of Homeland Security—could be working in buildings owned by the very "international criminals or malign foreign powers they are tasked with investigating."[32]

Beyond the national security threats that kleptocracy poses is the humanitarian devastation that it inflicts, especially on poor countries. By definition, all government corruption is a crime against the people—a theft of resources (or a distortion of decisions) that could have advanced the public good but instead were diverted for private gain. Roads and bridges, schools and hospitals, access to justice and clean water, a decent distribution of income—all suffer as a result.

I discovered this viscerally when I lived and taught in Nigeria in the last year of its larcenous Second Republic, in 1982–1983. I watched a kleptocratic political class loot and destroy a democracy and a society, until economic chaos and public anger were so pervasive that students were demonstrating in the streets to urge the military to come back to power. After the generals did so in a New Year's Eve coup, Nigerians discovered that the military was just as venal as the politicians—and even less inclined to circulate some of its plunder around.

Hence, when formal democratic institutions were restored in Nigeria in 1999, they came with greater immunity against future military intervention. Since then, some halting steps have been taken to control corruption, lifting Nigeria from the very bottom few countries to merely the bottom fifth of Transparency International's annual rankings of corruption.[33] But despite earning more than $300 billion in oil revenue since its independence in 1960, Nigeria remains one of the world's poorest countries, in terms of both per capita income and human well-being.

In 2014, while preparing to deliver a lecture in Nigeria, I wondered what difference it would have made if, instead of ranking near the bottom when it came to governance, Nigeria had a similar level to that of nearby Ghana—a genuine democracy that rates near the middle among countries in controlling corruption. What if, instead of having one of every eight of its children die before the age of five, Nigeria had Ghana's rate of child mortality, of one death out of every fourteen? The difference in child deaths over time would have exceeded the death toll of the Nigerian civil war of 1967–1970: more than one million people. And that difference is *entirely due to bad governance.*[34] This is why the former U.N. high commissioner for human rights, Navi Pillay, said in 2013 that "the money lost to corruption every year could feed the world's hungry eighty times over."[35] In poor countries, kleptocracy kills on a grand scale.

Clearly, kleptocracy is a paramount threat to democracy, the rule of law, national security, social justice, and human well-being. But fortunately, it is a menace that we can do something about.

Recovering from Kleptocracy: A 10-Step Program

Beyond the moral imperative, there is one overriding reason to make the battle against kleptocracy a global priority. It would help revive democratic progress in the world.

Just as widespread corruption threatens the legitimacy of democratic rule, its rot undermines autocracies as well. Predatory corruption is the soft underbelly of authoritarian rule. If these dictators' pillaging of their countries was revealed and internationally prosecuted, the domestic and international support base for their rule would begin to unravel.

The most important condition for fighting kleptocracy is political will. Kleptocracy is not just megacorruption; it is the movement and laundering of stolen money across national borders. Kleptocracy thrives not just because the legal and political systems in the countries of origin are debased but because powerful interests in the world's wealthy democracies—"including bankers, real estate brokers, accountants, lawyers, wealth managers, and public-relations agents,"[36] not to mention American state governments—want to cash in on this debasement. This complicity is degrading and endangering our democracies.

The path to reform is not mysterious. It requires closing the loopholes that permit international criminal actors—whether drug lords, terrorists, or corrupt politicians—first, to place their illicit funds in legitimate banks and businesses in the West, using front individuals, anonymous companies, and sophisticated lawyers; second, to layer the money, concealing its origins by transferring it "through multiple bank secrecy jurisdictions" or anonymous shell companies, trusts, and limited partnerships; and third, to circulate the illicit money in the bloodstream of the legitimate economy through the purchase of assets like real estate. When a former Ukrainian prime minister buys a $5 million home in Marin County, California, for example, that should be a red flag.[37]

A 10-step program can close loopholes in the U.S. legal system, strengthen enforcement mechanisms, and generate broader momentum for an international war on kleptocracy. While I offer these steps with the United States in mind, they invoke general principles that all liberal democracies should rally behind. (Many of these reforms are drawn from the superb work of the Kleptocracy Initiative.)[38]

1. **End anonymous shell companies.** Federal law should require the real ownership of all U.S. companies and trusts to be disclosed and listed in a register, which would be accessible at least to law-enforcement agencies and ideally to the public (as is done in the United Kingdom). Deception by owners or agents to mask real ownership should meet with serious civil or criminal penalties. Moreover, the United States should encourage other states to adopt similar laws requiring full transparency in business ownership.

2. **End anonymous real estate purchases.** Washington should require all real estate purchases in the United States to reveal the true owner behind the purchase. Real estate agents, lawyers, and other professionals and firms involved in these transactions should have to undertake serious due diligence to verify the true identity of the purchaser, with biting penalties for negligence or deliberate noncompliance. And a new law should forbid *any* U.S. government agency (especially those conducting sensitive work) from leasing office space from unknown owners or from any owner or business linked to an authoritarian or corrupt government.

3. **Modernize and strengthen the Foreign Agents Registration Act.** We should close the loophole that enables many agents for foreign principals to simply register under less

onerous reporting requirements as lobbyists. We need an integrated system for reporting all lobbying and public relations advocacy on behalf of foreign interests. This line of work has exploded in recent years, with "an estimated 1,000 U.S. lobbyists working for foreign principals" and receiving "half a billion dollars for their services annually,"[39] but almost no one is ever prosecuted for noncompliance with the law. The U.S. Justice Department has a staff of only eight people working to enforce FARA;[40] the department needs more staff, more investigative powers, and more painful civil or criminal penalties for violations.

4. **Strengthen prohibitions and monitoring of political contributions by foreign actors.** Foreign political and campaign contributions are forbidden in the United States (except by permanent residents), but only comprehensively at the federal level, and some foreign contributions could be filtering in through donations made by lobbyists and agents for foreign actors. Foreign contributions to *all* candidates and political campaigns, at every level of government, should be prohibited in the United States, and all political contributions by foreign agents should be monitored by a well-staffed federal agency. Other democracies around the world should also ban foreign financial contributions to their political parties and campaigns.

5. **Ban former U.S. officials and members of Congress from lobbying for or representing foreign governments.** Soon after entering the White House in January 2017, President Trump signed an executive order restricting the future lobbying activities of his political appointees and banning them for life from lobbying for foreign governments or political parties.[41] This lifetime ban should be embedded in law and extended to retired members of Congress as well. And the Justice

Department should maintain a list of foreign businesses, foundations, and organizations that, because of links to their authoritarian governments, are also off-limits for representation by former U.S. officials. We may even want to go further: do we really want to allow some future retired American official or member of Congress to work for a company effectively controlled by the Kremlin or the Chinese Communist Party?

6. **Modernize the anti-money-laundering system.** The current U.S. system has a key flaw: it relies on someone to report suspicious activity, rather than empowering the Treasury Department's Financial Crimes Enforcement Network to conduct its own investigations. As a result, money launderers "face a less than 5 percent risk of conviction" in the United States, according to the Financial Action Task Force, an independent intergovernmental body that fights money laundering.[42] We need a robustly funded and staffed watchdog mechanism that applies to financial institutions as well as to the "enablers" of money laundering—lawyers, investment advisers, real estate agents, and so on. In addition, the United States should adopt something like Britain's landmark 2017 legislation, which holds that if a foreign person with links to crime or public wealth in his home country makes an extravagant purchase (for example, property or jewels) that seems to be beyond his explainable means, law-enforcement agencies can investigate the source of the money. If the source is found to be corrupt or the individual cannot account for his or her wealth, the assets can be seized.

7. **Increase the resources that the United States and other rule-of-law states devote to monitoring, investigating, and prosecuting grand corruption and money laundering.** This should include greater cooperation among various national

intelligence and law-enforcement agencies to identify illicit funds and property and track and disrupt money laundering.

8. **Strengthen cooperation among democracies in fighting kleptocracy and ending "golden visas."** Because Russian kleptocracy represents such a serious common threat, NATO is a logical forum for the Western democracies to share intelligence, upgrade and harmonize their laws and strategies, and cooperate in tracking, sanctioning, and apprehending suspects. This will prevent kleptocrats from obscuring their wealth by playing off one jurisdiction against another.[43] More must be done to call out countries with lax enforcement and help them plug loopholes, perhaps through a new State Department office to coordinate U.S. antikleptocracy efforts. One especially high priority for standardizing these rules should be closing down the racket in securing residency and citizenship abroad; it is far too easy for the rich to buy a pathway to citizenship in major democracies such as the United States, Britain, Canada, and Australia—and it is easier still in small EU countries that give kleptocrats a gateway to the rest of the European Union.[44]

9. **Raise public awareness about kleptocracy in Russia and other offending states.** The people of Russia—and other deeply corrupt states—deserve to know exactly who is pillaging their wealth, laundering it, and extravagantly investing it abroad. The Kleptocracy Initiative recommends establishing a Fund for the Russian People, into which seized assets could be deposited until such time as they could be returned to "a state governed by the rule of law."[45] But why not create such a fund—and publicize the details of known cases of money laundering and asset seizures—for all of the world's leading kleptocracies? And why not offer fast-track asylum and financial rewards to whistle-blowers from all countries who expose

colossal government corruption that is laundered through the
United States and other advanced democracies?

10. **Increase international support for investigative journalism, NGOs, and official institutions working to monitor
and control corruption around the world.** The best lines of
defense against kleptocracy are usually found within the countries where it originates. This demands more than rewards for
a few daring whistle-blowers. We need to do much more to
support the frontline defenders of the global rule of law. Courageous journalists are working at great risk to expose grand
corruption and increase government accountability in their
troubled countries. NGOs like the local chapters of Transparency International are lobbying to plug loopholes in monitoring and reporting, establish effective freedom-of-information
laws, and give anticorruption agencies more power, resources,
and autonomy. In many corrupt, low-grade democracies, dedicated civil servants and even some political appointees are
trying against great odds to strengthen their countries' institutions to fight endemic corruption. All these efforts need our
financial and technical support—as well as our diplomatic
backing, to help spare brave anticorruption activists from arrest and assault. A prime example of the kind of global effort
that merits support from democracy-promotion foundations
and private philanthropies is the International Consortium of
Investigative Journalists, which broke the Panama Papers
story and now draws together more than 220 investigative
journalists and more than 100 media organizations from some
80 countries to collaborate on in-depth investigative stories.[46]

These ten steps constitute an ambitious but feasible agenda for a serious assault on global kleptocracy. We might reach for one more distant
star in the future: U.S. district court judge Mark Wolf has proposed es-

tablishing an international anticorruption court with a global role similar to that of the International Criminal Court. Where national judicial
systems are capable of investigating and prosecuting grand corruption,
they would continue to do so. But in countries whose judicial systems
are too weak, politicized, or corrupt to act, the new court could step in.
Such a court might not only punish global corruption but help return its
rotten fruit back to the country of origin once a more transparent government was in place. Today, the concept is no more than a gleam in the
eye of some farsighted international lawyers. But many innovations have
started audaciously. Quoting a line often attributed to Nelson Mandela,
Judge Wolf says, "It's always impossible until it happens."[47]

The Autocrats' Accomplice

We cannot reverse the worldwide surge of authoritarianism unless we
rein in its accomplice, kleptocracy. Increasingly, the destruction of democracy, the repression of civil liberties, the plundering of public wealth,
and the international laundering of this loot are intertwined in what
amounts to a death embrace for freedom and the rule of law. While the
West's liberal democracies now account for less than half of the global
economy,[48] they remain the principal financial and cultural destinations
for ill-gotten wealth. This gives these democracies enormous leverage.
They must use it.

This is a question of survival, not just morality. Kleptocracy is a cancer that is eating away at the vital organs of our own democracies—our
norms, our rule of law, even our electoral processes. Fighting back is
essential to the defense of freedom.

ELEVEN

A FOREIGN POLICY FOR FREEDOM

We must be staunch in our conviction that freedom is not the sole prerogative of a lucky few, but the inalienable and universal right of all human beings. . . . The objective I propose is quite simple to state: to foster the infrastructure of democracy, the system of a free press, unions, political parties, universities, which allows a people to choose their own way to develop their own culture, to reconcile their own differences through peaceful means.

—RONALD REAGAN, ADDRESS TO THE BRITISH
PARLIAMENT, JUNE 8, 1982

T he most obvious response to the ill winds blowing from the world's autocracies is to help the winds of freedom blowing in the other direction. The democracies of the West cannot save themselves if they do not stand with democrats around the world.

This is truer now than ever, for several reasons. We live in a globalized world, one in which models, trends, and ideas cascade across borders. Any wind of change may gather quickly and blow with gale force. People everywhere form ideas about how to govern—or simply about which forms of government and sources of power may be irresistible—based on what they see happening elsewhere. We are now immersed in a fierce global contest of ideas, information, and norms. In the digital age, that contest is moving at lightning speed, shaping how people think about their political systems and the way the world runs. As doubts about and threats to democracy are mounting in the West, this is not a contest that the democracies can afford to lose.

Globalization, with its flows of trade and information, raises the stakes for us in another way. Authoritarian and badly governed regimes increasingly pose a direct threat to popular sovereignty and the rule of law in our own democracies. Covert flows of money and influence are subverting and corrupting our democratic processes and institutions. They will not stop just because Americans and others pretend that we have no stake in the future of freedom in the world. If we want to defend the core principles of self-government, transparency, and accountability in our own democracies, we have no choice but to promote them globally.

It is not enough to say that dictatorship is bad and that democracy, however flawed, is still better. Popular enthusiasm for a lesser evil cannot be sustained indefinitely. People need the inspiration of a positive vision. Democracy must demonstrate that it is a just and fair political system that advances humane values and the common good.

To make our republics more perfect, established democracies must not only adopt reforms to more fully include and empower their own citizens. They must also support people, groups, and institutions struggling to achieve democratic values elsewhere. The best way to counter Russian rage and Chinese ambition is to show that Moscow and Beijing are on the wrong side of history; that people everywhere yearn to be free; and that they can make freedom work to achieve a more just, sustainable, and prosperous society.

In our networked age, both idealism and the harder imperatives of global power and security argue for more democracy, not less. For one thing, if we do not worry about the quality of governance in lower-income countries, we will face more and more troubled and failing states. Famine and genocide are the curse of authoritarian states, not democratic ones. Outright state collapse is the ultimate, bitter fruit of tyranny. When countries like Syria, Libya, and Afghanistan descend into civil war; when poor states in Africa cannot generate jobs and improve their citizens' lives due to rule by corrupt and callous strongmen; when Central American societies are held hostage by brutal gangs and klepto-cratic rulers, people flee—and wash up on the shores of the democra-cies. Europe and the United States cannot withstand the rising pressures of immigration unless they work to support better, more stable and ac-countable government in troubled countries. The world has simply grown too small, too flat, and too fast to wall off rotten states and pre-tend they are on some other planet.

Hard security interests are at stake. As even the Trump administra-tion's 2017 National Security Strategy makes clear, the main threats to U.S. national security all stem from authoritarianism, whether in the form of tyrannies from Russia and China to Iran and North Korea or in the guise of antidemocratic terrorist movements such as ISIS.[1] By sup-porting the development of democracy around the world, we can deny these authoritarian adversaries the geopolitical running room they seek. Just as Russia, China, and Iran are trying to undermine democracies to bend other countries to their will, so too can we contain these autocrats' ambitions by helping other countries build effective, resilient democra-cies that can withstand the dictators' malevolence.

Of course, democratically elected governments with open societies will not support the American line on every issue. But no free society wants to mortgage its future to another country. The American national interest would best be secured by a pluralistic world of free countries— one in which autocrats can no longer use corruption and coercion to gobble up resources, alliances, and territory.

If you look back over our history to see who has posed a threat to the United States and our allies, it has always been authoritarian regimes and empires. As political scientists have long noted, no two democracies have ever gone to war with each other—ever. It is not the democracies of the world that are supporting international terrorism, proliferating weapons of mass destruction, or threatening the territory of their neighbors.

For all these reasons, we need a new global campaign for freedom. Everything I am proposing in this book plays a role in that campaign, but in this chapter, I am concerned more narrowly with the ways that we can directly advance democracy, human rights, and the rule of law in the twenty-first-century world.

As with any policy area, many of the challenges can be somewhat technical, requiring smart design and the careful management of programs and institutions. Those operational debates I leave for another venue. Here, I make a more basic case for four imperatives. First, we must support the democrats of the world—the people and organizations struggling to create and improve free and accountable government. Second, we must support struggling and developing democracies, helping them to grow their economies and strengthen their institutions. Third, we must pressure authoritarian regimes to stop abusing the rights and stealing the resources of their citizens, including by imposing sanctions on dictators to make them think hard about their choices and separate them from both their supporters and the people at large. Finally, we need to reboot our public diplomacy—our global networks of information and ideas—for today's fast-paced age of information and disinformation. For the sake of both our interests and our values, we need a foreign policy that puts a high priority on democracy, human rights, and the rule of law.

Minding Our Own Business

Not everyone agrees, of course. Plenty of critics and skeptics call this approach foolish, arrogant, or misplaced. Over the past decade, these objections have intensified even as the need to buttress democracy has grown increasingly urgent. But many of these critics are smart and principled, and they deserve a response.

Perhaps the most common critique is that the way other people run their governments is none of our business—that we should keep our arrogant noses out of other people's affairs.[2] I'd argue that supporting democracy is very much our business; in fact, it is a compelling national interest of the United States.

This doesn't mean that we should push "our" model (or any one specific form) of democracy. Nor does promoting democracy require an arrogant tone. In countless lectures in authoritarian countries, and in working with democratic activists from Nigeria to Nepal, I have found that openness and humility count for a lot. When prodemocracy programs and speakers present the United States in a balanced light, honestly reflecting on its democratic shortcomings, it preempts a lot of suspicion and criticism. Such candor and self-confidence say that we are all on a journey toward better, freer, more accountable government, and that both old and young democracies gain from partnership. And most of all, they show that in a real democracy, even those speaking or working on its behalf are willing—and free—to be critical.

A second critique argues that we should not push such "Western" values as democracy and human rights on non-Western societies. This kind of cultural relativism has always struck me as a deeper form of arrogance. It suggests that freedom, while precious to people in the West, isn't needed by people from other cultures. Or it implicitly argues that people elsewhere don't have the same innate rights as Westerners do. But since the end of World War II, many international treaties and declarations have codified civil and political rights as *universal* human rights. This critique also suggests that liberal democratic values—individual rights, political accountability, and limited government—have their roots only in the Western Enlightenment, when in fact one can point to rich, relevant, and resonant intellectual traditions about self-government and human dignity in many other cultures.³ And finally, as we have seen, this argument simply doesn't accord with the public-opinion surveys, which show that the desire for democratic, accountable government is broadly and even intensely shared across cultures.

Well, fine, says a third critique, but we need to put "America first," and that means backing authoritarian allies whenever we have to—even when they are corrupt and unsavory figures like Egypt's dictator, Abdel Fattah al-Sisi. However, no serious strategy for expanding democracy argues that we should engage *only* with democratic rulers. Clearly, Saudi Arabia is not going to become a democracy tomorrow, and Western interests require working, if not cordial, relationships with many authoritarian countries. But they do not require that we ignore, condone, or, even worse, support brazen violations of human rights, such as the merciless Saudi military campaign in Yemen, which has displaced more than two million people and left eight million in need of emergency food, or the Saudi regime's shocking murder of Jamal Khashoggi.⁴

Even when dealing with autocrats friendly to Washington, we can—and must—raise human rights concerns, support advocates for freedom and accountability, and encourage political reform. The old line about Nicaraguan strongman Anastasio Somoza, often attributed to President Franklin Roosevelt—"He may be a son of a bitch, but he's *our* son of a bitch"—only goes so far in securing the national interest. After all, Somoza fell to an anti-American revolution. So did the U.S.-backed shah of Iran. In Congo, Haiti, and Somalia, chaos has followed the collapse of corrupt but pro-American dictatorships. When we uncritically back such regimes and just assume that they will hang on, it often ends badly—both for their people and for us. Secretary of State Condoleezza Rice had it right in her 2005 speech in Cairo: "For sixty years, my country, the United States, pursued stability at the expense of democracy in this region, here in the Middle East—and we achieved neither."⁵

Of course, any mention of the George W. Bush administration provokes a fourth critique: Wait, you mean democracy promotion, as in

Iraq? But the ill-fated and ill-advised war of choice in 2003 should not discredit the project of advancing democracy. We should never go to war for the purpose of fostering democratic change, and we should never invoke the cause of democracy to justify an otherwise foolish decision to invade a sovereign state. One can oppose the decision to invade Iraq (as I did in 2003) and still believe that we should assist *peaceful* efforts to build democracy around the world—even in Iraq (as I also tried to do in 2004, as a U.S. adviser in post-Saddam Iraq). After all, supporting democracy is not about the use of force, and it's not about imposing our will or our values. Rather, it's a long-term bet on peaceful processes of democratic change, and on the people trying to bring them about.

A fifth critique says that democracy will take care of itself once countries develop and grow rich. Forget about promoting democracy, these critics say: just support economic development, public health, and education, and political change will follow later.

But there is no evidence that authoritarian rule provides a surer path to economic development than democracy does. And in Africa, it is the democracies whose economies have generally been growing faster since the mid-1990s, while all of the continent's development disasters have occurred in authoritarian states.[6] So why should we condemn people to decades of corrupt tyranny when it isn't necessary for economic growth— and probably impedes it?

Sixth, we often hear an ostensibly budget-conscious critique, from both the Donald Trump right and some on the Bernie Sanders left: We need to worry about our own needs in the United States, rather than fret about other nations' problems; we just can't afford to keep dishing out these huge sums to help other countries.

In fact, our investments in democracy are a great bargain. When Americans are asked what percent of the federal budget is spent on foreign aid, the average answer is about 30 percent.[7] Not even close. Foreign aid in all forms—*including* the $9 billion we give annually in security assistance—represents only 1 percent of the annual federal budget. By a generous estimate, U.S. development assistance comes to only about $30 billion annually, and democracy and governance assistance is just some 8 percent of that (about $2.3 billion in 2018).[8] Throw in the public-diplomacy efforts to support U.S. international broadcasting and counter the authoritarians' influence operations, and the amount we spend to promote democracy, freedom, and accountability around the world is still much less than 1/10 of 1 percent of the federal budget.

Finally, some critics argue that it's too risky to try to help out democrats abroad, or warn that we can't make a difference. However, from Portugal to South Africa and Chile, international assistance has repeatedly helped tip the balance toward democracy in countries trying to leave autocracy behind.

Today, many democracies are decaying or are at risk of backsliding into authoritarian rule. Does anyone really think that people in the Philippines, Tunisia, or Ukraine will be better off—or that the United States will be more secure—if these countries fall back into autocracy? And could life in desperate, disintegrating autocracies like Venezuela and Zimbabwe be worse under democracy?

There is no guarantee that an attempt at democracy will succeed. But it would be beneath our heritage for the United States to tell the people of Egypt or Libya *not* to demand freedom, or to tell the people of Iran or Russia *not* to protest a stolen election, or to tell the people of Cambodia or Venezuela *not* to rally against an opposition leader's arrest. It is not America's place to tell those who long for liberty to wait for it. And shunning them is not consistent with who we are as a people.

Helping Burma's Democrats

Over more than four decades traveling around the world trying to understand what makes democracy work, I've come to no stronger conclusion than this: democracy is built not by abstract economic or historical forces but by people. Where we find people risking and sacrificing for liberty, struggling for democracy, fighting corruption, resisting human rights abuses, building grassroots organizations, educating their fellow citizens, and advocating for the same freedoms we sometimes take for granted, we need to support them.

In my research, teaching, and travels, I have met thousands of activists, intellectuals, and politicians working for freedom and good governance in their home countries. They have inspired me, kept me focused, and spurred me to write this book.

Zin Mar Aung was twelve years old when she witnessed the "88 revolution" in Burma.[9] The 1988 uprising against a quarter century of military dictatorship began with protests among university students in Yangon (formerly known as Rangoon) and quickly marshaled hundreds of thousands of people from all walks of life. As Zin Mar saw students march past her house, she was moved to bring them food and water. The protests spread from the universities to the high schools, and she struggled to understand: What is democracy? What are human rights? Why are these young people—some of them former students of her schoolteacher father—protesting?

Then, on September 18, the military staged a bloody coup to restore order. Zin Mar saw soldiers shoot their fellow citizens in the streets of Yangon and watched her father scramble to hide potentially incriminating statements about freedom, for fear that their home might be searched.

In May 1990, the Burmese military organized elections for a parliament that would write a constitution. Not quite yet fourteen, Zin Mar became an active supporter of the dissident Aung San Suu Kyi and her National League for Democracy (NLD). The NLD won those elections in a landslide, but rather than hand over power, the military refused to recognize the results. Hearing only the government line on state radio and television, she turned, as so many Burmese did, to the BBC and the Voice of America to get truthful news.

Several years later, her most powerful democracy lessons came every weekend outside the Yangon residence of Aung San Suu Kyi, when the Lady (as she was known) would emerge from her house to meet with supporters and answer questions. There, Zin Mar learned about the Czech dissident Václav Havel, about other struggles for democracy, and about why citizen participation is vital to a good society. She joined a poetry club that doubled as an underground student movement at her university. She and her friends started going to the American Center (a cultural center and library sponsored by the U.S. diplomatic mission) and the British Council (a similar U.K. entity) to learn English. At the American Center, they discovered leaders like Lincoln and Martin Luther King Jr. and talked about America's struggles to perfect its democracy and secure civil rights.

In 1998, on the tenth anniversary of the 88 uprising, Zin Mar was arrested at a protest rally, after she read a poem calling for the military to recognize the results of the 1990 election. Hundreds of others were also swept up in the new wave of repression. Zin Mar was swiftly sentenced without trial to twenty-eight years in prison.

Zin Mar would spend the next eleven years in jail, nine of them in solitary confinement. She willed herself to survive. She liked music and maintained her spirit by singing revolutionary songs from Burmese politics. In 2007, the regime started releasing political prisoners. She refused to sign a pledge to stay out of politics. It cost her another two years of her life.

Finally, in 2009, Zin Mar was released. Before long, she was forming organizations to conduct civic education, promote ethnic tolerance, and aid former prisoners of conscience, especially women. She connected with other former activists and political prisoners, some of whom she met anew at the American Center. They started talking about why the movement had come up short and realized that they needed a deeper strategy. The democratization of Burma would take a long time. They had to combat the idea, which the military had drummed into two generations of Burmese, that democracy was incompatible with Asian culture. They had to create active, informed citizens.

In September 2011, Zin Mar joined with other former political prisoners to launch the Yangon School of Political Science, which has sought to educate a new generation of Burmese citizens about democracy. Half a century of military authoritarianism had left an intellectual wasteland. The Yangon School moved quickly to fill the gap, and it has been my honor to teach there and help stock their library (which will include this book). In 2012, Zin Mar Aung received the U.S. State Department's International Woman of Courage Award, but her highest honor came in 2015, when she was elected to parliament as a member of the NLD. Today, she works from both inside and outside the system to represent citizen concerns, roll back military domination, and promote democracy.

Zin Mar's life underscores some important lessons about the international dimensions of democratic change. Early on, she drew inspiration from U.S. and British resources on democratic values, institutions, and struggles. Later, those countries provided safe spaces for reading and discussion. Sustained economic and diplomatic sanctions by the United States and other Western democracies (as well as the World Bank) left the Burmese regime more isolated and stressed. Key military officers came to fear that Myanmar (as the country is now formally called) would become a vassal state of China if it did not forge other economic and political partnerships. This helped spur the military to embark on a path of constitutional reform beginning in 2008.

Zin Mar was released the following year, and Aung San Suu Kyi was released from years of house arrest in late 2010. In 2012, her party entered parliament after winning forty-three of the forty-four seats it contested in by-elections. As the transition got going, a new American ambassador, Derek Mitchell, made advancing democratic reforms the central focus of U.S. diplomacy. Zin Mar and the Yangon School obtained international support for their civic work. New members of the country's parliament have received extensive training from the U.S.-based National Democratic Institute (of which Mitchell is now president), enhancing their skill and confidence. For some democratic MPs with strong activist credentials but only rudimentary education, that training has addressed such basic needs as how to set up a Facebook account, do internet research, and achieve proficiency in English.

Today, Burma is stuck in transition; the military remains the most powerful political force in the country, and Aung San Suu Kyi's leadership has been tainted by her callousness—or worse—in the face of attacks on the country's Muslim minorities. Burma's democrats need financial support from the United States and Europe to build the infrastructure of democracy: representative institutions, parties, and a robust civil society of independent associations, media outlets, and think tanks. And they need the West to press the military to cease its ongoing abuses and permit genuine democratic reforms. Zin Mar's story is inspiring, but her country's future is unclear.

Supporting Democrats Worldwide

One of the most noble—and cost-effective—things that the United States does in the world is to support people such as Zin Mar Aung. Some of this support comes from grants by nongovernmental foundations, including the National Endowment for Democracy (a private, nonprofit foundation funded largely by the U.S. Congress) and private groups like the Open Society Foundation, Freedom House, and the Ford Foundation.[10] These groups (along with the State Department and the U.S. Agency for International Development, or USAID) support a plethora of efforts to educate people about democracy, defend human rights, monitor elections, empower women, combat corruption, extend the freedom of the press, and more. The endowment's two party institutes, the National Democratic Institute and the International Republican Institute, work worldwide to help strengthen democratic parties, legislatures, and local governments, combat vote fraud, increase government openness, and fight disinformation.

While the United States is the largest spender in democracy assistance, it is far from the only one. The European Union, individual European countries (especially Germany and the Scandinavians), Canada, and Australia also provide important support. So do a few emerging democracies, such as Taiwan.

People must secure their own freedom, but such democracy assistance can make a big difference. International support for democratic parties, trade unions, civic education, and election monitoring contributed to the democratic transitions in the Philippines, Poland, Nicaragua, Chile, Zambia, South Africa, and many other countries in the 1980s and '90s. It facilitated electoral transitions to democracy in Serbia, Georgia, and Ukraine in the early 2000s and in Gambia in 2015.

Autocrats like Vladimir Putin accuse organizations like the National Endowment for Democracy of engineering "regime change." Hardly. These organizations invest in smart, spirited citizens seeking freedom, openness, and accountability in their countries. But those independent citizens and groups chart their own course.[11] If transitions to more open rule occur, international assistance helps these actors build the culture and the institutions of sustainable democracy. In poor countries with traumatic histories of repression and conflict—including Burma, Nepal, Liberia, and Sierra Leone—this international support makes it possible for civil society to function, for representative institutions to gain a footing, and for democracy to have a chance.

In recent years, democracy assistance efforts have increasingly emphasized tackling corruption and fighting human rights abuses. Consider Latin America, where Brazil's so-called Lava Jato (car wash) bribery scandal brought down a president of Brazil and implicated elected officials in nearly a dozen other countries. Projects supported by the National Endowment for Democracy are training journalists in investigative reporting; monitoring corruption cases and tracking money laundering; and convening civil servants, legal authorities, journalists, and civil-society leaders to discuss reforms.

You can't fight corruption and abuse of power without strong, independent media. In February 2017, when *The Washington Post* adopted its new motto, "Democracy dies in darkness," it could also have said, "Autocracy wilts in sunlight." Every dictator tries to control, corrupt, or close free media outlets, and for good reason. Nothing threatens the concentration of power as much as honest, probing reporting about its abuses. Transitions to democracy share a common thread: independent journalists who report news and voice critiques that the state-controlled media won't touch. Whether it's the underground samizdat press, passed from hand to hand in the Soviet era; the Serbian B92 radio station, whose vigorous reporting exposed the pointless wars and violent repression of the pitiless Slobodan Milošević; or *Malaysiakini*, the online newspaper in Malaysia that opened up new space for truthful reporting, independent media outlets give the lie to the state's propaganda and rip the cover off its venality, arrogance, and incompetence. Hence, a significant share of National Endowment for Democracy grants now support online and alternative media, independent social media content, training in professional standards, enhanced digital security for media and NGOs operating in autocracies, and local efforts to expose authoritarian propaganda. Even under ruthless regimes like Russia today, the endowment's grants are helping intrepid journalists report the news that the state media suppresses or distorts.[12]

Among the endowment's leading Africa grantees is Maka Angola, a website for investigative journalism and democracy advocacy led since 2008 by its founding editor, Rafael Marques de Morais.[13] Over the past two decades, Marques's reports have exposed the links between the regime's plundering of Angola's vast oil and diamond wealth and its rampant human rights abuses, as well as oil multinationals' degradation of the environment. He has detailed shocking abuses in the criminal justice system, including a man who was now in his eighth year of "preventive detention" after having gotten drunk and fallen asleep in a stranger's minivan. Marques has appealed passionately for transparency and the rule of law as the only antidote to wanton misrule.[14]

Marques, who has won numerous prizes for journalistic excellence, shows how resolute reporting and bold activism go hand in hand in the struggle for freedom. It takes great courage to walk that road. Marques was first arrested and charged with defamation in 1999 for an article titled "The Lipstick of Dictatorship," which bluntly called José Eduardo dos Santos, Angola's strongman president, a dictator and held him squarely responsible for "the destruction of the country."[15] Thrown into Luanda's dreaded Viana Prison, Marques won the confidence of his fellow inmates and uncovered atrocious state crimes, including a cell in which the prisoners were starving because they had no relatives to bring them food. When he complained about the situation, he was punished with eleven days in solitary confinement, where he slept on a cement floor surrounded by cockroaches.

Three things saved Marques: a defiant will, a sharp wit, and robust outside support. The Committee to Protect Journalists persistently publicized his case. The Open Society Foundation (whose programs in Angola he was managing) came to his defense. For the first time, the Catholic bishops of Angola rallied behind a victim of political persecution. After forty days, he was released when the U.S. ambassador to the United Nations, Richard Holbrooke, made it clear that he intended to see Marques in prison when he visited Angola. Marques was later convicted of causing "injury" to President dos Santos's reputation but was dismissed with a fine and a suspended sentence.

Marques didn't let up. Using prison records given to him by an inmate, he exposed other prison abuses, such as a warden who used prisoners as slave laborers on his farm. He unmasked cavalier waste by the government of Angola's oil-rich Cabinda province, which—in a single year—spent $2.4 million on Christmas gifts even while most of its people were trapped in extreme poverty. He documented sadistic human rights abuses against anyone who got in the way of diamond mining by the Angolan regime's crony companies. After Marques published a 2011 book documenting widespread torture and murders of villagers living near the diamond mines,[16] he filed crimes-against-humanity charges against seven Angolan army generals. They in turn pressed defamation charges, threatening Marques with a $1.6 million penalty and nine years in prison. He shrugged: "I'm not afraid to go to jail," he said, "because it will be an opportunity to do human rights work inside the jail."[17] In July 2018, he and his journalist codefendant were acquitted of defamation charges by a provincial court.[18]

Help Democracies, Pressure Autocracies

To survive, democracies must deliver. People don't expect miracles at the start of a new democracy, but they do expect that the new system will at least gradually improve the economy and reduce corruption. Democracies are often born amid crisis, so any strategy for advancing rule by the people must support new and fragile republics in tough times. The biggest success stories in international assistance—the Marshall Plan after World War II and the enlargement of the European Union after the end of the Cold War—involved big, bold bets to support emerging democracies, steering transformative levels of aid and investment to Western Europe and then (two generations later) to Eastern Europe.

Today, we again need daring investments to support democracy in troubled strategic places. Consider Ukraine. In 2014, when Russia's authoritarian ally, Viktor Yanukovych, was forced from power by popular protests, the Kremlin went to war against democracy, conquering a piece of Ukraine's territory (Crimea), assaulting the country's eastern region, and trying to strangle its economy.

It is difficult to imagine a more strategically important country for democracy than Ukraine, the biggest independent state between Russia and the European Union, and a nation with nearly a third the population of Russia. Yet simply pouring money into Ukraine's chronically corrupt system is hardly a promising bet for democracy. We need tough love: invest heavily in Ukraine, but only if its government—led by an elected president, Petro Poroshenko, who straddles the past and the future—adopts difficult reforms to make effective use of foreign aid and save the country from Kremlin sabotage.[19]

Ukraine is the classic swing state. It could stride forward, for the first time in its history, toward genuine democracy and the rule of law. Or it could remain so trapped in the parasitic clutches of corrupt oligarchs that it is captured by an expansionist Kremlin. Helping Ukraine's democrats requires carefully calibrated support. Ukraine's civil society needs financial and technical assistance from Europe and the United States to help it build public pressure for reforms.[20] Ukraine also deserves defensive military equipment (such as antitank missiles) to fend off Russian military aggression. But its government must also show that it is serious about reducing corruption and modernizing the state to merit the levels of financial assistance required to revive the economy and win reelection.

A somewhat similar dynamic holds true in Tunisia, the lone Arab country to have become a viable democracy after throwing off tyranny during the 2011 Arab Spring. With its higher levels of education and economic development, its secular traditions, and its distance from the region's hottest cauldrons of conflict, Tunisia is the Arab country best positioned to develop a lasting democracy. But since parliamentary elections in 2014, Tunisia has seen many of the same problems as Ukraine—a weakening of the will for economic and political reform, a resurgence of corruption, and the resurfacing of crooked elites from the old order.

So a similarly delicate balancing act is needed: combining support for Tunisia's democrats with a tough-love strategy that conditions transfor-

mative levels of economic aid on the government's willingness to implement sweeping reforms. Carefully conditioned aid can help sweep away
the old networks of crony capitalism and promote a new kind of reform
coalition, uniting young people who want economic opportunity, entrepreneurs who want a level playing field, and citizens who want government transparency.[21]

Since around 2000, foreign aid experts have recognized the need to
link economic assistance to better governance. In my early travels and
research, I had seen how unconditional aid let venal government officials skim off their countries' resources without delivering much in
return. By the 1990s, I began to argue that large aid flows to such governments simply perpetuated endemic corruption. Under such circumstances, aid was just like oil: free income to be stolen and squandered. I
urged the World Bank, USAID, and anyone else who would listen to
sharply reduce aid to governments that would not reform, to channel as
much of it as possible through NGOs, and to reward reform-minded,
democratic governments with increased assistance.[22]

Because so much of the U.S. foreign-assistance budget is constrained
by congressional earmarks, which direct aid to very specific purposes, I
didn't get very far. But in 2002, President George W. Bush initiated a
new development-aid mechanism, the Millennium Challenge Account,
to reward the countries that showed a more serious commitment to
development. The new Millennium Challenge Corporation, which administers the account, was directed to measure countries' performance
on democratic governance, economic openness, and investments in their
people, and poor countries that ranked highly on these measures qualified for significant new aid grants. The countries themselves propose
the priorities for spending this aid, crafted in consultation with their
civil societies and private sectors. The logic is straightforward: "By fo-
cusing on economic growth in countries with good governance, U.S.
development dollars have a bigger impact on poverty reduction."[23]

There is a flip side of this game of incentives: sanctions to punish particularly bad governments. Generally, sanctions (or the threat thereof) work only when they reinforce domestic pressures for change and when the target countries have economic, geopolitical, social, or cultural ties with the country imposing the sanctions. The denser the U.S. ties of trade, investment, and partnership, the more the target country has to lose from sanctions, and the more leverage Washington can apply. This dynamic has let the United States pressure authoritarian regimes at critical moments: in South America in the late 1970s and early '80s, then later in the Philippines, South Korea, Taiwan, and white supremacist South Africa.

The problem is that the United States often has deep ties with autocratic regimes because they have things we want—typically oil (as in Saudi Arabia, other Gulf states, Nigeria, Angola, and Azerbaijan) or security cooperation (as with Egypt, Pakistan, Ethiopia, and Kenya). The question then becomes, What are we willing to risk to press for democracy and human rights?

U.S. administrations have often proved overly timid, overestimating the risks that such regimes will cut all cooperation and underestimating their needs for American support. But some caution is understandable. Most American diplomats and policy makers are in their positions for limited periods of time, which reinforces the instinct to avoid a rupture for which they can be blamed. More important, pushing the envelope of risk requires a bold vision of America's true national interest, which can come only with farsighted presidential leadership.

To influence the behavior of a really bad regime, like Iran, North Korea, Venezuela, or Zimbabwe, sanctions need broad international cooperation, at least among the Western democracies. That generally comes only in pursuit of urgent security concerns, such as nuclear proliferation or terrorism.

Sanctions are no panacea. Reckless regimes can turn elsewhere—principally toward Russia and China, but also to Iran and some others—if the Western democracies threaten to suspend assistance. Sanctioned regimes can also use their state-run media to spin a narrative of national victimization, blaming the West for dire economic straits caused by an inept autocrat. Half a century of American sanctions failed to bring about political change in Cuba; all they did was isolate the country and feed the Castro regime's anti-American blame game.

Fortunately, sanctions aimed nationwide are not the only form of pressure in our international toolbox. We also have narrower sanctions that can impose real pain on autocrats and their cronies without hurting the larger society. In drawing attention to the ruling elites' greed and oppression, these targeted sanctions can help divide the people from their leaders while sowing divisions within the ruling class. And that, in turn, can help spur democratic change.

Diplomacy for Democracy

In June 2012, Derek Mitchell arrived in Burma to become the first American ambassador to that beautiful Asian country since the 1988 crackdown spurred the United States to downgrade diplomatic relations. He had held high-level positions in the Obama administration on Asia policy and organized 1990s prodemocracy programs in Asia and the former Soviet Union. Mitchell hit the ground running, with an intimate knowledge of Burma and the kinds of things that the United States can do to foster democracy. During his nearly four years as ambassador, he repeatedly told the country's authorities, its political opposition, and civil society how important democracy was to U.S.-Burmese relations.

"Countries can tell if an ambassador is going through the motions or really cares," Mitchell told me. "I never missed an opportunity to talk about democratic processes and mind-sets in virtually every public engagement."[24] He quoted Washington, Jefferson, and Lincoln, and he invoked elements of the American experience that he felt would resonate in a large, ethnically complex country—such as the U.S. federal system and America's struggle "to build unity amidst diversity." And he used the U.S. embassy's hugely popular Facebook page as a forum to promote democratic values.

A determined, vigorous diplomat can do democracy a great service. As ambassador, Mitchell worked to embed democratic principles— "community consultation, choice, transparency, and accountability"— in virtually every U.S. assistance program. How the United States did things, he argued, was as important as what it did. So he and other American diplomats "held regular media interviews—putting a premium on independent and local media outlets—apologized when we made mistakes, and tried to convey openly the successes and shortcomings of what we did." Mitchell also pressed American businesses to pursue high standards of corporate social responsibility. And then, a year and a half before Burma's November 2015 elections, Mitchell gathered all the ambassadors from key donor countries to begin coordinating intensive international efforts to support the voting. The result was not a full transition to democracy—the country's military-imposed constitution ruled that out—but it did produce and give some power to the first democratically elected parliament in more than half a century.

Mitchell's story reinforces some crucial lessons.[25] Above all, individuals matter. Diplomats who care about democracy and human rights— and who model democratic norms and principles as they go about their duties—can strengthen democratic actors and nudge recalcitrant forces in the right direction.

Moreover, assistance really helps. When Burma's political opening began in 2010, the country's political and civic landscape had been flattened by five decades of sometimes nearly totalitarian rule. It was as if a giant meteor had hit the country's media and civil society, crushing most of what was there and hurling the remnant far afield. But generous international aid programs helped civil society and competitive politics to reemerge within just a few years.

Ambassadors can do a lot more than make lofty statements or offer small grants. By visiting imprisoned dissidents, showing up at demonstrations, or monitoring show trials, diplomats can raise the costs of state repression—and perhaps even deter it. By engaging harassed activists or oppressed communities, diplomats can shine a light on human rights abuses and gradually diminish them. By pressing forcefully in private for reforms, warning of sanctions for intransigence, and offering rewards for democratic progress, diplomats can reinforce local campaigns for freedom and accountability.

Sometimes, as during Michael McFaul's turbulent two-year ambassadorship in Russia during the Obama administration, the authoritarian tide is irrepressible, and diplomats must work hard to keep hope alive among beleaguered democrats.[26] In other moments, as in the Philippines in 1986, Chile in 1988, and South Africa in the early 1990s, exceptional American ambassadors (such as Stephen Bosworth, Harry Barnes, and Princeton Lyman, respectively) can help steer moral and material support to a country's democratic forces and help tip an uncertain political process in the direction of liberty.

Let the Word Go Forth

In the digital age, information is power. What people think, value, and believe can determine the future of systems of government. This is why the Kremlin and the Chinese Communist Party have invested so heavily in their global information operations. They seek to project glowing portraits of their political models, to promote authoritarian values, to censor critical reporting, and to sow doubt, discord, and disinformation about the democracies of the world—and democracy itself. And as global public-opinion trends show, they are getting at least some results. With American democracy looking increasingly dysfunctional and Donald Trump pursuing his brash "America first" chauvinism, public approval of

U.S. global leadership has plunged around the world, leaving the United States in a virtual tie with Russia and China.[27]

No improvements in global communications will improve America's standing if it offers the rest of the world only sneers and fears. But more sensible rhetoric and policies also will not reverse the tide by themselves. To shore up democracy against the new authoritarian tide, we need a new campaign of information and ideas.

Unfortunately, the U.S. government is not set up for this fight, even if the president were interested. Washington once had just the instrument needed to wage this campaign. The U.S. Information Agency (USIA) was established in 1953 to explain U.S. policies, promote American values, counter Communist propaganda and disinformation, and manage international broadcasting efforts like the Voice of America. It oversaw numerous publications, broadcasts in more than two dozen languages, and a wide variety of cultural and educational exchanges.

Not everything the agency did worked; some of its spin was crude enough to damage U.S. credibility. But at its best, USIA promoted democratic ideas, knowledge, and people-to-people exchanges in ways that transcended conventional diplomacy. In 1999, however, the agency died a quiet death as part of a Clinton administration deal with Senator Jesse Helms, the North Carolina Republican who then chaired the Senate Foreign Relations Committee, to spare cuts to other budgets for U.S. global engagement. The agency's operational functions were merged into the State Department, while authority over international broadcasting was given to a separate board of governors (recently reconfigured as the U.S. Agency for Global Media). American public diplomacy and global cultural engagement continued, of course, but they lost some of their edge, focus, and resources.

Amid today's autocratic surge, we need a vigorous reboot of public diplomacy *for* democracy. The best way to do that would be to create what James Clapper, the former director of national intelligence, has

called "a USIA on steroids to fight this information war a lot more aggressively."[28] But reviving a government entity that has been laid to rest
is never an easy political lift.

At a minimum, the State Department needs vigorous, high-profile
leadership of this mission. Since the position was created in October
1999 as part of the Clinton-Helms deal, twelve individuals have held the
role of undersecretary of state for public diplomacy and public affairs,
with an average tenure of about a year and a half. Few have had much
experience in public diplomacy, and none has had the stature of Edward R. Murrow, the legendary reporter whom President John F.
Kennedy tapped to lead USIA in 1961. To wage a global war against
emboldened authoritarians, we need a capable general.[29]

Few things better project America's "soft power" and democratic values than educational and cultural exchanges. China is dramatically expanding its people-to-people exchanges, with huge increases in funding
for students, journalists, and civic and political leaders to visit and study
in China. The last thing we should be doing is cutting funding for ours.

The flagship of these programs—the Fulbright fellowships—has
helped more than 370,000 Americans study and teach abroad and helped
bring foreigners from more than 160 countries to study in American
universities. Some sixty foreign Fulbright alumni have gone on to become their countries' heads of state.[30] Take it from me: the year I spent
teaching in Nigeria in 1982–1983 on a Fulbright lectureship gave me an
enduring connection to that country and a priceless education in democratic development.

The isolationist Trump administration has targeted these exchanges
for radical cuts. Fortunately, in 2017, the Fulbright program's many supporters rallied to defeat a proposed cut of nearly half of its $235 million
annual budget, but the administration came back to propose a 71 percent budget cut for the 2019 fiscal year.[31]

Beyond defending our exchange programs, we must expand, deepen, and accelerate U.S. international broadcasting to meet the fierce challenge posed by China and Russia (as well as Iran and terrorist groups like ISIS). That means new energy for the Voice of America and America's regional "freedom broadcasters," such as Radio Free Europe, Radio Free Asia, and Alhurra (Arabic for "the free one"). Such international broadcasting must be fiercely committed to the truth. As Murrow put it during his testimony to Congress while directing USIA in 1963, "truth is the best propaganda and lies are the worst. To be persuasive we must be believable; to be believable we must be credible; to be credible we must be truthful."[32]

In 2016, the Obama administration created a promising new unit within the State Department, the Global Engagement Center, "to recognize, understand, expose, and counter foreign state and non-state propaganda and disinformation efforts" threatening U.S. national security.[33] As one reporter said, this was "Washington's answer to the Internet Research Agency," the Russian troll factory that hacked America's 2016 election.[34] But under the Trump administration, the new center was stymied by "administrative incompetence," policy divisions, and a lack of commitment from Trump's hapless first secretary of state, Rex Tillerson, who failed to spend more than $100 million that Congress had allocated to counter Russian disinformation.[35]

Nevertheless, the concept remains critical to a global campaign for freedom: an authoritative, nimble, well-resourced, technologically innovative center to combat authoritarian propaganda through rapid digital responses and compelling alternative narratives. Without adopting the penchant for falsehood of the Kremlin and Trump, America's global diplomats should learn an important lesson from them: telling and repeating a compelling story can move people politically. That messaging needs to be both rapid and factual, both passionate and respectful, both vivid and responsible. It needs to stream on multiple media, in a wide range of languages, and to be conveyed on social media by our ambassadors as well. It also needs to respond to what other societies are thinking and feeling about the United States. Open-minded listening is a prerequisite to "winning hearts and minds."[36]

We also need to rethink how we convey knowledge about democracy. For decades, American libraries and cultural centers have helped people worldwide to learn about U.S. history, democracy, gender equality, civil rights, and many other topics that may be difficult to study in autocratic societies' schools and libraries. These "American spaces" remain important physical places for people to read and think and meet in safety. But the number of people who use them is limited, especially under Big Brother regimes. The digital age permits us to transmit knowledge at previously unimagined levels.

With a moderate commitment of resources, the United States and other democracies could translate both classic works and fresh thinking on democracy into Chinese, Russian, Arabic, Farsi, Vietnamese, and more; broadcast massive open online courses (MOOCs) offering free instruction in such subjects as constitutional design, human rights, civil-military relations, and nonviolent civil resistance; support youth exchanges such as the Young African Leaders Initiative, which brings seven hundred young African leaders to America each year as "Mandela fellows"; and help develop new tools and open platforms for digital communication and learning.

We should also fight for free and open access to the internet in autocratic countries. Expanding broadband access to the internet in lower-income countries, and making computers more widely available in schools across the developing world, will help spur a knowledge revolution that will benefit the cause of freedom. Most poor people will access the internet on their smartphones; courses, videos, and other materials about democracy and human rights should be designed with small screens and big hopes in mind.

Web users in authoritarian countries also need new tools to circumvent state censorship of the internet and enhance their security in cyberspace. In recent years, the State Department has helped to fund such efforts, and, as I note in the next chapter, Jigsaw (a division of Google) has created promising new tools to help protect journalists, civil-society groups, and individuals from cyber attacks and online abuse.[37] We should continue supporting the development of new tools and open platforms.

We should also try a simple but creative gambit: mass-producing flash drives in the name of democracy. Today's miniature flash drives can hold as much information (thirty-two gigabytes or more) as an entire desktop computer just a few years ago. We can put multiple courses' worth of books, articles, and video-based MOOCs on these tiny pieces of metal, plastic, and circuitry. Because they are so small, they can be easily hidden or disguised as other objects, such as lipstick. In countries lacking internet freedom, flash drives may be the best way to circulate large quantities of democratic ideas. To paraphrase Rafael Marques, these could be the lipstick that brings down dictatorship.

Keeping Faith

The world's democracies should remember one thing above all else: we have the better ideas. Some people may accept authoritarian rule as useful or necessary at a certain historical moment. But even with the spectacular rise of China, and aside from some self-serving rulers and their cliques, few people in the world today celebrate authoritarianism as a superior system, morally or practically. Even in the world's most tenacious autocracies—such as China, Russia, Iran, Venezuela, and Vietnam—many people want to understand what democracy is and how it can be achieved. Even many dictators and generalissimos know and fear democracy's allure.

We should bet heavily on this battle of information and ideas because if we do, we will win. Dictatorships cannot satisfy the fundamental human aspiration for freedom, dignity, and self-determination. All they can do is confuse and sully it. As the Dalai Lama wrote in 1999, "respect for human rights, freedom of speech, the equality of all human beings, and the rule of law" are "necessary conditions of a civilized society." He declared, "It is the responsibility of the democratic free world to come to the aid of those countries" struggling for democracy.[38] It is this humble, Buddhist spiritual leader—not China's ruthless strongman, Xi Jinping—who stands on the right side of history, beckoning us to our better angels.

TWELVE

MAKING THE INTERNET SAFE FOR DEMOCRACY

I think in the back deep-deep recesses of our minds, we knew something bad could happen. We have created tools that are ripping apart the social fabric of how society works.

—CHAMATH PALIHAPITIYA, FORMER FACEBOOK SENIOR EXECUTIVE, 2017[1]

n 2006, two of my students told me about something called Face-book. I had never heard of the social-networking site; I was barely aware of YouTube (which had launched only the previous year), and I had not yet really focused on how information and communication technologies were changing politics. But as often happens in academia, professors discover through their students. I hired them both as research assistants, and with their help, I began to delineate a phenomenon I called *liberation technology*.

Around the world, new information technologies—the internet, email, text messaging, photo sharing, and other forms of social media—were letting people transcend government censorship, document human rights abuses, expose vote fraud, organize demonstrations, reveal corruption, and create a new public sphere of free expression.[2] These technologies had further democratized American politics, and in 2008, they probably made the difference in enabling Barack Obama to out-organize Hillary Clinton and win the Democratic nomination for president. I was captivated.

The following year, I cofounded a new program at Stanford to study the ways that digital tools were being used to counter censorship and repression—and to empower citizens, improve public health, and generally make society more open, decent, and just.[3] My students, academic colleagues, and I were inspired by the activists using social media to mobilize the mass protests of the Arab Spring, including the demonstrators who poured into Tahrir Square in Cairo and brought down the Egyptian dictator Hosni Mubarak in February 2011.[4] We learned of young Chinese bloggers using clever memes to evade censorship, challenge Communist Party propaganda, and report human rights abuses; the daring Malaysian online newspaper *Malaysiakini*, which exposed corruption, ethnic discrimination, and police brutality; and a Kenyan nonprofit organization, Ushahidi, which developed software to pinpoint incidents of postelection violence in that country in 2008.[5] Hence the term "liberation technology"—a play on the concept of liberation theology, the Catholic movement that has fought repression, poverty, and injustice in Latin America.

But as inspiring uses of the new digital tools advanced, so did authoritarian ones. In particular, China and Russia threw resources into monitoring, blocking, disrupting, and hacking the online work of independent media and civil society. So did Iran after the 2009 opposition Green Movement protests, and most of the Arab states after the Arab Spring.

By 2011, democrats and autocrats were vying for control of cyberspace. Even in liberal democracies, privacy rights were coming under pressure from state and corporate actors while cyber bullying and abusive language were becoming commonplace online. Not only were authoritarian states trying to monitor, filter, and control access to the internet; they were also seeking to break the net into national pieces, use it to divide their citizens, and develop new digital tools of repression, such as facial-recognition technology.[6]

Back then, I was optimistic that democratic norms and actors would prevail in cyberspace. Today, the internet is a much grimmer place. Yet the situation is far from hopeless. Several creative initiatives are seeking to reverse the ill winds of polarization, disinformation, manipulation, and government repression that are now degrading freedom online. We can make the internet a safer place for democracy, but it will require a concerted partnership among democratic governments, technology companies, civil-society groups, and individual "netizens."

Unfriending Democracy

By mid-2018, an estimated 3.2 billion people (more than 40 percent of the world's population) used social media, and that number was growing at the astonishing rate of 13 percent annually. Facebook remains the most popular platform, with more than 2 billion users and by far the deepest level of user engagement, but other platforms—including You-Tube, WhatsApp, Instagram, and WeChat—have more than 1 billion users or are driving quickly toward that threshold.[7] By August 2017, two thirds of Americans said they get at least some of their news via social media, and far more Americans now frequently consume news on social media than through newspapers and radio.[8]

As social media have become the dominant means for transmitting news, opinions, and political appeals, the dangers they pose to democracy have become clearer and more urgent. Indeed, it is precisely their radical democratization of information flows—removing editorial filters and standards, thus enabling anyone anywhere to act as a journalist, filmmaker, or pundit—that have helped make social media a threat to democracy. As Facebook CEO Mark Zuckerberg observed in a remarkable November 2018 post, "One of the things I've learned is that when you connect two billion people, you will see all the beauty and ugliness of humanity."[9]

Yet the perils posed by social media also spring from other deep-seated features. The economic incentive of social media platforms is to grab people's attention, because more user time spent on a site means more ad revenue. That often privileges content that is provocative, emotive, or downright outrageous. Of course, that is true for all commercial media, because, as Zuckerberg notes, "left unchecked, people will engage disproportionately with more sensationalist and provocative content."[10] However, lacking any space limits, advance editorial filters, or scheduling constraints, social media convey information instantly, and their dense, decentralized networks enable wide diffusion of these information flows. These two features—high speed and wide spread—enable digital posts to go viral, capturing attention for cynical lies and ardent truths alike.

Moreover, social media are by nature open to manipulation. Even if all the big platforms were to forbid fake or anonymous users (as Facebook already technically does), it would be difficult and costly to establish every user's true identity. And automation now enables rapid distribution of malicious information on a colossal scale by fake accounts (though Facebook is regularly removing astonishing numbers of those fake accounts). This makes social media distinctively vulnerable to manipulation by malign forces, domestic and foreign.

These problems overlap, but we can (with the aid of an excellent recent synthesis by the Omidyar Group[11]) identify a number of interconnected dangers that social media pose to democracy. Social media intensify political polarization, in part by propagating false information, whether deliberately or inadvertently; the more outrageous the content, the further it travels. As confidence in all sources of information—and the very notion of objective truth—disintegrates, so does the legitimacy of the established media. This clears the field for governments, political parties, movements, and leaders to spread false and divisive messages and to forge direct, carefully targeted ties with their followers. Polarization then deepens, draining the public sphere of the civility and mutual respect that make for a healthy democratic society. As everything becomes digitized and tracked, individual privacy and freedom suffer along with democracy.

Of course, polarization did not begin with the digital age. It ravaged modern democracies, from the United States to Germany, well before the era of television, let alone the internet. But social media make it quick and easy to find the like-minded, to bond with them, and to disparage those who disagree.

Digital platforms continually feed users news, search results, friend suggestions, and updates that fit their interests, biases, and even shopping preferences. This generates a feedback loop that constantly refines people's data profiles and promotes "self-segregation into like-minded groups," otherwise known as "echo chambers."[12] These also act as "filter bubbles," sheltering people "from information that might challenge the [partisan] messages sent to them."[13]

That echoes one of the classic insights from early research in sociology: people with crosscutting social ties—those who frequently interact with people of different ethnicities, religions, and political opinions—tend to be more moderate in their views. Such people are "cross-pressured"; their fellow workers may lean heavily in one direction, their fellow church members in another. But if those healthy cross pressures evaporate, people become caught up in more narrow worlds of shared beliefs, fears, and resentments.[14]

When it gets really bad, people can come to live in different factual universes. Not only do they follow radically different news sources, such as Fox or MSNBC, but their friends send them news—or propaganda—that reinforces their biases. They grow less tolerant of opposing views and less willing even to listen to them, dismissing opposing opinions as based on "fake news." And sometimes, that may be correct.

In today's digital realm, distortion of the truth takes two forms: "disinformation" (the deliberate creation and propagation of false information) and "misinformation" ("the inadvertent sharing of false information," including rumor and satire).[15] Fabricated and misleading content readily goes viral on social media, because falsehood is often more entertaining and gripping than truth—and it is becoming easier and easier to generate in convincing digital form.

The greatest danger, however, is industrial-scale truth distortion as governments and political groups launch highly organized information operations—like the Russian hacking of the 2016 U.S. election—"to achieve a strategic and/or geopolitical outcome."[16] These operations employ fake digital accounts (both human and bots) in a coordinated effort to amplify outrage and intimidate opposition. And often they succeed, making people ever angrier and more polarized.

It isn't only the Kremlin's massive Internet Research Agency in St. Petersburg that can hack a U.S. election. In 2016, one small Macedonian town with few jobs and lots of internet-savvy youth hungry for work became, according to *Wired* magazine, "the registered home of at least 100 pro-Trump websites, many of them filled with sensationalist, utterly fake news." These sites brought each young creator thousands or tens of thousands of dollars in ad revenue.[17]

As people become more deeply isolated in their own information silos, they become more inclined to believe and distribute bad information. Paying little attention to sourcing or credibility, they pounce on stories that confirm their biases. This only intensifies in the heat of an election campaign. The top twenty fake news stories in the 2016 U.S. election (including such whoppers as "Pope Francis endorses Donald Trump" and "Hillary Clinton sells weapons to ISIS") were more widely shared and commented upon than the top twenty true stories, concluded a Brookings Institution report.[18] One lunatic story—alleging that a

Washington pizza parlor was harboring child sex slaves, with the knowledge of Hillary Clinton—propelled a North Carolina man to race to the
nation's capital with an assault weapon to stage what he imagined might
be a rescue.[19] Mercifully, no one was killed. But media professionals and
international monitors have worried that the proliferation of malicious
rumors, along with Trump's escalating "enemy of the people" attacks on
the media, would soon lead to direct violence against American journalists.[20] And in October 2018, a fanatical Trump supporter from Florida
was arrested for sending explosive devices to the New York office of
CNN and to numerous critics of the president.[21]

Once people buy into false stories, it is very hard to debunk them;
human beings become emotionally invested in what they believe. In
fact, the effort to persuade them that they are wrong may only prompt
them to dig in deeper.[22] Hence disinformation intensifies radicalization
and polarization. And it may also drive others to tune out of politics "by
fanning cynicism regarding the candidates and the election," as my
Stanford colleague Nathaniel Persily has put it.[23]

The destructive scope of disinformation will increase exponentially in
the coming years. Rapid advances in artificial intelligence will enhance
"deep fakes," videos that manipulate images and voices to make it appear
that individuals have said or done outrageous things.[24] These highly re-
alistic fakes will provoke outrage and even violence, as people view seemingly convincing proof of hoaxes that could previously be promoted only
through cruder forms of forgery. To make matters worse, public awareness of this budding technology also threatens to undermine the credibility of authentic video evidence. In the years ahead, citizens may well
find it harder and harder to believe their eyes and ears.

As doubt and distrust are becoming routine, the traditional media—
from *The Wall Street Journal* and NPR to ABC News—are losing credibility and legitimacy. These old-school media outlets have long sought
to determine and explain the facts, fairly, rigorously, and accurately. In
doing so, they elevated the legitimacy of experts, and even sometimes of

governments and other established institutions such as universities and courts. By contrast, social media elevate what is popular, buzzy, and viral. For a time, this meant rising trust in information coming from peers or social media platforms, as opposed to more established institutions.[25] But amid the pervasive disinformation online, we now risk a broader loss of confidence in all channels of information and authority.[26]

All of this renders society more vulnerable to political manipulation by those who would manufacture fake streams of public opinion, through bots and trolls disguised as authentic individuals. The most notorious example of this was the Kremlin's social media intervention in the 2016 American election, but all modern authoritarian regimes now manipulate, manage, vilify, and amplify public opinion online. Governments' growing manipulation of social media content is now one of the leading drivers of the steady eight-year decline in global internet freedom, as documented by Freedom House.[27] And no dictatorship manipulates social media more massively, with more frightening implications for freedom, than China.

Political campaigns and politicized news sites in many democracies manipulate online content as well, but less brazenly. One study found that bots generated nearly 18 percent of campaign-related tweets in the final phase of the 2016 election and about a quarter of those during the Clinton-Trump presidential debates.[28] In the United States, right-wing online media outlets, led by the nativist Breitbart, were much more polarizing than their leftist counterparts—that is, far more likely to amplify false and misleading claims and to spin them into a larger narrative compelling enough to infiltrate the mainstream media. Polarization did not just happen irresistibly; it was consciously driven from the right.[29]

Populist leaders like Donald Trump, Philippine president Rodrigo Duterte, and Indian prime minister Narendra Modi use their tweets to build direct relationships with their followers, unmediated by journalistic filters or checks. Social media enable illiberal leaders to "normalize hateful or cynical views themselves, or implicitly approve the messages of their social media supporters."[30] At the extreme, autocrats and demagogues can use Facebook and other platforms to propagate hate speech that incites deadly violence against minorities, as with the Rohingya and other Muslims in Burma.[31]

As digital society grows more polarized and disinformation crowds out deliberation, the quality of online discourse is deteriorating, thereby degrading the public square. Since rival online communities can no longer agree on the facts and have little overlap in their social networks or metanarratives, there is little to restrain their emotions. Argument is replaced with invective. Racism and hate speech flow freely.

The anonymity of much online expression intensifies the challenge. The ability to mask one's identity on, say, Twitter (or to defy the rules and do so on Facebook anyway) further emboldens ugly and hateful expression, as well as cyber bullying and the online abuse of women and minorities. Trolls and bots, serving extremist or foreign agendas, can wade into online conversations to stoke the flames of social discord. As those holding opposing political views defame and scream at one another online, they become even more mutually contemptuous and distrustful.

But tolerance, civility, and trust are not the only qualities that are decaying on the internet. We are losing our personal privacy and autonomy as well. Today, social media platforms—and governments—are watching and recording every click we take, every search we make, every thing we buy, and every app we try (to paraphrase the famous song by the Police).

Technology firms—including not only Facebook, Google, and Instagram but also online shopping sites like Amazon—store, share, and sell this data through precision advertising. Beyond the alarming implications for individual privacy, these companies are creating a brave new world of personal manipulation. When these bits of data are interpreted, using (as the Omidyar Group puts it) new statistical tools of "big data analysis, combined with computational psychology and behavioral and demographic analysis," they can profile the personality and nudge the behavior of each user with a previously unimaginable level of accuracy.[32]

This doesn't just mean more sales of books, music, shoes, and socks. It also has transformed politics. In 2016, this gold mine of big data enabled the right-wing political-consulting firm Cambridge Analytica to microtarget advertising and messaging for the Trump and Brexit campaigns. Even though Cambridge Analytica was forced to shut down over its scandalous misuse of the Facebook data of more than eighty million users, the deployment of troves of personal data to microtarget voters with tailored messages is here to stay. And so are the attendant threats to individual privacy and social coherence.

Social media and ecommerce companies are not the only ones tracking every breath of online life; dictatorships are too. Increasingly, authoritarian governments are using the internet as a vast web for political surveillance, repression, and control.

China is leading the way, building a sweeping surveillance state that aims to assess every digital footprint of every Chinese citizen and then compile each person's "social credit score." Writing a social media post critical of the government, sharing news online deemed "unpatriotic," or being photographed near a protest by a state surveillance camera— any of these things could generate a low score, making it difficult to get a passport or even a train ticket.

China's major cities are now blanketed by surveillance cameras, with the visual data being checked by powerful facial-recognition software. A massive content-filtering operation, often known as the Great Firewall of China, blocks *The New York Times* and a host of other "dangerous" Western sites and social media platforms. An army of internet police quickly purges the web of foreign content and dangerous ideas.[33] China's internet companies are now obliged to do the content filtering, leaving the state free to conduct more sophisticated levels of monitoring and to mobilize proregime commentary, often in the form of trendy memes and tweets by members of the Communist Youth League, who are rewarded for their patriotism. And the party can also divert attention by flooding the web with entertainment and other distracting content, especially when criticism spikes over some new scandal or case of regime corruption.

Sadly, authoritarian and illiberal governments around the world think China has shown them the secret formula. China is readily sharing its Orwellian tools with other autocratic regimes, threatening an "Arab Spring in reverse" in which digital technology enables "state domination and repression at a staggering scale."[34] Authoritarian states are becoming more adept and aggressive at blocking and purging criticism; tracking, harassing, and arresting skeptical journalists and bloggers; and using bots and trolls to drive favorable social media commentary and to demonize their opponents. Increasingly, dictatorships require internet platforms to store users' data in the country, where the regime can demand access to it. As in China, these increasingly comprehensive digital footprints can then be mined to more aggressively shape, constrain, and punish the expression and behavior of citizens.

Autocrats can also use dedicated denial-of-service (DDoS) attacks to overwhelm the websites of opposition groups and independent media outlets (including those based abroad) with swarms of disabling traffic. If all else fails, the strongmen can slow down the internet or simply shut it down for a while. In these and many other ways, authoritarian regimes are determined to keep the internet safe for autocracy.[35]

Saving the Internet for Democracy

Reclaiming the internet will require government responses, corporate reforms, and technological innovations. The race to preserve freedom and civility online will at best involve a good deal of trial and error.

Technology companies and governments alike should proceed with some humility. Many steps to defend democracy from one problem— such as disinformation and hate speech—risk exacerbating another: the assault on freedom of expression. Political and corporate responses therefore need to be grounded in democratic values.

The Oxford professor Timothy Garton Ash has laid out ten principles of free speech, which offer a wise starting point.[36] His precepts acknowledge that people everywhere must be free to express themselves and to exchange information and ideas. This requires eschewing taboos but respecting religious freedom. It requires "uncensored, diverse, trustworthy media" and a free internet. It rejects violent intimidation and embraces "robust civility"—the ability to talk about even controversial topics, but in a decent and serious way. Just as democracy in the real world rests on citizen participation, so too will democracy online ask a lot of individual netizens. We will all need to be educated to use the internet in an active, discerning, and respectful fashion.

FIGHTING BOTS, TROLLS, AND DISINFORMATION

The hard-driving, poorly regulated tech companies helped create many of these problems, and they can do many things to ameliorate them. For one thing, they can flag sources of information that have been repeatedly identified by professional fact checkers as purveyors of false, malicious, or sloppy information. In March 2017, after a public outcry, Facebook began flagging what it called "disputed" news—items that clearly had no basis in fact. That experiment backfired, drawing extra attention to disinformation and even sometimes reinforcing belief in it, and the company began instead to suggest more factual "related" news items.[37] Other platforms also use such tags, including Wikipedia, which has made them an organic element of its laudable effort to crowdsource a free, open, online encyclopedia. But more research is needed to determine the effects of tagging news articles for disputed or dubious quality.

In March 2018, under pressure, Facebook announced a new set of measures to guard the integrity of election campaigns against foreign and other anonymous interventions. These included an accelerating effort by Facebook to identify and disable fake accounts, which are a major vehicle for spewing inflammatory falsehoods. Facebook says that it is now using advances in machine learning to block "millions of fake accounts each day at the point of creation before they can do any harm."[38]

The larger challenge for social media companies is to use artificial intelligence to ferret out and block all bots. In addition, Facebook claims it is working to diminish one of the main incentives for distributing false information—money—by adjusting its algorithms to demote (that is, show less often and prominently) the content generated by spammers trying to profit from disinformation.[39] It also vows to demote "borderline content so it gets less distribution and engagement."[40]

Artificial intelligence also has great promise for identifying hoaxes, but it can do only so much. Human judgment remains indispensable in fighting disinformation. In early 2018, Facebook increased the number of people it employs to review content and improve digital security from 10,000 to 20,000. (By November it reported a total staff of 30,000 devoted to enforcing its community standards and reviewing more than two million pieces of content each day.)[41] Facebook says that it is also deepening partnerships with fact-checking organizations to identify and debunk false news stories as quickly as possible, including an arrangement it made with the Associated Press for the 2018 midterm elections. By mid-2018, Facebook was working with mainstream news outlets in fourteen countries, including France, Italy, and India, to "scrub news stories, photos, and videos for misleading information."[42] Stories identified as false are demoted in Facebook's news feed, reducing their future views, the company says, by an average of more than 80 percent.

Google has taken some similar steps to combine human vetting with artificial intelligence to more accurately "flag hoaxes, conspiracy theories, and false and/or offensive information."[43] The algorithms for Google searches are then updated to push down dodgy material and favor more authoritative news.[44]

Yet Facebook has not accepted responsibility for its inadequate response to Russia's subversive misuse of its platform in the 2016 election campaign. According to the investigative reporting of *The New York Times*, Mark Zuckerberg and Facebook COO Sheryl Sandberg stubbornly "ignored warning signs" of widespread "suspicious Russia-linked activity on its site" and then "sought to conceal them from public view." Moreover, when it was revealed that Cambridge Analytica (the political data firm affiliated with the Trump campaign) had gained access to the data of possibly tens of millions of Facebook users, the company "sought to deflect blame and mask the extent of the problem," while trashing critics like George Soros with cynical hardball tactics aided by a political opposition-research firm.[45]

Clearly, internet companies cannot be effective in combatting disinformation if they don't deal transparently with their users and the public. Still, the companies are recognizing (at least implicitly) that they are not just aggregators or conveyors of information, but in effect, publishers who bear some responsibility for their content. However, "content moderation" (as it is called) presents its own slippery slope toward unaccountable censorship. Human content moderators are human; they make mistakes. And the companies' machine-learning algorithms—which set the automatic rules for making such decisions—may incorporate political or racial biases that mass-reproduce unfairness. Resourceful actors have manipulated these companies' vetting rules "to effectively censor their political opponents." And when faced with individual or community complaints—not to mention fierce pressure from authoritarian regimes—the platforms often take the path of least resistance and capitulate, silencing voices that "span the political spectrum and the globe," including activists trying to document racism, war crimes, and police brutality.[46]

If freedom is to be preserved online, the internet companies' growing efforts to moderate content must meet certain standards of transparency and accountability. In February 2018, internet freedom advocates like the Electronic Frontier Foundation, the American Civil Liberties Union, and New America came together to delineate three principles. First, the digital companies should regularly publish the numbers of posts they remove and of accounts they suspend or terminate. Second, when content is removed or an account suspended, the companies should tell the user why. And third, the companies should provide a mechanism for timely appeal of these decisions.[47]

The scale of the challenge is staggering. In November 2018, Facebook released a detailed report on its annual removal of content for violations of its "community standards" relating to hate speech, graphic violence, terrorism, cruelty, and nudity.[48] Most of the removals were due to spam (nearly 4 billion pieces) and fake accounts (over 2 billion), but in the twelve-month period from October 2017 through September 2018, Facebook took action on 15 million posts related to terrorism, nearly 10 million related to hate speech, 2 million involving bullying, and about 100 million involving nudity and sexual activity.[49] Any review mechanism must therefore be prepared to vet a huge number of appeals of decisions to remove content, and in a manner that is seen to be fair and responsive to general principles rather than corporate interests. To hear user appeals on its content decisions, Facebook has pledged to create "an independent body . . . whose decisions would be transparent and binding."[50] This would be a major step forward for fairness and transparency. However, a better approach would be for the major internet platforms (such as Facebook, YouTube, Twitter, LinkedIn, and Reddit) to jointly fund a fully independent review mechanism for appeals of all their content-removal decisions. To process the likely volume of complaints, the mechanism would need to have full-time professional staff and panels of at least part-time "judges" who would be assigned to various cases, perhaps (as with the appellate court structures of many democracies) with varying sizes of review panels depending on the gravity and potential significance (for future precedent) of the case. One value of such a voluntary initiative, based on a partnership between the corporations and civil society, is that it would probably preempt calls for government regulation of content, with all the worrisome implications that could have for freedom of expression.

None of this really grapples with the deeper problem of the algorithms that determine what information rises to the top and goes viral. Until all the major internet companies are willing to allow real transparency and public engagement around this highly sensitive aspect of their operations—which drives to the core of their business model, and hence their profitability—outrageous content will always have an edge over the facts.

Fortunately, the tech sector (both for-profit and philanthropic) is investing in independent research and professional journalism as well. Omidyar Network has announced a $100 million initiative "to fund investigative journalism, combat the spread of mis- and disinformation online, increase citizen engagement, and restore trust in institutions."[51] The $14 million News Integrity Initiative at the City University of New York aims to help new and old media alike do better at combating media manipulation and online vitriol.[52] Google is supporting academic initiatives to better understand and combat false news, and the company helped to found First Draft, which is doing research, fact checking, education, and training to fight false news and manipulated videos.[53]

These often rather modest efforts are still in their early days, and they don't come close to relieving the vast responsibility that the internet titans bear. Social media firms still have huge financial incentives to welcome attention addiction; fake news will still move faster than its ethical foes; and the pressure to debunk rapidly can exist in tension with the need for thoroughness and accuracy. For now, conspiracy theories and propaganda still pervade search engines and sites like YouTube.

Elevating facts requires robust journalism, especially thriving, serious newspapers committed to keeping reporting separate from editorializing (and clearly walled off from paid ads and sponsored content). It also demands a central role for professional fact-checking organizations such as PolitiFact, FactCheck.org, and the myth-busting Snopes.com. And it will benefit from efforts like the Trust Project of Santa Clara University in California, which is working to identify the key disclosures—"about the news outlet, author, and commitments behind a story"—that "make it easy for the public to identify the quality of news." Digital platforms like Facebook, Google, and Bing can then use this information to prioritize more trustworthy news.[54]

In Ukraine, which is fighting both a real war with Russia and an online battle against Russian disinformation, the civic organization Stop-Fake is using journalists, editors, IT specialists, translators, and ordinary citizens to spot and refute Kremlin propaganda. With support from foreign democracies and foundations, StopFake is defending the information space in Ukraine against one of the most dedicated assaults on truth in any democracy—and thereby strengthening citizens' media literacy and the capacity of Ukraine's media to identify fakes.[55]

To diminish the influence of malicious information, democracies must generate more good information. As Stephen King, a former BBC executive who is now a partner at Omidyar Network, has observed, "First and foremost, our response must be founded on the belief that truth exists, that it's precious, and that it's best protected through robust reporting and well-informed debate."[56]

RESISTING FOREIGN INTERFERENCE
AND ELECTORAL MANIPULATION

It has long been illegal for foreigners to contribute to U.S. federal election campaigns, but it is now hard to discover whether they have intervened online. The tech companies can do a lot to help here.

After the 2016 fiasco, Facebook began requiring political advertisers in the 2018 U.S. midterm elections to verify their identity with a government-issued ID; provide their physical mailing address, which is then verified by mail; and disclose which candidate, organization, or business they represent. These ads are now clearly identified as political ads, with a disclosure of who paid for them. Facebook also launched a public archive of all political ads showing how much money was spent on each ad, how widely they were viewed, and by which demographics. All social media platforms should be required to post all their political ads in such an online, publicly accessible archive for at least a year, along with the groups paying for them.[57]

In one sense, democracies have an advantage in trying to identify foreign digital influence in their elections: they can openly enlist the help of ordinary netizens through crowdsourcing. The superb investigative journalists at ProPublica have launched a crowdsourcing tool, the Political Ad Collector. Once users install this bit of software in their web browsers and log into Facebook, the software automatically collects the ads displayed on their newsfeeds and determines which ones are political. Those are then conveyed back to ProPublica and stored for analysis in a public database.[58]

Social media companies could go further to brand state propaganda channels for what they are. Democracies should not impose blanket bans on authoritarian state networks like Russia's RT and Sputnik. But they can at least "identify and label" this material as propaganda.[59]

COMBATING HATE SPEECH AND INTOLERANCE

The cyber world is increasingly infested with bigotry and bullying. Artificial intelligence can help demote or remove hate speech, personal abuse, and incitements to violence and terrorism.[60] Banning anonymous or fake accounts is the right policy: people behave better when their identities are known, but their inhibitions evaporate when they cannot be held accountable for hateful or abusive posts. Yet in authoritarian countries banning anonymity comes with a cost, because people who criticize the government with their real names take huge risks.

The problem in combating hate speech is not so much technological as political and moral: What constitutes intolerably offensive speech? At what point does purging verbal intolerance threaten the bedrock principle of free expression? Even if liberal democrats can agree to ban explicit incitement to violence, removing any content that some group might find offensive is a slippery slope to a censored world.

A better approach is for companies and communities to stigmatize and marginalize hateful speech. The Southern Poverty Law Center urges individuals and communities to denounce major, organized purveyors of hate and intolerance. But it also advises: "Do not debate hate group members on conflict-driven talk shows or public forums. Your presence lends them legitimacy and publicity."[61]

The best way to counter hate speech is with better speech—with messages and stories that reject bias, defend minorities, and promote inclusion. These need to be advanced in the digital realm and the physical world alike. If acceptance, pluralism, and diversity are not taught thoughtfully and modeled sincerely in our schools and civic organizations, they will not prevail in cyberspace either.

RECONCILING GOVERNMENT REGULATION WITH DEMOCRATIC VALUES

As social media's threats to democracy become increasingly urgent, and as the online titans' responses prove partial and sluggish, policy makers are coming under increasing pressure to *do something*. But legislating under crisis conditions rarely produces wise policy, even when policy makers fully understand the potential drawbacks. A rush to regulation online risks doing democracy more harm than good.[62]

Freedom of speech is a core value in the United States, with its sweeping interpretation of the First Amendment. Other countries seek a different balance between freedom and decency. With its Nazi history, Germany has little tolerance for hate speech, and its public has demanded action to constrain it online. Germany's Bundestag responded in June 2017 with the Network Enforcement Act, which requires social media platforms to "delete illegal, racist, or slanderous comments and posts" (including hate speech or Holocaust denial) within twenty-four hours of being notified of it, or be liable for fines that could rise to fifty million euros.[63] The act is well intentioned but misguided. The law is both broad and ambiguous, which could lead private companies to err on the side of censorship to avoid heavy penalties.[64] It sets a bad precedent at a time when illiberal governments are increasingly eager to constrain internet freedom.

Democratic governments should avoid censorship, but they can certainly compel transparency in online political advertising. In October 2017, Senators Mark Warner, Amy Klobuchar, and John McCain introduced the Honest Ads Act to extend to social media the same type of disclosure provisions for campaign advertising that now apply to television, radio, and print media. Large digital platforms would be required to make "reasonable efforts" to ensure that foreign nationals do not buy ads to try to influence U.S. election campaigns; they would also have to keep a complete, publicly available digital record of advertisers who spent more than $500 on political ads in the previous year. Twitter announced its support of the bill, followed by Facebook, which initially lobbied against it.[65] But as a recent Atlantic Council report argued, the law should go further—to prohibit foreigners from funding "issue ads in campaign contexts," to require social media firms to prominently "identify the sponsors and funders of all content," and to empower the Federal Election Commission to enforce these new provisions.[66]

Lawmakers can also do more to protect our privacy online. The European Union's General Data Protection Regulation, implemented in May 2018, gave users more control over their personal data. Digital platforms and tech companies can no longer act as if "other people's personal information belongs to them just because it happens to be sitting on their servers."[67] Now, they must store data in a way that protects European users' identity (for example, through encryption) and must make the highest level of privacy the default setting in users' options so that personal data is not made available to others without their explicit consent. The companies must now give European users ongoing, clear, and accessible means for controlling the use of their personal information.[68] They must grant people the "right to be forgotten" by deleting their data on request, under a much wider range of circumstances. They must inform users within seventy-two hours of a breach of their personal data. And they face much more legal liability and much stiffer financial penalties if users' personal data is stolen or misused.

While some tech companies adopted the new EU standards globally to avoid inadvertently violating Europeans' new legal rights, others pulled back, complaining about the costs of compliance. As the new EU measure approached, Facebook removed its users in Asia, Africa, and Latin America from Irish jurisdiction, and thus from the regulation's protection.[69] For now, unfortunately, citizens of the world's democracies enjoy quite different levels of protection for their digital privacy.

All this is unfolding amid growing unease over the sheer bulk and power of the internet titans. Many politicians and critics are suggesting that the major tech companies be broken up—particularly Google and Facebook, which together gobble up 85 percent of online advertising revenue. These massive firms' market dominance and our utter dependence on them give these companies some of the character of utilities and make some government regulation inevitable. At a minimum, as Senator Warner has suggested, some of their most blatantly anticompetitive practices should be addressed.[70]

Some have gone further and advocated antitrust action. They should consider two cautions. First, massive technological investment will continue to be needed to use artificial intelligence to track down, expel, or demote bots, trolls, fake accounts, and malicious actors—and very large companies are much better positioned to make the gigantic investments in technological innovation and human monitoring that battle requires. Second, the major Western tech companies face mounting global competition from Chinese giants like Alibaba and Tencent, which are not truly private companies but entities answerable to the biggest monopoly player of all, the Chinese Communist Party. Western companies, which carry at least some sensitivity to democratic values of openness and pluralism, should not be handicapped in this struggle.

EDUCATING DIGITAL CITIZENS

Even if tech companies, independent media, and democratic governments do everything possible to combat the perils of social media, one major vulnerability will remain: the users themselves. We cannot make the internet safe for democracy without educating citizens—ideally from a very young age—to use it safely, skeptically, and respectfully.

Recent research shows that young people across the United States, from middle school to college, are woefully unprepared to assess the veracity of information they encounter online. As two leading researchers, Sam Wineburg and Sarah McGrew of the Stanford History Education Group, noted after studying nearly eight thousand students, "At every level, we were taken aback by students' lack of preparation: middle school students unable to tell the difference between an advertisement and a news story; high school students taking at face value a cooked-up chart from the Minnesota Gun Owners Political Action Committee; college students credulously accepting a .org top-level domain name as if it were a Good Housekeeping seal."[71]

A key part of the problem is that young people are not being trained to engage in what is called "civic online reasoning." To the extent that today's students receive instruction in media literacy, it tends to involve a checklist of some ten to thirty questions (for example, whether a website lists a contact person and looks professional). Such checklists might ferret out the cheapest and crudest fakes, but they can hardly distinguish between an independent research institute and a sophisticated Russian front operation.[72]

The problem with the checklist approach is simply the way people of all ages use the internet: we read vertically, burrowing down into a website, page, or article to gather more information within the confines of the site. But that can often take us deeper down a rabbit hole of illusion.

The descent into credulity may deepen in response to a site's other superficial features: the trappings of authority, the appearance of documentation, the allure of high-quality graphics. The key to real digital media literacy, argue Wineburg, McGrew, and their colleagues in the Stanford History Education Group, is getting readers to step outside a given website or article and read *laterally*—that is, to open a new tab (or, better yet, several) to independently check out the person or organization and its qualifications, funding, and credibility.

This is the method that professional fact checkers use to evaluate online information, and it is strikingly similar to the patterns of physical interaction that generate more nuanced, patient, and tolerant attitudes in the offline world. But navigating the net this way requires training and some cultural reorientation, stressing skepticism about unknown sources of information, embrace of the critical method, and active consumption of the internet rather than passive. It is no coincidence that these are core features of offline democratic culture as well.

Wineburg, McGrew, and their colleagues recommend other steps to cultivate more responsible digital citizens. One is to train students to be more discerning and selective consumers of search-engine results. Another is to make informed but questioning use of Wikipedia as "a useful starting place for online research" and a valuable source of references for further reading.[73] Students can also build up immunity against online deception through carefully controlled exposure to malicious websites that disguise their true backers and peddle misleading information.[74]

Instruction in online media literacy needs to begin early, certainly before high school.[75] Some high school classes now teach students how stories go viral and how filter bubbles divide people. Students need reinforcement from their other studies, bringing to their online activity the same respect for evidence, grounding in statistics, and facility in critical reasoning that one hopes they are getting in other subjects.[76]

Adults could use similar programs of instruction. Public schools and libraries should offer free courses on the responsible and discerning use of the internet. And our political leaders and civic organizations should encourage people of all ages to be more civil and thoughtful on social media. Recently, Wineburg told a group of educators that we do not yet have "adequate awareness of what it means to be a responsible digital citizen, that you don't just forward or retweet an outrageous news item simply because it accords with your biases. We need to have a view of this as digital litter and launch a digital anti-littering campaign like the one against physical littering forty years ago."[77]

Defending Freedom on the Web

The global fight for freedom is inseparable from the fight for internet freedom. The world's democracies will need to make this cause a major theme of their diplomacy and foreign aid. Just as states should be called out and penalized for violating their citizens' rights in the offline world, so too should constrictions of internet freedom have consequences.

Liberal democracies should pressure other governments to halt disruptions and slowdowns of internet service for political ends; to cease digital assaults on news media and civil-society organizations; to end harassment of and physical assaults on online journalists and activists; to stop punishing citizens for using encrypted communications apps like Signal; to terminate Russian- and Chinese-style state programs to disseminate fake news, demonize opponents, and distort online discussions; and to roll back draconian laws that restrict online freedom in the name of "cyber security."

Defending digital freedom requires supporting those on its front lines. Individuals and organizations at risk need technological help. For many years, nonprofit organizations and private companies, sometimes with the assistance of the United States and other democracies, have been developing tools to evade digital censorship—for example, by using proxy websites to access blocked web pages and using virtual private networks to tunnel under censorship walls while remaining anonymous. It will take constant innovation to keep these tools sharp as technologically sophisticated autocracies seek to blunt them.

Jigsaw, a technology incubator within the larger corporate structure of Google, has developed some of the most promising innovations of this kind.[78] Its Project Shield uses Google's mammoth digital infrastructure to give independent news, human rights, and prodemocracy organizations a free, "multi-layered defense system" against DDoS attacks. Password Alert is a free Chrome browser extension that alerts journalists and activists of attempts to steal their passwords. Outline is a free, downloadable tool that enables vulnerable journalists and news organizations to quickly and safely create their own virtual private networks.

Another leading innovator here is the Electronic Frontier Foundation, a San Francisco–based nonprofit that offers helpful tools such as HTTPS Everywhere, which routinely encrypts users' communications with many major websites, and Privacy Badger, which blocks spying ads and invisible trackers.[79] If reading this chapter has made you nervous, you might want to download some of these safeguards.

Citizens, companies, crooks, and states are locked in a complex, constantly shifting struggle to determine whether the internet will be a venue for advancing human freedom or constraining it. Free societies, whose openness to innovation has produced so much of the digital revolution, are well positioned to prevail—but only if the democracies of the world summon the financial resources, technological innovation, diplomatic capital, and moral resolve to win. Their survival is at stake.

THIRTEEN

REVIVING AMERICAN DEMOCRACY

> If we fail to meet our problems here, no one else in the world
> will do so. If we fail, the heart goes out of progressives around
> the world.
>
> —ELEANOR ROOSEVELT, ADDRESS TO THE FOUNDING OF
> AMERICANS FOR DEMOCRATIC ACTION, 1947[1]

W e cannot prevail against the ill winds of Russian fury, Chinese opportunism, and authoritarian populism unless we reverse the decline of American democracy. George Kennan made this point half a century ago in a prescient passage near the end of his 1946 Long Telegram from Moscow: "Every courageous and incisive measure," he wrote, to solve the "internal problems of our own society, to improve self-confidence, discipline, morale and community spirit of our own people, is a diplomatic victory over Moscow worth a thousand diplomatic notes and joint communiqués."[2]

To make American *democracy* great again, we must forthrightly confront—across party and ideological lines—the assaults on truth, science, the news media, the judicial system, immigrants, minorities, the civil service, and our democratic allies that President Donald Trump has deliberately unleashed. Containing his illiberal actions and authoritarian inclinations is now the paramount challenge for our democratic system.

But we need a deeper look into the mirror. The decline of American democracy did not begin with Trump's election—although he certainly accelerated it well before that with his deceitful, racist campaign questioning President Obama's legitimacy and birth in the United States. The erosion of democratic norms and institutions does not come solely from a single party—even if many Republicans in Congress and in some statehouses have in recent years been particularly willing to violate democratic principles in pursuit of total victory at any cost. And the political polarization that cripples our governance and degrades our civic life owes its existence to many factors and actors reaching across ideology, party, and geography. The Trump phenomenon may be the nadir of this process, but it is not the totality of it.

Deep social, technological, and economic forces are driving American democracy's polarization and decay. I do not pretend to have answers to all of these problems, including ways to reduce economic inequality, combat institutional racism, and create meaningful new jobs in the face of relentless automation.

I will focus here on political reform and civic vigilance, largely because this is what I know best. If we don't fix our political process, we will have no hope of adopting the substantive reforms that will make America a more just society and a more vibrant economy. Moreover, some plausible and promising political reform ideas are looking increasingly achievable in the near to medium term.

This chapter will discuss seven remedies to our democratic woes. Above all, we need to change the method we use to elect public officials so that we provide voters with more choice and give politicians more incentives for moderation, civility, and compromise. We also need to eliminate gerrymandering, an undemocratic scourge. We need to expand voting rights and defeat partisan efforts at voter suppression. We need a fairer way of electing the president, particularly by retiring the Electoral College. We need Congress to change its rules to make each house work far better. We need campaign-finance and lobbying reforms to reduce the tide of unaccountable money in politics. And finally, we need to defend our voting systems against foreign sabotage. Eminently practical ideas are now circulating for achieving each of these objectives; none of them requires a constitutional amendment, and all of them can be avidly pursued even while Donald Trump remains in office.

If this book's diagnosis of democracy's growing problems seems gloomy, the future need not be. We should take heart in the reformist energy that is starting to bubble up from the grass roots of American society—in no small part, because of citizens' dismay over Trump.

There are tantalizing signs that we may be entering a new reform era in the United States. Like the earlier such era, from the late nineteenth century to 1920, this one rises from a broad societal reaction against concentrated wealth, unaccountable power, deepening corruption, and brazen subjugation of the public interest. As with the Progressive era, we now hear an increasingly loud if somewhat inchoate demand for greater economic fairness, less power for special interests and pluto-crats, and a more vigorous and open democracy. A century ago, mobili-zation around similar sentiments gave us women's suffrage, a professional civil service, the direct election of senators, and new federal institutions to regulate monopolies, preserve forests, and protect the quality of food and drugs.

One key Progressive-era reform was the ballot initiative, letting citi-zens push policy reforms directly before a statewide electorate. This has sometimes gone too far; in my home state of California, the prolifera-tion of such costly initiatives finally led to amendments in 2014 to allow for reasoned compromise between an initiative's proponents and the legislature before proceeding to a public vote.[3] But the ballot initiative remains one of the most promising tools that citizens have to improve outmoded rules and invigorate American democracy. And the people are using it to enact historic reforms—none more promising than in the state of Maine.

The Battle for Ranked-Choice Voting

Cara Brown McCormick was born in 1968, a turbulent year of protests, assassinations, and social upheaval. Her father, Roger Glenn Brown, was a CIA analyst on China who had landed in political trouble after publishing an article calling for the United States to recognize China. Her mother had marched in 1974 to demand President Richard Nixon's impeachment—Cara's earliest political memory. "I grew up thinking that America was a wonderful place with some serious flaws," she recalls, a place in which "it wasn't okay to lie, and Nixon got what was coming to him. There was corruption, but it wouldn't stand."[4] After she graduated from UCLA, she worked on Democratic campaigns and joined a political consulting firm. When it denied her a raise, she left and started her own company, working mainly for Democratic candidates. She moved from California to Maine, got married, had kids, but retained her firm and her steady engagement with political campaigns.

McCormick grew increasingly troubled by our politics. "Voters were forced to choose between opposite poles," she told me. "There was a duopoly controlling our politics, and it was killing the country." In 2010, she worked for the independent candidate for governor of Maine, Eliot Cutler, a popular and moderate environmental lawyer. But some Democrats peeled away from Cutler near the end, worrying that they would "waste their vote." He narrowly lost to Paul LePage, a vulgar Republican populist who proved to be an eerie harbinger of Donald Trump.

McCormick worked again for Cutler's 2014 campaign for governor. Left-leaning Maine voters proved even more fearful of wasting a vote on the independent candidate and helping reelect the "belligerent, foul-mouthed and polarizing governor,"[5] who had told the NAACP to "kiss my butt" and compared the IRS to the Gestapo.[6] LePage won, with a larger plurality than in 2010. McCormick, along with many of her fellow Mainers, realized that the "only thing that would eliminate the spoiler problem" that had twice stymied Cutler's otherwise plausible independent candidacy was an "instant runoff"—that is, what election experts call *ranked-choice voting.*

As noted in chapter 2, under ranked-choice voting, people do not just vote for their first choice for an office. Instead, they rank the candidates in order of their preference. If no candidate wins an outright majority, the candidate with the lowest number of first-place votes is eliminated, and the second-preference votes of his or her supporters are redistributed to the remaining candidates. The process continues until someone wins a majority.

It is an elegant, deeply democratic idea. Votes aren't wasted: if a voter's favorite candidate falls short, her vote is transferred to her next choice down the line. Voters can weigh the merits of several candidates, and candidates have to appeal for the second- or third-preference votes of their rivals' supporters.

McCormick joined with other creative moderates in Maine, including Kyle Bailey, who had managed the 2012 initiative that made Maine the first state in the nation to legalize same-sex marriage at the ballot box. These reformers crafted an initiative to institute ranked-choice voting for all state and federal elections in Maine (save presidential ones) and managed to collect the more than sixty thousand signatures needed to place the reform on the November 2016 ballot. After suffering through years of LePage, who was widely viewed as "an embarrassment,"[7] Mainers seemed ready for electoral reform.

Long a state that rewarded moderation—in the form of such distinguished senators as Margaret Chase Smith, Edmund Muskie, William Cohen, Olympia Snowe, and now Susan Collins and Angus King—Maine seemed the perfect battleground for ranked-choice voting. With support from national philanthropists and activists seeking to depolarize American politics, the campaign gained credibility, volunteers, funding, and endorsements. Despite widespread opposition from the two party establishments, especially the Republicans, ranked-choice voting prevailed in the 2016 election, by 52 percent to 48 percent.

That seemed to be a happy ending for the reform push, but it was only the beginning. Maine's Republican Party launched a dogged campaign to block and bury ranked-choice voting. Many of the state's Democrats also publicly or surreptitiously joined in, not wanting to risk losing the governorship to an independent. Initially, the party establishments argued that the new ranked-choice voting method would be confusing to voters, costly to implement, or even (somehow) undemocratic. Some warned that the confusion would depress voter turnout.

None of this proved consistent with the evidence: ranked-choice voting has worked well in roughly a dozen U.S. municipalities, in more than a century of voting for the lower house of Australia's parliament, and, more recently, for the Best Picture Oscar. So its opponents switched tacks. When Maine's voters adopted ranked-choice voting in 2016, its foes charged that it violated Maine's state constitution, which requires that state general elections be decided by plurality vote. In a May 2017 advisory opinion, Maine's State Supreme Court agreed, but it left intact the use of ranked-choice voting for all primary elections and for general elections for U.S. Senate and House seats. The legislature seized the opportunity to try to kill ranked-choice voting altogether. In October 2017, it passed a bill to suspend its use for any office and to kill it entirely after December 2021 unless the state's constitution was somehow amended by then (which the legislators knew it would not be).

But the people of Maine did not go gently into that good night. Uniquely among American states, Maine's constitution provides for something called "the people's veto referendum," which enables any six registered voters to submit a proposed veto of a legislative bill to Maine's secretary of state. They then have ninety days from the end of the legislative session to gather the required signatures of registered voters (now more than 61,000) to place the referendum on the ballot.

The state legislature passed the poison bill on October 23, 2017, in the middle of the night, in a special one-day session called for that lone purpose. That ensured that the referendum to save ranked-choice voting would take place amid a primary election, when independents (its most likely supporters) would have no candidates to vote for, and thus would presumably be less likely to vote. The reformers' grassroots signature drive would now have to wrestle with the Thanksgiving and Christmas holidays and the depths of a harsh Maine winter.

The reformers also faced foot-dragging from Maine secretary of state Matthew Dunlap, and a wording[8] of the ballot question so convoluted that an ordinary voter could hardly determine whether restoring ranked-choice voting meant a yes or no vote. But the grassroots campaign for the people's veto began electronically sending petitions across the state to copy shops and drove them to volunteer gatherers. On November 7, a municipal election day, due to superior organization and determination, they obtained 33,000 signatures from voters by standing outside polling stations.

Some 1,800 volunteers continued to gather signatures throughout some brutally cold days in December and January—with Portland's highs hovering at or well below freezing. "Every week, it was another blizzard, and there was even a weather phenomenon called a bomb cyclone," recalls McCormick. "Our fingers were frozen to the bone; we had to go into our cars to warm up." Voters asked, "Didn't we already vote for this a year ago? Why do we have to sign this again?"

The shenanigans of Maine's political establishment frustrated people, but it also fired them up. Even people and opinion leaders who hadn't voted for ranked-choice voting the first time signed up for the second round. It had become not just a matter of electoral mechanics but a question of whether a bunch of politicians could trash the popular will.

When the petitions were due on February 2, the ranked-choice-

voting forces handed in a more than ample 77,000 signatures. The subsequent referendum campaign drew the support of the actress Jennifer
Lawrence, the *New York Times* editorial board,[9] and two Nobel Prize–
winning economists.[10] It also raised over a million dollars in funding,
much of it from national philanthropists seeking democratic reform.[11]
And Phish drummer Jon Fishman, who lives in Lincolnville, staged a
concert in support.

Once the signatures were certified, Maine's voters would get the chance
to decide—through the people's veto referendum—whether ranked-
choice voting would be used again. As Maine's voters headed to the polls
on June 12, 2018, Governor LePage declared ranked-choice voting "the
most horrific thing in the world"—ahead of terrorism, the opioid crisis,
and North Korea's nuclear weapons. He threatened not to certify the
election—an option he legally did not have.[12]

The people's veto referendum prevailed by eight percentage points—
twice the margin of the original victory for ranked-choice voting in
2016. "When we won," McCormick later told me, "there was a feeling
of vindication that we had gotten something back that had been stolen
from us. But even more gratifying was that we proved to one another
that democracy is not just a theory in a book; it can be a living practice
and a devotion."[13]

In November 2018, the people's faith in ranked-choice voting was
vindicated, when Maine became the first state in American history to
elect a member of Congress through the instant runoff process. In a
close contest for Maine's Second Congressional District, Jared Golden,
a thirty-six-year-old Marine Corps veteran, came from slightly behind
in the tally of first-preference votes to defeat the Republican incumbent,
Bruce Poliquin. Golden's narrow margin of victory came from the vote
transfers from two minor independent candidates. In a final gasp of resistance to reform, Poliquin went to federal court to try to stop the instant runoff count, but a federal judge turned down his case.

The victory for ranked-choice voting in Maine energized national

interest in the idea—just as a growing number of municipalities, political scientists,[14] thoughtful media outlets,[15] foundations,[16] and reformers[17] were coming to view it as the most promising *achievable* reform for
making American politics more civil, democratic, and amenable to compromise.

The logic is compelling. By removing the specter of wasted votes,
ranked-choice voting makes it easier for independents in the creative
center of American politics to run—and for voters seeking relief from
withering, zero-sum, partisan warfare to back them. If the independents
come up short in the early rounds of voting, citizens can always use their
lower-preference votes to retreat to a more partisan default. Third-party
candidates also get the same more serious chance to appeal to voters
without being tagged a "spoiler." All of this is likely to make elections
fairer, more competitive, more interesting, and yet more encouraging of
moderation.

Ranked-choice voting also makes it harder for extreme candidates to
capture their party's nominations in the primaries. Such candidates may
still get through, but they can't do so merely by appealing to a tiny slice
of the most militant voters in a fragmented race.

Ranked-choice voting would also solve another built-in problem in
some states, like Texas, which require second-round runoffs if no candidate wins a majority of their party's primary vote. Such low-turnout runoff elections put a premium on mobilizing the most committed voters,
who also tend to be the most ideological. In 2010, for instance, that
dynamic let the more extreme candidate, Ted Cruz, come from second
place to beat Texas's more centrist lieutenant governor in the runoff for
the Republican U.S. Senate nomination. Using the instant runoff in the
primaries makes particular sense in deeply Democratic states like New
York or deeply Republican ones like Mississippi, where a party's nomination is virtually tantamount to election.

In most states and districts, using ranked-choice voting in the general
election will require candidates to broaden their base and reach beyond

it—exactly what many Americans say they want. Even in a deep-red or deep-blue state, ranked-choice voting may open up the possibility of a new kind of race—one in which, for example, the real contest is not between the two establishment parties but, say, between a Tea Party Republican and an independent who is still fairly conservative but tempered enough to win the second-place votes of most Democrats along with the first-place votes of most independents and some more moderate Democrats and Republicans. As voters and politicians get accustomed to the altered logic of electoral politics under ranked-choice voting, we might see competitive races for senator and governor again in deep-red southern states and deep-blue states like California.

Ranked-choice voting could also mean more civil politics. After all, it is hard to "go negative" against multiple opponents—particularly if you think you will probably need the second- and third-preference votes of their followers later on. Voters in municipalities with ranked-choice voting view their election campaigns as less negative than do voters in cities without it.[18]

Some experts worried that the slightly more complex ballot of ranked-choice voting might depress turnout and discourage minority voters, but California cities that have adopted it have seen no drop in turnout—and a marked increase in the election of minority candidates.[19] In an exciting three-way race for mayor in 2018, San Francisco for the first time elected an African American woman, London Breed—who was also the most moderate of the three candidates.

Logically, ranked-choice voting should stimulate voter turnout, because it generates more competitive races with a wider range of candidates to interest diverse voters. As *The Economist* noted, "A study of 79 elections in 26 American cities" found that ranked-choice voting "was associated with a 10% increase in turnout compared with [non-ranked-choice-voting primaries] and run-off elections, and San Francisco's race had the highest primary turnout in years."[20] This sort of voting is not a silver bullet—but it is a considerable step forward, and a movement that should gain momentum from coast to coast.

The Vital Center

What so destructively polarizes American politics is not that our politicians have strong political views. It is that they dread compromising, even when they know it will be better for the country than today's chronic gridlock. Our politicians' fear is not bad policy outcomes; it is losing their bids for renomination in low-turnout party primaries that have, as former House member Mickey Edwards has put it, "become powerful magnets for the most committed, and most ideological, voters."[21]

The problem has reached existential proportions with the Trump presidency. Moderate Republican senators like Jeff Flake and Bob Corker declined to run for reelection in 2018 not because they lost interest in politics but because they were keenly aware that they could not win a primary fight without slavish loyalty to the new American Caesar and his worldview—as most Republican nomination races confirmed in 2018. Our primary system has become one of the principal problems of American democracy.

One obvious fix, again, would be to use ranked-choice voting in primary and general elections, which should make it easier for incumbent legislators to depart from party orthodoxy and still get renominated and reelected. But this innovation may not be enough to spare relative moderates from the wrath of party purists in low-turnout party primaries. We could try to increase voter turnout in party primaries by moving them to dates when more voters can easily cast ballots. But we should also consider giving incumbents who lose a primary another path to reelection by allowing them to run as independents in the general election.

In forty-six of the fifty states, however, that path is now blocked by something called the "sore-loser" rule.[22] This rule prevents candidates from having their name on the general-election ballot if they lose a party primary. When a congressional incumbent is defeated in a primary, it is almost always curtains for his or her legislative career. In the Trump era, this has led House and Senate Republicans to either fall in line or bow out. But if states adopted ranked-choice voting and got rid of their sore-loser rules, some of these incumbents might find their spine. They might be emboldened to stand their ground and fight the extremist tide, knowing that if they lost their party primary they could come back and run as an independent in the general election, drawing support from across the spectrum.

Some experts have also suggested that ranked-choice voting be combined with "proportional representation," a system that allocates seats in multimember districts to parties based on their proportions of the vote in each district. In this scenario, voters would rank not individual candidates but party-run (and possibly independent) slates of candidates. In 2017, Representative Don Beyer and two of his Democratic colleagues proposed such a system for the U.S. Congress. Their Fair Representation Act would create multimember districts of three to five members in larger states, then use proportional representation and ranked-choice voting to choose the winners. This has attracted interest from the *New York Times* editorial board and the columnist David Brooks.[23]

Such systems appeal to our sense of fairness. In a state like Massachusetts, where all nine House seats are held by Democrats, a proportional-representation system of three three-member districts would likely give Republicans two to three seats. Instead of each having six Republicans and one Democrat, Alabama and South Carolina would have a fairer balance too. Ohio, where Democrats won only four of sixteen House seats in 2016 and 2018, despite winning 42 and then 48 percent of the vote, would more nearly approach an even balance. In fact, most districts with three or more members would likely have at least one member from each of the two major parties.[24]

But reformers should be mindful of the Hippocratic oath: first, do no harm. In a three-seat district, proportional representation guarantees a seat to any party or candidate with a minimum of 25 percent of the vote plus one (and typically less). In a four-seat district, the minimum threshold declines to a fifth of the vote plus one, and so on. Once you start lowering the threshold for victory from a majority (or a sizable plurality) to 25, 20, or 16 percent, something big changes. Yes, the system becomes "fairer" and more inclusive. But it may also become more fragmented. Ranked-choice voting would reduce the danger by holding instant runoffs until a candidate cleared the largest mathematical threshold (in a three-seat district, 25 percent plus one). But even in this scenario, proportional representation is still a sharp departure from the more consensual logic of requiring a winning candidate to garner a majority of the votes in a single-member district.

America's two major parties could split apart. We could have a Tea Party tussling with a pro-trade Republican Party. We could have a pragmatic, liberal Democratic Party wrangling with a new, Bernie Sanders–style Progressive Socialist Party.

All this might increase voter participation, but it would hardly make it easier for Congress to forge coalitions to pass legislation. Instead, Congress might be pulled even further to the extremes by pressure from America's newly emboldened left and right flanks.

Nor is the foreign experience of proportional representation encouraging. (Just ask an Israeli or an Italian.) Moderate proportional representation did work well for many decades in post–World War II Germany, but what had long been a center-leaning, three-party system has now become a more fragmented six-party one, with the far-right nativists of Alternative for Germany winning over 12 percent of the seats in recent voting.[25] Under stress, proportional-representation systems risk empowering the extremes as establishment parties hemorrhage support to more militant alternatives.

Ending a Blight on Democracy

Another fixable problem is a particularly pernicious one: the partisan gerrymandering of congressional and state-legislature districts.[26] Such deliberate distortions typically produce a gross advantage for the party that controls the once-a-decade redistricting process. Since Republicans have, over the past two decades, controlled more state legislatures and thus had the advantage in drawing district boundaries, Democrats have had to win a disproportionately large margin in the popular vote in order to win the House.[27] In 2018, their margin of seats won was close to their national margin of victory in the popular vote, but only because they won many close contests. Gerrymandering stifles competition by protecting incumbents. And it feeds decennial spasms of hyperpartisanship: as redistricting approaches, legislators rally ever more intensely behind their parties, using computer models and political muscle to squeeze every last ounce of partisan benefit from the process.[28]

These bitter battles are unworthy, unseemly, and undemocratic. The best way to fix gerrymandering is straightforward: take redistricting out of the hands of the partisan state legislatures and give it to nonpartisan commissions, as Arizona, California, Idaho, and Washington State have already done. As the superb civic organization RepresentUs suggests, independent commissioners should be "people who are openly vetted, act with complete transparency, come from across the political spectrum, and abide by strict criteria to ensure fair and accurate representation for all voters."[29]

In May 2018, three quarters of Ohio voters approved a referendum with creative inducements for the state's legislature to achieve bipartisan consensus on a redistricting plan. In a grassroots campaign with echoes of the Maine drama on ranked-choice voting, some 4,000 volunteers in Michigan gathered more than 425,000 signatures from February through May 2018 to place an initiative on the ballot giving redistricting power to a nonpartisan commission.[30] On November 6, that proposition won by nearly a million votes, with over 60 percent approval. Voters in three other states—Colorado, Missouri, and Utah—also eliminated partisan gerrymandering that night. As a result, roughly a third of all House seats will be redrawn by independent commissions or nonpartisan experts by 2022.[31] But most states still give complete or ultimate redistricting authority to their legislatures, which proceed in highly partisan fashion wherever a single party dominates.

Partisan redistricting is also being challenged on legal grounds. In November 2016, a federal court in Wisconsin struck down the state's contorted assembly district map as unconstitutional. But in a cautious and narrowly argued decision in June 2018, the U.S. Supreme Court sent the issue back to the lower courts rather than rule in principle against highly partisan redistricting. That August, a North Carolina federal court reached a similar decision about that state's redistricting plan—imposed in 2016 for the express purpose of minimizing the number of U.S. House districts in which a Democrat might win—but the court soon decided there wasn't time to redraw districts for the 2018 election. In November, North Carolina Republicans held on to their lopsided margin of ten of the state's thirteen seats. A separate lawsuit challenged the highly skewed Democratic redistricting plan in reliably blue Maryland.

In January 2018, the Pennsylvania Supreme Court struck down the state's 2011 redistricting map, ruling that it "clearly, plainly, and palpably" violated the state's constitution by undermining the ability of citizens to vote in "free and 'equal' elections." Nonpartisan redistricting then made a difference. When Pennsylvania's Republican-controlled legislature and Democratic governor could not agree on a new map, the court itself redrew the map in a way much more likely to level the playing field.[32] And it did. In the November 2018 midterm elections, the Republicans won only nine of the state's eighteen congressional seats, down from thirteen in 2016.

Partisan gerrymandering of electoral districts is an abomination against democratic principles, and its days fortunately appear to be numbered.

Let the People Vote

In theory, if more people voted in primary elections that were partially or fully open to all voters, moderates would have a better chance of winning, because they would likely be facing a broader, more ideologically diverse electorate rather than the more familiar array of devotees who usually vote in American primaries. But voter turnout in primary elections remains stubbornly low. When separated from a presidential primary, regular primary turnout tends to average around 20 percent of eligible voters—and may run as low as 10 percent in some states.[33]

Timing may have something to do with this, notes Elaine Kamarck of the Brookings Institution. Currently, the state primaries stretch over seven months deep into "the dog days of summer. To a certain extent, this calendar is a creation of incumbents who, confident in their small core of primary voters, liked the fact that very few people would vote."[34]

Instead, Kamarck urges the states and parties to consolidate state primary elections into a few big "national primary" days. That would stimulate voter interest, galvanize media attention, and make it easier to get voters to the polls. But nationalizing state primary elections could make them even more intensely partisan.

Another option for boosting turnout would be to move state primary elections (for all offices save president) to September, when more voters are paying attention and have returned from their summer holidays. Currently only five northeastern states vote then, shortly after Labor Day. September primaries would also make for shorter, less costly campaigns, but they could give an advantage to well-funded, well-known incumbents.

The best bets for increasing state primary election turnout are the kinds of steps that would increase voter participation more generally. That means making it easier to register to vote, ideally through automatic voter registration. The United States lags well behind most advanced democracies in voter registration and turnout; one in four eligible Americans isn't even registered to vote.[35]

Oregon provides a model for how to do better. In 2016, it became the first state in the country to automatically register eligible voters based on motor-vehicle registration or other interactions with the government that demonstrate U.S. citizenship.

Oregon's new system substantially increased voter registration in 2016, particularly among racial minorities, young people, and the poor. It also increased voter turnout, which rose by four percentage points over 2012 even though Oregon didn't have a U.S. Senate race in 2016 and Hillary Clinton had the left-leaning state's presidential electoral votes pretty much locked up.[36] By April 2018, twelve states had adopted automatic voter registration, and nineteen others were considering legislation to implement it.[37] That November, voters in Michigan and Nevada adopted it by ballot initiative. Same-day registration at the polling place and online voter registration would also help.

We could also increase turnout by expanding opportunities to vote early and by mail, which can reduce the costs of voting and of staffing the polls.[38] Many Americans like voting early; one in three already do it. But thirteen states still bar early voting.[39]

Finally, we should either move voting from our now traditional Tuesdays to the weekend (ideally on both Saturday and Sunday) or make election day in November a national holiday (perhaps by moving Presidents' Day to that date).[40] Most major democracies do something like this. Holding voting on a workday makes it harder to cast your ballot, especially for blue-collar workers with inflexible schedules.[41]

The beauty of these reforms is that they are both achievable and effective. There are two changes we should resist, however. One is online voting, for which reliable, hacker-proof technology is simply not ready. The second is voter suppression—the active efforts of partisan Republican politicians in some (mostly southern) states to make it more difficult to vote, particularly through discriminatory laws requiring the presentation of photo IDs, which disproportionately target racial minorities. In Georgia in 2018, Secretary of State Brian Kemp—the Republican nominee for governor—used a law requiring an "exact match" of name spellings to suspend 53,000 predominantly African American voter registration applications.[42]

This is why America needs to fully restore the Voting Rights Act, one of the most successful pieces of civil rights legislation in U.S. history. The act was weakened by a 2013 Supreme Court ruling, which threw out the formula requiring certain states with a history of racist voter suppression to obtain federal permission before changing their voting requirements. As recent experience shows, this measure is still needed to protect African Americans' most fundamental rights.[43] We also need to protect voters from being unfairly purged from the voter rolls, and we need criminal penalties to punish the spread of intimidating and deceptive messages designed to keep minorities from voting. Federal legislation has been proposed to address both of these problems.[44] Congress should pass it and dare any president not to sign.

The Democratic Way to Elect a President

Any serious discussion about problems with American democracy comes quickly around to the Electoral College. One of the most common questions I am asked when I travel abroad is "Why do you Americans allow the loser of the popular vote to sometimes become president?" I try to explain the background—that our Founders feared unchecked populism and so designed a number of constitutional filters on the popular passions (including, until a century ago, an indirectly elected Senate). In the *Federalist Papers*, Alexander Hamilton explained that the Electoral College was meant to ensure the election of an eminently qualified candidate, and to guard against the election of a candidate with "[t]alents for low intrigue, and the little arts of popularity."[45]

That was then. This is now. We have been stuck with the anachronism of the Electoral College, and all the tortured arguments in its defense, for far too long. The United States is less democratic today because of a system that, as *The Economist* acidly and accurately put it, "America's founders jury-rigged in part to square the needs of democracy with the demography of slavery."[46] That Americans have—twice in less than two decades—peacefully accepted the ascension of presidents who lost the popular vote is a testament to the strength of our democratic culture; that Americans have had to do so is a testament to the deficiency of our democratic institutions.

The most obvious way to get rid of the Electoral College would require a constitutional amendment—a far-fetched prospect in this era of polarization. But there is a promising shortcut: the National Popular Vote Interstate Compact. By this ingenious initiative, eleven states (including populous New York and California) and the District of Columbia have adopted a bill requiring that their electoral votes be cast for the winner of the *national* popular vote. The bill only takes effect once the states that have passed it account for at least 270 electoral votes (a majority). Currently, states in the compact account for 172 electoral votes, but the bill has passed one legislative chamber in states that account for another 89 electoral votes. While this admirable initiative will not prevail in time for the 2020 election, it could get to 270 electoral votes in the not-too-distant future. The organizers take particular hope from the fact that even many Republicans believe, as a matter of principle, that the winner of the national popular vote should be president and dislike the way the current system concentrates presidential campaigning on a few key swing states.[47]

The Electoral College is not the only factor upholding today's dysfunctional two-party duopoly. Another is the rules for access to the presidential debates. No independent or third-party candidate has a chance of winning the White House without participating in the autumn debates, but no serious third candidate has emerged since Ross Perot in the 1990s because, in part, the post-Perot debate rules make it virtually impossible for one to qualify. The Commission on Presidential Debates requires a third candidate to average 15 percent of the vote in presidential preference polls seven weeks before the election. As a recent Harvard Business School study noted, this creates "an insurmountable 'Catch-22' "[48]: a candidate who had not contested in the party primaries would not be able to achieve the name recognition and national attention to score 15 percent in the polls without spending close to a billion dollars (and if a candidate ran in the primaries, the "sore-loser" rules would keep him off the general-election ballot in most states).[49]

The most democratic way to choose an American president is clear: by ranked-choice voting in a direct, national popular vote, with reasonable rules for entry into the autumn debates. But such a national system would require a constitutional amendment to end the Electoral College, as well as legislation to implement ranked-choice voting nationwide.

That is clearly a long way off. In the meanwhile, there are other ways to improve the way we choose our presidents. One could be achieved entirely by civil-society groups and the media.

Candidates for president must now run a gauntlet of low-turnout nomination contests that begins with the Iowa caucuses in January, followed in February by the New Hampshire and South Carolina primaries. In 2020, the contest will then become fast and furious as eight states—including California, Texas, Massachusetts, and Virginia—hold their primaries on March 3. But the increasing frontloading of the presidential primary calendar and the unrepresentative nature of the primary electorate—which is much more partisan and ideological than the general voting public—intensifies polarization.

So what if the first expression of presidential voter preference came not from Iowa's caucuses but from the whole, sprawling, diverse country—in the form of a random sample of the American electorate, drawn together over a weekend to deliberate on the issues, hear the candidates speak, and then register their preferences through ranked-choice voting? This national "deliberative poll"—putting America in one room—would be far more representative of the entire nation. It would emphasize issues over personalities while giving voters a chance to size up each candidate in person. And this method of deliberative polling has already been applied more than one hundred times in twenty-eight different countries.[50]

A Congress That Works

Americans disagree on a lot these days, but they are united in their view of Congress: throughout 2018, only some 15 to 20 percent of Americans approved of the job it was doing.[51] The best way to a more workable Congress—one better able to strike bargains and pass legislation with bipartisan majorities—is to elect more senators and representatives who are ideologically moderate or at least flexible enough to compromise.

Congress today simply isn't very democratic. The majority party leaders in the House and the Senate tightly control the agenda and can prevent popular bills from reaching the floor. The House used to mainly consider bills under an "open" rule that allows free debate and wide amendment; now, most bills come to the floor under a "closed" rule that prohibits changes. This elevation of power over dissent has been the work of both political parties over time, making the House an increasingly embittered arena of zero-sum political combat.

The Senate was never a terribly democratic idea to begin with, but its internal procedures and culture have also eroded in recent years. The key problems include the growing use of the filibuster and senatorial holds (which enable a lone senator to prevent a motion from reaching a floor vote unless there is a three-fifths vote to end debate). These tools enable the minority to grind the body to a halt.[52]

These problems could be attenuated, argues Mickey Edwards, who served eight terms in the House, by changing the rules to sharply pare back the use of senatorial filibusters and holds (which used to be rare occurrences) and to guarantee that any amendment on a House bill with at least one hundred cosponsors will have a full hearing and a recorded floor vote. The nonpartisan political-reform group No Labels would go further, allowing House members to anonymously sign a discharge petition to bring a bill to the floor over the resistance of the majority leaders. This would enable moderate members of the majority party to push forward bipartisan compromises without fearing retaliation from their leaders.[53] No Labels also recommends requiring an up-or-down Senate vote on any presidential nominee within ninety days, without which the nominee would be confirmed by default.[54]

Along with many other former members of Congress, Edwards also argues passionately that fostering better personal relationships across the partisan divide is crucial to promoting civility and problem solving on Capitol Hill. He recommends longer workweeks and more opportunities for members to travel on congressional business and socialize with one another. Some years ago, No Labels proposed a profound change to the congressional work schedule: instead of a Tuesday-to-Thursday legislative schedule that has members constantly traveling back home to raise money and see constituents, have Congress in session three weeks a month and let members go home the remaining full week.[55]

Somewhat paradoxically, we might achieve a better Congress by modestly loosening the requirements for openness in committee hearings, legislative negotiations, and floor debates. Transparency is important in any democracy, but when opposing politicians cannot retreat from the cameras' glare to privately explore painful concessions and unconventional solutions, it becomes that much harder to reach compromise. Having to negotiate in public, or with the expectation that deliberations will be leaked, drives lawmakers back into politically safe, fixed positions. But if they can talk candidly in private, politicians can explore risky trade-offs that they don't have to acknowledge unless they get a successful deal.[56]

There is also a tension between purity and pragmatism when it comes to congressional earmarks, the widely reviled provisions in spending bills that direct money to a specific project or purpose, usually in a member's state or district. Earmarks are hardly ideal, but paralyzing gridlock is worse. Congress could improve its members' bargaining flexibility by restoring some greater capacity to logroll, giving members side payments in the form of spending earmarks in exchange for agreements on legislation. If the side payments are transparent, necessary to achieve a decent deal, and proportional to the good achieved by the legislation, people are apt to see them as justifiable.[57]

The key point underlying all these ideas is that reform is possible. In almost all of these instances, each chamber can simply change its own rules, without the more complicated process of lawmaking. The catch is that members would have to want a Congress that works—and that will happen only when their constituents demand it.

Defending Our Elections

No amount of tinkering with our legislative machinery will matter unless Americans have confidence that our elections are honest and fair. As I've already suggested, this puts a high premium on ending partisan gerrymandering and voter suppression. But that still leaves two big challenges to electoral integrity: the corrupting influence of money in

American politics and the newer danger of foreign (or other) hacking of our voting machines.

Most Americans take it for granted that the results announced on election night represent an honest count of the votes. Notwithstanding Donald Trump's insinuations, there is simply no evidence of significant vote fraud of the old-fashioned kind, in which people voted multiple times, stuffed ballot boxes, or impersonated actual voters. But Russia's penetration of state election websites and voter-registration databases in twenty-one states during the 2016 election cycle has exposed a profound vulnerability in American democracy. With "aging technology, inadequate security, and a patchwork system of election administration with widely varying degrees of sophistication and resources," warn Wendy Weiser and Alicia Bannon of the Brennan Center for Justice, our "twentieth century voting system is not suitable for the twenty-first century."[58]

The most urgent danger is computerized voting systems, such as touch-screen voting, that record votes directly into a computer's memory without leaving a verifiable paper trail. No election in any democracy should ever take place without a paper record that can be audited or recounted.[59] In the age of hacking, high-tech computer-based systems open up our elections to digital rigging that might be undetectable or virtually impossible to prove. But despite Russia's assault on the 2016 elections, roughly a dozen American states still use electronic voting machines that do not produce a verified paper audit trail of our votes.[60] And many other voting machines and state voter-registration databases are simply antiquated. Even without rigging the vote count, a malicious hacker could cause havoc—and even sway the results—by breaking into vulnerable registration systems and purging voters from the rolls.

We urgently need to modernize and harden our voting systems. In March 2018, Congress gave the states (many of them financially strapped) $380 million to upgrade their voter-registration systems, replace insecure voting machines, and implement postelection vote-audit systems. But this is only about 10 percent of the total that Congress appropriated in 2002 to upgrade voting systems—and thirty-three states say that they need to replace their voting machines before the 2020 election.[61] Congress must help them. Fixing our voting infrastructure goes to the heart of our democracy; it should not be a partisan issue.

Securing our voting systems is a relatively technical challenge. Reducing the influence of money in our politics will be far tougher and more political. But the current flood of increasingly unregulated cash into our politics is devastating our democracy.

At a minimum, we should seek full disclosure of *all* campaign contributions and spending beyond truly trivial sums. We must require transparency in online ads while making it much more difficult for foreign actors to purchase them or otherwise intervene in an American election campaign. The Supreme Court's 2010 *Citizens United* decision made this far harder, because the court in effect deemed independent groups' ability to spend unlimited amounts of money a constitutionally protected form of free speech.

Unless and until that lamentable decision is reversed, the best we can do is to ensure full disclosure of the sources of all donations designed to influence elections. The major loophole now is the vast amount of spending done by so-called social welfare organizations—501(c)(4)s under the IRS code. These groups can spend unlimited amounts of undisclosed dark money on politics and election campaigns, so long as that amounts to less than half of their total expenditures (with the rest usually coming with "issue" education).[62] Incredibly, these funds are tax exempt.

In the 2016 election cycle, the largest of these "social welfare" groups, an arm of the National Rifle Association, spent some $35 million in tax-exempt contributions; seven of the top ten dark-money groups were Republican or conservative.[63] Some states, such as California, now require major nonprofit campaign spenders to disclose the identity of their donors; a bill proposed by two Democratic members of Congress would impose a similar national requirement. But partisans and special-interest groups will fight such sensible reforms tooth and nail, and it will take determined citizen advocacy to beat them back.

Another useful campaign-finance reform would crack down on the supposedly independent political action committees (known as super PACs) that raise and spend unlimited amounts of money to support presidential candidates. As the Brennan Center for Justice has noted, the laws requiring the super PACs to be independent from the candidates and their campaigns have become a joke, rendering "candidate contribution limits virtually meaningless."[64]

Neither Republicans nor Democrats should put up with this. Instead, we could sensibly raise the limits on campaign contributions from individuals—but then vigorously enforce the requirement for the independence of super PACs. Proposed federal legislation from Representative David Price, a North Carolina Democrat, would close several practical loopholes that now enable close de facto coordination between super PACs and their presidential candidates; some states (including California and Minnesota) have already adopted similar measures.[65]

It is hard to imagine Congress passing mandatory campaign-spending limits or providing for full public financing of campaigns. But we could do more to induce candidates to accept spending limits in exchange for public support. In 2017, the city of Seattle implemented a system of public campaign financing called *democracy vouchers*. Each registered voter is given four vouchers worth $25, which he or she can assign to any candidate who opts into the program by agreeing to certain spending limits and by raising a minimum number of contributions of at least $10. Candidates who participated in this program raised a significantly larger share of their funding from the city's residents.[66]

A kindred reform would have governments, at all election levels, match small individual contributions to candidates. This would put a premium on candidates who inspire a broad base of voters to contribute— and reduce dependence on special interests. RepresentUs would go further. Its comprehensive American Anti-Corruption Act would give every voter a credit to use to make a political donation, but candidates and political action committees could receive those credits only if they agreed to fund-raise solely from small donors.[67] None of these reforms will end the flood of unregulated money into our politics, but unless we start shutting that spigot, our democracy will continue to drown.

Draining the Swamp

A better democracy also requires lobbying reform to reduce the influence of wealthy special interests and foreign governments. In October 2016, candidate Trump proposed a ban on executive-branch appointees lobbying the federal government for five years after leaving office; a five-year ban on lobbying by former members of Congress and their staffs; a lifetime ban on senior executive-branch officials lobbying for foreign governments; and a law to prevent registered foreign lobbyists from raising campaign funds in the United States.[68] Trump's plan constituted a step in the right direction. As mentioned earlier, once he took office in January 2017, President Trump issued an executive order banning departing officials from lobbying their own agencies for five years and from ever lobbying for a foreign government or foreign political party.[69]

But far more comprehensive reform is needed. RepresentUs has proposed banning serving members of Congress and senior congressional staff from even exploring future private employment and banning lobbyists from contributing to presidential or congressional election campaigns.[70] All these provisions should be enshrined in law, with one addition: members of Congress should also be banned from *ever* lobbying for foreign governments.[71]

But we need more than just rule changes. Unlike most advanced democracies and even many emerging ones, the United States lacks a coherent national agency to enforce laws and standards against corruption by major public officeholders. The current structure—scattered across the Office of Government Ethics, the Department of Justice, the inspectors general of the various cabinet departments and agencies, and more—is weak, piecemeal, and ineffective.[72]

In May 2018, the Roosevelt Institute, a liberal think tank, proposed creating a fully independent Public Integrity Protection Agency to remedy this. The new agency's director would appoint the inspectors general who serve as watchdogs of the executive branch's departments and would be a nonpartisan figure appointed for an extended but fixed term.[73] I would go even further and give this agency oversight on congressional ethics as well. Donald Trump is right when he calls today's Washington a swamp. But he is now the worst creature in it, and only new rules and institutions can dry it up.

Defying America's Demagogue

The most urgent problem with American democracy today is Donald Trump, and as this book goes to press, the fate of his presidency remains uncertain. He could be impeached, disgraced, and even conceivably removed from office if Senate Republicans can somehow belatedly find their spine. Or he could be reelected, opening the potential for much graver and more lasting damage to our democratic institutions and culture.

Our system has already done much to normalize this highly abnormal and dangerous president. The media, after all, must still cover the White House. Congress must still negotiate with him. Republican members of Congress must find their way within a party he has remade in his nativist image. And an unsettling number of people in his administration and outside it have sought to curry his favor by issuing obsequious praise or declining to publicly confront his transgressions.

The conventional wisdom in Washington has been that our democratic institutions—Congress, the courts, the media—are working to draw limits and defend constitutional norms. But with a new scandal or rhetorical outrage breaking virtually every day, reporters have been hard-pressed to fix the public's attention on the larger pattern of abuse. Meanwhile, Fox News continues to cheerlead for the president and mislead its viewers while the seductions of Twitter and cable-news shouting matches have moved some other members of the media away from their constitutionally protected mission of holding powerful people accountable.

The courts have shown significant independence and integrity, at least thus far. But the Supreme Court erred in blessing a lightly disguised version of Trump's promised ban on letting Muslims into the country. And will the judiciary's commitment to constitutionalism hold if Trump has six more years to stack the judiciary with appointees who share his political views?

In the first two years of Trump's presidency, the greatest system failure has been in Congress. It has failed to provide concerted moral and political pushback, especially from members of Trump's own party, who—aside from the late, great John McCain and a few other honorable exceptions—have lacked the courage even to denounce Trump's degradations of democracy, let alone vote against them.

What the republic needs now is a group of Republicans to draw the line, as six Republican senators did in 1950 when they signed onto Senator Margaret Chase Smith's stirring Declaration of Conscience against Joe McCarthy. From the floor of the Senate on June 1, the Republican from Maine declared: "I do not want to see the Republican Party ride to political victory on the Four Horsemen of Calumny—Fear, Ignorance, Bigotry, and Smear. . . . While it might be a fleeting victory for the Republican Party, it would be a more lasting defeat for the American people."[74]

The single most important condition for defending democracy against Trump's calumnies is for *Republican* members of Congress to rise on principle, in much the way Smith did in 1950, in both votes and rhetoric. If she could summon the courage, so can Republican senators today. It is more daring to oppose a president than a fellow senator, but in 1950, Smith was a freshman and the only woman in the Senate, and McCarthy was riding high in public opinion and political momentum. In the end, democracy is only as strong as the courage of the people whose responsibility it is to defend it.

That sets out another clear test of patriotism as we look toward 2020: one brave Republican needs to mount a resolute, civic-spirited primary challenge to Trump. Fine words alone will not cut it in our hour of emergency. In recent American political history, all of our one-term presidents—Gerald Ford, Jimmy Carter, and George H. W. Bush— were badly wounded by serious primary challengers on their way to defeat in November; Lyndon Johnson was deterred from running in 1968 by Eugene McCarthy's moral victory in the New Hampshire primary. Trump deserves the same.

A long list of Republican heavyweights—including John Kasich, Mitt Romney, Nikki Haley, Ben Sasse, Jeff Flake, Larry Hogan, and Bob Corker—understand the peril that Trump poses to their country and their party. They will face abuse and invective for running against him, and he will likely win the primary fight. But any challenger may well reap political rewards when the Republican Party shakes off the fever of Trumpism. And they will certainly be rewarded by the verdict of history. Most Republican leaders know all too well how unfit Trump is for his office, how dangerous he is for his country, and how corrosive he is for democratic values. They should act like it.

Nor should we let senior members of Trump's administration off the hook. They have seen his autocratic temperament and behavior up close. They should turn their private horror over his conduct into forthright public criticism.

The Democratic Party faces a different dilemma. If it does not op-pose Trump's assaults on democratic norms, it will fail its core constitu-encies and the country at large. But if the party condemns everything Trump says and does with equal vigor, it will make it impossible for the public to distinguish between the defense of core democratic values and the waging of more normal political battles over issues.

Democrats must clearly separate two forms of opposition to Trump. First is the normal partisan and ideological resistance that one party mounts to the policy agenda of a president from the opposing party. The second level involves statements and acts that threaten democracy itself. Democrats must clearly distinguish this as a higher, more urgent level of opposition—one that demands cooperation from Republicans similarly worried about what Trump means for the republic. Here the focus must be on the defense of institutions and norms—freedom of the press, judicial independence, congressional oversight, individual rights—that transcend the standard cut and thrust of policy debate. Trump came to power by splitting Americans apart. He will be driven from power only when Americans come together.

To restore American democracy, we will need new and broad alli-ances. Liberals, conservatives, and independents who want politics to be more open and competitive—and less toxic and polarizing—must join together to fight for reforms like ranked-choice voting and an end to gerrymandering.

A growing number of Americans are ready—indeed hungry—for a renewal of our civic virtues. Beneath the surface of our broken national politics, they are making gains. What is missing is the national vision and leadership to renovate and reinvigorate our democracy. If we cannot summon the courage to defend our founding values, the light of the American experiment may dim, flicker, and go out.

FOURTEEN

CONCLUSION: A NEW BIRTH OF FREEDOM

Power is stubborn. It has to be moved. And it can only be moved by us.

—LAURENE POWELL JOBS, COMMENCEMENT ADDRESS
TO MIAMI DADE COLLEGE, MAY 5, 2018[1]

Tell your brother that he's gotta rise up.
Tell your sister that she's gotta rise up.

—LIN-MANUEL MIRANDA, "MY SHOT," FROM *Hamilton*

In Frank Capra's 1946 movie *It's a Wonderful Life*, the uncle of a generous banker named George Bailey innocently misplaces a large deposit, which will let a greedy rival take over the bank and the entire town. Despondent, George (played by Jimmy Stewart) prepares to jump from the town bridge on Christmas Eve. At the last moment, a guardian angel intervenes and shows George all the good deeds that would never have been performed if not for him. "You've been given a great gift, George," the angel says. "A chance to see what the world would be like without you."

If there is a silver lining to the disaster that has been Donald Trump's presidency, it is this: as Trump has insulted our closest democratic allies, undermined NATO, and encouraged the breakup of the European Union; as he has pulled the United States out of the global climate accord, the Iranian nuclear deal, and the Trans-Pacific Partnership; as he has started gratuitous trade wars with friends and foes alike; as he has excused and befriended Vladimir Putin and a grim list of other brutal dictators; as he has made common cause with nativist bigots abroad and at home; as he has revived the old, nasty, and specious slogan "America first"; and as he has shaken every moral and strategic pillar of the post–World War II liberal order, we are all being given a glimpse into the possible future: a chance to see what the world would look like without American leadership and steadfastness.

For democrats everywhere, this is a frightening prospect. But for the belligerent autocrats in China and Russia, it is a gift: a startling, almost too-good-to-be-true opportunity to bring down the global architecture of norms and alliances that has kept the peace in Europe and the Pacific for nearly three quarters of a century—and enabled an unprecedented expansion of democracy and freedom.

The global crisis of democracy has been long in coming. It did not start with Donald Trump, and it will not end when he leaves the White House. Yet American moral and geopolitical leadership—our defense of democratic norms, our assistance to democratic governments and movements, our support for freer trade and broader economic development, and our willingness to deter aggression and denounce oppression—has enabled waves of democratic expansion to roll forward across the world.

To be sure, the United States has often been inconsistent and imperfect in its foreign policy. But over more than a century, it has also been what former secretary of state Madeleine Albright rightly called "the indispensable nation" for democracy—indispensable in advancing human rights, indispensable in stirring democratic hopes, indispensable in building the international institutions and alliances that have enabled freedom to thrive.

Ideals matter in world politics, but so does power—and the United States, for all its flaws and blunders, has been the rare great power to fuse both might and right to create space for the expansion of democracy. Since the end of World War II, a strong, steadfast American presence has kept the democracies of Europe and the more pluralistic states of Asia from throwing in their lot with the Soviet Union, Maoist China, and their successor dictatorships. Take away American power, presence, and principles, and most Asian states would jump on the bandwagon of the emerging Chinese imperium in Asia. Remove America as the bonding cement of NATO and a counterweight to Russia's ambitions in former Soviet states like Ukraine and Georgia, and it will doom hopes for freedom throughout the former USSR—probably even in the Baltic states—and cast a long, dark shadow over the remaining democracies of Central and Eastern Europe. The European Union might not survive such a U.S. retreat, and if the EU did, it would feel intense pressure to reconcile with a resurgent Russian empire. The world without us would be a far more frightening and dangerous place, with muscular, corrupt dictatorships dominating large swaths of the globe through both blatant coercion and covert subversion.

To borrow a phrase from Bill Clinton, the power of our example has mattered more than the example of our power.[2] The assistance we have provided and the example we have shown have helped inspire and support democratic change in Latin America, Africa, and even—after a long, sordid period of unquestioning U.S. support for Arab dictatorships—the Middle East. We have often erred and failed to live up to our best traditions. But on balance, American ideals, broadcasts, grants, and diplomacy have pressured autocracies to change, warned them not to resort to devastating repression, and opened up space for people around the world to claim their own inalienable rights. Take all of that away, and it is not clear when—or if—the transitions to democracy would have occurred in such places as Argentina, Brazil, and Chile; South Korea, Taiwan, and the Philippines; South Africa, Ghana, and Tunisia; and all the countries once locked behind the Iron Curtain.

Until recently, American power and principle have helped enable many societies to make peaceful transitions to democracy. American resolve has kept the ill winds of Russian rage, Chinese ambition, and populist authoritarianism from reaching hurricane force. But today, another gale is raging: that of America's own political decay, rooted in cynical politicians, calcified systems, and complacent citizens, tarnishing the overall luster of democracy and pulling America away from the world. If we do not soon reverse this retreat, democracy worldwide will be at risk.

Already, we have seen twelve consecutive years of erosion in global levels of freedom, with many more countries declining than gaining each year, according to Freedom House. We have seen a gathering tide of democratic breakdowns, with the proportion of democracies (among countries with populations over one million) slipping back in recent years to barely half. But the numbers do not capture the full extent of the danger. Behind the statistics is a steady, palpable corrosion of democratic institutions and norms in a wide range of countries. A new global narrative is on the rise, hailing strongman rule—not parliamentary rules—as the way to govern in difficult times.

Slow descents have a way of lulling us into complacency. Things aren't so bad, we tell ourselves; they're just slipping a bit. But we ignore gradual decay at our peril. In Ernest Hemingway's *The Sun Also Rises*, the freewheeling, hard-drinking Mike Campbell is asked how he went bankrupt. "Two ways," he says. "Gradually and then suddenly."[3] The demise of democracy is often like that too.

In Venezuela, the collapse started gradually, over a protracted period of corruption and complacency. The country had once been a vibrant liberal democracy, blessed with bountiful oil wealth, but the people grew steadily more alienated from a self-serving political class that was not delivering. This paved the way for a leftist, populist demagogue, Hugo Chávez, first to try to seize power by military coup and then to triumph through the ballot box.

Much of the decay of democracy in Latin America has been like this. In Mexico, Brazil, and Peru, widespread corruption, increasing crime, and feckless governance have thrown citizen confidence and the party system into crisis. As a result, democracy is now at risk across the region.

A similar erosion is painfully clear in Turkey, a Muslim NATO ally. For years after Recep Tayyip Erdogan and his Justice and Development Party came to power, they seemed to just be religious or social conservatives willing to abide by democratic rules. Western observers and governments ignored warnings from liberal Turks as Erdogan slowly tightened the screws on dissent and pluralism. Then, after a failed coup in July 2016, he crushed all political opposition. Turkish democracy died in two ways: "Gradually and then suddenly."

We would like to think that American democracy is immune. It is not. Democracies are not gifts or miracles; they are painstakingly built forms of government, and none of them are invincible if citizens succumb to cynicism and complacency in perilous times.

We are at a precarious moment—the most dangerous I have seen in my forty-year career as a scholar of democracy. Several major democracies are either hanging from a populist thread—as in Poland and the Philippines—or showing large and growing signs of strain. Immigrant bashing, ethnic chauvinism, and anti-Muslim bigotry are threatening the civic fabric of many democracies we had previously considered stable, including countries in the liberal heart of Western Europe and now even the United States. If democracy could be effectively extinguished in an EU member state like Hungary, then who is immune? If an illiberal demagogue deeply contemptuous of the media, the courts, the opposition, and the truth could win the American presidency, then what ground is safe?

The problems span the globe. We should not underestimate the danger of religious intolerance, now on the rise in Indonesia and India. Like Erdogan, Narendra Modi, India's Hindu-chauvinist prime minister, is a charismatic, ambitious populist and social conservative who extols religious virtues. Like Erdogan, Modi has amassed enough power to sideline one restraining institution after another. India's countervailing power centers—the higher courts, the civil service, the media, and independent organizations—are strong. But will Indian democracy withstand a prolonged period of one-party dominance and religious intolerance? History teaches us—all of us—to take nothing for granted.

In Africa, democratic institutions are increasingly under assault. South Africa's wantonly corrupt president, Jacob Zuma, and his kleptocratic cabal have mercifully lost power in South Africa, but the country's deeper problems of corruption and extreme, racially fraught poverty and inequality remain. Aside from Ghana, democracy has been either decaying or failing to take root in most other larger African states, such as Kenya, Tanzania, and Nigeria. As we have seen, despite the pervasive poverty that supposedly leads people to choose bread over freedom, most Africans still passionately want democratic and accountable government. But they need help. Instead, the current world realities of Chinese swagger, European distraction, and American retreat are enabling African autocrats to have their way.

In the Middle East, the lone Arab democracy still standing after the 2011 revolutions is Tunisia. Its breakthrough was extraordinary but fragile, and it is now struggling amid its own ill winds: a reeling economy, powerful Gulf autocrats who would like to see democracy wither, and political survivors from the old dictatorship reluctant to give up the corrupt privileges and authoritarian practices of the past. In Egypt, after the fall of the longtime Mubarak dictatorship, the military has now crushed all opposition and dissent. The oil-rich Gulf states now believe that they have forced the genie of the Arab Spring back into the bottle of state repression. Meanwhile, the Middle East's one long-standing democracy, Israel, has been drifting increasingly toward an illiberal populism that consigns its own Arab citizens to second-class citizenship—and the Palestinians of the West Bank to none at all.[4]

And this could be just the beginning of the drop. Suppose that the drift in U.S. global leadership persists and even intensifies. Suppose that illiberal populism gains an even stronger footing in the United States and Western Europe. Suppose that autocratic leaders conclude that we just don't care anymore—that there is scant price to be paid for abandoning democracy. Among the world's fifty most populous countries, slightly less than half are now democracies, but that could well plunge to just a third or less, even as the possibilities for democratic renewal dry up in swing states that might have moved or returned to democracy under more favorable international conditions.

Here's how that story might unfold. A third reverse wave of global democratic failures would see much of Central and Eastern Europe joining Hungary in silent defection from democracy. With the European Union's eastern flank swinging truculently away from liberal values and its western core absorbed with anti-immigrant passions and meltdowns of national self-confidence, the EU could break apart.

A reelected Donald Trump would feel himself free to more brazenly advance an isolationist, despot-friendly, pro-Kremlin posture. Without its foundation, NATO could then disintegrate too, freeing Vladimir Putin to achieve his ultimate dream: the resurrection of the Greater Russian Empire, a new heir to the Soviet Union whose demise he has long considered a tragedy.

The Baltics would again be abandoned to a ruthless Russian bear. Hopes for democracy in Ukraine, Moldova, Georgia, and Armenia would drown in a wave of Kremlin coups and aggressions. A despotic Russia would once again surround itself with client and puppet states that would do its bidding.

The lengthening shadow of authoritarianism would also reach out from Beijing. An increasingly assertive and nationalist China would demand and compel submission to its growing strategic ambitions—not just in southeast Asia and the South China Sea but in the Indian Ocean, all the way to the Middle East at one end and deep into the Pacific Ocean at the other.

As China continued its march to technological supremacy and global leadership, a declining, demoralized, and discredited United States would have to decide whether to go to war to defend democratic Taiwan from being forcibly absorbed into China's Communist dictatorship. Surging Chinese despotism would threaten the freedom of much of the rest of democratic Asia, even if Japan, South Korea, and other U.S. allies—at best exposed, at worst forsaken—were able to resist Beijing's growing efforts to penetrate and compromise their democratic political systems.

It would be a hinge in history. How would democracy in Latin America fare in the face of this massive shift in global power and momentum, with the corrupting influence of Chinese money eroding democratic forces in party politics, the media, and government? How would the brave dissidents and demonstrators who cherish the values of self-government and human rights argue for the moral force of democracy as an idea with China on the march and America in retreat? How many weak and tentative democracies would survive in Africa as its elites saw ever more clearly which way the winds of global power were blowing? How many multinational companies would conclude that their interests compelled them to ride the dictators' bandwagon? How many global broadcasters and social media companies would resist the autocrats' demands for censorship and complicity?

In such a near future, my fellow experts would no longer talk of "democratic erosion." We would be spiraling downward into a time of democratic despair, recalling Daniel Patrick Moynihan's grim observation from the 1970s that liberal democracy "is where the world was, not where it is going."[5] The world pulled out of that downward spiral—but it took new, more purposeful American leadership. The planet was not so lucky in the 1930s, when the global implosion of democracy led to a catastrophic world war, between a rising axis of emboldened dictatorships and a shaken and economically depressed collection of self-doubting democracies.

These are the stakes. Expanding democracy—with its liberal norms and constitutional commitments—is a crucial foundation for world peace and security. Knock that away, and our most basic hopes and assumptions will be imperiled.

The problem is not just that the ground is slipping. It is that we are perched on a global precipice. That ledge has been gradually giving way for a decade. If the erosion continues, we may well reach a tipping point where democracy goes bankrupt suddenly—plunging the world into depths of oppression and aggression that we have not seen since the end of World War II. As a political scientist, I know that our theories and tools are not nearly good enough to tell us just how close we are getting to that point—until it happens.

The Fire Beneath the Ash

All this is reason for resolve, not panic. If there is a silver lining to this picture of widespread democratic erosion, it is that many authoritarian regimes don't look all that stable either. Remember how the Soviet Union went politically bankrupt: first gradually (with signs of sclerosis that few observers took seriously enough), then suddenly.

Several big and seemingly resilient dictatorships are facing tough times. The Islamic Republic of Iran had a near death experience in 2009 with the protests that came to be known as the Green Movement. The regime survived and cracked down ruthlessly, but Iranians continue to defy the ayatollahs audaciously even as Iran's economy sputters. The theocracy is much more fragile than it appears.

The same is true about Ethiopia, Africa's second-most-populous country, with more than 100 million people.[6] The besieged regime there

recently turned to the youthful Abiy Ahmed, who became prime minister in April 2018 and launched political reforms to open up the country's
fearful, decrepit authoritarian system. His sudden emergence has been
compared with Mikhail Gorbachev's. Abiy has rallied young people and
ethnic outsiders in a country fed up with political repression, regional
conflict, elite land grabs, and domination by a narrow ethnic minority.[7]
None of this ensures a transition to democracy, but it has opened the
door.

China and Vietnam are among the world's most seemingly stable dictatorships, but each regime confronts two classic dilemmas of successful
authoritarianism. As their economies have boomed, their societies are
becoming more educated, sophisticated, and diverse—and less likely to
remain indefinitely content with the absence of freedom and transparency. And China's and Vietnam's monolithic, one-party regimes are susceptible to political earthquakes should a sudden crisis provoke intense
demands for change and accountability that cannot be fulfilled from
within the system. But this kind of change is unlikely to happen if China's citizens think their Communist regime is on an intoxicating path to
global domination.

Many experts argue that the Chinese Communist Party has found a
formula for perfect dictatorship, utilizing social media and other feedback mechanisms to respond to discontent before it becomes politically
threatening. But the supposed authoritarian strength of the Chinese
system, its lack of transparency, may ultimately be its downfall. Few
people really know what is happening inside Beijing's corridors of power,
except that limits on President Xi Jinping's authority are disappearing
even as Communist Party surveillance and control are intensifying. This
is chafing on many businesspeople and professionals who have traveled
to (or even lived in) the West and know the appeals of liberty and the
rule of law.

Among the planet's fifty most populous countries are a number of
nondemocracies that have at least the formal architecture of competi-

tive, multiparty elections, such as Pakistan, Bangladesh, Turkey, Nigeria, Tanzania, Kenya, Mozambique, and Morocco. It is easier for a country to embrace democracy when the formal structures are already in place and some surprise development—a split in the ruling party, a shift in popular sentiment, a crisis in the military—pushes the system from the façade of democracy to the real thing. That will not happen in all of these countries, but it will happen in some—if the world's most powerful democracies will support the forces of democratic change while bringing pressure to bear on recalcitrant autocrats.

History has a way of surprising us, for ill but also for good. If we needed another lesson in hope, Malaysia provided it in May 2018, when one of the world's most durable autocracies came crashing down after six decades in power. Malaysia's one-party regime had once seemed invulnerable, using massive institutional advantages—including control over the media, business, the financial system, and the judiciary—to keep "winning" decisive parliamentary majorities even when it lost majority support. But after nearly a decade in power, Prime Minister Najib Razak and his ruling party were so badly repudiated at the polls— winning barely a third of the vote—that even their entrenched advantages could not save them. The spark for their demise was the breathtaking corruption scandal described in chapter 10, in which billions of dollars in public funds simply disappeared—including, reportedly, $700 million into Najib's personal accounts.[8] Criminal investigations and filings by the U.S. Justice Department and other international authorities were critical in documenting the web of kleptocracy.[9] With the ruling party divided, the opposition unified, and the public livid over the staggering corruption, Malaysia experienced the first democratic change of government in its history.

Malaysia's drama is characteristic of many elected authoritarian regimes: they seem stable, until they are not. Their strength—that they can claim legitimacy through repeated multiparty elections—is also their weakness. Lacking the discipline that comes with the real risk of electoral defeat and lacking the checks that come with an independent judiciary, a free press, and a vigorous civil society, such regimes are at chronic risk of a public revolt—either at the ballot box or on the streets—when corruption and human rights abuses reach intolerable levels. The familiar tools of control—electoral fraud, censorship, intimidation of the opposition—work only to a point. When the regime's abuses grow too extreme, or when the society grows more prosperous and better educated, people become less willing to put up with an arrogant, self-serving autocracy. They increasingly long for voice, accountability, and the rule of law—and become more willing to take personal risks to achieve them.

Two factors often send such regimes over the cliff. One is long-term change: social and economic development that creates a more educated, resourceful, and demanding public. That lets opposition crystallize first and foremost in the cities, among the professional classes, and among the young (notably today's smartphone generation). The second factor is divisions within the regime, which can fracture its leadership and open the way for new working alliances. Both factors were crucial in Malaysia. We can expect them to surface in other autocracies, and we should encourage them when they do.

Like Malaysia, Russia has also seen a new generation rise up with economic growth and better access to information. They too want real elections, free expression, genuinely accountable government, and the rule of law—in other words, democracy. These better-educated and younger Russians—some as young as twelve years old—are not going away.[10]

Their widespread street demonstrations in December 2011—the largest in Russia since the fall of the Soviet Union—alarmed and infuriated Vladimir Putin, prompting him to punish Secretary of State Hillary Clinton and the United States, which he accused of fomenting the unrest. But people mobilized again in some twenty-six cities across Russia to protest Putin's inauguration to a fourth presidential term.[11] And with

Donald Trump in the White House, whom does Putin have to blame now? Electoral autocracies look strong—until they're not. Beneath the surface of domineering calm, there now stirs in Russia a generation of young, urban, educated citizens who are fed up with kleptocracy and will not be silent.

Deep down, Putin knows this, which is why he will not allow the level of electoral opposition that has existed in Malaysia. Russia's March 2018 presidential election was a charade in which the only serious opposition candidate, Alexei Navalny, was barred from running. Putin is a kleptocrat of titanic proportions, but we shouldn't overestimate his regime's stability. His kleptocracy has immense control over money, propaganda, and means of coercion. But its insecurity is just as immense.

This is why Putin is so unnerved by the fall of other autocracies. Putin waged a relentless propaganda assault against my Stanford colleague Michael McFaul from the moment he arrived in Moscow as U.S. ambassador in January 2012. One motive for the Kremlin's campaign was a 2005 article that McFaul had written in the *Journal of Democracy* analyzing the conditions that facilitated the "color revolutions" against electoral fraud in Serbia, Georgia, and Ukraine between 2000 and 2004, bringing about transitions to democracy in each case.[12] Putin feared that McFaul had come to promote the conditions in Russia for democracy: political space for opposition, an unpopular incumbent, a united opposition, and rifts within the regime. Any autocrat who fears that an American ambassador could bring down a regime as resourceful and ruthless as Russia's cannot really, deep down, be confident.

Another crucial factor in the collapse of an autocracy is brave opposition leadership. Putin's most charismatic and effective opponent, Boris Nemtsov, was shot to death a short distance from the Kremlin in February 2015. In Malaysia, the opposition leader Anwar Ibrahim's reputation was slandered repeatedly, and he spent nearly half of the last two decades in solitary confinement.

In November 2014, shortly before the final phase of his legal appeal against a second trumped-up conviction on bogus sodomy charges, Anwar gave a learned address at Stanford University on "Islam and Democracy." It was a bold, forthright declaration of Islam's compatibility with liberal democracy—including freedom of religion, freedom of conscience, freedom of expression, and the rule of law. It frontally denounced Malaysia's rising ethnic and religious bigotry, in the name of Islam. And it closed by invoking Abu al-Qasim al-Shabbi, an early-twentieth-century Tunisian poet whose words later inspired Tunisian and Egyptian protesters during the Arab Spring. "If the people will to live," Anwar quoted the poet as saying, "the chains are certain to be broken."

After the intense applause died down and the rush of student and faculty admirers subsided, I pulled Anwar aside for a short stroll on Stanford's pastoral campus. I had something difficult to ask him privately, and the poignancy of the moment hung in the air. If he returned to Malaysia, his conviction would probably be upheld, leaving him to face another long spell in prison, probably again in solitary confinement. It was ten years since he had been released from his first such stint. He was sixty-seven years old. I worried that he might not survive another long sentence.

"Why not stay here?" I asked—but really, it was an appeal. "You can get political asylum in the United States. You can work from here for democracy in Malaysia."

"I have to go back," Anwar replied. "The struggle is there at home. If I don't return, the regime will paint me as a coward and a fugitive from justice, and I will lose legitimacy."

There is no other word for this than courage, a word too often used but too little seen in our time. At the time, I was struck by the realization that I was seeing it in the moment, in the flesh. I didn't know if I would see it again. But I have—repeatedly.

Two and a half years later, at the Oslo Freedom Forum, I met Vladimir Kara-Murza, the journalist and associate of Boris Nemtsov whom the Kremlin twice came very close to assassinating with a rare poison. Our May 2017 Oslo meeting came just three months after the second attempt on Kara-Murza's life. Each time, the Moscow doctor who had cared for Kara-Murza had warned his wife that her husband's vital organs were shutting down, leaving him with only a 5 percent chance of pulling through. After his second recovery, the doctor warned him sternly, "If there is a third attempt, you will not survive."

In Norway, I asked Kara-Murza his plans, and his answer was virtually identical to Anwar's in 2014. "When I've fully recovered, I will return to Russia," he said. I was aghast. I had only just met him, but I pleaded with him not to travel back to Russia while Putin was still in power. He was unmoved. "I have to return at some point," he said. "If I do not go back, I will lose touch with the struggle, and it will diminish my ability to effect change."

Such courage should inspire us all. We can rally ourselves to action out of fear and anger—justified reactions in the age of Trump, Orbán, and Putin. But fear can be paralyzing, and anger can be polarizing. It is better to be driven by conviction and hope—by the conviction that freedom is worth risking everything to defend, and by the hope, confirmed by countless national struggles including our own, that if people who value liberty and justice can draw together smartly and steadfastly, they can prevail.

We live in frightening times, but it was not simply fear and alarm that propelled me to write this book. It was the hope and inspiration that I have drawn from democracy activists around the world who chose to risk it all for freedom. I think of Zin Mar Aung, spending eleven years in solitary confinement in Burma, refusing to buckle under to military dictatorship. I think of Rafael Marques de Morais, defying death threats and prison terms to expose kleptocracy in Angola. I think of Kenyans like Maina Kiai, an indefatigable human rights defender and former U.N. champion of free association, and John Githongo, a journalist and anticorruption activist, who have persisted despite risks to their livelihoods and lives. Over three decades, Kenya's corrupt power brokers have tried to warn or buy Kiai off. "What do you want?" they asked. "Just name it." He never wavered: "These are my values," he would reply. "This is who I am. I have been fighting for democracy and justice my whole life."[13]

This is what autocrats worry about: the refusal of all these activists to just give up, even in the face of cruelty, calumny, and crackdown. This is the fear that gnaws at tyrants—whether in Tehran or Cairo, Moscow or Beijing—and keeps them from sleeping soundly. Al-Shabbi's most famous poem—the one that was widely quoted by prodemocracy protesters during the 2011 Arab Spring—includes these lines:

Wait! Don't be fooled by the spring, the clearness of the sky,
    or the light of the dawn;
for on the horizon lies the horror of darkness, rumble of thunder,
    and blowing of winds.
Beware, for below the ash there is fire.[14]

Avoiding "America Alone"

It is a cliché to say we stand at a turning point; but we do. The danger of a killer wave of democratic breakdowns is real and growing. The winds of Russian rage, Chinese ambition, and American complacency are gusting. These give political space and comfort to autocrats around the world looking to tighten their grip. One form of backsliding builds on another. As geopolitical momentum swings behind today's illiberal populists, they sense new possibilities for riding economic anxiety and ethnic and religious prejudice to power. Watching and aiding one another, aspiring autocrats discover new techniques for stirring fear, polarizing publics, and eroding constitutional checks on their power.

We can still reverse these ill winds. We can even help generate a new burst of freedom in the world. But it will not happen without vigorous American leadership—to support democrats, pressure autocrats, and counter the malign expansion of Russian and Chinese power.

Global leadership does not mean American global dominance. Those days are gone. But American leadership is flatly incompatible with Trump's relentless insistence that the United States is being cheated by its friends and allies and must now insist on putting its interests above all others. Of course, every country puts its national interests first. But the constant trumpeting of "America first" is heard around the world as "America only," and that propels us down the self-defeating path of "America alone."

Reversing the alarming worldwide trends of authoritarian advance and democratic decay requires first and foremost the steadfast embrace of our alliances. That means an unflinching U.S. commitment to NATO, and to its crucial Article 5 provision for mutual defense—reaffirming that an attack on any alliance member is an attack on them all. It means support for the European Union as not only a crucial economic and political complement to NATO but also an indispensable building bloc of a larger community of democratic nations. And it means reviving our commitment to other communities of shared democratic resolve, including, in our own backyard, the Organization of American States.

Broad democratization will be slower to come to Asia, but as China casts its shadow over the region, we have two key advantages we can harness. First, most Asians—and most Asian governments—desperately want an alternative to Chinese hegemony. That alternative will never again be American hegemony but rather a fluid balance of power in which no superpower dominates the region and Asian countries are free to determine their own fates. This can happen only if the United States remains heavily engaged in Asia, to ensure that its sea lanes remain open, to help buck up Taiwan and other democratic governments against Chinese military intimidation, to support the growth of democratic norms and institutions, and to build up regional economic alternatives to Chinese control.

The second advantage is that Asia continues to be a region of rapid economic and social transformation. Xi Jinping and other Asian autocrats may insist that only the China model is a compelling fit with "Asian values," but as levels of education, information, and income rise, Asians are moving in a different direction, toward greater aspirations for freedom and autonomy. Even in China's own backyard, democratic ideals—which are, after all, *universal* values—have the advantage. But they aren't likely to triumph without support from Europe, Japan, and above all the United States.

All this may sound like the quaint idealism of a more hopeful, bygone era—before the elevation of Donald Trump and his miserly, transactional, soulless approach to world affairs. But within Congress, the career foreign service, and the professional national security bureaucracy—and even among many of Trump's own appointees to senior foreign policy positions—there remains a strong commitment to American leadership in Europe and Asia, as well as to energetic American initiatives worldwide to defend human rights, support democracies, promote economic growth, foster freer trade, combat terrorism, and counter the power projection of Russia, China, and Iran.

Yes, much of the Republican base has swallowed Trump's cynical, pro-Putin, and inward-turning approach to the world. But this appears more as a tribal embrace of Trump—as leader, symbol, and aggrieved cause—than a resolute foreign policy conviction. We can still reassert American democratic leadership in the world and launch a new generation of public broadcasting and diplomacy to convey democratic values and rebut misinformation in the digital age.

But this will be done only with a different president. The longer that Trump stays in power, the deeper and more lasting will be the damage to America's standing in the world, our democratic alliances, our career diplomats, soldiers, and spies—and thus to our capacity to rebound from the immense damage that Trump is inflicting on the liberal world order, which has secured the highest levels of freedom and human development and the longest stretch of peace between major powers in modern history.

Against Complacency

The threats to democracy and the assaults on truth, tolerance, and human dignity are growing. But there may be a silver lining. "Ill blows the wind that profits nobody," wrote Shakespeare in *Henry VI Part 3*. The time of Trump may yet rally those who believe in democracy—of all nationalities, ages, ethnicities, faiths, genders, and political parties—to come together to defend it.

If the greatest problem with today's Russia is its simmering rage and the greatest challenge with today's China is its vaulting ambition, the greatest blight on American democracy is our profound complacency. We have taken far too much for granted for far too long.

As the 2018 midterm elections were approaching, a student of mine at Stanford, Matthew Wigler, spent the summer interviewing voters and candidates in swing congressional districts across the United States. In the Central Valley of California, he encountered a twenty-year-old Hispanic American woman who was disgusted with Donald Trump and his policies on immigration, guns, and (in her words) "locking up kids." But she conceded that she wasn't likely to cast her ballot that November. "I'm all for voting, but sometimes I get lazy," she said.[15]

She isn't alone. Even in presidential election years, voter turnout in the United States is among the lowest in the advanced democracies.[16] The nonvoters tend to be younger, less educated, and disproportionately Latino or Asian American.[17] Turnout is also being discouraged by apathy, by a lack of competition and choice, and by Republican-backed laws in more than a dozen states that make it harder to register, vote early, or vote at all without a certain type of state-issued photo ID.[18] We cannot revitalize our democracy unless we mobilize more people to care, become informed, and actually vote. In 2018, voter turnout sharply rose for a midterm election, but revitalizing our democracy will require a massive grassroots effort to reach and rouse nonvoters, as well as legal action and electoral reforms to combat voter suppression and imbue elections with greater choice.

Readers have already seen my agenda for renewing American democracy. It's ambitious, but it's attainable. Against all odds, confronting a resourceful and cynical pack of established politicians, the voters of Maine prevailed in 2018, changing their electoral system to allow for greater competition. That took dogged efforts by grassroots citizen activists, and their victory has ignited nationwide interest in ranked-choice voting and other reforms to open up our elections to wider, more meaningful choice. Momentum for electoral reform is gathering in Massachusetts, Minnesota, Wisconsin, California, and New Mexico. And increasingly, partisan gerrymandering is under assault from legal challenges and bottom-up efforts to put an end to this bane of democracy.

It is not just liberal cities or progressive states that are seeing a new burst of reformist energy. Bills and voter initiatives to end gerrymandering, fight corruption, improve transparency, and strengthen voting rights are also passing in red states like Alaska, Missouri, North Dakota, and Utah, and in swing states like Arizona, Colorado, Nevada, and Ohio.[19] The common thread in all these changes is that citizens are organizing to bring about change. In Alaska, RepresentUs sponsored an anticorruption initiative to limit lobbyists' gifts to politicians, strengthen conflict-of-interest rules, and halt legislators' per diems if they fail to pass a budget on time. With the voter initiative drawing 84 percent support in preelection polls, Alaska's Republican-controlled legislature preemptively passed its provisions into law in July 2018 rather than risk a voter tsunami in November.[20]

But changing the law is not the only path to reducing polarization and rebuilding a more workable democracy. A new bipartisan initiative, With Honor, has begun supporting military veterans of both parties who run for Congress pledging to embrace bipartisan problem solving and a civil tone over unrelenting partisanship.[21] In November 2018, the organization helped elect nearly half of the roughly forty military veterans it endorsed for the House, raising the number of veterans in Congress to its highest level in nearly a decade.[22] They included Jared Golden, the former marine who prevailed through ranked-choice voting in Maine, and Dan Crenshaw—a former Navy SEAL who lost an eye in Afghanistan, and who won over *Saturday Night Live* viewers across the spectrum with a Veterans Day message of national unity and a gracious willingness to accept *SNL* star Pete Davidson's apology for his previous juvenile mocking of Crenshaw's eye patch. Other bipartisan organizations, such as No Labels and the Bipartisan Policy Center, are working to create a political climate in which Republicans and Democrats cooperate to address the nation's urgent problems.

If we are resolute, the time of Trump could still be followed by a new Progressive era that revives the founding spirit of American democracy, a time in which ordinary people rise up to reclaim power from giant corporations, opaque special interests, and entrenched partisan oligarchies.

But it is up to us. This is an existential moment for American democracy. We could rescue it from the howling gales of bigotry, fear, nativism, prejudice, and misinformation. But we could also lose it. That is the central warning of this book: we could lose our democracy—or see it so degraded by abuse of power, deliberate divisiveness, and the steady erosion of our civil liberties that it fails to protect or inspire, at home or abroad. We would like to think that American democracy is immortal and impervious. We would like to think that it can't happen here. But it can.

We cannot be so arrogant or complacent as to assume that there is some natural and unbridgeable point at which the subversion of our democratic norms and institutions is bound to stop. No democratic constitution is self-enforcing. It takes people in positions of authority and responsibility to defend it. Republicans in Congress have so far failed that test. The media have been more steadfast, but some staunchly conservative outlets appear ready to follow Trump wherever he may lead. The judiciary has often ruled wisely, but it has yet to be fully tested; it is not immune from the pulls of partisan polarization, and it has already indulged some of Trump's outrages.

That brings us to the last line of defense: "we the people." You and I—all of us—are America's ultimate barrier against a descent into tyranny. And that barrier will not stand unless it is constantly reinforced.

Democracy will not reform itself by some hidden or automatic process. It takes citizens to awaken from their inertia, apathy, or fear. No one else will demand change for us.

If you fear for our democracy, vote—and get everyone you can to vote. Elections now are about much more than policy choices on health care, the environment, or the economy, vital though such issues are. In the era of Donald Trump and the partisan corrosion of democracy, our votes will determine the fate of our constitutional checks and balances and of our rights under the rule of law.

If you are fed up with caustic polarization, conflicts of interest, and abuse of power, work for change. Find an organization in your state or your community that is campaigning for democratic reform—groups like RepresentUs, FairVote, and Common Cause—and join their efforts. Or support think tanks like the Niskanen Center and advocacy groups like No Labels that are thoughtfully seeking to bridge our divides. Fight bigotry by backing organizations like the ACLU, the NAACP, and the Southern Poverty Law Center, or any church, mosque, or synagogue appealing for racial and religious diversity. Follow the excellent research and advocacy of groups working to defend our democracy in this hour of danger, including the Brennan Center for Justice, the Center for Responsive Politics, the Sunlight Foundation, Protect Democracy, and Stand Up Republic.[23] Spread the news among your friends and followers on social media—with words that restore rather than shred a culture of civility.

I have devoted my life to the study of democracy, but I am a citizen like any other. My vote counts for no more than anyone else's. So my ultimate appeal goes out to my fellow citizens: join the movement for a better, fairer, and more transparent democracy. It may seem like a long and difficult struggle, but it needn't be a dreary one. Along the way, you will meet neighbors, make friends, and find people who will uplift you. You will encounter outrage and frustration, but you will also find the meaning and the joy that come from connecting in a noble common cause—ultimately, one that will change the course of history. Vote and advocate for a foreign policy that supports democratic allies and movements around the world. Help educate young people about the history of the struggle for liberty and self-government—this wondrous and perishable gift that each generation must discover, embrace, and renew.

This is the duty of democratic citizenship: to fight for the values of our republic as if our own freedom is at stake. It is.

ACKNOWLEDGMENTS

Since the publication of *Squandered Victory* and *The Spirit of Democracy* in the previous decade, it had always been my intention to write another book for a broad readership, but until 2016 I had never imagined that it would need to be one so full of apprehension and even alarm about the fate of democracy. With Donald Trump's election to the presidency in November 2016 and the rising tide of illiberal populism then sweeping the world, the notion of writing a book like this assumed increasing urgency, but it took an invitation from Penguin Press executive editor Warren Bass to bring me from the idea to the book. For creatively advising me and faithfully representing me in what became a deeply gratifying relationship with Penguin Press, I offer again a profound vote of thanks to my agent and friend Scott Mendel.

I am honored that this was the first book signed up by Warren Bass in his tenure at Penguin Press, and I cannot overstate the enormous debt I owe him. Warren was not simply my editor but an indispensable partner in this endeavor from beginning to end, helping me to envision, structure, and proportion a book that would engage readers outside the cloistered halls of academia. Beyond that, Warren's gifted and rigorous editing through several drafts of each chapter helped immeasurably to make the manuscript more readable, logical, and ardent. To the extent this book succeeds in informing and inspiring a diverse array of readers who care about freedom, much of the credit goes to Warren.

I want to thank heartily as well the superb team I had the privilege to work with at Penguin Press. Caroline Sydney worked with Warren in editing the manuscript and preparing it for publication. After Warren returned to *The Wall Street Journal* in October 2018, Caroline ably managed the final editing and production of the book with exceptional diligence, aplomb, and good cheer. Trent Duffy did a thorough, careful, and perceptive job of copyediting the manuscript. I am grateful as well to Bruce Giffords, to Cohen Carruth for excellent work in preparing the index, and to Jane Cavolina for fact checking.

In preparing this book, I benefited from the superb research assistance of Leo Kirby, a second-year student in Stanford's M.A. Program in International Studies, who managed and analyzed the data in this book and also helped in identifying developments with regard to social media, and three undergraduate assistants: Sarah Goodman, Jayaram Ravi, and Ryan Chandra, who worked energetically to gather information and keep me up to date on the rapidly evolving political developments in Europe, the United States, and other parts of the world. I am also grateful to Sarahi Zaldumbide, whose support of my professional work and of our Global Digital Policy Incubator at Stanford also aided me considerably.

While I was writing this book I was also cochairing the Working Group on Chinese Influence Activities in the United States. The two projects overlapped almost completely in time, and the research and findings of the Working Group have significantly shaped my understanding of the challenge China poses to democracy in the United States and around the world. I especially want to thank my cochair, Orville Schell, and our project coordinator, Kyle Hutzler, but I am indebted as well to the many other members of the Working Group from whom I learned. My thinking about the new form of authoritarian threat to the integrity of democratic institutions, called "sharp power," has also been informed by the work of my colleagues at the International Forum for Democratic Studies of the National Endowment for Democracy, especially Christopher Walker and Jessica Ludwig. I also want to thank Chris Walker and my coleader of the Global Digital Policy Incubator, Eileen Donahoe, for their insights on and their helpful critical reading of my chapter on social media, and my Stanford colleague Francis Fukuyama, who read and commented helpfully on a number of the chapters.

Many of the articles cited in this book appear in the publication I have coedited for the past twenty-nine years, the *Journal of Democracy*. Without my deep immersion in the work of that journal, I would not have had the breadth of knowledge to attempt to analyze so many countries and issues affecting the fate of freedom worldwide. For their partnership and for all that they have helped me understand, I thank all of my colleagues at the *Journal*, especially my coeditor, Marc F. Plattner. Similarly, I would like to thank my many colleagues at the Hoover Institution and the Freeman Spogli Institute for International Studies at Stanford University, who have provided me with the fertile intellectual climate to address these issues.

My biggest debt is owed to the activists and practitioners who have devoted their lives to the struggle to achieve, defend, or improve democracy and who gave patiently of their time and insights during the course of this book project. I particularly want to thank the seven people to whom this book is dedicated, Zin Mar Aung, Vladimir Kara-Murza, Maina Kiai, Rafael Marques de Morais, Cara McCormick, Nicholas Opiyo, and Joshua Wong, as well as Carl Gershman, Derek Mitchell, and Kenneth Wollack (who also graciously gave of their time in interviews). But my profound gratitude extends much further, to the remarkable staff, grantees, and fellows associated with the National Endowment for Democracy, the World Movement for Democracy, and the Draper Hills Summer Fellows Program of the Center for Democracy, Development, and the Rule of Law, one of my intellectual homes at Stanford.

I hasten to stress that none of the above-named organizations or individuals bears any responsibility for this book's tone or content—not to mention any errors of fact or interpretation. As a university lecturer deeply committed to a rigorously nonpartisan stance in the classroom, I take no pleasure in having had to condemn here so harshly the actions and rhetoric of a sitting president, and at times many others in his party. I hope the reader will judge that this was not done from any partisan motive—many in the president's own party have come to the same alarming conclusions.

Finally, I want to thank my late mother for imparting to me some of my passion for democracy, which began with the 1960 presidential election and the riveting Kennedy-Nixon television debate. I am deeply grateful to my friends and family for their devotion and understanding. And I especially thank my sister and brother-in-law, Linda and Rob Raznick, for their love and infectious laughter throughout the trying year of writing this book.

NOTES

EPIGRAPHS

Alexander Hamilton, *The Federalist* 1, www.constitution.org/fed/federa51.htm.
John F. Kennedy, Inaugural Address, January 20, 1961, https://www.presidency.ucsb.edu /documents/inaugural-address-2.
Madeleine Albright, *Fascism: A Warning* (New York: HarperCollins, 2018), 87.

CHAPTER 1: INTRODUCTION: THE CRISIS

1. Hannah Arendt, *On Revolution* (London: Penguin, 1963), 11.
2. Sinclair Lewis, *It Can't Happen Here* (New York: Doubleday Doran, 1935), 71.
3. Jonathan Freedland, "Who Is to Blame for This Awful US Election?," *The Guardian*, November 7, 2016, www.theguardian.com/us-news/2016/nov/07/who-is-to-blame-us-election -trump#img-4.
4. Christina Coleburn, "Donald Trump's History of Praising Dictators," NBC News, July 6, 2016, www.nbcnews.com/politics/2016-election/donald-trump-s-history-praising-dictators -n604801.
5. Daniel A. Bell, *The China Model* (Princeton, N.J.: Princeton University Press, 2015).
6. Michel J. Crozier, Samuel P. Huntington, and Joji Watanuki, *The Crisis of Democracy: A Report on the Governability of Democracies to the Trilateral Commission* (New York: New York University Press, 1975), 6, 8, http://trilateral.org/download/doc/crisis_of_democracy.pdf.

CHAPTER 2: WHY DEMOCRACIES SUCCEED AND FAIL

1. Alexis de Tocqueville, *Democracy in America* (New York: Alfred A. Knopf, 1945), vol. 1, ch. 14, 246.
2. This is a central insight of all the classic works on the conditions for democracy, including Seymour Martin Lipset, *Political Man: The Social Bases of Democracy* (Garden City, N.Y.: Doubleday, 1960); Robert A. Dahl, *Polyarchy: Participation and Opposition* (New Haven: Yale University Press, 1971); Juan J. Linz, *The Breakdown of Democratic Regimes: Crisis, Breakdown, and Reequilibration* (Baltimore: Johns Hopkins University Press, 1978).
3. This type of system has been called *competitive authoritarianism*. See Steven Levitsky and Lucan Way, *Competitive Authoritarianism: Hybrid Regimes After the Cold War* (Cambridge: Cambridge University Press, 2010).

4. Francis Fukuyama, *The Origins of Political Order: From Prehuman Times to the French Revolution* (New York: Farrar, Straus and Giroux, 2011).
5. Robert D. Putnam, *Making Democracy Work: Civic Traditions in Modern Italy* (Princeton, N.J.: Princeton University Press, 1993).
6. "Corruption Perceptions Index 2016," Transparency International, January 25, 2017, www.transparency.org/news/feature/corruption_perceptions_index_2016.
7. Lipset, *Political Man*; Dankwart Rustow, "Transitions to Democracy: Toward a Dynamic Model," *Comparative Politics* 2 (April 1970): 337–63.
8. Alex Rowel and David Madland, "New Census Data Show Household Incomes Are Rising Again, but Share Going to Middle Class Is at Record Low," Center for American Progress, September 12, 2017, www.americanprogress.org/issues/economy/news/2017/09/12/438778/new-census-data-show-household-incomes-rising-share-going-middle-class-record-low/.
9. Eleanor Krause and Isabel V. Sawhill, "Seven Reasons to Worry About the American Middle Class," Brookings Institution, June 5, 2018, www.brookings.edu/blog/social-mobility-memos/2018/06/05/seven-reasons-to-worry-about-the-american-middle-class/.
10. Lucian W. Pye, "Political Science and the Crisis of Authoritarianism," *American Political Science Review* 84, no. 1 (1990): 15.
11. Alex Inkeles, "National Character and Modern Political Systems," in *Psychological Anthropology: Approaches to Culture and Personality*, ed. Francis L. K. Hsu (Homewood, Ill.: Dorsey, 1961), 195–98.
12. Sidney Hook, *Reason, Social Myths, and Democracy* (1940; repr., New York: Cosimo, 2009), 290.
13. Steven Levitsky and Daniel Ziblatt, *How Democracies Die* (New York: Crown, 2018), 106.
14. Guillermo O'Donnell and Philippe C. Schmitter, *Transitions from Authoritarian Rule: Tentative Conclusions About Uncertain Democracies* (Baltimore: Johns Hopkins University Press, 1986), 38. This point also figures prominently in Rustow's seminal "Transitions to Democracy."
15. Lipset, *Political Man*, 45.
16. Samuel P. Huntington, *The Third Wave: Democratization in the Late Twentieth Century* (Norman: University of Oklahoma Press, 1991), 60.
17. John Holm, "Botswana: A Paternalistic Democracy," in *Democracy in Developing Countries: Africa*, ed. Larry Diamond, Juan J. Linz, and Seymour Martin Lipset (Boulder, Colo.: Lynne Rienner, 1988), 199.
18. These arguments are developed in much greater detail in Juan J. Linz, "Presidential or Parliamentary Democracy: Does It Make a Difference?," in *The Failure of Presidential Democracy: Comparative Perspectives*, ed. Juan J. Linz and Arturo Valenzuela (Baltimore: Johns Hopkins University Press, 1994), 3–87.
19. James Madison, *The Federalist* 51, February 6, 1788, www.constitution.org/fed/federa51.htm.
20. "General Powers of Special Counsel," *Code of Federal Regulations*, title 28, ch. 6, part 600, www.gpo.gov/fdsys/pkg/CFR-2001-title28-vol2/pdf/CFR-2001-title28-vol2-part600.pdf.
21. Neal Katyal, "Trump or Congress Can Still Block Mueller," *Washington Post*, May 19, 2017, www.washingtonpost.com/posteverything/wp/2017/05/19/politics-could-still-block-muellers-investigation-i-know-i-wrote-the-rules/?utm_term=.de03cd4cc8ed.
22. Alina Mungiu-Pippidi, "The Quest for Good Governance: Learning from Virtuous Circles," *Journal of Democracy* 27 (January 2016): 95–109.
23. Larry Diamond, *The Spirit of Democracy: The Struggle to Build Free Societies Throughout the World* (New York: Times Books/Henry Holt, 2008), 80–81.

CHAPTER 3: THE MARCH AND RETREAT OF DEMOCRACY

1. Samuel P. Huntington, *The Third Wave: Democratization in the Late Twentieth Century* (Norman: University of Oklahoma Press, 1991), 316.
2. Ibid., 17.
3. Ibid., 13–31. Huntington's counts exclude countries of less than one million population and include a few that were probably only quasi-democratic.
4. Ibid., 91–95; quote from 95.
5. Ibid., 94.
6. Jeane Kirkpatrick, "Dictatorships and Double Standards," *Commentary Magazine* 68 (November 1979): 34–45.

7. Ronald Reagan, Inaugural Address, January 20, 1981, at John Woolley and Gerhard Peters, American Presidency Project, www.presidency.ucsb.edu/ws/?pid=43130.

8. "Five Shopping Sprees So Wild, They Made History," *New York* ("The Cut"), April 15, 2013, www.thecut.com/2013/04/5-shopping-sprees-so-wild-they-made-history.html#.

9. George P. Shultz, *Turmoil and Triumph: My Years as Secretary of State* (New York: Scribner's, 1993), 630.

10. National Democratic Institute for International Affairs, "Reforming the Philippine Electoral Process: Developments, 1986–88," 1991, 11–15, www.ndi.org/sites/default/files/233_ph _reforming.pdf; Melissa Estok, Neil Nevitte, and Glenn Cowan, "The Quick Count and Election Observation," National Democratic Institute for International Affairs, 2002, www .ndi.org/sites/default/files/1417_elect_quickcounthdbk_1-30.pdf.

11. Shultz, *Turmoil and Triumph*, 625.

12. Ibid., 623–41.

13. Nick Davies, "The $10Bn Question: What Happened to the Marcos Millions?," *The Guardian*, May 7, 2016, www.theguardian.com/world/2016/may/07/10bn-dollar-question-marcos -millions-nick-davies.

14. Shultz, *Turmoil and Triumph*, 975–80.

15. "Tiananmen Square Protest Death Toll 'Was 10,000,'" BBC, December 23, 2017, www.bbc .com/news/world-asia-china-42465516.

16. I count as "liberal" democracies those states that receive from Freedom House one of the two best scores, a 1 or a 2, on both 7-point indexes of political rights and civil liberties. See the annual "Freedom in the World" reports.

17. Michael McFaul, "Transitions from Postcommunism," *Journal of Democracy* 16 (July 2005): 5–19.

18. Steven Levitsky and Lucan Way, "The Myth of the Democratic Recession," *Journal of Democracy* 26 (January 2015): 45–58; Bruce Jones and Michael O'Hanlon, "Democracy Is Far from Dead," *Wall Street Journal*, December 10, 2017, www.wsj.com/articles/democracy-is-far-from -dead-1512938275.

19. Miriam Kornblith, "The Referendum in Venezuela: Elections Versus Democracy," *Journal of Democracy* 16 (January 2005): 124–37; Larry Diamond, *The Spirit of Democracy: The Struggle to Build Free Societies Throughout the World* (New York: Times Books/Henry Holt, 2008), 67–70.

20. Ivan Krastev, "New Threats to Freedom: Democracy's 'Doubles,'" *Journal of Democracy* 17 (April 2006): 54.

21. Freedom House, "Freedom in the World 2018," 7, https://freedomhouse.org/sites/default /files/FH_FITW_Report_2018_Final_SinglePage.pdf.

22. "Philippines: Duterte's 'Drug War' Claims 12,000-Plus Lives," Human Rights Watch, January 18, 2018, www.hrw.org/news/2018/01/18/philippines-dutertes-drug-war-claims-12000 -lives; "Philippine Chief Justice Sereno, Duterte's Critic, Removed," Al Jazeera, May 11, 2018, www.aljazeera.com/news/2018/05/philippine-chief-justice-sereno-duterte-critic-removed -180511065453926.html.

23. See the stunning postelection analysis by former Brazilian president Fernando Henrique Cardoso, who observed, "Of the four presidents elected after the 1988 Constitution took effect, two were impeached, one is in jail for corruption and the other is me.": Fernando Henrique Cardoso, "How the Unthinkable Happened in Brazil," *Washington Post*, October 29, 2018, www.washingtonpost.com/news/theworldpost/wp/2018/10/29/bolsonaro/?utm_term= .7648c87b479f.

CHAPTER 4: THE AUTHORITARIAN TEMPTATION

1. "Europe's Populists Are Waltzing into the Mainstream," *The Economist*, February 3, 2018, www.economist.com/news/briefing/2018/02/03/europes-populists-are-waltzing-into-the -mainstream.

2. "Excerpts, Hungarian 'Lies' Speech," BBC, September 19, 2006, http://news.bbc.co.uk/2/hi /europe/5359546.stm.

3. Jacques Rupnik, "Hungary's Illiberal Turn: How Things Went Wrong," *Journal of Democracy* 23 (July 2012): 134.

4. Miklós Bánkuti, Gábor Halmai, and Kim Lane Scheppele, "Hungary's Illiberal Turn: Disabling the Constitution," *Journal of Democracy* 23 (July 2012): 139.

5. Ibid., 140.

6. János Kornai, "Hungary's U-Turn: Retreating from Democracy," *Journal of Democracy* 26 (July 2015): 40.

7. Arch Puddington and Tyler Roylance, "The Freedom House Survey for 2016: The Threat of Populists and Autocrats," *Journal of Democracy* 28 (April 2017): 112.

8. Kornai, "Hungary's U-Turn," 46.

9. Miklós Haraszti, "Behind Viktor Orbán's War Against Refugees in Hungary," *Huffington Post*, September 8, 2015 (updated December 6, 2017), www.huffingtonpost.com/miklos-haraszti /viktor-orban-hungary-refugees_b_8100906.html.

10. Ibid.

11. "Hungary: Opinion Editorial by U.N. High Commissioner for Human Rights Zeid Ra'ad al Hussein," United Nations Human Rights: Office of the High Commissioner, www.ohchr.org /EN/NewsEvents/Pages/DisplayNews.aspx?NewsID=22765.

12. Jan Werner-Müller, *What Is Populism?* (Philadelphia: University of Pennsylvania Press, 2016).

13. Steven Levitsky and Daniel Ziblatt, *How Democracies Die* (New York: Crown, 2018), 118–19.

14. Bojan Bugarič and Tom Ginsburg, "The Assault on Postcommunist Courts," *Journal of Democracy* 27 (July 2016): 69.

15. Jacques Rupnik, "Surging Illiberalism in the East," *Journal of Democracy* 27 (October 2016): 79.

16. Joanna Fomina and Jacek Kucharczyk, "Populism and Protest in Poland," *Journal of Democracy* 27 (October 2016): 63.

17. Ibid., 65.

18. Marc Santora, "Poland Purges Supreme Court, and Protesters Take to the Streets," *New York Times*, July 3, 2018, www.nytimes.com/2018/07/03/world/europe/poland-supreme-court -protest.html.

19. Jan Gross, "Poles Cry for 'Pure Blood' Again," *New York Times*, November 17, 2017.

20. Giuseppe Sedia, "PiS Leader Kaczynski Meets with Hungarian PM Viktor Orban: What Does It Mean?," *Krakow Post*, January 11, 2016, www.krakowpost.com/11017/2016/01 /kaczynski-orban-meeting.

21. Jacques Rupnik, "Evolving or Revolving? Central Europe Since 1989," Eurozine, December 15, 2017, www.eurozine.com/evolving-or-revolving-central-europe-since-1989/.

22. Rupnik, "Surging Illiberalism in the East," 82.

23. Organization for Economic Cooperation and Development: Data, https://data.oecd.org /migration/foreign-born-population.htm.

24. Rupnik, "Surging Illiberalism in the East," 81.

25. Ibid., 80.

26. Seymour Martin Lipset, *Political Man: The Social Bases of Politics* (1960; repr., Baltimore: Johns Hopkins University Press, 1981), ch. 5.

27. Ibid., ch. 4.

28. Sławomir Sierakowski, "How Eastern European Populism Is Different," *The Strategist*, February 2, 2018, www.aspistrategist.org.au/eastern-european-populism-different/.

29. Martin Eiermann, Yascha Mounk, and Limor Gultchin, "European Populism: Trends, Threats, and Future Prospects," Tony Blair Institute for Global Change, 5, December 29, 2017, https://institute.global/insight/renewing-centre/european-populism-trends-threats -and-future-prospects.

30. Rupnik, "Surging Illiberalism in the East," 79.

31. Ibid.

32. Bugarič and Ginsburg, "The Assault on Postcommunist Courts," 74.

33. Patrick Kingsley, "As West Fears the Rise of Autocrats, Hungary Shows What's Possible," *New York Times*, February 11, 2018.

34. Alastair Macdonald, "EU Parliament Pushes Hungary Sanctions for Orban Policies," Reuters, September 12, 2018, www.reuters.com/article/us-eu-hungary/eu-parliament-pushes-hungary -sanctions-over-orban-policies-idUSKCN1LS1QS.

35. Gabriela Baczynska and Robert-Jan Bartunek, "EU Piles Pressure on Poland over Courts Independence," Reuters, June 26, 2018, www.reuters.com/article/us-eu-poland/eu-piles -pressure-on-poland-over-courts-independence-idUSKBN1JM0YT.

36. The Lisbon Treaty, article 7, www.lisbon-treaty.org/wcm/the-lisbon-treaty/treaty-on -european-union-and-comments/title-1-common-provisions/7-article-7.html.

37. Ivan Krastev, "The Specter Haunting Europe: The Unraveling of the Post-1989 Order," *Journal of Democracy* 27 (October 2016): 91, 92.

38. "EU Migration to and from the U.K.," Migration Observatory at the University of Oxford, August 30, 2017, www.migrationobservatory.ox.ac.uk/resources/briefings/eu-migration-to-and -from-the-uk/.

39. Robert Ford and Matthew Goodwin, "Britain After Brexit: A Nation Divided," *Journal of Democracy* 28 (January 2017): 18, 19.

40. "AfD: What You Need to Know About Germany's Far-Right Party," Deutsche Welle, www.dw .com/en/afd-what-you-need-to-know-about-germanys-far-right-party/a-37208199.

41. Alissa J. Rubin, "Macron Decisively Defeats Le Pen in French Presidential Race," *New York Times*, May 7, 2017, www.nytimes.com/2017/05/07/world/europe/emmanuel-macron-france -election-marine-le-pen.html.

42. Tom Turula, "Sweden's Foreign-Born Population Is Nearing 1.7 Million—Finland and Iraq Have the Biggest Communities," Nordic Business Insider, March 3, 2017, https://nordic .businessinsider.com/swedens-foreign-born-population-is-nearly-17-million-people—finns -are-the-biggest-group-2017-3.

43. Hortense Goulard and Cynthia Kroet, "Dutch Party Wants to Outlaw Mosques, Islamic Schools, Koran," *Politico*, August 26, 2016 (updated March 14, 2017), www.politico.eu/article /far-right-dutch-politician-backs-mosques-koran-ban-islamic-schools/.

44. Eiermann, Mounk, and Gultchin, "European Populism," 7.

45. "Europe's Populists Are Waltzing into the Mainstream."

46. Seymour Martin Lipset and Earl Raab, *The Politics of Unreason: Right-Wing Extremism in America, 1790–1977* (Chicago: University of Chicago Press, 1978).

47. Ibid.; Ronald Inglehart and Christian Welzel, *Modernization, Cultural Change, and Democracy: The Human Development Sequence* (Cambridge: Cambridge University Press, 2005); Lee Drutman, Larry Diamond, and Joe Goldman, "Follow the Leader: Exploring American Support for Democracy and Authoritarianism," Democracy Fund Voter Study Group, March 2018, www.voterstudygroup.org/publications/2017-voter-survey/follow-the-leader.

48. Rupnik, "Evolving or Revolving?"

49. Associated Press, "Bannon to France's Far Right: 'Let Them Call You Racist . . . Wear It as a Badge of Honor,'" *Politico*, March 10, 2018, www.politico.com/story/2018/03/10/steve-bannon -france-national-front-marine-le-pen-454183.

50. Chris Megerian, "What Trump Has Said Through the Years About Where Obama Was Born," *Los Angeles Times*, September 16, 2016, www.latimes.com/politics/la-na-pol-trump -birther-timeline-20160916-snap-htmlstory.html.

51. Jeremy Diamond, "Donald Trump: Ban All Muslim Travel to U.S.," CNN, December 8, 2015, www.cnn.com/2015/12/07/politics/donald-trump-muslim-ban-immigration/index.html.

52. Jenna Johnson and Abigail Hauslohner, "'I Think Islam Hates Us': A Timeline of Trump's Comments About Islam and Muslims," *Washington Post*, May 20, 2017, www.washingtonpost .com/news/post-politics/wp/2017/05/20/i-think-islam-hates-us-a-timeline-of-trumps -comments-about-islam-and-muslims/?utm_term=.498737dca1d1.

53. Donald Trump's 2016 acceptance speech to the Republican National Convention, with capitalization per the original, https://assets.donaldjtrump.com/DJT_Acceptance_Speech.pdf.

54. Bill Kaufman, "When the Left Was Right," *American Conservative*, May 19, 2008, www .theamericanconservative.com/articles/when-the-left-was-right/.

55. Ibid.

56. Sam Reisman, "Trump Tells Crowd to 'Knock the Crap out' of Protestors, Offers to Pay Legal Fees," Mediaite, February 1, 2016, www.mediaite.com/online/trump-tells-crowd-to -knock-the-crap-out-of-protesters-offers-to-pay-legal-fees/.

57. Maxwell Tani, "Trump: I'll Consider Paying Legal Fees for the Man Who Allegedly Threw a Sucker Punch at One of My Rallies," *Business Insider*, March 13, 2016, www.businessinsider .com/donald-trump-legal-fees-punch-protester-2016-3.

58. Nick Corasaniti and Maggie Haberman, "Donald Trump Suggests 'Second Amendment People' Could Act Against Hillary Clinton," *New York Times*, August 9, 2016, www.nytimes.com /2016/08/10/us/politics/donald-trump-hillary-clinton.html; Jessica Taylor, "Trump's Second Amendment Rhetoric Again Veers into Threatening Territory," NPR, September 16, 2016, www.npr.org/2016/09/16/494328717/trumps-second-amendment-rhetoric-again-veers-into -threatening-territory.

59. Oliver Laughland and Sam Tielman, "Trump Loyalists Plan Own Exit Poll Amid Claims of 'Rigged' Election," *The Guardian*, October 20, 2016, www.theguardian.com/us-news/2016/oct/20/citizens-for-donald-trump-exit-poll-roger-stone-rigged-election-claim.
60. Levitsky and Ziblatt, *How Democracies Die*, 61.
61. Rick Hampson, "Donald Trump's Attacks on the News Media: A Not-So-Short History," *USA Today*, March 10, 2016, www.usatoday.com/story/news/politics/onpolitics/2016/03/10/donald-trump-versus-the-media/81602878/.
62. "Donald Trump Steps Up His Attack on the Media," *The Economist*, August 15, 2016; Taylor, "Trump's Second Amendment Rhetoric."
63. Levitsky and Ziblatt, *How Democracies Die*, 21–24.

CHAPTER 5: THE DECLINE OF AMERICAN DEMOCRACY

1. "T.R.B. from Washington," *The New Republic*, November 9, 1968, 4.
2. Peter Baker, "Nixon Tried to Spoil Johnson's Vietnam Peace Talks in '68, Notes Show," *New York Times*, January 2, 2017, www.nytimes.com/2017/01/02/us/politics/nixon-tried-to-spoil-johnsons-vietnam-peace-talks-in-68-notes-show.html.
3. "A Chronology of Violations of Democratic Principles by the Presidential Administration of Donald Trump," in Steven Levitsky and Daniel Ziblatt, *How Democracies Die* (New York: Crown, 2018), 176–80.
4. David Z. Morris, "Trump, Playing to His Base, Pardons Anti-Immigrant Sheriff Joe Arpaio," *Fortune*, August 26, 2017, http://fortune.com/2017/08/26/donald-trump-pardons-joe-arpaio.
5. John Shattuck, Amanda Watson, and Matthew McDole, "Trump's First Year: How Resilient Is Liberal Democracy in the U.S.?," Carr Center for Human Rights, Harvard University, February 15, 2018, 10; Glenn Kessler, Salvador Rizzo, and Meg Kelly, "President Trump Has Made 3,251 False or Misleading Claims in 497 Days," *Washington Post*, June 1, 2018, www.washingtonpost.com/news/fact-checker/wp/2018/06/01/president-trump-has-made-3251-false-or-misleading-claims-in-497-days/?utm_term=.34447309159f.
6. Levitsky and Ziblatt, *How Democracies Die*, 178.
7. Neil K. Katyal and George T. Conway III, "Trump's Appointment of Acting Attorney General Is Unconstitutional," *New York Times*, November 8, 2018, www.nytimes.com/2018/11/08/opinion/trump-attorney-general-sessions-unconstitutional.html.
8. Shattuck, Watson, and McDole, "Trump's First Year," 27.
9. Trump tweet, June 13, 2018, https://twitter.com/realDonaldTrump/status/1006891643985854464.
10. Trump tweet, June 24, 2018, https://twitter.com/realDonaldTrump/status/1010900865602019329.
11. James Hohmann, "Why Trump Flippantly Accusing Democrats of 'Treason' Is Not a Laughing Matter," *Washington Post*, February 6, 2018, www.washingtonpost.com/news/powerpost/paloma/daily-202/2018/02/06/daily-202-why-trump-flippantly-accusing-democrats-of-treason-is-not-a-laughing-matter/5a792a2130fb041c3c7d7657/?utm_term=.5fd9344d5d47.
12. Philip Rucker and Robert Costa, "Bob Woodward's New Book Reveals a 'Nervous Breakdown' of Trump's Presidency," *Washington Post*, September 4, 2018, www.washingtonpost.com/politics/bob-woodwards-new-book-reveals-a-nervous-breakdown-of-trumps-presidency/2018/09/04/b27a389e-ac60-11e8-a8d7-0f63ab8b1370_story.html?utm_term=.02d35ac650bf. See also Michael Wolff, *Fire and Fury: Inside the Trump White House* (New York: Henry Holt, 2018).
13. Madeleine Albright, *Fascism: A Warning* (New York: HarperCollins, 2018), 246.
14. Margaret Sullivan, "Trump's Vicious Attack on the Media Shows One Thing Clearly: He's Running Scared," *Washington Post*, August 23, 2017, www.washingtonpost.com/lifestyle/style/trumps-vicious-attack-on-the-press-shows-one-thing-clearly-hes-running-scared/2017/08/23/4fc1a6a2-8802-11e7-a50f-e0d4e6ec070a_story.html?utm_term=.d456749d1ad5.
15. Shattuck, Watson, and McDole, "Trump's First Year," pp. 12–13.
16. Michael Tackett and Michael Wines, "Trump Disbands Commission on Voter Fraud," *New York Times*, January 3, 2018, www.nytimes.com/2018/01/03/us/politics/trump-voter-fraud-commission.html; "Trump's Election Commission Is Fully Transparent About Its Purpose: Voter Obstruction," editorial, *Washington Post*, July 23, 2017, www.washingtonpost.com

/opinions/mr-trumps-election-commission-is-fully-transparent-about-its-purpose-voter
-obstruction/2017/07/23/43169900-6e51-11e7-96ab-5f38140b38cc_story.html?utm_term=
.1ae02f694482.

17. Steve Denning, "Trump: Replacing Sessions with Whitaker Appears to Obstruct Justice,"
Forbes, November 8, 2018, www.forbes.com/sites/stevedenning/2018/11/08/trump-why
-appointing-whitaker-risks-appearing-to-obstruct-justice-in-plain-sight/#3c3058f31b69.

18. *Trump, President of the United States, et al. v. Hawaii et al.*, 585 U.S. (2018), www.supremecourt
.gov/opinions/17pdf/17-965_h315.pdf.

19. Jake Tapper and Devan Cole, "Architect of bin Laden Raid: Trump 'Threatens the Constitution' When He Attacks the Media," CNN, November 18, 2018, www.cnn.com/2018/11/18
/politics/donald-trump-william-mcraven/index.html.

20. Norman L. Eisen, Caroline Frederickson, and Laurence H. Tribe, "Is Devin Nunes Obstructing Justice?," *New York Times*, February 12, 2018.

21. Gallup Poll, "Presidential Approval Ratings—Donald Trump," http://news.gallup.com/poll
/203198/presidential-approval-ratings-donald-trump.aspx, accessed September 12, 2018.

22. Thomas L. Friedman, "A President with No Shame and a Party with No Guts," *New York
Times*, July 17, 2018, www.nytimes.com/2018/07/17/opinion/trump-putin-republicans.html.

23. Jeff Flake, Speech from the Senate Floor, October 24, 2017, www.cnn.com/2017/10/24
/politics/jeff-flake-retirement-speech-full-text/index.html.

24. Eric Lipton and Alexander Burns, "NRA's Muscle Built on Votes, Not Donations," *New York
Times*, February 25, 2018; Christopher Ingraham, "Most Gun Owners Don't Belong to the
NRA and They Don't Agree with It Either," *Washington Post*, October 15, 2015, www
.washingtonpost.com/news/wonk/wp/2015/10/15/most-gun-owners-dont-belong-to-the
-nra-and-they-dont-agree-with-it-either/?utm_term=.87f475c6ee86.

25. For a clear overview of these rules and extensive documentation of campaign spending by the
largest groups, see the excellent Open Secrets website of the Center for Responsive Politics,
www.opensecrets.org/outsidespending/.

26. Robert Maguire, "$1.4 Billion and Counting in Spending by Super PACs, Dark Money
Groups," Open Secrets: Center for Responsive Politics, November 9, 2016, www.opensecrets
.org/news/2016/11/1-4-billion-and-counting-in-spending-by-super-pacs-dark-money
-groups/.

27. Sean Sullivan, "What Is a 501(c)(4), Anyway?," *Washington Post*, May 13, 2013, www
.washingtonpost.com/news/the-fix/wp/2013/05/13/what-is-a-501c4-anyway/?utm_term=
.2df3572ed3d9.

28. The top five were the NRA, the Chamber of Commerce, the 45 Committee, Americans
for Prosperity, and the American Future Fund, according to "Political Nonprofits: Top Election Spenders," Open Secrets: Center for Responsive Politics, www.opensecrets.org
/outsidespending/nonprof_elec.php?cycle=2016.

29. "Political Nonprofits (Dark Money)," Open Secrets: Center for Responsive Politics, www
.opensecrets.org/outsidespending/nonprof_summ.php?cycle=2018&type=viewpt; "2018 Outside Spending, by Group," Open Secrets: Center for Responsive Politics, www.opensecrets
.org/outsidespending/summ.php?disp=O, accessed November 9, 2018.

30. Brendan Fischer and Maggie Christ, "Three Money in Politics Trends You May Have Missed
in 2017," Campaign Legal Center, August 13, 2018, www.campaignlegalcenter.org/news
/blog/three-money-politics-trends-you-may-have-missed-2017.

31. Patrik Jonsson, "In Richard Lugar Defeat, a Tea Party Road Map for Revamping Washington?," *Christian Science Monitor*, May 9, 2012, www.csmonitor.com/USA/Elections/Senate
/2012/0509/In-Richard-Lugar-defeat-a-tea-party-road-map-for-revamping-Washington.

32. Freedom Works, "Hold Your Elected Officials Accountable," http://congress.freedomworks
.org/, accessed February 20, 2018.

33. Ibid.

34. Shane Goldmacher and Nick Corasaniti, "A Trump-Fueled 'Wipeout' for House Republicans
in Northeast," *New York Times*, November 7, 2018, www.nytimes.com/2018/11/07/nyregion
/house-republicans-election-northeast.html.

35. Thomas Mann and Norman Ornstein, *It's Even Worse Than It Looks* (New York: Basic Books,
2012).

36. Josh Kraushaar, "The Most Divided Congress Ever, at Least Until Next Year," *National Jour-*

nal, February 6, 2014, www.nationaljournal.com/2013-vote-ratings/the-most-divided
-congress-ever-at-least-until-next-year-20140206.

37. Morris Fiorina, *Unstable Majorities: Polarization, Party Sorting, and Political Stalemate* (Stanford, Calif.: Hoover Institution Press, 2017), 18.

38. Adam Nagourney and Sydney Ember, "Election Consolidates One-Party Control over State Legislatures," *New York Times*, November 7, 2018, www.nytimes.com/2018/11/07/us/politics /statehouse-elections.html.

39. Christopher Hare, Keith T. Poole, and Howard Rosenthal, "Polarization in Congress Has Risen Sharply. Where Is It Going Next?," *Washington Post*, February 13, 2014, www .washingtonpost.com/news/monkey-cage/wp/2014/02/13/polarization-in-congress-has -risen-sharply-where-is-it-going-next/?utm_term=.020cd24d51c5.

40. "The Polarization of the Congressional Parties," updated March 21, 2015, https://legacy .voteview.com/political_polarization_2014.htm.

41. Fiorina, *Unstable Majorities*.

42. Drew DeSilver, "The Polarized Congress of Today Has Its Roots in the 1970s," Pew Research Center, June 12, 2014, www.pewresearch.org/fact-tank/2014/06/12/polarized-politics-in -congress-began-in-the-1970s-and-has-been-getting-worse-ever-since/.

43. Mann and Ornstein, *It's Even Worse Than It Looks*, 31–43.

44. Jonathan Rodden, *Why Cities Lose: Political Geography and Representation in Industrialized Societies* (New York: Basic Books, forthcoming).

45. Fiorina, *Unstable Majorities*, 206.

46. Francis Fukuyama, *Identity: The Demand for Dignity and the Politics of Resentment* (New York: Farrar, Straus and Giroux: 2018).

47. Fiorina, *Unstable Majorities*, 211.

48. "2016 U.S. Presidential Election Map by County and Vote Share," Brilliant Maps, November 29, 2016, http://brilliantmaps.com/2016-county-election-map/.

49. Fiorina, *Unstable Majorities*, ch. 2.

50. Jane C. Tim, "They're Still Drawing Crazy-Looking Districts. Can't It Be Stopped?," NBC News, September 21, 2017, www.nbcnews.com/politics/elections/they-re-still-drawing-crazy -looking-districts-can-t-it-n803051.

51. Rodden, *Why Cities Lose*.

52. "List of Most-Listened-To Radio Programs," Wikipedia, https://en.wikipedia.org/wiki/List _of_most-listened-to_radio_programs.

53. Nathaniel Persily, "The 2016 U.S. Election: Can Democracy Survive the Internet," *Journal of Democracy* 28 (April 2017): 72; Joshua A. Tucker et al., "From Liberation to Turmoil: Social Media and Democracy," *Journal of Democracy* 28 (October 2017): 49.

54. Center for Humane Technology, "Our Society Is Being Hijacked by Technology," http:// humanetech.com/problem#team.

55. Persily, "The 2016 U.S. Election," 65.

56. Ibid., 66.

57. Center for Humane Technology, "Our Society Is Being Hijacked by Technology."

58. David M. J. Lazer et al., "The Science of Fake News," *Science* 359, March 9, 2018, http:// science.sciencemag.org/content/359/6380/1094.full.

59. Soroush Vosoughi, Deb Roy, and Sinan Aral, "The Spread of True and False News Online," *Science* 359, March 9, 2018, http://science.sciencemag.org/content/359/6380/1146.full.

60. On its 10-point democracy index, *The Economist* tracked a similar decline, putting the United States for the first time in the category of "flawed democracies": see "Democracy Index 2017: Free Speech Under Attack," Economist Intelligence Unit, www.eiu.com/topic/democracy -index.

61. Freedom House, "Freedom in the World 2018," 3. https://freedomhouse.org/sites/default /files/FH_FITW_Report_2018_Final_SinglePage.pdf.

62. Sarah Binder, "Polarized We Govern?," Brookings Institution, May 27, 2014, www.brookings .edu/research/polarized-we-govern/.

63. Shattuck, Watson, and McDole, "Trump's First Year," p. 57.

64. "Top Spenders, 2017," Open Secrets: Center for Responsive Politics, www.opensecrets.org /lobby/top.php?indexType=s&showYear=2017.

65. Maggie Christ and Brendan Fisher, "Three Money in Politics Trends You May Have Missed

in 2017," Campaign Legal Center, December 28, 2017, www.campaignlegalcenter.org/news
/blog/three-money-politics-trends-you-may-have-missed-2017.

66. See, for example, Kurt Weyland and Raúl L. Madrid, "Liberal Democracy: Stronger Than
    Populism, So Far," *The American Interest*, March–April 2018, 24–28; Francis Fukuyama, "Is
    American Democracy Strong Enough for Trump?," *Politico*, January 23, 2017, www.politico
    .com/magazine/story/2017/01/donald-trump-american-democracy-214683.

67. Shattuck, Watson, and McDole, "Trump's First Year," 15.

68. Linda Greenhouse, "A Conservative Plan to Weaponize the Federal Courts," *New York Times*,
    November 23, 2017, www.nytimes.com/2017/11/23/opinion/conservatives-weaponize
    -federal-courts.html.

69. Wendy R. Weiser, "Voter Suppression: How Bad? (Pretty Bad)," *The American Prospect*, Octo-
    ber 1, 2014, http://prospect.org/article/22-states-wave-new-voting-restrictions-threatens
    -shift-outcomes-tight-races; Shattuck, Watson, and McDole, "Trump's First Year," 31–32.

70. Michael Lewis, *The Fifth Risk* (New York: W. W. Norton, 2018).

71. Niraj Chokshi, "Assaults Increased When Cities Hosted Trump Rallies, Study Finds," *New
    York Times*, March 16, 2018, www.nytimes.com/2018/03/16/us/trump-rally-violence.html
    ?smprod=nytcore-ipad&smid=nytcore-ipad-share.

72. Daryl Johnson, "I Warned of Right-Wing Violence in 2009. Republicans Objected. I Was
    Right," *Washington Post*, August 21, 2017, www.washingtonpost.com/news/posteverything
    /wp/2017/08/21/i-warned-of-right-wing-violence-in-2009-it-caused-an-uproar-i-was-right
    /?nid&utm_term=.59ceb6093359.

73. Ibid.

CHAPTER 6: RUSSIA'S GLOBAL ASSAULT

1. Alexia Fernández Campbell, "The 7 Most Revealing Exchanges from Comey's Senate Testimony," *Vox*, June 8, 2017, www.vox.com/2017/6/8/15761794/comey-hearing-revealing
   -exchanges. Zeeshan Aleem, "Watch Comey's Impassioned Statement About Why Russia's
   Interference Was So Nefarious," *Vox*, June 8, 2017, https://www.vox.com/policy-and-politics
   /2017/6/8/15762574/comey-trump-russia.

2. George F. Kennan, "The Long Telegram," February 22, 1946, 13, www.trumanlibrary.org
   /whistlestop/study_collections/coldwar/documents/pdf/6-6.pdf.

3. "Putin's Asymmetric Assault on Democracy in Russia and Europe: Implications for U.S. National Security," Minority Staff Report, U.S. Senate Committee on Foreign Relations, January 10, 2018, 8, www.foreign.senate.gov/imo/media/doc/FinalRR.pdf.

4. Karen Dawisha, *Putin's Kleptocracy: Who Owns Russia?* (New York: Simon & Schuster, 2014).

5. Kennan, "The Long Telegram."

6. Ellen Barry, "Rally Defying Putin's Party Draws Tens of Thousands," *New York Times*, December 10, 2011, www.nytimes.com/2011/12/11/world/europe/thousands-protest-in-moscow
   -russia-in-defiance-of-putin.html.

7. Elise Labott, "Clinton Cites 'Serious Concerns' About Russian Election," CNN, December 6,
   2011, www.cnn.com/2011/12/06/world/europe/russia-elections-clinton/index.html.

8. David M. Herszenhorn and Ellen Barry, "Putin Contends Clinton Incited Unrest over Vote,"
   New York Times, December 8, 2011, www.nytimes.com/2011/12/09/world/europe/putin
   -accuses-clinton-of-instigating-russian-protests.html; Steve Gutterman, "Putin Says U.S.
   Stoked Russian Protests," Reuters, December 8, 2011, www.reuters.com/article/us-russia
   /putin-says-u-s-stoked-russian-protests-idUSTRE7B610S20111208.

9. Michael Crowley and Julia Ioffe, "Why Putin Hates Clinton," *Politico*, July 25, 2016, www
   .politico.com/story/2016/07/clinton-putin-226153.

10. Michael McFaul, *From Cold War to Hot Peace: An American Ambassador in Putin's Russia* (Bos-
    ton: Houghton Mifflin Harcourt, 2018).

11. Julia Ioffe, "What Putin Really Wants," *The Atlantic*, January–February 2018, www.theatlantic
    .com/magazine/archive/2018/01/putins-game/546548/.

12. Raphael Satter, "Inside Story: How Russians Hacked the Democrats' Emails," Associated
    Press, November 4, 2017, www.apnews.com/dea73efc01594839957c3c9a6c962b8a.

13. U.S. Intelligence Community Assessment, "Assessing Russian Activities and Intentions in Re-
    cent U.S. Elections," January 6, 2017, www.dni.gov/files/documents/ICA_2017_01.pdf.

14. Satter, "Inside Story."
15. Crowley and Ioffe, "Why Putin Hates Clinton."
16. Ken Dilanian, "Intelligence Director Says Agencies Agree on Russian Meddling," NBC News, July 21, 2017, www.nbcnews.com/news/us-news/intelligence-director-says-agencies -agree-russian-meddling-n785481.
17. U.S. Intelligence Community Assessment, "Assessing Russian Activities," 1.
18. Kevin Breuninger, "Russians Penetrated U.S. Voters Systems, DHS Cybersecurity Chief Tells NBC," CNBC, February 7, 2018, www.cnbc.com/2018/02/07/russians-penetrated-us-voter -systems-nbc-citing-top-us-official.html.
19. Dan Mangan and Mike Calia, "Special Counsel Mueller: Russians Conducted 'Information Warfare' Against U.S. During Election to Help Donald Trump Win," CNBC, February 16, 2018, www.cnbc.com/2018/02/16/russians-indicted-in-special-counsel-robert -muellers-probe.html.
20. Scott Shane and Mark Mazzetti, "Inside a Three-Year Russian Campaign to Influence U.S. Voters," *New York Times*, February 16, 2018, www.nytimes.com/2018/02/16/us/politics/russia -mueller-election.html.
21. Craig Timberg, Elizabeth Dwoskin, Adam Entous, and Karoun Demirjian, "Russian Ads, Now Publicly Released, Show Sophistication of Influence Campaign," *Washington Post*, November 1, 2017, www.washingtonpost.com/business/technology/russian-ads-now-publicly -released-show-sophistication-of-influence-campaign/2017/11/01/d26aead2-bf1b-11e7 -8444-a0d4f04b89eb_story.html?utm_term=.60ca97898685.
22. "Jill Stein: Democratic Spoiler or Scapegoat?," Five Thirty Eight, December 7, 2016, https:// fivethirtyeight.com/features/jill-stein-democratic-spoiler-or-scapegoat/.
23. Greg Walters, "The State Department Has a Secret Plan to Counter Russian Propaganda. It May Be Too Late," Vice News, March 6, 2018, https://news.vice.com/en_ca/article/vbpkd9 /the-state-department-has-a-secret-plan-to-counter-russian-propaganda-it-may-be-too-late.
24. Ibid.
25. Ben Nimmo, "How a Russian Troll Fooled America," Digital Forensic Research Lab, Atlantic Council, November 14, 2017, https://medium.com/dfrlab/how-a-russian-troll-fooled-america -80452a4806d1.
26. Ibid.
27. Shelby Holliday and Rob Barry, "Russian Influence Campaign Extracted Americans' Personal Data," *Wall Street Journal*, March 7, 2018, www.wsj.com/articles/russian-influence-campaign -extracted-americans-personal-data-1520418600.
28. Satter, "Inside Story."
29. Jo Becker, Adam Goldman, and Matt Apuzzo, "Russian Dirt on Clinton? 'I Love It,' Donald Trump Jr. Said," *New York Times*, July 11, 2017, www.nytimes.com/2017/07/11/us/politics /trump-russia-email-clinton.html.
30. "Read the Emails on Donald Trump Jr.'s Russia Meeting," *New York Times*, July 11, 2017, www .nytimes.com/interactive/2017/07/11/us/politics/donald-trump-jr-email-text.html.
31. Danielle Kurtzleben, "Here's How Many Bernie Sanders Supporters Ultimately Voted for Trump," NPR, August 24, 2017, www.npr.org/2017/08/24/545812242/1-in-10-sanders -primary-voters-ended-up-supporting-trump-survey-finds.
32. Harry Enten, "How Much Did WikiLeaks Hurt Hillary Clinton?," Five Thirty Eight, December 23, 2016, https://fivethirtyeight.com/features/wikileaks-hillary-clinton/.
33. Tim Meko, Denise Lu, and Lazaro Gamio, "How Trump Won the Presidency with Razor-Thin Margins in Swing States," *Washington Post*, November 11, 2016, www.washingtonpost .com/graphics/politics/2016-election/swing-state-margins/; Philip Bump, "Donald Trump Will Be President Thanks to 80,000 People in Three States," *Washington Post*, December 1, 2016, www.washingtonpost.com/news/the-fix/wp/2016/12/01/donald-trump-will-be -president-thanks-to-80000-people-in-three-states/?utm_term=.972f41a7926c. Jane Mayer reports that the Russian hackers might also have obtained Democratic polling data that showed a strong propensity of many likely Democrats in the midwestern battleground states to defect from Clinton and possibly vote for a third-party candidate: "How Russia Helped Swing the Election for Trump," *The New Yorker*, October 1, 2018, www.newyorker.com /magazine/2018/10/01/how-russia-helped-to-swing-the-election-for-trump.
34. Kathleen Hall Jamieson, *Cyberwar: How Russian Hackers and Trolls Helped Elect a President*

(New York: Oxford University Press, 2018); Mayer, "How Russia Helped Swing the Election for Trump."

35. James R. Clapper, *Facts and Fears: Hard Truths from a Life in Intelligence* (New York: Viking, 2018), 396.
36. Natasha Bertrand, "Trump's Top Intelligence Officials Contradict Him on Russian Meddling," *The Atlantic*, February 13, 2018, www.theatlantic.com/politics/archive/2018/02/the-intelligence-community-warns-congress-russia-will-interfere-in-2018-elections/553256/.
37. "Tracking Russian Influence Operations on Twitter," German Marshall Fund, Alliance for Securing Democracy, http://dashboard.securingdemocracy.org/, accessed March 8, 2018.
38. Laura Rosenberger and Jamie Fly, "Shredding the Putin Playbook," *Democracy: A Journal of Ideas* 47 (Winter 2018), https://democracyjournal.org/magazine/47/shredding-the-putin-playbook/.
39. Susan Glasser, "The Russian Bots Are Coming. This Bipartisan Duo Is on It," *Politico*, February 26, 2018, www.politico.com/magazine/story/2018/02/26/russia-social-media-bots-propaganda-global-politico-217084.
40. "Putin's Asymmetric Assault on Democracy in Russia and Europe."
41. "Testimony of John Lansing, CEO and Director of the Broadcasting Board of Governors, Before the Committee on Security and Cooperation in Europe," September 14, 2017, 3, www.bbg.gov/wp-content/media/2017/09/BBG_Helsinki-Commission_CEO-John-Lansing-Testimony.pdf.
42. Peter Pomerantsev, *Nothing Is True and Everything Is Possible: The Surreal Heart of the New Russia* (New York: Public Affairs, 2014).
43. "Testimony of John Lansing."
44. Dan Zak, "Whataboutism," *Washington Post*, August 18, 2017, www.washingtonpost.com/lifestyle/style/whataboutism-what-about-it/2017/08/17/4d05ed36-82b4-11e7-b359-15a3617c767b_story.html?utm_term=.e58e80e1102a.
45. Sophie Tatum, "Trump Defends Putin: 'You Think Our Country's So Innocent?,'" CNN, February 6, 2017, www.cnn.com/2017/02/04/politics/donald-trump-vladimir-putin/index.html.
46. Jane Mayer, "Christopher Steele: The Man Behind the Trump Dossier," *The New Yorker*, March 12, 2018, www.newyorker.com/magazine/2018/03/12/christopher-steele-the-man-behind-the-trump-dossier.
47. Alex Hern, "Russian Troll Factories: Researchers Damn Twitter's Refusal to Share Data," *The Guardian*, November 15, 2017, www.theguardian.com/world/2017/nov/15/russian-troll-factories-researchers-damn-twitters-refusal-to-share-data.
48. Patrick Wintour, "Russian Bid to Influence Brexit Vote Detailed in New U.S. Senate Report," *The Guardian*, January 10, 2018, www.theguardian.com/world/2018/jan/10/russian-influence-brexit-vote-detailed-us-senate-report.
49. Jeremy Diamond, "Trump Opens NATO Summit with Blistering Criticism of Germany," CNN, July 11, 2018, https://edition.cnn.com/2018/07/10/politics/donald-trump-nato-summit-2018/index.html.
50. Rosenberger and Fly, "Shredding the Putin Playbook."
51. David Alandate, "How Russian Networks Worked to Boost the Far Right in Italy," *El País*, March 1, 2018, https://elpais.com/elpais/2018/03/01/inenglish/1519922107_909331.html.
52. "Putin's Asymmetric Assault on Democracy," 41. See also "Testimony of John Lansing."
53. "Putin's Asymmetric Assault on Democracy," 37–53.
54. Ibid., 51–52.
55. Joseph Nye, *Soft Power: The Means to Success in World Affairs* (New York: Public Affairs, 2004).
56. Christopher Walker and Jessica Ludwig, "Introduction: From 'Soft Power' to 'Sharp Power,'" in Juan Pablo Cardenal et al., "Sharp Power: Rising Authoritarian Influence," National Endowment for Democracy, December 5, 2017, 8, 13, www.ned.org/sharp-power-rising-authoritarian-influence-forum-report/.
57. Jonathan Marcus, "Are Russia's Military Advances a Problem for NATO?," BBC News, August 11, 2016, www.bbc.com/news/world-europe-37045730; Jonathan Marcus, "Zapad: What Can We Learn from Russia's Latest Military Exercise?," BBC News, September 20, 2017, www.bbc.com/news/world-europe-41309290.
58. John Garnaut, "How China Interferes in Australia, and How Democracies Can Push Back,"

Foreign Affairs, March 9, 2018, www.foreignaffairs.com/articles/china/2018-03-09/how-china-interferes-australia.

CHAPTER 7: CHINA'S STEALTH OFFENSIVE

1. "Summary of the 2018 National Defense Strategy of the United States," Department of Defense, 2, www.defense.gov/Portals/1/Documents/pubs/2018-National-Defense-Strategy-Summary.pdf.
2. Melissa Davey, "Author Vows Book Exposing Chinese Influence Will Go Ahead After Publisher Pulls Out," *The Guardian*, November 12, 2017, www.theguardian.com/australia-news/2017/nov/13/author-vows-book-exposing-chinese-influence-will-go-ahead-after-publisher-pulls-out; "Australian Book on China's 'Silent Invasion' Withdrawn at Last Minute Amid Legal Threats," Radio Free Asia, November 13, 2017, www.rfa.org/english/news/china/book-11132017110421.html.
3. John Garnaut, "How China Interferes in Australia, and How Democracies Can Push Back," *Foreign Affairs*, March 9, 2018, www.foreignaffairs.com/articles/china/2018-03-09/how-china-interferes-australia.
4. Clive Hamilton, *Silent Invasion: China's Influence in Australia* (Melbourne: Hardie Grant, 2018), 9.
5. Katharine Murphy, "Sam Dastyari's Loyalty to Australia Questioned After He Tipped Off Chinese Donor," *The Guardian*, November 28, 2017, www.theguardian.com/australia-news/2017/nov/29/sam-dastyaris-loyalty-to-australia-questioned-after-he-tipped-off-chinese-donor.
6. Primrose Riordan, "China's Veiled Threat to Bill Shorten on Extradition Treaty," *The Australian*, December 5, 2017, www.theaustralian.com.au/national-affairs/foreign-affairs/chinas-veiled-threat-to-bill-shorten-on-extradition-treaty/news-story/ad793a4366ad2f94694e89c92d52a978.
7. Hamilton, *Silent Invasion*, 3.
9. Garnaut, "How China Interferes in Australia." This amount, and all other money figures in this section, have been converted from Australian into U.S. dollars.
10. "Australia Passes Foreign Interference Laws Amid China Tension," BBC, June 28, 2018, www.bbc.com/news/world-australia-44624270.
11. Christopher Walker, Shanthi Kalathil, and Jessica Ludwig, "How Democracies Can Fight Authoritarian Sharp Power," *Foreign Affairs*, August 16, 2018, www.foreignaffairs.com/articles/china/2018-08-16/how-democracies-can-fight-authoritarian-sharp-power.
12. Garnaut, "How China Interferes in Australia."
13. Hamilton, *Silent Invasion*, 137.
15. Amy Qin, "Worries Grow in Singapore over China's Calls to Help the 'Motherland,'" *New York Times*, August 5, 2018, www.nytimes.com/2018/08/05/world/asia/singapore-china.html.
16. Martin Hala, "China in Xi's 'New Era': Forging a New 'Eastern Bloc,'" *Journal of Democracy* 29 (April 2018): 86.
17. Minxin Pei, "China in Xi's 'New Era': A Play for Global Leadership," *Journal of Democracy* 29 (April 2018): 37–51; Shanthi Kalathil, "China in Xi's 'New Era': Redefining Development," *Journal of Democracy* 29 (April 2018): 52–58.
18. www2.compareyourcountry.org/oda?cr=oecd&lg=en.
19. Kai Schultz, "Sri Lanka, Struggling with Debt, Hands a Major Port to China," *New York Times*, December 12, 2017, www.nytimes.com/2017/12/12/world/asia/sri-lanka-china-port.html.
20. Jamie Tarabay, "With Sri Lankan Port Acquisition, China Adds Another 'Pearl' to Its 'String,'" CNN, February 4, 2018, www.cnn.com/2018/02/03/asia/china-sri-lanka-string-of-pearls-intl/index.html.
21. Wenyuan Wu, "China's 'Digital Silk Road': Pitfalls Among High Hopes," *The Diplomat*, November 3, 2017, https://thediplomat.com/2017/11/chinas-digital-silk-road-pitfalls-among-high-hopes/.
22. Kalathil, "Redefining Development."
23. Zhao Lei, "Satellite Will Test Plan for Communications Network," *China Daily*, March 5, 2018, www.chinadaily.com.cn/a/201803/05/WS5a9c9a3ba3106e7dcc13f807.html.

24. Kalathil, "Redefining Development."
25. Pei, "A Play for Global Leadership," 41.
26. Ibid.
27. David Shambaugh, "China's Soft-Power Push: The Search for Respect," *Foreign Affairs*, July–August 2015, www.foreignaffairs.com/articles/china/2015-06-16/china-s-soft-power-push.
28. Minxin Pei, "China's Moment of Truth," *Nikkei Asian Review*, August 7, 2018, https://asia.nikkei.com/Opinion/China-s-moment-of-truth.
29. "China and Africa: A Despot's Guide to Foreign Aid," *The Economist*, April 16, 2016, www.economist.com/news/middle-east-and-africa/21697001-want-more-cash-vote-china-united-nations-despots-guide-foreign.
30. Anne-Marie Brady, "Magic Weapons: China's Political Influence Activities Under Xi Jinping," Wilson Center, September 28, 2017, www.wilsoncenter.org/article/magic-weapons-chinas-political-influence-activities-under-xi-jinping. For a more detailed account, see *Chinese Influence and American Interests: Promoting Constructing Vigilance*, Report of the Working Group on Chinese Influence Activities in the United States, Hoover Institution, November 2018.
31. Brady, "Magic Weapons," 2.
32. Pei, "A Play for Global Leadership," 46.
33. Garnaut, "How China Interferes in Australia."
34. Pei, "A Play for Global Leadership," 45.
35. Shambaugh, "China's Soft-Power Push."
36. Ibid. The 2016 U.S. estimate for public diplomacy includes cultural exchanges and other items that may not be included in the estimate of China's effort: see U.S. Department of State, "2017 Comprehensive Annual Report on Public Diplomacy and International Broadcasting," www.state.gov/pdcommission/reports/274698.htm.
37. Thorsten Benner et al., "Authoritarian Advance: Responding to China's Growing Political Influence in Europe," Report of the Global Public Policy Institute and the Mercatur Institute for China Studies, February 2018, 22, www.merics.org/sites/default/files/2018-02/GPPi_MERICS_Authoritarian_Advance_2018_1.pdf.
38. Ibid., 24.
39. John Fitzgerald, "China in Xi's New Era: Overstepping Down Under," *Journal of Democracy* 29 (April 2018): 62.
40. Ibid.
41. Ibid., 60.
42. Ibid.
43. Ibid., 61.
44. Ibid.
45. *Chinese Influence and American Interests*, 4.
46. Eleanor Albert, "China's Big Bet on Soft Power," Council on Foreign Relations, February 9, 2018, www.cfr.org/backgrounder/chinas-big-bet-soft-power; Pei, "A Play for Global Leadership," 46.
47. "On Partnerships with Foreign Governments: The Case of Confucius Institutes," American Association of University Professors, June 2014, www.aaup.org/report/confucius-institutes.
48. Pei, "A Play for Global Leadership," 46.
49. Edward Wong, "China Denies Entry to an American Scholar Who Spoke Up for a Uighur Colleague," *New York Times*, July 7, 2014, www.nytimes.com/2014/07/08/world/asia/us-scholar-who-supported-uighur-colleague-is-denied-entry-to-china.html.
50. Benner et al., "Authoritarian Advance," 27–29.
51. Shambaugh, "China's Soft-Power Push."
52. Mike Ives, "Chinese Student in Maryland Is Criticized at Home for Praising U.S.," *New York Times*, May 23, 2017, www.nytimes.com/2017/05/23/world/asia/chinese-student-fresh-air-yang-shuping.html.
53. Stephanie Saul, "On Campuses Far from China, Still Under Beijing's Watchful Eye," *New York Times*, May 4, 2017, www.nytimes.com/2017/05/04/us/chinese-students-western-campuses-china-influence.html.
54. Benner et al., "Authoritarian Advance," 20.
55. Hala, "China in Xi's 'New Era,'" 87.
56. Ibid.
57. David Barboza, Marc Santora, and Alexandra Stevenson, "China Seeks Influence in Europe,

One Business Deal at a Time," *New York Times*, August 12, 2018, www.nytimes.com/2018/08
/12/business/china-influence-europe-czech-republic.html.

58. Hala, "Forging a New 'Eastern Bloc,' " 86–87; see also Benner et al., "Authoritarian Advance," 20.

59. Benner et al., "Authoritarian Advance," 7.

60. Jason Horowitz and Liz Alderman, "Chastised by E.U., a Resentful Greece Embraces China's
Cash and Interests," *New York Times*, August 26, 2017, www.nytimes.com/2017/08/26/world
/europe/greece-china-piraeus-alexis-tsipras.html.

61. Benner et al., "Authoritarian Advance," 18.

62. Juan Pablo Cardenal, "China in Latin America," in Cardenal et al., "Sharp Power: Rising
Authoritarian Influence," National Endowment for Democracy, December 5, 2017, 34, www
.ned.org/sharp-power-rising-authoritarian-influence-forum-report/.

63. *Chinese Influence and American Interests*, 101–18.

64. Shambaugh, "China's Soft-Power Push."

65. Bethany Allen-Ebrahimian, "This Beijing-Linked Billionaire Is Funding Policy Research at
Washington's Most Influential Institutions," *Foreign Policy*, November 28, 2017, http://
foreignpolicy.com/2017/11/28/this-beijing-linked-billionaire-is-funding-policy-research-at
-washingtons-most-influential-institutions-china-dc/.

66. Erik Larson, "HNA's NYC-Based Charity Registers with N.Y. Attorney General," Bloomberg, September 29, 2017, www.bloomberg.com/news/articles/2017-09-29/hna-s-nyc-based
-charity-registers-with-n-y-attorney-general-j86923jj.

67. "HNA Foundation Says Not Seeking Tax Exempt Status," Reuters, July 15, 2018, www.reuters
.com/article/us-hna-taxation/hna-foundation-says-not-seeking-tax-exempt-status
-idUSKBN1K50PD; Alexandra Stevenson, "HNA Will Transfer Co-Chairman's Stake as
Ownership Doubts Linger," *New York Times*, July 13, 2018, www.nytimes.com/2018/07/13
/business/hna-co-chairman-death-stake.html.

68. Michael Forsythe and Alexandra Stevenson, "Behind an $18 Billion Donation to a New York
Charity, a Shadowy Chinese Conglomerate," *New York Times*, July 26, 2017, www.nytimes
.com/2017/07/26/business/hna-group-billion-donation-new-york-charity.html; Prudence
Ho, "HNA Charity Names CEO, Pledges to Give Away $200 Million," Bloomberg, Decem-
ber 15, 2017, www.bloomberg.com/news/articles/2017-12-15/hna-group-charity-names-ceo
-pledges-to-give-away-200-million.

69. Margaret Vice, "In Global Popularity Contest, U.S. and China—Not Russia—Vie for First,"
Pew Research Center, August 23, 2017, www.pewresearch.org/fact-tank/2017/08/23/in-global
-popularity-contest-u-s-and-china-not-russia-vie-for-first/.

70. Julie Hirschfeld Davis, Sheryl Gay Stolberg, and Thomas Kaplan, "Trump Alarms Lawmakers with Disparaging Words for Haiti and Africa," *New York Times*, January 11, 2018, www
.nytimes.com/2018/01/11/us/politics/trump-shithole-countries.html.

71. "What Does China Really Spend on Its Military?," China Power, December 28, 2015, https://
chinapower.csis.org/military-spending/.

72. Nikita Vladimirov, "Russia, China Making Gains on U.S. Military Power," *The Hill*, March 18,
2017, http://thehill.com/policy/defense/324595-russia-china-making-gains-on-us-military
-power.

73. Steven Lee Myers, "With Ships and Missiles, China Is Ready to Challenge U.S. Navy in the
Pacific," *New York Times*, August 29, 2018, www.nytimes.com/2018/08/29/world/asia/china
-navy-aircraft-carrier-pacific.html.

74. The definitive recent report is Michael Brown and Pavneet Singh, "China's Technology
Transfer Strategy: How Chinese Investments in Emerging Technology Enable a Strategic
Competitor to Access the Crown Jewels of U.S. Innovation," Defense Innovation Unit Experimental (DIUx), January 2018, https://diux.mil/library. See also Jane Perlez, Paul Mozur,
and Jonathan Ansfield, "China's Technology Ambitions Could Upset the Global Trade Order," *New York Times*, November 7, 2017, www.nytimes.com/2017/11/07/business/made-
in-china-technology-trade.html; David Barboza, "How This U.S. Tech Giant Is Backing
China's Tech Ambitions," *New York Times*, August 4, 2017, www.nytimes.com/2017/08/04
/technology/qualcomm-china-trump-tech-trade.html.

75. Paul Mozur and Jane Perlez, "China Bets on Sensitive U.S. Start-Ups, Worrying the Pentagon,"
March 22, 2017, www.nytimes.com/2017/03/22/technology/china-defense-start-ups.html.

76. Pei, "A Play for Global Leadership," 44.

CHAPTER 8: ARE PEOPLE LOSING FAITH IN DEMOCRACY?

1. Amartya Sen, "Democracy as a Universal Value," *Journal of Democracy* 10 (July 1999): 12.
2. Juan J. Linz and Alfred Stepan, *Problems of Democratic Transition and Consolidation: Southern Europe, South America, and Post-Communist Europe* (Baltimore: Johns Hopkins University Press, 1996), 5–7; Larry Diamond, *Developing Democracy: Toward Consolidation* (Baltimore: Johns Hopkins University Press, 1999), 64–71.
3. Roberto Stefan Foa and Yascha Mounk, "The Democratic Disconnect," *Journal of Democracy* 27 (July 2016): 5–17.
4. Ibid., 7.
5. Lee Drutman, Larry Diamond, and Joe Goldman, "Follow the Leader: Exploring American Support for Democracy and Authoritarianism," Democracy Fund Voter Study Group, March 2018, www.voterstudygroup.org/publications/2017-voter-survey/follow-the-leader.
6. The Pew Research Center found a notably lower number, 46 percent, but satisfaction with democracy is a more volatile measure that moves with the state of politics and the economy.
7. Richard Wike at al., "Globally, Broad Support for Representative, Direct Democracy," Pew Research Center, October 16, 2017, www.pewglobal.org/2017/10/16/globally-broad-support -for-representative-and-direct-democracy/.
8. Drutman, Diamond, and Goldman, "Follow the Leader," figure 11.
9. Ibid., 18–27.
10. Joe Ruiz, "Trump Again Questions Maxine Waters' Intelligence, Says She's 'Very Low IQ,'" CNN, March 11, 2018, www.cnn.com/2018/03/10/politics/trump-waters-low-iq-individual /index.html; Christina Caron, "Trump Mocks LeBron James's Intelligence and Calls Don Lemon 'Dumbest Man' on TV," *New York Times*, August 4, 2018, www.nytimes.com/2018/08 /04/sports/donald-trump-lebron-james-twitter.html.
11. Wike et al., "Globally, Broad Support," 26–29.
12. Drutman, Diamond, and Goldman, "Follow the Leader," 6–7.
13. Abraham Maslow, "A Theory of Human Motivation," *Psychological Review* 50 (July 1943): 370–96.
14. Ronald Inglehart and Christian Welzel, *Modernization, Cultural Change, and Democracy: The Human Development Sequence* (Cambridge: Cambridge University Press, 2005), 54; see also Ronald Inglehart, *Culture Shift in Advanced Industrial Society* (Princeton, N.J.: Princeton University Press, 1990).
15. Inglehart and Welzel, *Modernization*, 60.
16. Ronald F. Inglehart, "The Danger of Deconsolidation: How Much Should We Worry," *Journal of Democracy* 27 (July 2016): 22.
17. Online data analysis of the 2016 Latinobarometer performed at www.latinobarometro.org /latOnline.jsp; "Informe 2017," Corporación Latinobarómetro, www.latinobarometro.org /latNewsShow.jsp. A different measure of support for democracy, whether people think "democracy is always preferable" or agree that "sometimes an authoritarian government can be preferable," shows lower levels of average support (only 53 percent in 2017) and the same moderate but steady decline, from 61 percent in 2010.
18. The data is from the fourth round of the Asian Barometer, covering fourteen countries in east and southeast Asia, conducted between June 2014 and June 2016 (depending on the country): see www.asianbarometer.org/survey/survey-timetable. I consider here only seven of those fourteen nations, the ones with some democratic experience, leaving out Singapore, Malaysia, and Communist countries like China and Vietnam, where constraints on freedom of thought and expression make it difficult to interpret the data.
19. "Asian Barometer Survey of Democracy, Governance, and Development," www.asianbarometer .org/pdf/core_questionnaire_wave4.pdf.
20. Online data analysis performed at afrobarometer.org. Data was subsequently posted for some additional African countries.
21. The question on media scrutiny is from 2014–2016; it was not asked in the most recent survey.
22. Online data analysis performed at www.arabbarometer.org/content/online-data-analysis.
23. The six countries are Algeria, Jordan, Lebanon, Morocco, Palestine (both the West Bank and Gaza), and Tunisia. This data from the fourth wave of the Arab Barometer was accessed online on August 4, 2018.

24. Michael Robbins, "Tunisia Five Years After the Revolution: Findings from the Arab Barometer," Arab Barometer, May 15, 2016, www.arabbarometer.org/country/tunisia.
25. The sources for the data are the Pew 2017 survey for the G-7 and the aforementioned regional barometers for the others. The question used for the G-7 asks about support for representative democracy.
26. "Do Africans Still Want Democracy?" (news release), Afrobarometer, November 22, 2016, http://afrobarometer.org/sites/default/files/press-release/round-6-releases/ab_r6_pr15_Do _Africans_want_democracy_EN.pdf.

CHAPTER 9: MEETING THE AUTOCRATS' CHALLENGE

1. John McCain, "Remarks at the 2017 Munich Security Conference," February 17, 2017, www .mccain.senate.gov/public/index.cfm/speeches?ID=32A7E7DD-8D76-4431-B1E7 -8644FD71C49F.
2. George F. Kennan, "The Long Telegram," February 22, 1946, 15–15½, www.trumanlibrary .org/whistlestop/study_collections/coldwar/documents/pdf/6-6.pdf.
3. Data from "GDP Per Capita," World Bank, https://data.worldbank.org/indicator/NY.GDP .PCAP.CD?locations=RU. Per capita income in Russia (in current U.S. dollars—that is, for the respective year) was $3,428 in 1990 but fell to $1,331 by 1999.
4. "Why Is Russia's Growth in Life Expectancy Slowing?," Moscow Times, August 30, 2015, https:// themoscowtimes.com/news/why-is-russias-growth-in-life-expectancy-slowing-49224.
5. Kennan, "Long Telegram," 17.
6. Fareed Zakaria, The Post-American World: Release 2.0 (New York: W. W. Norton, 2011), 2.
7. Kennan, "Long Telegram," 17.
8. Alex Horton, "The Magnitsky Act, Explained," Washington Post, July 14, 2017, www .washingtonpost.com/news/the-fix/wp/2017/07/14/the-magnitsky-act-explained/?utm_term =.6f1b885c6cce.
9. Ian Talley, "Trump Administration Sanctions Russia for Interference in U.S. Elections," Wall Street Journal, March 15, 2018, www.wsj.com/articles/trump-administration-sanctions -russians-for-interference-in-u-s-elections-1521124200; Ian Talley, "U.S. Targets Allies of Putin in Latest Round of Sanctions," Wall Street Journal, April 6, 2018, www.wsj.com/articles /u-s-targets-russian-oligarchs-in-new-sanctions-1523018826/.
10. "Russian Businessmen, Officials on New U.S. Sanctions List," Reuters, April 6, 2018, www .reuters.com/article/us-usa-russia-sanctions-factbox/russian-businessmen-officials-on-new-u -s-sanctions-list-idUSKCN1HD22K?il=0.
11. "No Longer Safe Assets: Invest in Russia at Your Own Risk After U.S. Sanctions, Strategist Says," CNBC, April 10, 2018, www.cnbc.com/2018/04/10/invest-in-russia-at-your-own-risk -after-us-sanctions-strategist-says.html.
12. "Western Allies Expel Scores of Russian Diplomats over Skripal Attack," The Guardian, March 27, 2018, www.theguardian.com/uk-news/2018/mar/26/four-eu-states-set-to-expel -russian-diplomats-over-skripal-attack.
13. Oliver Bullough, "Forget the Pledges to Act—London Is Still a Haven for Dirty Russian Money," The Guardian, September 30, 2018, www.theguardian.com/commentisfree/2018 /sep/30/forget-pledges-to-act-london-still-haven-for-dirty-russian-money; John Gunter, "Sergei Skripal and the Fourteen Deaths Under Scrutiny," BBC, March 7, 2018, www.bbc .com/news/world-europe-43299598.
14. Anne Applebaum, "Why Does Putin Treat Britain with Disdain? He Thinks He's Bought It," Washington Post, March 16, 2018, www.washingtonpost.com/opinions/global-opinions/why -does-putin-treat-britain-with-disdain-he-thinks-hes-bought-it/2018/03/16/9f66a720-2951 -11e8-874b-d517e912f125_story.html?utm_term=.2c73148b40da.
15. Ibid.
16. Wealthy foreigners looking for golden visa options among Western democracies—including the United States, Canada, and Britain—can find more than a dozen of them at the "Corpocrat" website: https://corpocrat.com/2015/10/20/25-immigrant-investor-citizenship -programs-in-the-world/.
17. Teri Schultz, "'Golden Visas': EU Offers the Rich Bigger Bang for the Buck," Deutsche Welle, March 17, 2018, www.dw.com/en/golden-visas-eu-offers-the-rich-bigger-bang-for -the-buck/a-42947322.

18. David Z. Morris, "Vladimir Putin Is Reportedly Richer Than Bill Gates and Jeff Bezos Combined," *Fortune*, July 29, 2017, http://fortune.com/2017/07/29/vladimir-putin-russia-jeff-bezos-bill-gates-worlds-richest-man/. See also Rob Wile, "Is Vladimir Putin Secretly the Richest Man in the World?," *Money*, January 23, 2017, http://time.com/money/4641093/vladimir-putin-net-worth/.

19. Laura Rosenberger and Jamie Fly, "Shredding the Putin Playbook," *Democracy: A Journal of Ideas* 47 (Winter 2018), https://democracyjournal.org/magazine/47/shredding-the-putin-playbook/.

20. Michael W. Sulmeyer, "How the U.S. Can Play Cyber-Offense," *Foreign Affairs*, March 22, 2018, www.foreignaffairs.com/articles/world/2018-03-22/how-us-can-play-cyber-offense.

21. Rebecca Smith, "Russian Hackers Reach U.S. Utility Control Rooms, Homeland Security Officials Say," *Wall Street Journal*, July 23, 2018, www.wsj.com/articles/russian-hackers-reach-u-s-utility-control-rooms-homeland-security-officials-say-1532388110?mod=mktw.

22. Christopher Walker and Jessica Ludwig, "Introduction: From 'Soft Power' to 'Sharp Power,'" in Juan Pablo Cardenal et al., "Sharp Power: Rising Authoritarian Influence," National Endowment for Democracy, December 5, 2017, 22–24, www.ned.org/sharp-power-rising-authoritarian-influence-forum-report/.

23. This is one of the recommendations of our report, *Chinese Influence and American Interests: Promoting Constructive Vigilance*, Report of the Working Group on Chinese Influence Activities in the United States, Hoover Institution, November 2018.

24. Eli Meixler, "Joshua Wong, Hong Kong's Most Prominent Pro-Democracy Activist, Has Been Jailed Again," *Time*, January 17, 2018, http://time.com/5105498/joshua-wong-hong-kong-prison/.

25. Cynthia Brown, "The Foreign Agents Registration Act (FARA): A Legal Overview," Congressional Research Service, December 4, 2017, 13, https://fas.org/sgp/crs/misc/R45037.pdf.

26. *Chinese Influence and American Interests*, x.

27. This structure is described at length in *Chinese Influence and American Interests*, 131–41.

28. Michael Brown and Pavneet Singh, "China's Technology Transfer Strategy," Defense Innovation Unit Experimental (DIUx), January 2018, 23–26, https://admin.govexec.com/media/diux_chinatechnologytransferstudy_jan_2018_(1).pdf.

29. Alexandra Yoon-Hendricks, "Congress Strengthens Reviews of Chinese and Other Foreign Investments," *New York Times*, August 1, 2018, www.nytimes.com/2018/08/01/business/foreign-investment-united-states.html.

30. Alejandra Reyes-Velarde, "Chinese Gaming Company Buys Remaining Stake of Grindr," *Los Angeles Times*, January 8, 2018, www.latimes.com/business/la-fi-tn-grindr-kunlun-20180108-story.html.

31. Keith Griffith, "Fears Mount That China's Spymasters Will Cruise Grindr for Personal Data to 'Out People' After a Chinese Tech Firm Bought the Gay Dating App for $400m," *Daily Mail*, January 12, 2018, www.dailymail.co.uk/news/article-5264963/Grindr-sale-Kunlun-sparks-fears-Chinese-spying.html.

32. Brown and Singh, "China's Technology Transfer Strategy," 24.

33. "Sizing Up the Gap in Our Supply of STEM Workers," New American Economy, March 29, 2017, https://research.newamericaneconomy.org/report/sizing-up-the-gap-in-our-supply-of-stem-workers/.

34. Robert Farley, "The Consequences of Curbing Chinese STEM Graduate Student U.S. Visas," *The Diplomat*, June 15, 2018, https://thediplomat.com/2018/06/the-consequences-of-curbing-chinese-stem-graduate-student-us-visas/.

35. Compete America, Partnership for a New American Economy, and U.S. Chamber of Commerce, "Understanding and Improving the H-1B Visa Program," April 2015, 4, www.newamericaneconomy.org/wp-content/uploads/2015/04/Briefing-Book-on-Understanding-and-Improving-H-1B-Visas-4-24-2015.pdf.

CHAPTER 10: FIGHTING KLEPTOCRACY

1. Oliver Bullough, "The Rise of Kleptocracy: The Dark Side of Globalization," *Journal of Democracy* 29 (January 2018): 33.

2. Rosalind S. Helderman and Alice Crites, "The Russian Billionaire Next Door: Putin Ally Is Tied to One of D.C.'s Swankiest Mansions," *Washington Post*, November 29, 2017, www

.washingtonpost.com/politics/the-russian-tycoon-next-door-putin-ally-is-tied-to-one-of-dcs
-swankiest-mansions/2017/11/28/15f913de-cef6-11e7-81bc-c55a220c8cbe_story.html?utm
_term=.c8691ab5bc77.

3. "Treasury Designates Russian Oligarchs, Officials, and Entities in Response to Worldwide
   Malign Activity" (press release), U.S. Department of Treasury, April 6, 2017, https://home
   .treasury.gov/news/press-releases/sm0338.

4. Helderman and Crites, "The Russian Billionaire Next Door."

5. Ken Silverstein, "Oleg Deripaska and the Buying of Washington: Controversial Oligarch
   Funds Local Think Tanks," *Harper's*, October 24, 2008, https://harpers.org/blog/2008/10
   /oleg-deripaska-and-the-buying-of-washington-controversial-oligarch-funds-local-think
   -tanks/. The Council on Foreign Relations reports that Deripaska's company, Basic Element,
   joined its corporate-membership program in 2007 for a year; the council says that it has not
   had a relationship with Basic Element (or Deripaska) since 2008: email communication, September 6, 2018.

6. Andrew Higgins and Kenneth P. Vogel, "Two Capitals, One Russian Oligarch: How Oleg
   Deripaska Is Trying to Escape U.S. Sanctions," *New York Times*, November 4, 2018, www
   .nytimes.com/2018/11/04/world/europe/oleg-deripaska-russia-oligarch-sanctions.html.

7. Ibid.

8. Cynthia Gabriel, "The Rise of Kleptocracy: Malaysia's Missing Billions," *Journal of Democracy*
   29 (January 2018): 69.

9. Ibid., 70.

10. Belinda Li, "Why Miami Matters," Kleptocracy Initiative, June 26, 2017, http://
    kleptocracyinitiative.org/2017/06/why-miami-matters/.

11. Ben Judah and Belinda Li, "Money Laundering for Twenty-First Century Authoritarianism:
    Western Enablement of Kleptocracy," Kleptocracy Initiative, the Hudson Institute, Decem-
    ber 2017, 7, https://www.hudson.org/research/14020-money-laundering-for-21st-century
    -authoritarianism.

12. Alexander Cooley, John Heathershaw, and J. C. Sharman, "The Rise of Kleptocracy: Laun-
    dering Cash, Whitewashing Reputations," *Journal of Democracy* 29 (January 2018): 44.

13. Ibid.

14. Ilya Zaslavskiy, "How Non-State Actors Export Kleptocratic Norms to the West," Kleptoc-
    racy Initiative, the Hudson Institute, September 2017, 2, https://s3.amazonaws.com/media
    .hudson.org/files/publications/Kleptocratic_Norms.pdf.

15. Statement of Charles Davidson, executive director of the Kleptocracy Initiative, to the Com-
    mittee on the Judiciary, U.S. Senate, November 28, 2017, www.judiciary.senate.gov/imo
    /media/doc/Davidson%20Testimony.pdf.

16. Zaslavskiy, "How Non-State Actors," 24.

17. Rick Noack, "He Used to Rule Germany. Now, He Oversees Russian Energy Companies and
    Lashes Out at the U.S.," *Washington Post*, August 12, 2017, www.washingtonpost.com/news
    /worldviews/wp/2017/08/08/he-used-to-rule-germany-now-he-oversees-russian-energy
    -companies-and-lashes-out-at-the-u-s/?utm_term=.ae9dab6a03da.

18. Gerald Knaus, "Europe and Azerbaijan: The End of Shame," *Journal of Democracy* 26 (July
    2015): 6, 10.

19. Brett L. Carter, "The Rise of Kleptocracy: Autocrats Versus Activists in Africa," *Journal of
    Democracy* 29 (January 2018): 55–56.

20. David Bensoussan, "Dominique Strauss-Kahn au chevet du président congolais Denis
    Sassou-Nguesso," *Challenges*, August 30, 2017, www.challenges.fr/economie/dominique
    -strauss-kahn-dsk-au-chevet-du-president-congolais-denis-sassou-nguesso-aupres-du-fmi
    _496094; David Bensoussan, "La banque Lazard au chevet du Congo," *Challenges*, Jan-
    uary 4, 2018, https://www.challenges.fr/economie/quand-la-banque-lazard-dirigee-par
    -mathieu-pigasse-rejoint-dominique-strauss-kahn-et-stephane-fouks-au-chevet-du-congo
    _558075.

21. Sassou-Nguesso's expenditures on Washington, D.C., lobbying firms have been tracked and
    aggregated by University of Southern California political scientist Brett L. Carter, who has
    shared his statistical results with me. Specific evidence can be found in these articles: Anu
    Narayanswamy, "Corruption Charges Prompt Congo to Lobby Congress," Sunlight Founda-
    tion, September 25, 2009, https://sunlightfoundation.com/2009/09/25/corruption-charges

-prompt-congo-to-lobby-congress/; Carol D. Leonnig, "Congo's Heavy Use of D.C. Lobbyists Prompts Questions," *Washington Post*, August 25, 2010, www.washingtonpost.com/wp-dyn/content/article/2010/08/25/AR2010082505238.html.

22. Carter, "The Rise of Kleptocracy," 60.
23. Ibid., 61; Nicolas Beau, "Rwanda, lorsque Paul Kagamé achetait 'Jeune Afrique' en 2004," Mondafrique, March 10, 2005, https://mondafrique.com/rwanda-lorsque-paul-kagame-achetait-jeune-afrique-en-2004/.
24. Monica Mark, "Nigerian Police Recover Part of Sani Abacha's $4.3bn Hoard from Robbers," *The Guardian*, October 5, 2012, www.theguardian.com/world/2012/oct/05/nigeria-sani-abacha-jewellery-police.
25. Norimitsu Onishi, "Portugal Dominated Angola for Centuries. Now the Roles Are Reversed," *New York Times*, August 22, 2017, www.nytimes.com/2017/08/22/world/europe/angola-portugal-money-laundering.html.
26. Net worth is estimated as of September 13, 2018: "#924, Isabel dos Santos," *Forbes*, www.forbes.com/profile/isabel-dos-santos/.
27. "World Mortality 2017," United Nations, www.un.org/en/development/desa/population/publications/pdf/mortality/World-Mortality-2017-Data-Booklet.pdf.
28. Onishi, "Portugal Dominated Angola." However, Portugal has prosecuted the former Angolan vice president. Conor Gaffey: "Portugal Charges Angolan Vice-President with Corruption," *Newsweek*, February 17, 2017, www.newsweek.com/manuel-vicente-angola-portugal-557906.
29. Bullough, "Rise of Kleptocracy: The Dark Side," 35.
30. Casey Michael, "The United States of Anonymity," Kleptocracy Initiative, the Hudson Institute, November 2017, 3. https://s3.amazonaws.com/media.hudson.org/files/publications/UnitedStatesofAnonymity.pdf.
31. Ibid., 3.
32. "Office Space: Who Really Owns Real Estate Leased by the U.S. Government?," Kleptocracy Initiative, January 30, 2017, http://kleptocracyinitiative.org/2017/01/office-space/. For the Government Accountability Office's report, see www.gao.gov/products/GAO-17-195.
33. This ranking is based on a survey of international experts and businesspeople: "Corruption Perceptions Index 2017," Transparency International, www.transparency.org/news/feature/corruption_perceptions_index_2017?gclid=CjwKCAjwiPbWBRBtEiwAJakcpKPbB7q9v42Q4EcdREVv7TTqPONV5pn-eLt6M-K39oaerRFiQLlBNhoCRdEQAvD_BwE.
34. Larry Diamond, *In Search of Democracy* (London: Routledge, 2016), 26.
35. "Judge Mark Wolf on Kleptocracy and the International Anti-Corruption Court," National Endowment for Democracy, June 6, 2017, www.ned.org/judge-mark-wolf-international-anti-corruption-court/. Pillay's statement was made in 2013.
36. Cooley, Heathershaw, and Sharman, "Rise of Kleptocracy: Laundering Cash," 40.
37. Judah and Li, "Money Laundering for Twenty-First Century Authoritarianism," 16–22; Bullough, "Rise of Kleptocracy: The Dark Side."
38. Ben Judah and Nate Sibley, "Countering Russian Kleptocracy," Kleptocracy Initiative, the Hudson Institute, April 2018, www.hudson.org/research/14244-countering-russian-kleptocracy. See also Cooley, Heatherstraw, and Sharman, "Rise of Kleptocracy: Laundering Cash."
39. Judah and Sibley, "Countering Russian Kleptocracy," 7.
40. Ibid.
41. Executive Order: Ethics Commitments by Executive Branch Appointees, January 28, 2017, www.whitehouse.gov/presidential-actions/executive-order-ethics-commitments-executive-branch-appointees/.
42. Judah and Sibley, "Countering Russian Kleptocracy," 9.
43. Bullough, "Rise of Kleptocracy: The Dark Side," 34–35.
44. Cooley, Heatherstraw, and Sharman, "Rise of Kleptocracy: Laundering Cash," 45–46.
45. Judah and Sibley, "Countering Russian Kleptocracy," 15.
46. "About," International Consortium of Investigative Journalists, www.icij.org/about/.
47. "Judge Mark Wolf on Kleptocracy."
48. Robbie Gramer, "Infographic: Here's How the Global GDP Is Divvied Up," *Foreign Policy*, February 24, 2017, http://foreignpolicy.com/2017/02/24/infographic-heres-how-the-global-gdp-is-divvied-up/.

CHAPTER 11: A FOREIGN POLICY FOR FREEDOM

1. "National Security Strategy of the United States of America," The White House, December 2017, www.whitehouse.gov/wp-content/uploads/2017/12/NSS-Final-12-18-2017-0905.pdf.

2. The ensuing discussion has been inspired by the work of the Democracy and Human Rights Working Group of the McCain Institute for International Leadership; see www.mccaininstitute.org/advancing-freedom-promotes-us-interests/.

3. Amartya Sen, "Democracy as a Universal Value," *Journal of Democracy* 10 (July 1999): 3–17; Kim Dae Jung, "Is Culture Destiny?," *Foreign Affairs* 73 (November–December 1994): 189–94; His Holiness the Dalai Lama, "Buddhism, Asian Values, and Democracy," *Journal of Democracy* 10 (January 1999): 3–7; Abdou Filali-Ansary, "Muslims and Democracy," *Journal of Democracy* 10 (July 1999): 18–32.

4. Glen Carey and Sarah Algethami, "How the Saudis Turned the Yemen War into a Humanitarian Crisis," Bloomberg, October 19, 2018, www.bloomberg.com/news/articles/2018-10-19/how-saudis-turned-yemen-war-into-humanitarian-crisis-quicktake/.

5. Condoleezza Rice, remarks at the American University of Cairo, June 20, 2005, https://2001-2009.state.gov/secretary/rm/2005/48328.htm.

6. Steven Radelet, *Emerging Africa: How Seventeen Countries Are Leading the Way* (Washington, D.C.: Center for Global Development, 2010).

7. Jon Greenberg, "Most People Clueless on U.S. Foreign Aid Spending," *Politifact*, November 9, 2016, www.politifact.com/global-news/statements/2016/nov/09/john-kerry/yep-most-people-clueless-us-foreign-aid-spending/.

8. The core annual appropriation to the flagship democracy-assistance program, the National Endowment for Democracy, was in turn only $170 million: www.appropriations.senate.gov/imo/media/doc/FY18-OMNI-SFOPS-SUM.pdf.

9. Like many scholars and people from the country, I use Burma interchangeably with the formal name of the country, Myanmar (given to the nation by its military regime in 1989, a year after it had killed thousands of its own citizens in suppressing the 1988 popular uprising). However, because of the provenance of the new name, I typically use "Burma."

10. The National Endowment for Democracy is a family of congressionally funded but nongovernmental assistance efforts. The endowment makes grants directly through its grants program and its Center for International Media Assistance. Other endowment grants and assistance programs are delivered through the International Republican Institute, the National Democratic Institute, the Solidarity Center, and the Center for International Private Enterprise (which represent the two U.S. political parties, labor, and business, respectively).

11. Daniel Twining and Kenneth Wollack, "Russia's Nefarious Meddling Is Nothing Like Democracy Assistance," *Washington Post*, April 10, 2018, www.washingtonpost.com/opinions/russias-nefarious-meddling-is-nothing-like-democracy-assistance/2018/04/10/b8942f20-3ce2-11e8-a7d1-e4efec6389f0_story.html?utm_term=.580cef1963b6.

12. See Open Internet for Democracy, an initiative sponsored by the National Endowment for Democracy: https://openinternet.global/about-open-internet-democracy-initiative.

13. Maka Angola can be found at www.makaangola.org/en/.

14. Rafael Marques, "Angola's Oil Curse," Alternet, December 17, 2004, www.alternet.org/story/20780/angola%27s_oil_curse; Rafael Marques, "Lundas: The Stones of Death. Angola's Deadly Diamonds," March 9, 2005, http://cdm16064.contentdm.oclc.org/cdm/ref/collection/p266901coll4/id/3098; Rafael Marques, "Operation Kissonde: The Stones of Death," Chesapeake Digital Preservation Group: Legal Information Archive, 2006, www.business-humanrights.org/sites/default/files/reports-and-materials/Operation-Kissonde-Rafael-Marques-Sep-2006.pdf; Rafael Marques, "A New Diamond War," *Washington Post*, November 6, 2006, www.washingtonpost.com/wp-dyn/content/article/2006/11/05/AR2006110500775.html; Rafael Marques de Morais, "Blood Diamonds: Corruption and Torture in Angola," www.tintadachina.pt/pdfs/626c1154352f7b4f96324bf928831b86-insideENG.pdf; Rafael Marques de Morais, "Eight Years for Falling Asleep in a Parked Car," *The Guardian*, April 29, 2016, www.theguardian.com/world/2016/apr/29/angolas-punitive-prison-system-rafael-marques-de-morais.

15. "Rafael Marques on Trial," Committee to Protect Journalists, March 31, 2000, https://cpj.org/reports/2000/03/angola-marques-00.php.

16. Marques, "Blood Diamonds: Corruption and Torture in Angola."

17. Tracy McVeigh and David Smith, "Champion of Freedom Defies Angola's President, Generals and the Power of Diamond Companies," *The Guardian*, March 21, 2015, www.theguardian .com/world/2015/mar/22/rafael-marques-de-morais-defies-angolas-president-generals-and -the-power-of-diamond-companies.

18. "Angola: Index Welcomes Acquittal of Rafael Marques de Morais," Index on Censorship, July 9, 2018, www.indexoncensorship.org/2018/07/angola-index-welcomes-acquittal-rafael -marques-de-morais/.

19. Veronika Melkozerova and Josh Kovensky, "Donors: Ukraine Will Get Aid in 2018 After Government Renews Fight Against Corruption, Adopts Crucial Reforms," *Kyiv Post*, January 11, 2018, www.kyivpost.com/ukraine-politics/donors-ukraine-will-get-aid-2018 -government-renews-fight-corruption-adopts-crucial-reforms.html.

20. For a listing of U.S. Agency for International Development assistance programs in Ukraine, see www.usaid.gov/ukraine/documents/1863/usaidukraine-annual-report-2017.

21. Robert Kubinec, "How Foreign Aid Could Hurt Tunisia's Transition to Democracy," *Washington Post*, December 19, 2016, www.washingtonpost.com/news/monkey-cage/wp/2016/12 /19/how-foreign-assistance-can-hurt-not-help-tunisias-democratic-transition/?utm_term= .b3bd771c2174.

22. U.S. Agency for International Development, "Foreign Aid in the National Interest: Promoting Freedom, Security, and Opportunity," 2002, www.au.af.mil/au/awc/awcgate/usaid/foreign _aid_in_the_national_interest-full.pdf.

23. "About MCC," Millennium Challenge Corporation, www.mcc.gov/about.

24. Email exchange with Derek Mitchell, May 21, 2018.

25. For a comprehensive survey of tools and lessons, see Jeremy Kinsman and Kurt Bassuener, eds., *A Diplomat's Handbook for Democracy Development Support* (Waterloo, Ont.: Center for International Governance Innovation, 2013).

26. Michael McFaul, *From Cold War to Hot Peace: An American Ambassador in Putin's Russia* (Boston: Houghton Mifflin Harcourt, 2018).

27. Julie Ray, "World's Approval of U.S. Leadership Drops to New Low," Gallup, January 18, 2018, http://news.gallup.com/poll/225761/world-approval-leadership-drops-new-low.aspx.

28. "Clapper Calls for U.S. Information Agency 'on Steroids' to Counter Russian Propaganda," *Washington Times*, January 5, 2017, www.washingtontimes.com/news/2017/jan/5/james-clapper -calls-us-information-agency-steroids.

29. William A. Rugh, "Repairing American Public Diplomacy," *Arab Media and Society*, February 8, 2009, www.arabmediasociety.com/repairing-american-public-diplomacy/.

30. Carol Morello, "That Knock on a Congressman's Door Could Be a Fulbright Scholar with a Tin Cup," *Washington Post*, June 8, 2017, www.washingtonpost.com/world/national-security /that-knock-on-a-congressmans-door-could-be-a-fulbright-scholar-with-a-tin-cup/2017/06 /08/06aa1984-4baf-11e7-bc1b-fddbd8359dee_story.html?utm_term=.64f13122d582.

31. Fulbright Association website, https://fulbright.org/stand-for-fulbright-2018/.

32. Quoted in Christian Mull and Matthew Wallin, "Propaganda: A Tool of Strategic Influence," American Security Project, September 2013, 1, https://www.americansecurityproject.org /ASP%20Reports/Ref%200138%20-%20Propaganda%20-%20A%20tool%20of%20 strategic%20influence%20-%20%20Fact%20Sheet.pdf.

33. This language is from the authorizing legislation passed in late 2016: see www.state.gov/r /gec/.

34. Abigail Tracy, "'A Different Kind of Propaganda': Has America Lost the Information War?," *Vanity Fair*, April 23, 2018, www.vanityfair.com/news/2018/04/russia-propaganda-america -information-war.

35. Issie Lapowsky, "The State Department's Fumbled Fight Against Russian Propaganda," *Wired*, November 22, 2017, www.wired.com/story/the-state-departments-fumbled-fight-against -russian-propaganda/; Gardiner Harris, "State Dept. Was Granted $120 Million to Fight Russian Meddling. It Has Spent $0," *New York Times*, March 4, 2018, www.nytimes.com/2018 /03/04/world/europe/state-department-russia-global-engagement-center.html.

36. Much of my thinking in this section has been informed by an excellent report from the Aspen Institute: Richard Kessler, "Reforming American Public Diplomacy: A Report of the Annual Aspen Institute Dialogue on Diplomacy and Technology," Aspen Institute Communications and Society Program, 2015, http://csreports.aspeninstitute.org/documents/ADDTech14 %20Report.pdf.

37. "How Can Technology Make People in the World Safer?," Jigsaw, https://jigsaw.google.com /projects/.
38. Dalai Lama, "Buddhism, Asian Values, and Democracy," 7.

CHAPTER 12: MAKING THE INTERNET SAFE FOR DEMOCRACY

1. Max Fisher, "With Alex Jones, Facebook's Worst Demons Abroad Begin to Come Home," *New York Times*, August 8, 2018, www.nytimes.com/2018/08/08/world/americas/facebook -misinformation.html.
2. Joshua A. Tucker et al., "From Liberation to Turmoil: Social Media and Democracy," *Journal of Democracy* 28 (October 2017): 49.
3. An archived description of our Stanford program can be found at http://cddrl.fsi.stanford .edu/docs/about_libtech.
4. Philip N. Howard and Muzammil M. Hussain, "The Upheavals in Egypt and Tunisia: The Role of Digital Media," *Journal of Democracy* 22 (July 2011): 35–48.
5. Larry Diamond, "Liberation Technology," *Journal of Democracy* 21 (July 2010): 69–83.
6. See the essays in Larry Diamond and Marc F. Plattner, eds., *Liberation Technology: Social Media and the Struggle for Democracy* (Baltimore: Johns Hopkins University Press, 2012).
7. Dave Chaffey, "Global Social Media Research Summary," Smart Insights, March 28, 2018, www.smartinsights.com/social-media-marketing/social-media-strategy/new-global-social -media-research/.
8. Elisa Shearer and Jeffrey Gottfried, "News Use Across Social Media Platforms," Pew Research Center, September 7, 2017, www.journalism.org/2017/09/07/news-use-across-social -media-platforms-2017/; Kristin Bialik and Katerina Eva Matsa, "Key Trends in Social and Digital News Media," Pew Research Center, October 4, 2017, www.pewresearch.org/fact -tank/2017/10/04/key-trends-in-social-and-digital-news-media/.
9. Mark Zuckerberg, "A Blueprint for Content Governance and Enforcement," Facebook, November 15, 2018, www.facebook.com/notes/mark-zuckerberg/a-blueprint-for-content -governance-and-enforcement/10156443129621634/.
10. Ibid.
11. Anamitra Deb, Stacy Donohue, and Tom Glaisyer, "Is Social Media a Threat to Democracy?," Omidyar Group, October 1, 2017, www.omidyargroup.com/wp-content/uploads/2017/10 /Social-Media-and-Democracy-October-5-2017.pdf.
12. Ibid., 6.
13. Nathaniel Persily, "Can Democracy Survive the Internet?," *Journal of Democracy* 28 (April 2017): 72.
14. Seymour Martin Lipset, *Political Man: The Social Bases of Politics* (1960; repr., Baltimore: Johns Hopkins University Press, 1981), 74–79.
15. Deb, Donohue, and Glaisyer, "Is Social Media a Threat to Democracy?," 7. I resist using the term "fake news," which Donald Trump has appropriated to stigmatize truthful reporting that is not to his liking.
16. Jen Weedon, William Nuland, and Alex Stamos, "Information Operations and Facebook," Facebook, April 27, 2017, https://fbnewsroomus.files.wordpress.com/2017/04/facebook-and -information-operations-v1.pdf.
17. Samanth Subramanian, "Fake News Factory to the World: Welcome to the Macedonian Fake-News Complex," *Wired*, February 15, 2017, www.wired.com/2017/02/veles-macedonia -fake-news/.
18. Darrell M. West, "How to Combat Fake News and Disinformation," Brookings Institution, December 18, 2017, www.brookings.edu/research/how-to-combat-fake-news-and -disinformation/.
19. Marc Fisher, John Cox, and Peter Hermann, "Pizzagate: From Rumor, to Hashtag, to Gunfire in D.C.," *Washington Post*, December 6, 2016, www.washingtonpost.com/local/pizzagate-from -rumor-to-hashtag-to-gunfire-in-dc/2016/12/06/4c7def50-bbd4-11e6-94ac-3d324840106c _story.html?noredirect=on&utm_term=.58ac7f5ffef6.
20. Reuters, "Trump's Attacks on Media May Lead to Real Violence: U.N. Expert," *U.S. News & World Report*, August 2, 2018, www.usnews.com/news/world/articles/2018-08-02/trumps -attacks-on-media-may-lead-to-real-violence-un-expert; Rick Noack, "Can Anti-Media Rhetoric Spark Violence? These German Researchers Reached a Startling Conclusion,"

Washington Post, July 30, 2018, www.washingtonpost.com/news/worldviews/wp/2018/07/30/can-anti-media-rhetoric-spark-violence-these-german-researchers-reached-a-startling-conclusion/?noredirect=on&utm_term=.46bada56f159.

21. William K. Rashbaum, Alan Feuer, and Adam Goldman, "Outspoken Trump Supporter in Florida Charged in Attempted Bombing Spree," *New York Times*, October 26, 2018, www.nytimes.com/2018/10/26/nyregion/cnn-cory-booker-pipe-bombs-sent.html.

22. Craig Silverman, "'Death Panel' Report Reaches Depressing Conclusions: The Media Is Ineffective at Dispelling False Rumors," *Columbia Journalism Review*, May 27, 2011, https://archives.cjr.org/behind_the_news/death_panels_report_reaches_de.php.

23. Persily, "Can Democracy Survive the Internet?," 69.

24. A YouTube deep-fake video of the actor Jordan Peele ventriloquizing Barack Obama in a simulated video message—produced to educate the public about the potential of artificial intelligence to deceive in this way—had been viewed more than 5 million times on YouTube by November 2018: see www.youtube.com/watch?v=cQ54GDm1eL0.

25. Deb, Donohue, and Glaisyer, "Is Social Media a Threat to Democracy?," 9.

26. Pen America, "Faking News: Fraudulent News and the Fight for Truth," October 12, 2017, 4, https://pen.org/wp-content/uploads/2017/11/2017-Faking-News-11.2.pdf.

27. See the annual Freedom House Reports: Freedom on the Net 2017, https://freedomhouse.org/report/freedom-net/freedom-net-2017; Freedom on the Net 2018, https://freedomhouse.org/report/freedom-net/freedom-net-2018.

28. Bence Kollanyi, Philip Howard, and Samuel Woolley, "Bots and Automation over Twitter During the 2016 U.S. Election," November 17, 2016, http://comprop.oii.ox.ac.uk/wp-content/uploads/sites/89/2016/11/Data-Memo-US-Election.pdf.

29. Robert Faris et al., "Partisanship, Propaganda, and Disinformation: Online Media and the 2016 U.S. Presidential Election," Berkman Klein Center for Internet and Society at Harvard University, August 16, 2017, https://cyber.harvard.edu/publications/2017/08/mediacloud.

30. Deb, Donohue, and Glaisyer, "Is Social Media a Threat to Democracy?," 10.

31. Fisher, "With Alex Jones, Facebook's Worst Demons."

32. Deb, Donohue, and Glaisyer, "Is Social Media a Threat to Democracy?," 11.

33. Anna Mitchell and Larry Diamond, "China's Surveillance State Should Scare Everyone," *The Atlantic*, February 2, 2018, www.theatlantic.com/international/archive/2018/02/china-surveillance/552203/.

34. Daniel Benaim and Holly Russon Gilman, "China's Aggressive Surveillance Technology Will Spread Beyond Its Borders," *Slate*, August 9, 2018, https://slate.com/technology/2018/08/chinas-export-of-cutting-edge-surveillance-and-facial-recognition-technology-will-empower-authoritarians-worldwide.html.

35. Tucker et al., "From Liberation to Turmoil," 50–52.

36. Timothy Garton Ash, *Free Speech: Ten Principles for a Connected World* (New Haven: Yale University Press, 2016); "An Introductory Guide to the Ten Principles," Free Speech Debate, January 10, 2017, https://freespeechdebate.com/media/new-video-content-on-free-speech-in-2017/.

37. Laura Italiano, "Facebook Gives Up on 'Flagging' Fake News," *New York Post*, December 22, 2017, https://nypost.com/2017/12/22/facebook-gives-up-on-flagging-fake-news/.

38. "Hard Questions: What Is Facebook Doing to Protect Election Security?," Facebook, March 29, 2018, https://newsroom.fb.com/news/2018/03/hard-questions-election-security/.

39. Aja Romano, "Mark Zuckerberg Lays Out Facebook's Three-Pronged Approach to Fake News," *Vox*, April 3, 2018, www.vox.com/technology/2018/4/3/17188332/zuckerberg-kinds-of-fake-news-facebook-making-progress/.

40. By "borderline," Facebook means content that it will not prohibit but that comes closer to violating its community standards, such as offensive speech that doesn't quite rise to the level of hate speech or "click and bait misinformation": see Zuckerberg, "A Blueprint for Content Governance and Enforcement."

41. Ibid.

42. Jonathan Vanian, "Facebook Expanding Fact-Checking Project to Combat Fake News," *Fortune*, June 21, 2018, http://fortune.com/2018/06/21/facebook-fake-news-fact-checking/.

43. Swapna Krishna, "Google Takes Steps to Combat Fake News 'Snippets,'" Engadget, January 31, 2018, www.engadget.com/2018/01/31/google-tackles-fake-news-in-snippets/.

44. Ben Gomes, "Our Latest Quality Improvements for Search," Google, April 25, 2017, https://blog.google/products/search/our-latest-quality-improvements-search/.

45. Sheera Frenkel, Nicholas Confessore, Cecilia Kang, Matthew Rosenberg, and Jack Nicas, "Delay, Deny and Deflect: How Facebook's Leaders Fought Through Crisis," *New York Times*, November 14, 2018, https://www.nytimes.com/2018/11/14/technology/facebook-data-russia -election-racism.html.

46. David Greene, "Alex Jones Is Far from the Only Person Tech Companies Are Silencing," *Washington Post*, August 12, 2018, www.washingtonpost.com/opinions/beware-the-digital -censor/2018/08/12/997e28ea-9cd0-11e8-843b-36e177f3081c_story.html?utm_term= .7415b30c723f.

47. "The Santa Clara Principles," https://newamericadotorg.s3.amazonaws.com/documents /Santa_Clara_Principles.pdf.

48. Facebook, Community Standards, www.facebook.com/communitystandards/. In Zuckerberg's "A Blueprint for Content Governance and Enforcement," he concedes that Facebook's review teams "make the wrong call in more than 1 out of every 10 cases."

49. Facebook, Transparency, Community Standards Enforcement Report, November 2018, https://transparency.facebook.com/community-standards-enforcement.

50. Zuckerberg, "A Blueprint for Content Governance and Enforcement."

51. Deb, Donohue, and Glaisyer, "Is Social Media a Threat to Democracy?," 15.

52. "News Integrity Initiative," City University of New York: Craig Newmark Graduate School of Journalism, www.journalism.cuny.edu/centers/tow-knight-center-entrepreneurial -journalism/news-integrity-initiative/.

53. "About First Draft," First Draft, https://firstdraftnews.org/about/.

54. "The Trust Project," Santa Clara University: Markkula Center for Applied Ethics, www.scu .edu/ethics/focus-areas/journalism-ethics/programs/the-trust-project/.

55. "About Us," Stop Fake, www.stopfake.org/en/about-us/.

56. Stephen King, "Trust Starts with Truth," *The Telegraph*, April 5, 2017, www.telegraph.co.uk /news/2017/04/04/ebay-founder-pierre-omidyar-commits-100m-fight-fake-news-hate/.

57. Seth Copen Goldstein, "Solving the Political Ad Problem with Transparency," Free Speech Debate, November 17, 2017, https://freespeechdebate.com/discuss/solving-the-political-ad -problem-with-transparency/.

58. Julia Angwin and Jeff Larson, "Help Us Monitor Political Ads Online," ProPublica, September 7, 2017, www.propublica.org/article/help-us-monitor-political-ads-online.

59. Daniel Fried and Alina Polyakova, "Democratic Defense Against Disinformation," Atlantic Council, February 2018, 11, www.atlanticcouncil.org/publications/reports/democratic-defense -against-disinformation.

60. YouTube claims that its advances in machine learning enable it to "take down nearly 70% of violent extremism content within 8 hours of upload and nearly half of it in 2 hours": John Shinai, "Facebook, Google Tell Congress They're Fighting Extremist Content with Counter-propaganda," CNBC, January 17, 2018, www.cnbc.com/2018/01/17/facebook-google-tell -congress-how-theyre-fighting-extremist-content.html.

61. "Ten Ways to Fight Hate: A Community Response Guide," Southern Poverty Law Center, August 14, 2017, www.splcenter.org/20170814/ten-ways-fight-hate-community-response -guide.

62. Eileen Donahoe, "Don't Undermine Democratic Values in the Name of Democracy," *American Interest*, December 12, 2017, www.the-american-interest.com/2017/12/12/179079/.

63. Melissa Eddy and Mark Scott, "Delete Hate Speech or Pay Up, Germany Tells Social Media Companies," *New York Times*, June 30, 2017, www.nytimes.com/2017/06/30/business/germany -facebook-google-twitter.html.

64. Eileen Donahoe, "Protecting Democracy from Online Disinformation Requires Better Algorithms, Not Censorship," Council on Foreign Relations, August 21, 2017, www.cfr.org/blog /protecting-democracy-online-disinformation-requires-better-algorithms-not-censorship.

65. Taylor Hatmaker, "Twitter Endorses the Honest Ads Act, a Bill Promoting Political Ad Transparency," Techcrunch, April 10, 2018, https://techcrunch.com/2018/04/10/twitter-honest-ads -act/.

66. Fried and Polyakova, "Democratic Defense Against Disinformation," 7–8.

67. Natasha Lomas, "WTF Is GDPR?," Techcrunch, January 20, 2018, https://techcrunch.com /2018/01/20/wtf-is-gdpr/.

68. Ibid.

69. Mark Scott and Nancy Scola, "Facebook Won't Extend EU Privacy Rights Globally, No Matter What Mark Zuckerberg Says," *Politico*, April 19, 2018, www.politico.eu/article/facebook-europe-privacy-data-protection-markzuckerberg-gdpr-general-data-protection-regulation-eu-european-union/.
70. Mark Warner, "Potential Policy Proposals for Regulation of Social Media," https://regmedia.co.uk/2018/07/30/warner_social_media_proposal.pdf.
71. Sam Wineburg and Sarah McGrew, "Most Teens Can't Tell Fake from Real News," *PBS NewsHour*, December 13, 2016, www.pbs.org/newshour/education/column-students-cant-google-way-truth.
72. Joel Breakstone et al., "Why We Need a New Approach to Teaching Digital Literacy," *Phi Delta Kappan* 99 (March 2018): 27–32, www.kappanonline.org/breakstone-need-new-approach-teaching-digital-literacy/.
73. They also recommend students be taught how to explore the "talk" page of Wikipedia entries so they can assess the "living dialogue" of evidence that is brought to bear on a claim.
74. Sarah McGrew et al., "The Challenge That's Bigger Than Fake News: Teaching Students to Engage in Civic Online Reasoning," *American Educator* (Fall 2017): 8–9, www.aft.org/sites/default/files/periodicals/ae_fall2017_mcgrew.pdf.
75. Pen America, "Faking News," 73.
76. Breakstone et al., "Why We Need a New Approach," 31.
77. Sam Wineburg, meeting attended by the author, June 7, 2018.
78. "How Can Technology Make People in the World Safer?," Jigsaw, https://jigsaw.google.com/projects/.
79. "Tools from EFF's Tech Team," Electronic Frontier Foundation, www.eff.org/pages/tools.

CHAPTER 13: REVIVING AMERICAN DEMOCRACY

1. Joseph P. Lash, *Eleanor: The Years Alone* (New York: W. W. Norton, 1972), 79.
2. George F. Kennan, "The Long Telegram," February 22, 1946, www.trumanlibrary.org/whistlestop/study_collections/coldwar/documents/pdf/6-6.pdf.
3. Patrick McGreevy, "Governor Brown Approves Major Changes in Legislative Process," *Los Angeles Times*, September 27, 2014, www.latimes.com/local/political/la-me-pc-gov-brown-oks-bill-allowing-changes-and-more-transparency-for-initiatives-20140926-story.html.
4. Here and below, all the quotes from Cara McCormick are from my telephone interview with her on September 3, 2018.
5. Colin Woodard, "Maine's Radical Democratic Experiment," *Politico*, March 27, 2018, www.politico.com/magazine/story/2018/03/27/paul-lepage-maine-governor-ranked-choice-voting-217715.
6. "Governor LePage's Most Controversial Quotes, 2010," *Bangor Daily News*, March 30, 2013, http://bangordailynews.com/2013/03/30/opinion/lepagequotes/.
7. Colin Woodard, "How Did America's Craziest Governor Get Reelected?," *Politico*, November 5, 2014, www.politico.com/magazine/story/2014/11/paul-lepage-craziest-governor-reelection-112583.
8. "Maine Question 1, Ranked-Choice Voting Delayed Enactment and Automatic Repeal Referendum (June 2018)," Ballotpedia, https://ballotpedia.org/Maine_Question_1,_Ranked-Choice_Voting_Delayed_Enactment_and_Automatic_Repeal_Referendum_(June_2018).
9. "Vote for Me! For Second Place, at Least?," editorial, *New York Times*, June 9, 2018, www.nytimes.com/2018/06/09/opinion/ranked-choice-voting-maine-san-francisco.html.
10. Eric Maskin and Amartya Sen, "A Better Electoral System for Maine," *New York Times*, June 10, 2018, www.nytimes.com/2018/06/10/opinion/electoral-system-maine.html.
11. Darren Fishell, "Who's Paying to Convince Mainers That Ranked-Choice Voting Suits Them," *Bangor Daily News*, June 11, 2018, http://bangordailynews.com/2018/06/08/politics/whos-paying-to-convince-mainers-that-ranked-choice-voting-suits-them/.
12. Edward D. Murphy and Peter McGuire, "As Mainers Vote in First Ranked-Choice Election, LePage Says He 'Probably' Won't Certify Referendum Results," *Portland Press Herald*, June 12, 2018, www.pressherald.com/2018/06/12/voters-turn-out-for-historic-election-day/.
13. Interview with Cara McCormick, September 3, 2018.

14. Lee Drutman, "All Politicians 'Game' the System. The Question Is How?" *Vox*, May 14, 2018, www.vox.com/polyarchy/2018/5/14/17352208/ranked-choice-voting-san-francisco.
15. "Multiple Choice: In Praise of Ranked-Choice Voting," *The Economist*, June 14, 2018, www .economist.com/united-states/2018/06/16/in-praise-of-ranked-choice-voting.
16. Kelly Born, "Maine's Ranked Choice Voting Could Lead the Way to a Healthier U.S. Democracy," Hewlett Foundation, August 16, 2018, https://hewlett.org/maines-ranked-choice -voting-could-lead-the-way-to-a-healthier-u-s-democracy/.
17. Fair Vote, "Ranked Choice Voting/Instant Runoff," www.fairvote.org/rcv#where_is_ranked _choice_voting_used; RepresentUs, "Ranked Choice Voting," https://act.represent.us/sign /ranked-choice-voting/.
18. Todd Donovan, Caroline Tolbert, and Kellen Gracey, "Campaign Civility Under Preferential and Plurality Voting," *Electoral Studies* 42 (June 2016): 157–63.
19. "Vote for Me! For Second Place, at Least?"
20. "Multiple Choice: In Praise of Ranked-Choice Voting."
21. Mickey Edwards, *The Parties Versus the People: How to Turn Republicans and Democrats into Americans* (New Haven: Yale University Press, 2012), 6.
22. Ibid., 44–45.
23. "Vote for Me! For Second Place, at Least?"; David Brooks, "One Reform to Save America," *New York Times*, May 31, 2018, www.nytimes.com/2018/05/31/opinion/voting-reform-partisanship -congress.html.
24. "A Congress for Every American," editorial, *New York Times*, November 10, 2018, https://www .nytimes.com/interactive/2018/11/10/opinion/house-representatives-size-multi-member .html.
25. "Germany's Election Results in Charts and Maps," *Financial Times*, September 24, 2017, www .ft.com/content/e7c7d918-a17e-11e7-b797-b61809486fe2.
26. Nolan McCarty, "Reducing Polarization: Some Facts for Reformers," *University of Chicago Legal Forum* 2015 (2016): 243–78.
27. "Extreme Gerrymandering: Democrats Need Near-Record Margin to Take House in 2018," Brennan Center for Justice, March 26, 2018, www.brennancenter.org/press-release/extreme -gerrymandering-democrats-need-near-record-margin-take-house-2018.
28. Thomas E. Mann, "We Must Address Gerrymandering," *Time*, October 13, 2016, http://time .com/collection-post/4527291/2016-election-gerrymandering/.
29. "Gerrymandering," RepresentUs, https://act.represent.us/sign/gerrymandering/. Hawaii and New Jersey now provide for commissions composed of politicians, which is less than ideal.
30. Aris Folley, "Michigan Court Orders Redistricting Measure to Go on Ballot," *The Hill*, June 8, 2018, http://thehill.com/regulation/legislation/391342-michigan-court-rules-voters -can-decide-on-redistricting.
31. Christian R. Grose, "Voters in Colorado, Michigan, Missouri, and Utah Endorse Independent Redistricting," Schwarzenegger Institute, November 2018, https://gallery.mailchimp.com /5216a8f2f16ed324741c940dd/files/6dc12574-9a71-4a0f-b454-c1e3e28236d3 /Schwarzenegger_Institute_Redistricting_Initiatives_Policy_Report.pdf.
32. Christopher Ingraham, "Pennsylvania Supreme Court Draws 'Much More Competitive' District Map to Overturn Republican Gerrymander," *Washington Post*, February 20, 2018, www .washingtonpost.com/news/wonk/wp/2018/02/19/pennsylvania-supreme-court-draws-a -much-more-competitive-district-map-to-overturn-republican-gerrymander/?utm_term= .0b16d2c0410c.
33. Hunter Schwarz, "Voter Turnout in Primary Elections This Year Has Been Abysmal," *Washington Post*, July 23, 2014, www.washingtonpost.com/blogs/govbeat/wp/2014/07/23/voter -turnout-in-primary-elections-this-year-has-been-abysmal/?utm_term=.f5bf8308f567.
34. Elaine C. Kamarck, "Increasing Turnout in Congressional Primaries," Brookings Institution, July 2014, 14, www.brookings.edu/wp-content/uploads/2016/06/KamarckIncreasing-Turnout -in-Congressional-Primaries72614.pdf.
35. Wendy Weiser, "Automatic Voter Registration Boosts Political Participation," Brennan Center for Justice, January 29, 2016, www.brennancenter.org/blog/automatic-voter-registration -boosts-political-participation; Drew DeSilver, "U.S. Trails Most Developed Countries in Voter Turnout," Pew Research Center, May 21, 2018, www.pewresearch.org/fact-tank/2018 /05/21/u-s-voter-turnout-trails-most-developed-countries/; Wendy Weiser and Alicia Ban-

non, "Democracy: An Election Agenda for Candidates, Activists and Legislators," Brennan Center for Justice, May 4, 2018, www.brennancenter.org/publication/democracy-election-agenda-2018.

36. Sean McElwee, Brian Schaffner, and Jesse Rhodes, "How Oregon Increased Voter Turnout More Than Any Other State," *The Nation*, July 27, 2017, www.thenation.com/article/how-oregon-increased-voter-turnout-more-than-any-other-state/.

37. "Automatic Voter Registration," Brennan Center for Justice, April 17, 2018, www.brennan center.org/analysis/automatic-voter-registration.

38. German Lopez, "Nine Ways to Make Voting Better," *Vox*, November 7, 2016, www.vox.com/policy-and-politics/2016/11/7/13533990/voting-improvements-election-2016.

39. Weiser and Bannon, "Democracy: An Election Agenda," 7.

40. Adam Bonica, "What's Good for Democracy Is Also Good for Democrats," *New York Times*, July 26, 2018, www.nytimes.com/2018/07/26/opinion/sunday/democracy-democrats-voters-disenfranchisment.html.

41. Tina Rosenberg, "Increasing Voter Turnout for 2018 and Beyond," *New York Times*, June 13, 2017, www.nytimes.com/2017/06/13/opinion/increasing-voter-turnout-2018.html.

42. Jelani Cobb, "Voter-Suppression Tactics in the Age of Trump," *The New Yorker*, October 29, 2018, www.newyorker.com/magazine/2018/10/29/voter-suppression-tactics-in-the-age-of-trump. This sorry incident—involving a grotesque conflict of interest on the part of Georgia's secretary of state—also underscores why the job of supervising elections at the state level should not be held by an elected (or appointed) partisan official, as is now the norm in the United States.

43. Weiser and Bannon, "Democracy: An Election Agenda," 9.

44. Ibid., 11–12.

45. Alexander Hamilton, "The Mode of Electing the President," *The Federalist* 68, www.congress.gov/resources/display/content/The+Federalist+Papers#TheFederalistPapers-68.

46. "The Minority Majority: America's Electoral System Gives the Republicans Advantages over Democrats," *The Economist*, July 12, 2018, www.economist.com/briefing/2018/07/12/americas-electoral-system-gives-the-republicans-advantages-over-democrats.

47. www.nationalpopularvote.com/.

48. Katherine M. Gehl and Michael E. Porter, "Why Competition in the Politics Industry Is Failing America," Harvard Business School, September 2017, 40, www.hbs.edu/competitiveness/Documents/why-competition-in-the-politics-industry-is-failing-america.pdf.

49. In 1992, Ross Perot exceeded 15 percent in public-opinion polls only after participating in the fall debates. I have been part of the effort to change this rule: see www.changetherule.org/.

50. "What Is Deliberative Polling?," Center for Deliberative Democracy, http://cdd.stanford.edu/what-is-deliberative-polling/; James S. Fishkin, *Democracy When People Are Thinking: Revitalizing Our Politics Through Public Deliberation* (New York: Oxford University Press, 2018).

51. "Congress and the Public," Gallup, https://news.gallup.com/poll/1600/congress-public.aspx.

52. Edwards, *The Parties Versus the People*, 114, 120.

53. "Make Congress Work: A No Labels Action Plan," No Labels, www.nolabels.org/wp-content/uploads/2017/04/MCW_Pages.pdf, p. 13.

54. Ibid.

55. Ibid., 14.

56. Bruce Cain, *Democracy More or Less: America's Political Reform Quandary* (New York: Cambridge University Press, 2015): 204–6; Sarah A. Binder and Frances E. Lee, "Make Deals in Congress," in *Solutions to Polarization in America*, ed. Nathaniel Persily (Cambridge: Cambridge University Press, 2015), 252.

57. Jane Mansbridge, "Helping Congress Negotiate," in Persily, ed., *Solutions to Polarization*, 268–69; Cain, *Democracy More or Less*, 160.

58. Weiser and Bannon, "Democracy: An Election Agenda," 15.

59. This is the cause of an outstanding nonprofit organization that I am proud to be associated with, Verified Voting: www.verifiedvoting.org/about-vvo/.

60. "The Verifier—Polling Place Equipment—November 2018," Verified Voting, www.verifiedvoting.org/verifier/; "Voting Methods and Equipment by State," Ballotpedia, https://ballotpedia.org/Voting_methods_and_equipment_by_state.

61. Weiser and Bannon, "Democracy: An Election Agenda," 15–16.

62. Sean Sullivan, "What Is a 501(c)(4), Anyway?," *Washington Post*, May 13, 2013, www .washingtonpost.com/news/the-fix/wp/2013/05/13/what-is-a-501c4-anyway/?utm_term= .48a8d4e5bbca. 501(c)(6) organizations, business leagues, fall under similar requirements.

63. See the excellent website Open Secrets, provided by the Center for Responsive Politics: www .opensecrets.org/dark-money/top-election-spenders.

64. Weiser and Bannon, "Democracy: An Election Agenda," 24.

65. Ibid., 25.

66. Ian Vandewalker, "Voucher-Funded Seattle Candidates Relied More on Constituents Than on Non-Constituent Donors," Brennan Center for Justice, June 1, 2018, www.brennancenter .org/blog/voucher-funded-seattle-candidates-relied-more-constituents-non-constituent -donors-part-two.

67. RepresentUs, "The American Anti-Corruption Act," https://anticorruptionact.org/whats-in -the-act/.

68. Russell Berman, "Donald Trump's Last-Ditch Plan to 'Drain the Swamp,'" *The Atlantic*, October 18, 2016, www.theatlantic.com/politics/archive/2016/10/donald-trumps-plan-to-drain -the-swamp/504569/.

69. Executive Order: Ethics Commitments by Executive Branch Appointees, January 28, 2017, www.whitehouse.gov/presidential-actions/executive-order-ethics-commitments-executive -branch-appointees/.

70. For the full text of the proposed American Anti-Corruption Act, see https://3pcd0f2kpjl33 pmc34996z9w-wpengine.netdna-ssl.com/wp-content/uploads/sites/4/2017/12/AACA -Revised-Full-Provisions-List-%E2%80%93-122F62F2017.pdf.

71. The Roosevelt Institute would go further and impose a lifetime lobbying ban on all departing senior executive branch officials and members of Congress: Rohit Chopra and Julie Margetta Morgan, "Unstacking the Deck: A New Agenda to Tame Corruption in Washington," Roosevelt Institute, May 2, 2018, 27, http://rooseveltinstitute.org/unstacking-deck/.

72. Alex Tucciarone, "Report Calls for Creation of Federal Enforcement Agency to Fight Corruption," Roosevelt Institute, May 2, 2018, http://rooseveltinstitute.org/report-calls-creation -federal-enforcement-agency-fight-corruption-washington/.

73. Chopra and Morgan, "Unstacking the Deck," 22.

74. Margaret Chase Smith, "Declaration of Conscience," U.S. Senate speech, June 1, 1950, www .senate.gov/artandhistory/history/resources/pdf/SmithDeclaration.pdf; reprinted in William Safire, ed., *Lend Me Your Ears: Great Speeches in History* (New York: W. W. Norton, 2004), 725.

CHAPTER 14: CONCLUSION: A NEW BIRTH OF FREEDOM

1. David Montgomery, "The Quest of Laurene Powell Jobs," *Washington Post*, June 11, 2018, www.washingtonpost.com/news/style/wp/2018/06/11/feature/the-quest-of-laurene-powell -jobs/?noredirect=on&utm_term=.bbd7caa64258.

2. Bill Clinton, Transcript of Speech to the Democratic Convention, August 27, 2008, www.npr .org/templates/story/story.php?storyId=94045962.

3. Ernest Hemingway, *The Sun Also Rises* (New York: Scribner, 1926), 141.

4. David M. Halbfinger and Isabel Kershner, "Israel Law Declares the Country the 'Nation-State of the Jewish People,'" *New York Times*, July 19, 2018, www.nytimes.com/2018/07/19 /world/middleeast/israel-law-jews-arabic.html.

5. Brad Roberts, introduction to *The New Democracies: Global Change and U.S. Policy*, ed. Brad Roberts (Cambridge, Mass.: MIT Press, 1990), ix.

6. Mohammed Ademo and Jeffrey Smith, "Ethiopia Is Falling Apart," *Foreign Policy*, January 11, 2018, https://foreignpolicy.com/2018/01/11/ethiopia-is-falling-apart/.

7. Jason Burke, "Ethiopian Prime Minister Vows to Stick to Reforms After Explosion at Rally," *The Guardian*, June 23, 2018, www.theguardian.com/world/2018/jun/23/explosion-rally-new -ethiopian-prime-minister-abiy-ahmed.

8. Hannah Ellis-Petersen, "Former Malaysian PM Najib Arrested in $4.5bn 1MDB Probe," *The Guardian*, July 3, 2018, www.theguardian.com/world/2018/jul/03/former-malaysian-leader -najib-arrested-in-45bn-graft-probe.

9. Cynthia Gabriel, "Malaysia's Missing Billions," *Journal of Democracy* 29 (January 2018): 69–75.

10. Michael A. McFaul, *From Cold War to Hot Peace: An American Ambassador in Putin's Russia* (Boston: Houghton Mifflin Harcourt, 2018).

11. Amie Ferris-Rotman and Anton Troianovski, "Russian Police Detain More Than 1,600 Pro-
    testing Putin's Fourth Presidential Term," *Washington Post*, May 5, 2018, www.washingtonpost
    .com/world/thousands-of-russians-rally-against-putin-ahead-of-inauguration/2018/05/05
    /3007a9a2-503d-11e8-b725-92c89fe3ca4c_story.html?utm_term=.d476f5dd5797.
12. Michael McFaul, "Transitions from Postcommunism," *Journal of Democracy* 16 (July 2005):
    5–19, www.journalofdemocracy.org/sites/default/files/McFaul-16-3.pdf.
13. Interview with Maina Kiai, March 10, 2018.
14. Abdul-Qasim Al-Shabbi, "To the Tyrants of the World," translated by Adel Iskandar. Aired on
    "The Role of Old and New Media in Egypt." Hosted by Melissa Block, *All Things Considered*,
    January 28, 2011.
15. Matthew Wigler, "Swing District," Medium, July 14, 2018, https://medium.com/swing
    -district-purple-america/diss-vs-piss-the-blue-wave-and-yellow-trickle-in-californias-central
    -valley-f302d5af2c4d.
16. Alicia Parlapiano and Adam Pearce, "For Every Ten U.S. Adults, Six Vote and Four Don't.
    What Separates Them?," *New York Times*, September 13, 2016, www.nytimes.com/interactive
    /2016/09/13/us/politics/what-separates-voters-and-nonvoters.html.
17. Gustavo López and Antonio Flores, "Dislike of Candidates or Campaign Issues Was Most
    Common Reason for Not Voting in 2016," Pew Research Center, June 1, 2017, www
    .pewresearch.org/fact-tank/2017/06/01/dislike-of-candidates-or-campaign-issues-was-most
    -common-reason-for-not-voting-in-2016/.
18. Tony Pugh, "Voter Suppression Laws Likely Tipped the Scales for Trump, Civil Rights
    Groups Say," McClatchy, November 10, 2016, www.mcclatchydc.com/news/politics
    -government/election/article113977353.html; Christopher Ingraham, "About 100 Million
    People Couldn't Be Bothered to Vote This Year," *Washington Post*, November 12, 2016, www
    .washingtonpost.com/news/wonk/wp/2016/11/12/about-100-million-people-couldnt-be
    -bothered-to-vote-this-year/?utm_term=.1ac01a89356a.
19. RepresentUs, "2018 Election Results," https://represent.us/election2018/.
20. Jen Johnson, "Victory! Voters in Alaska Just Passed a Sweeping Anti-Corruption Law,"
    RepresentUs, July 19, 2018, https://act.represent.us/sign/victory-in-alaska/.
21. "The Pledge," With Honor, https://www.withhonor.org/the-pledge.
22. Barbara Goldberg, "U.S. House Freshman Class Includes Most Veterans in Nearly a Decade,"
    Reuters, November 7, 2018, http://news.trust.org//item/20181107183710-ti1xo/.
23. Many of these are being supported by the philanthropic efforts of the Hewlett Foundation
    through its Madison Initiative: https://hewlett.org/strategy/madison-initiative/.

INDEX

Kennan, George F., 109–10, 111, 162, 163, 165–66, 253
Kennedy, John F., 7, 122, 222
Kennedy, Robert F., 13–14
Kenya, 22, 24, 228, 290, 299–300
Kerr, Miranda, 183
Khashoggi, Jamal, 204
Kiai, Maina, 299–300
King, Stephen, 243
Kirkpatrick, Jeane, 45
Kissinger, Henry, 44
kleptocracy, 12, 22, 111, 168, 170, 181–98, 295
  fighting of, 192–98
Kleptocracy Initiative, 184, 190, 193, 196
Klobuchar, Amy, 246
Knaus, Gerald, 186
knowledge elite, 95
Koch brothers, 91
Krastev, Ivan, 72
Ku Klux Klan, 7
Kunlun, 178
Kushner, Jared, 117
Kuwait, 54

Labour Party (Britain), 72
Lansing, John, 119
Latin America, 42, 43, 50, 139, 155, 211, 287, 289, 292
Latinobarometer, 155
Lava Jato (car wash) bribery scandal, 211
Law and Justice Party (PiS; Poland), 66–67
Lawrence, Jennifer, 260
laws, importance of, 6
League Party (Italy), 74
Lee, Mike, 92
Lee Kuan Yew, 147
Lee Teng-hui, 48
legitimacy, democratic, 16, 25–26, 27, 79–80, 149, 184, 192, 295–96
LePage, Paul, 256–57, 260
Le Pen, Marine, 5, 73, 120, 153
Levitsky, Steven, 28
Lewis, Sinclair, 1–2
liberal democracy, 19, 20
liberation technology, 227–28
Liberia, 211
libertarianism, 75
Libya, 54, 112, 201
Limbaugh, Rush, 99
Lincoln, Abraham, 102
Link, Perry, 136
Lipset, Seymour Martin, 25–26, 31, 69
lobbying, 103–4, 176, 182, 194–95, 255
  reform of, 279–80

Long Telegram, 109, 111, 162, 165, 253
Ludwig, Jessica, 124
Lugar, Richard, 48, 91
Lyman, Princeton, 220

McCain, John, 161, 246, 281
McCarthy, Eugene, 282
McCarthy, Joseph, 7, 102, 281, 282
McCormick, Cara Brown, 256–57, 259, 260
McFaul, Michael, 114, 220, 297
McGrew, Sarah, 248, 249
McRaven, William, 87
Macron, Emmanuel, 73, 171–72
Madison, James, 36
Maduro, Nicolás, 56
Magnitsky, Sergei, 168
Magnitsky Act, 168–69
Maine, 256–61, 304
Maka Angola, 212
Malawi, 52
Malaysia, 183, 212, 228, 295, 296, 297–98
Malaysiakini, 212, 228
Manafort, Paul, 117, 169, 182
Mandela, Nelson, 52, 198
Mann, Thomas, 93
manufacturing, movement to exurban and rural areas, 95
Marcos, Ferdinand, 46–48
Marcos, Imelda, 47
Marques de Morais, Rafael, 212–14, 299
Marshall Plan, 133, 214
Marx, Karl, 5
Maryland, 99, 267
Maslow, Abraham, 154
Massachusetts, 99, 264
massive open online courses (MOOCs), 224, 225
Mayer, Jane, 120–21
media, 64, 67, 79, 82, 83, 84, 85–86, 99–102, 105, 177, 187, 212–13, 242–43, 280, 281
  Chinese, 134–35, 172–73
  loss of legitimacy in, 233–34
  Trump's attacks on, 83, 84, 85–87, 233
Mexico, 22, 57, 148, 155, 289
Michigan, 116, 118, 266–67, 269
Middle East, 53
military coups, 55
Millennium Challenge Account, 216
Miller, Alexey, 169
Milošević, Slobodan, 212
Ministerial Conference of the Community of Democracies, 188
Minxin Pei, 132, 144
Miranda, Lin-Manuel, 285
misinformation, in digital realm, 232